ELVIN'S
DICTIONARY OF HERALDRY.

A
Dictionary of Heraldry

WITH UPWARDS OF TWO THOUSAND FIVE HUNDRED
ILLUSTRATIONS

BY

CHARLES NORTON ELVIN M.A.

AUTHOR OF "HAND-BOOK OF MOTTOES"
"ANECDOTES OF HERALDRY" ETC. ETC. ETC.

CLEARFIELD

G.N.ELVIN. DEL.

P.C.BAKER. Sc

Originally published
Great Britain, 1889

Reprinted for
Clearfield Company, Inc. by
Genealogical Publishing Co., Inc.
Baltimore, Maryland
1999

International Standard Book Number: 0-8063-0459-6

Made in the United States of America

ADVERTISEMENT.

HE aim of the present work is not to furnish an account of the antiquity and progress of Heraldry, but to provide as succinctly as possibly, and in Alphabetical order, a list of the terms met with in the Science, with their appropriate Illustrations.

Such a work it is hoped will be of great advantage to the Herald Painter and Engraver, as by means of it they will be enabled to refer, without trouble, to the subject they may desire to depict.

I propose, therefore, in the first place, to give the terms in a plain and concise form, so that any coat which is in strict conformity with the established rules of Heraldry, may easily be painted or engraved from the verbal Blazoning.

Secondly, I hope by the introduction of a great number of terms and Engravings, not to be found in any other Heraldic Glossary, to supply as complete a list as possible of those used in Coat Armour, and thus adapt the work not alone for the Practical Artist, but also for the Amateur, who desires to be able readily to blazon such coats as may fall under his observation.

CHARLES NORTON ELVIN.

ECKLING GRANGE,
 EAST DEREHAM, 1889.

LIST OF THE PRINCIPAL AUTHORITIES CONSULTED IN COMPILING THIS DICTIONARY.

ANSTIS, Register of the Order of the Garter, 1724.

ASHMOLE, The Institution, Laws and Ceremonies of the Order of the Garter, 1672.

BAKER, A Chronicle of the Kings of England, 1670.

BARONETAGES.

BERRY's Heraldry.

BLOOM's Heraldry, 1684.

BOSSEWELL, Works of Armorie, 1572.

BURNET, The Regal Armorie.

BURKE, Sir Bernard, Works.

BOYER, The Great Theatre of Honour and Nobility, 1729.

CAMBRIDGE, Camden Society.

CAMDEN, Remains of a greater work concerning Britaine, 1623.

CARTER, An Analysis of Honour and Armory, 1655.

CHALMERS, Caledonia, 1807.

CLARKE's Heraldry, 1829.

COAT's Heraldry, 1739.

COLLECTIONS of Coats of Arms.

COTMAN, Sepulchral Brasses in Norfolk, 1819.

COUNTY Histories.

DALLAWAY's Heraldry, 1793.

EDMONDSON's Heraldry, 1780.

EDWARD's, The Great Seal of England, 1837.

ELVEN's Heraldry, 1816 and 1829

FAVINE, Theatre of Honour and Knighthood, 1623.

FENN, Original Letters written in the Reign of Henry VI, Edward IV, and Richard III.

FROISSART Chronicles.

GIBBON, Introductio ad Latinam Blasoniam, 1682.

GLOSSARY of Architecture.

GOUGH, Sepulchral Monuments.

GRANTS of Arms.

GUILLIM's Heraldry, 1632.

HAINES' Monumental Brasses.

HAMPSON's Origines Patriciæ.

HEARNE's Works, 1720.

HERALDIC M.S.S.

HEYLIN, A Help to English History, 1709.

HOLME, (Randle), The Academy of Armorie, 1688.

JOHNSON, (Andr.), Notitia Anglicana, 1724.

KENT, Grammar of Heraldry, 1724.

LEIGH, (Gerard), The Accedence of Armorie, 1562.

LONG's Royal Descents, 1845.

LOWER, Curiosities of Heraldry, 1845.

MACKENZIE, Sir George, The Science of Heraldry, 1680.

MEYRICK's Ancient Armour.

MILLES, The Catalogue of Honor, 1610.

MONTAGUE, Guide to the Study of Heraldry.

MORGAN (Sylvanus), The Sphere of Gentry, 1661.

MOULE, Bibliotheca Heraldica Magnæ Britanniæ.

MOULE, Heraldry of Fish, 1842.

NICHOLS, J. G., The Herald and Genealogist.

NICHOLAS, Sir Harris, The Chronology of History.

NISBET's Heraldry, 1722.

NOBLE, History of the College of Arms

PRESTWICH, Sir J., Respublica, 1787.

ROLLS of Arms.

PEERAGES.

PORNEY's Heraldry, 1771.

SANDFORD's Genealogical History of the Kings of England, 1707.

SELDEN, Titles of Honour, 1672.

SHAW, Dresses and Decorations of the Middle Ages.

STODART, R. R., Scottish Arms.

STOTHARD, C. A., Monumental Effigies of Great Britain.

TANNER, Notitia Monastica, 1787.

UPTON, De Studio Militari libri quartuor, etc. cum notis Ed. Bissæi, 1654, fol.

WALKER & Richardson's Armorial Bearings of the Incorporated Companies of Newcastle upon Tyne.

WALLER, J. G. and L. A. B., Monumental Brasses.

WALLIS, The Arms, Crests, etc., of the Companies of the City of London, 1677, fol.

WEEVER, Ancient Funeral Monuments, 1681.

WILLEMENT's Regal Heraldry.

WYRLEY, W., The True use of Armorie, 1592.

YORK, The Union of Honour, 1640.

ABBREVIATIONS.

A., a., or *ar.* Argent.

az. Azure.

Bt. or *Bart.* Baronet.

betw. Between.

C.B. Companions of the Bath

chev. Chevron.

C.I. Companions of The Imperial Order of the Crown of India.

C.I.E. Companions of The Most Eminent Order of the Indian Empire.

C.M.G. Companions of St. Michael and St. George.

C.S.I. Companions of The Star of India.

disp. Displayed.

D.S.O. Companions of the Distinguished Service Order.

e.g. For Example.

engr. Engrailed.

erm. Ermine.

etc. or *&c.* and others.

ex. Example.

f. Figure.

Genealogies. For Abbreviations and Marks met with in Genealogies vid. term Genealogy.

G.C.B. Knights Grand Cross of the Bath.

G.C.H. Knights Grand Cross of the Hanoverian Guelphic Order.

G.C.I.E. Knights Grand Commanders of the Order of the Indian Empire.

G.C M.G. Knights Grand Cross of St. Michael and St. George.

G.C.S.I. Knights Grand Commanders of the Star of India.

G.M.M.G. Grand Master of St. Michael and St. George.

G.M.S.I. Grand Master of The Star of India.

gu. Gules.

guard. Guardant.

ib. (Ibid) The same place.

id. (Idem) The same.

i.e. (Id est) That is.

K.B. Knight of The Bath.

K.C.B. Knights Commanders of the Bath.

K.C.H. Knights Commanders of the Guelph or Hanoverian Guelphic Order.

K.C.I.E. Knights Commanders of The Indian Empire.

K.C.M.G. Knights Commanders of S. Michael and St. George.

K.C.S.I. Knights Commanders of the Star of India.

K.G. Knight of The Garter.

K.H. Knight of the Guelph, or The Royal Hanoverian Order.

Knt. Knight Bachelor.

K.P. Knight of St. Patrick.

K.T. Knight of The Thistle.

P. Plate.

pass. Passant.

per. Party-per.

ppr. Proper.

purp. Purpure.

q.v. (quod vide) Which see.

ramp. Rampant.

R.R.C. Lady of The Royal Red Cross.

sa. Sable

V.A. Royal Order of Victoria and Albert.

V.C. Victoria Cross.

vid. see.

viz. namely.

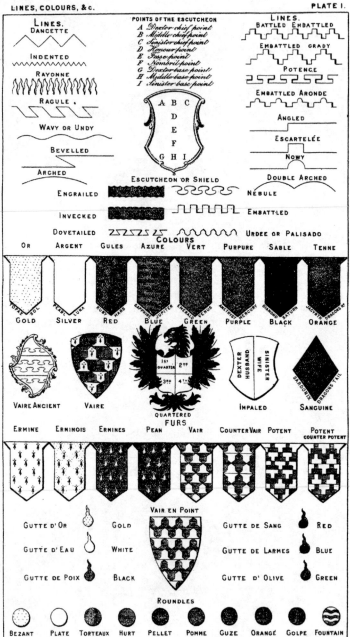

PLATE 1.

LINES. All the Ordinaries and Subordinaries are subject to the accidental forms of *Lines*, e.g., P. 3, 6, 12, 13, 14, etc.

POINTS OF THE ESCUTCHEON. Parts of the Shield denoting the position of the *Charges*.

COLOURS. Are divided into three classes, viz.: *Metals, Colours,* and *Furs.* See Tinctures.

METALS.

Or. Represented in engraving by Dots | Argent. Left quite plain

COLOURS.

Gules.	Represented in engraving by perpendicular lines	horizontal and perpendicular lines crossing each other
Azure.	Represented in engraving by horizontal lines	
		Tenne. Represented in engraving by diagonal lines from sinister to dexter crossed by horizontal lines
Vert.	Represented in engraving by diagonal lines from dexter to sinister	
Purpure.	Represented in engraving by diagonal lines from sinister to dexter	Sanguine. Represented in engraving by diagonal lines from dexter to sinister crossing each other
Sable.	Represented in engraving by	

The following paradigm will explain how some authors blazon Arms of Sovereigns by Planets, of Peers by Precious Stones, etc.

It was the adoption of such pedantries as this by the old writers that tended to make Heraldry repulsive and unintelligible to the modern apprehension.

The only recognised way now is to blazon all by the terms given under Metals, Colours, and Furs.

Or	Gold	Yellow	Sol	☉	Leo	Topaz
Argent	Silver	White	Luna	☾	Cancer	Pearl
Gules	Iron	Red	Mars	♂	Aries	Ruby
Azure	Tin	Blue	Jupiter	♃	Taurus	Sapphire
Vert	Copper	Green	Venus	♀	Gemini	Emerald
Purpure	Quick Silver	Purple	Mercury	☿	Sagittarius	Amethyst
Sable	Lead	Black	Saturn	♄	Capricorn	Diamond
Tenne		Orange	Dragon's Head	☊		Jacynth & Hyacinth
Sanguine		Murry	Dragon's Tail	☋		Sardonix

FURS.

Ermine. a white field with black spots	Vair in Point. the figures standing exactly one upon another flat upon flat
Erminois. a gold field with black spots	
Ermines. black field with white spots	
Pean. black field with gold spots	Vaire. when the figures forming the Vair are of more than two tinctures
Vair. white and blue, represented by figures of small escutcheons ranged in lines so that the base argent is opposite to the base azure	
	Vaire Ancient. represented by lines nebulée separated by straight lines
	Potent. resembles the head of crutches placed head to head
Conter Vair. the same as Vair only the figures are placed base against base and point against point	Potent counter potent. also termed VARRY CUPPA, and CUPPA, same as the last placed foot to head

GUTTE, a drop *(gutta)*

Gutte d' or	Drops of Gold.	Gutte de sang	Drops of Blood.
Gutte d' eau	,, ,, Water.	Gutte de larmes	,, ,, Tears.
Gutte de poix	,, ,, Pitch.	Gutte d' olive	,, ,, of Oil.

ROUNDLES.

Roundle or. is termed a Bezant	Roundle vert. is termed a Pome or Pomme
,, ar. ,, a Plate	,, sanguine ,, a Guze
,, gu. ,, a Torteaux	,, tenne ,, an Orange
,, az. ,, a Hurt	,, purpure ,, a Golpe
,, sa. ,, a Pellet	,, barry wavy ar. az a Fountain

PLATE 2.

Observe in Blazon the word Party may be omitted, e.g., Party per Pale, will be described as Per-Pale, Party per Fesse, by Per-Fesse, etc.

The Divisions of the Shield are termed Partition Lines.

1 Per Pale ar. and az. Collings
2 Per Fesse ar. and gu. Meelop
3 Per Fesse az. and or, on a Fesse Erm. betw. Two Boars pass. in chief of the second and in base a sprig of Mayflowers slipped and leaved ppr. Three Escallop shells gu. Tupper
4 Per Chevron ar. and sa. Aston
5 Per Saltire gu. and ar. Shelbury
6 Per Bend ar. and sa. Corket
7 Per Bend Sinister ar. & gu. Bayley
8 Per Pale and Per Chevron ar. and az. Branson
9 Per Cross, or Quarterly Erm. & gu. Stanhope
10 Per Pile and Fesse, or Per Bar and Pile ar. and sa. Crovile
11 Bendy of six ar. and gu. Midland
12 Bendy of eight ar. and gu. Minshaw
13 Barry of six erm. and gu. Hussey
14 Gu. three bars Nowy ar. Fainort
15 Barry Pily gu. and ar. Hoyland
16 Paly of six ar and az. Mails
17 Paly of eight ar. and gu. Lloyd
18 Ar. three Pales, or three Palets az. Thornton
19 Retierce, or Paly and Fesse of nine ar. and gu.
20 Paly of six ar. and sa. four bars gu. De Barry
21 Barry of six per pale indented ar. and gu. Peto
22 Gules Papelonne ar. or Counter Escallopée. Armourer
23 Ar. Masculy conjoined gu. Alan
24 Crests, Helmets and Lambrequins
25 Gyronny of six ar. and az. Branson
26 Gyronny of eight or and sa. Campbell
27 Masculy ar. and gu. Pogeys
28 Fusily ar. and gu. Duebeck
29 Gyronny of twelve ar. and az. Bassingborne, Elers
30 Gyronny of sixteen ar. and sa. Stapleford. For other examples of the gyron, see p. 19, f. 41, to 45

31 Lozengy or and sa. Bland
32 Paly Bendy, or Paly Lozengy, ar. and gu. Sydenham
33 Bendy Sinister Paly, or Paly Bendy Sinister
34 Barry bendy-sinister ar. and gu. Wenham
35 Barry bendy, or Barry lozengy ar. and gu. Ipre. Crispin
36 Barry of six indented ar. and az. Gill
37 Cheque, or Checky, ar. and gu. Alvers
38 Ar. Semée of Fleur-de-lis az. or ar. Semée-de-lis az. Potyn. Mortimer
39 Quarterly ar. and sa. six Roundles, three, two, and one counterchanged. Howison
40 Ar. Crucily sa. Patmore
41 Az. Gutté or Gutty d'eau. Winterbotham
42 Barry Paly, or Billettée counter billettée ar. and az.
43 Or a Double Tressure flory counter flory gu.
44 Ar. a canton gu. over all on a bend az. three garbs or, Fitton
45 Az. a Chevron lozengy engrailed or and gu. betw. three Plates each charged with a Martlet sa. Fletwood
46 Same Arms as No. 46. In Trick
47 Ar. a Fesse Weir ppr., or A Weir in Fesse. Williams
48 Flanched see in Dictionary
49 Per Fesse sa. and or a bend wavy counterchanged. Welnborn
50 Per Pale sa. and erm. a fesse counter-changed. Fitz Richard
51 Gu. on a mount vert., a Cave ppr. therefrom issuant a wolf at full speed reguardant ar. Williams

C.N. Elvin. Del.   P.C. Baker Sc.

PLATE 3.

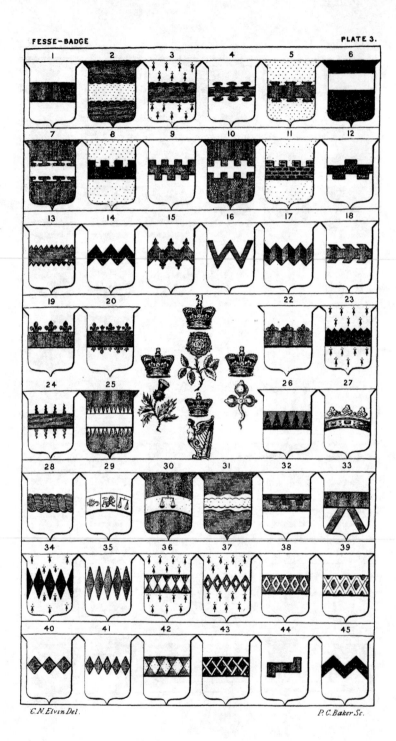

C.N.Elvin Del.

P.C.Baker Sc.

PLATE 3.

1 Fess or Fesse, Ar. a Fesse gu.
2 Fesse Engrailed
3 — Invecked, or Invected
4 — Nebulée, or Nebuly
5 — Dovetail
6 — Enhanced
7 — Potentée, or Counter Potent
8 — Crenelle, or Embattled
9 — Embattled, counter-embattled
10 — Bretessed
11 — Embattled-masoned
12 — with one embattle on the top, counter-embattled with two in the bottom
13 — Indented
14 — Dancettée
15 — Dancette-fleury counter-fleury. A fess dancette the upper points terminating in fleur-de-lis is borne by the name of Flowden
16 — Dancette of two pieces, or Fesse Emaunchée
17 — Dancettée gobony
18 — Raguly, counter-raguly
19 — Flory or Fleury
20 — Flory, counter-flory
21 See Badge in Dictionary
22 Fesse Treflée
23 — Indented on the top, or Fruille de scie
24 — Flamant on the sides
25 — Radiant, or Rayonne

26 Fesse Indented point in point
27 — Coronated on the top
28 — Wreathed, Tortilly, or Tortile
29 — Hemisphere, or Zodiac
30 — Arched, Champourne, or Eliptic-circle, thereon the sign libra
31 On a Fesse waved, or wavy, another Invecked
32 A Fesse per-fesse Crenelle
33 — Supported with two Stays cheveronwise
34 — of three fusils, or three fusils conjoined in fesse
35 — of Five fusils, or Five fusils conjoined in fesse
36 — Fusily
37 — of Five mascles, or Five mascles conjoined in fesse
38 On a Fesse, Five mascles conjoined; properly a fesse vert, masculy ar.
39 Fesse masculée
40 — of three lozenges, or three lozenges conjoined in fesse
41 — of Five lozenges, or Five lozenges conjoined in fesse
42 — lozengy or and az.
43 — sa. Fretty of the field
44 — Rectangled at both ends couped, the dexter to the base
45 — of Two chevrons conjoined, or Two chevrons coupled

PLATE 4.

1 Fesse Humettée, or couped. Ar. a fesse humettée gu.
2 — Voided, Sarcelle, or Recouise. Gu. a fesse ar. voided of the field
3 — Edged
4 — surmounted of another
5 — Bordered, or Fimbriated
6 — Nuée, or Nuage
7 — Eradicated, or Esclatte
8 — Escartele, or Escloppe
9 — Grice, Grady of three to the sinister, or Double escartelée
10 — Nowy, lozengy
11 — Indentee
12 — Nowy, Champaine, or urdée
13 — Nowy, quadrate
14 — Bottony, pometty, or nowy
15 — Debruised, fracted, or removed
16 — Ajouré
17 — Wiure, nebulée counter nebulée, or wiure nebulé counter-nebulée fixed in fesse
18 — of a Demi-belt, or a demi-belt fixed in fesse
19 — Double-beviled
20 — Bretessed, embattled-parted, or double-parted
21 Crest of Ireland. A Tower triple-towered or, from the portal a hart springing ar. attired and hoofed gold
22 Fesse Champaine, Urdée, or Warriated

23 Fesse Embattled-grady, cr Escartele grady
24 — Demi, or Demi fess
25 — Rompu, coppée, coupe, or double-downset
26 — Nebulée on the top, and Invecked on the bottom
27 — Beviled
28 — Rectangled, or angled
29 — between two greyhounds courant
30 On a fesse three lozenges
31 Az. two combs in fesse betw. a broken lance fesseways (or barways) or, one piece in chief the head respecting the dexter, the other half towards the sinister in base. Lombe
32 Per-fesse ar, and gu. six martlets countercharged. Fenwick
33 Per-fesse Nebuly az. and gu. Baker
34 Per-fesse, Escartelle, grady of three
35 Per-fesse Indented
36 Per-fesse Dancette
37 Per-fesse Dovetail
38 Per-fesse Crenelle
39 Bar, per base, erased
40 Fesse and Canton conjoined
41 — Billettée counter-billette
42 — Compony
43 — Counter-compony
44 — Chequy
45 — Quarterly

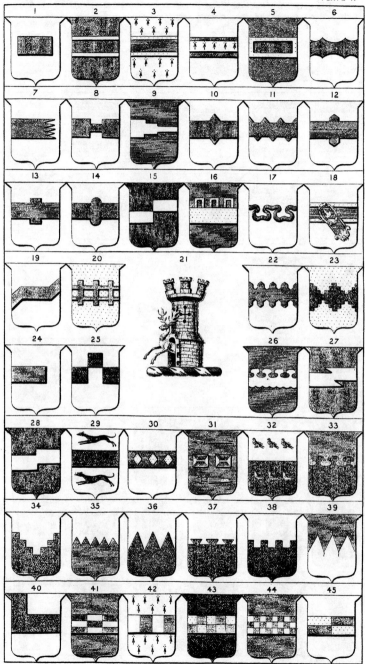

C.N.Elvin.Del.   P.C.Baker.Sc.

B

PLATE 5.

1 Bar. Ar. a Bar az.
2 Two Bars. Sa. two bars ar. arms of Brereton
3 Barrulet
4 Three Closets
5 Two Bars gemels
6 Three Bars gemels
7 Three Bars
8 Barry of eight
9 A Fesse cottised
10 A Fesse double cottised
11 Fesse treble cottised
12 Fesse charged with five music bars
13 Barry of six per-pale counter-charged
14 Fesse betw. two cottises fleury
15 — cottised potentée
16 — double cottised potent, counter-potent
17 — betw. two bars gemelle, embattled
18 — cottised-dancettée
19 A Fret
20 Fret couped
21 The Badge of Wales. A Dragon pass., wings elevated endorsed gu. upon a mount vert.
22 Fret engrailed. (For Triangular Frets see p. 42. f. 38.)
23 — fretted, or double fretted
24 — fleury at each point
25 — charged on each point with a pellet
26 — interlaced with an annulet
27 — throughout
28 Ar. on a Fret throughout gu. a rose in every interstice of the second, barbed vert., four hearts of the first. Gardiner

29 Fretty
30 Ar. Fretty sa. and semée of crescents of the second, or Ar. fretty sa. in each interstice a crescent of the last
31 An Orle
32 Per-Pale ar. and sa. an orle engrailed on both sides countercharged
33 A Double Orle, or an Orle of two pieces. (For Orle of three pieces see pl. 22, f. 25)
34 An Orle fretted with a pallet and barrulet
35 Gu. within an Orle ar. charged with eight mullets az. an armillary sphere or. Chamberlain
36 An Orle of eight estoiles. See Orle in Dictionary
37 Az. a Manche, or Maunch within an Orle of Fleur-de-lis or.
38 Erminois a crescent sa. within an Orle of Matlets gu. Roskell
39 Seven estoiles, or stars in orbicular form
40 Two Flasques, or Flanches
41 Two Voiders
42 Sa. a Stag's head cabosed betw. two Flanches ar. Parker
43 Gu. a lion ramp. or betw. two flanches erm. and a point in point of the last
44 Per-Pale sa. and ar. a Fleur-de-lis betw. two flanches, each charged with a Fleur-de-lis, all counter-charged. Also blazoned Per-Pale sa. and ar. two flanches and three Fleur-de-lis in fesse all countercharged. Robyns and White
45 Two square Flanches

PLATE 6.

1 Pile. Az. a pile erm.
2 — reversed or transposed
3 — issuing out of dexter base, in point bendways, also termed a Pile inverted in bend sinister
4 — indented
5 — reversed, or transposed indented
6 — embattled counter embattled
7 — reversed fitched, or undée at top, raguly, or with a crenelle on each side
8 — reversed goarée
9 — and two demi piles embowed, or flanched, and fixed to the sides
10 — Triple, or Triple-pointed
11 — in point bendwise, pierced lozengy
12 — charged with another engrailed
13 — in bend issuing out of the dexter corner. Ar. a pile issuant from the dexter chief point sa. fimberiated and engrailed gu.
14 Two Piles in point
15 Two Piles embowed fretting each other
16 Three Piles meeting in base, or three Piles in point
17 Pile betw. two Piles reversed
18 Pile transposed betw. two Piles
19 Three Piles issuing from the dexter barwise
20 Three Piles issuing out of sinister base in point bendways
21 Badge of the Prince of Wales. A plume of three ostrich feathers argent, enfiled by a coronet composed of fleur-de-lis and crosses-pattée alternately gold, and on an escroll az. edged or the motto Ich Dien
22 Three Piles, on a fesse surmounting the exterior ones, and debruised by the centre one, two crescents
23 A fesse in chief three Piles wavy

24 Pily counter-pily of seven traits (or pieces) the points ending in crosses pattée, three in chief and two in base
25 Three Piles issuing from the dexter in bend on each point a fleur-de-lis
26 A Pile triple, or triple-pointed in base bendwise, floried at the points
27 Issuing from a chief three piles
28 Two Piles reversed in point out of dexter and sinister base
29 Five Piles issuing from dexter bendways
30 Piles traversed, barwise
31 Pily of eight, traverse in point to sinister fesse
32 A Pile and cheveron countercharged
33 Three Piles issuing from the chief, surmounted by a cheveron, charged with three plates
34 On a Pile three pears slipped stalks upwards
35 On a Pile engrailed betw. two fish hauriant, a lion passant
36 Pile and Saltire countercharged. The blazon may be Ar. a Saltire sa. a pile countercharged
37 Three Piles within a bordure, or three piles gu. within a bordure az. plattée
38 Per-Pile traverse
39 Paly-pily, or Pily-paly
40 Pile square or tetragonell pyramid reversed
41 Three Piles solid and triangular couped
42 Piles fitched at the top also termed Piles wavy, fitched at both ends
43 Per Pile and cheveron countercharged
44 Per Pile reversed and per pale countercharged, or per pale and pile reversed countercharged
45 Per Pile transposed

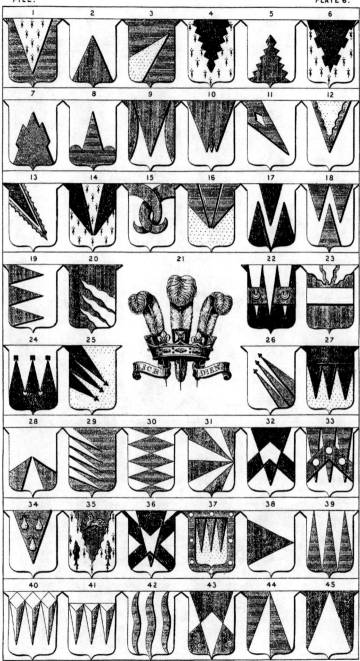

C.N.Elvin.Del.   P.C.Baker.Sc.

C.N.Elvin Del.

P.C.Baker Sc.

PLATE 7.

1 Cross. Ar. a Cross sa.
2 — between four Roses
3 On a Cross five fleur-de-lis
4 Cross surmounted by a Bendlet
5 — engrailed. Per pale az. and gu.
　　over all a cross engr. erm.
6 — raguly or raguled
7 — indented
8 — wavy, or undée
9 — watery, or a plain cross waved
10 — per-pale
11 — counter-quartered, or quarterly-
　　quartered, or quarterly a cross
　　countercharged
12 — point in point
13 — gobony, or componée
14 — counter componée, or counter
　　gobony
15 — chequy
16 — quarter-pierced
17 — rayonnated, or rayonnant
18 — corded
19 — clechée, recourse, or recoursie
20 — voided, also termed sarcelle.
　　Gu. a cross or voided of the
　　field
21 The Royal Banner, ditto of St.
　　George, St. Andrew, and St.
　　Patrick. The "Union Jack"
　　or National Banner, this flag is
　　blue, bearing the Red Cross of
　　St. George, the Saltire, or White
　　Cross of St. Andrew, and the
　　Red Saltire, or Cross of St.
　　Patrick, combined

22 Cross recercelled of another, also
　　blazoned cottised
23 — double voided, also termed
　　voided sarcelled
24 — fimbriated, or bordered
25 — surmounted of another
26 — double-parted
27 — double-parted and fretted
28 — triparted and fretted
29 — of three endorses surmounted of
　　as many barrulets
30 — treble-parted
31 — fillet
32 — fretted with an annulet. The
　　arms of Crusamell
33 — double-parted fretted with four
　　annulets
34 — lozengy-nowed, or lozengée-
　　nowed
35 — degraded
36 — pattée fixed, double-rebated
37 — nowy
38 — nowy-lozengy
39 — nowy-quadrat
40 — couped, at the top and flurt
41 — cable, or cablée
42 — cottised with eight demi fleur-de-
　　lis, properly a cross recercelled
　　with eight demi fleur-de-lis, their
　　bottoms towards the fesse point
　　conjoined
43 — nowed grady fixed
44 — nowed grady conjoined fitchée
45 — degraded and conjoined, or
　　issuing from twelve degrees

PLATE 8.

1 Cross lozengy, properly. Or a cross of nine lozenges az.
2 — lozengy. Ar. a cross lozengy or. and gu.
3 — of seven fusils
4 Five lozenges in cross
5 Cross of nine mascles, or masculy voided
6 — masculy
7 — mascle, or four mascles conjoined in cross
8 — of bezants. A cross bezantée is a plain cross strewed with bezants
9 — of roundles (hurts) ends tasselled
10 — of annulets
11 — of chains
12 — of four lozenges aboute
13 — of triangles, or twelve triangles in cross
14 — pall
15 — portate, portante, or portrate
16 — tron-onnée
17 — bretessed, a cross crossed, or a cross crosslet fixed
18 — crosslet also termed crosslet, crossell, crosset, or crucelet
19 — crosslet fitchée
20 — crosslet fitchée at the foot
21 Arms of a Bachelor. Ar. a chev. gu. betw. three martlets sa. The Shield ensigned with an helmet answering to his degree, mantled gu. doubled ar. Crest, on a wreath of the colours, Rocks ppr. issuant therefrom a demi lion ramp. or, holding a vine branch fructed also ppr. Motto Spectemur agendo in old English. Elvin

22 Cross crosslet double crossed
23 Cross crosslet on three grieces
24 — crosslet crossed
25 — of Jerusalem, or Jerusalem Cross, also termed a cross, crosslet cantoned with four crosses
26 — pattée crossed, also termed a cross crosslet pattée
27 — patriarchal grieced
28 — couped humette, or humetty
29 — couped and bordered
30 — couped voided. Az. a cross couped ar. voided of the field
31 — couped pierced circular
32 — nowy couped, properly a cross nowy quadrat couped
33 — Calvary, or cross of Christ
34 — couped pointed and voided, or a cross couped pointed and voided also termed Éguisce, or Aiguisé
35 — couped pointed and fimbriated, or, a cross points pointed and fimbriated
36 — bottonnée, pattée, also termed bottonee-masculed
37 — fitched at all points, pierced quarterly
38 — Lorrain voided
39 — masculy and pommettée, or clechée
40 — lambeauxed in all four
41 — blunted also termed mousue, or mossue
42 — couped fitchée double at the points, also termed chappe
43 — couped and fitchée at all points
44 — couped and fitchée at all points and pierced square
45 — estoile, or star-cross

PLATE 9.

1 Cross Pattée; also termed a Cross *Formée*
2 — Pattée pierced
3 — Pattée Fimbriated
4 — Pattée Concave
5 — Pattée Invecked
6 — Pattèe Engrailed
7 — Pattée Throughout, or Entire
8 — Pattée Fixed and Notched; also termed a Cross Pattée Escartelle or Demi Sarcelled
9 — Pattée Moline
10 — Pattée Quartered
11 — Pattée Pommettée, charged with another formée
12 —· Pattée Double Rebated
13 — Pattée Flory, or a Cross Pattée Fleury, or Florettée
14 — Pattée Fitchée, or Fitched
15 — Pattée Couped Fitched, or rebated, better say a Cross Pattée fitched rebated
16 — Pattée Double sarcelled at bottom
17 — Pattée Double Fitched
18 — Pattée Fitchée at the foot
19 — Pattée an engrail at each point
20 — Pattée Fitchée at all points
21 Arms of a Maid are always borne in a lozenge, Az. three swords one in pale point upwards, surmounted of the other two in saltire points downwards, ar. hilts and pommels or. Norton
22 Cross Pattée Crenellée
23 — Pattée Convexed, or a Cross pattée alisée, or globical
24 — Patriarchal pattée flory at the foot
25 Cross Pattée Fitchée Lambeaux, or a Cross Pattée Fitchée on a label of three points
26 — Pattée fitchée disjointed
27 — Pattée fitchée at all points (ancient)
28 — Patriarchal pattée
29 — Tau ends convexed, mounted upon three grieces
30 — Tau also termed St. Anthony's Cross, and Cross Commise
31 — Barbed, Barbée, Cramponée, or tournée
32 — Fusil at each end rebated
33 — Fusil at each end
34 — Double Portante
35 — Fourchée, Fourchy, or Furshe, also termed a Cross Miller rebated
36 — Couped treble-fitchée, also termed a Cross Fourchée of three points
37 — Couped fitchée of four at each end; also termed a Cross of sixteen points, or fitchée of sixteen
38 Long, or Passion Cross; also termed The Latin Cross
39 Long Cross couped with the felloe of a wheel conjoined at top
40 Long Cross, potent pomelled of three, the foot plain
41 Cross moline rebated
42 — couped fitchée, top fusil
43 — Fitchée, anciently called Furchée
44 — Pattée fusily fitchée
45 — Aiguise, or Equisée

PLATE 10.

1 Cross Moline, also termed Nyle, Anille, or Nelle
2 — Moline pierced lozengy
3 — Moline quarterly pierced
4 — Moline angled with acorns, or acorned as each angle
5 — Moline per cross, at each end at the centre of the extremities a leaf of three points
6 — Pattée in fesse and moline in pale
7 — Moline pomelled, or a cross moline pommetté
8 — Moline double-rebated
9 — Moline anchored
10 — Moline double-parted, voided flory, or a cross moline Sarcelled
11 — Anchored, Anchore, or Anchory. Also termed a cross pattée double fitched, or double fitchée of all four
12 — Double parted flory
13 — Patonce
14 — Patonce Fitchy
15 — Patonce angled with passion nails
16 — Patonce voided
17 — Flory
18 — Couped fleury, or Humetty flurty or florette
19 — Flory triparted, properly a cross-flory
20 — Bottonnee, or a cross Trefoil, or Treffle
21 Arms Impaled, i.e., Baron and Femme. Elvin impaling Norton. See pl. 8 and 9, fig. 21
22 Cross of the Capitals, of four pillars flurty and a leopard's face issuant
23 — Astragal, or Astrical with fleur-de-lis. Also termed a cross cornished flurt

24 Cross Miller, or a cross mill-rind
25 — Mill-rind voided and disjointed
26 — Triparted flory
27 — Pomelle, avelland, or cross pommelle flory
28 — Pomelled, Pommelle, or Crowned-pomel or bourdonnée
29 — Pomelle voided and removed
30 — Double-pomelled
31 — Pommelled and Crescented, also termed cross pommettée and crescente
32 — Couped crescented, also termed cross-crescented, or crescenty
33 — Ferrated, i.e. with horse-shoes at extremities
34 — Double-parted and anchored, or a cross double-parted and crescented
35 — Annulated, or a cross couped, at each end an annulet
36 — Annulated, rebated
37 — Annuly each fretted with a ring
38 — Degraded, nowed
39 — Crosslet, double-fitched (or fitchée) of all four rebated
40 — Double-fitched (or fitchée) and rebated of all four
41 — Entrailed
42 — Patriarchal thrice crossed potent the foot lambeaux
43 — Patriarchal pommettée upon three grieces
44 — Quarterly quartered couped, ends sarcelled and reverted
45 — Potent ends rounded, surmounted of a cross couped. It may be blazoned. Ar. a Cross Potent the ends rounded gu. voided per cross

C.N.Elvin Del.   P.C.Baker Sc.

PLATE 11.

1 Cross Pattée quadrat in the centre, this is also called the Cross of St. Cuthbert
2 — Cross of St. James
3 — of Athelstan, or Athelstone's Cross, i.e. on a mound, a cross botonnée
4 — Double triparted
5 — Double Avellaney, or a cross mascle fruitagée
6 — Fer-de-fourchette
7 — Potent, or Potence also termed a Cross Baton, or Batune
8 — Potent crossed, or a cross gemelle
9 — Potent engrailed
10 — Potent fitchée
11 — Potent Flory
12 — Potent pomelled and fitchée at foot
13 — Potent quadrat in the centre
14 — Potent, repotent
15 — Hamecon barbed at foot
16 — of Four pomels
17 — Caterfoil, or Cross Quatrefoil
18 — Potence of Saxon F. this is also termed Digamma
19 — with demi annulets inverted, or a cross demi anuled inverted
20 — Snagg
21 Arms of an Heiress or Co.-Heiress when married; the husband bear her arms in an Escutcheon of Pretence, as here shown. Arms in Pretence, quarterly or and gu. on a bend sa. five bezants. Stebbing
22 Cross of Four pruning hooks contrary embowed, by some called four coulters joined to a ball or bullet
23 — Fer-de-moline, pierced lozengy, or a cross moline nowy lozengy pierced

24 Cross Patriarchal pattée conjoined and annulated in the middle of the bottoms, or in the middle of the bottom cross. Also blazoned as two patriarchal crosses pattée conjoined and both annulated in the centre of the lower cross beam
25 — Lambeaux rebated
26 — on each stem the Saxon B
27 — Long, or Long Cross on Ball and top like the Roman P
28 — Coronated, or Coronetté
29 — Banister, or four banister-staves fixed crosswise to a roundle, each crowned at the ends
30 — Fruitagée
31 — Catoosed
32 — Moline invertant, Cercelée, or Sarcelée
33 — Avelane, or avellane
34 — with Caterfoils and trefoils
35 — grady pomelled
36 — Couped, anserated, or gringolée. See Decorated
37 — Long, or Long Cross raguled
38 — of four batunes fretted
39 — Potent rebated, also termed a Cross Cramponne; a Fylfot, or Gammadion
40 — Recercellée voided
41 — of Ermine, or Four Ermine-spots in cross, heads in fesse point
42 — of Malta, or Cross of St. John of Jerusalem. See also pl. 23, fig. 21
43 — Pendall, or Spindle
44 — Clechée properly means voided, but this cross is by some termed a cross clechée
45 — Capital, or Cornished

PLATE 12.

1 A Chief. Gu. a Chief or.
2 Ar. on a Chief vert. two mullets pierced or.
3 Az. in Chief three estoiles ar.
4 Chief Engrailed
5 — Invecked, or Invected
6 — Wavy, Wavée, or Undée
7 — Dancettée
8 — Urdée or Champaine, also termed embattled rebated at its corners
9 — Dove-tailed
10 — Quarterly, Potent counter-potent
11 — Neublée. Ar. Gutte-de-poix, a chief nebulée gu.
12 — Rayonée, Rayed, or Raise
13 — Indented. Ar. masoned sa., a chief indented of the second
14 — Crenellée
15 — of one Indent
16 — with one dovetail, also termed a Chief with one label or Lambeaux, or pattée
17 — Escartellée, also blazoned one embattlement in a chief
18 — with one embattlement
19 — Nowed
20 — Angled, or Rect-angled
21 Arms Quarterly. 1st and 4th ar. a chev. gu. betw. three martlets sa. Elvin 2nd and 3rd. Quarterly or and gu. on a bend sa. five bezants. Stebbing. Crest Blazoned at plate 8. fig. 21
22 A Chief Beveled
23 — Couped
24 — Bordered or rempli, also termed Cousu-Chief
25 — charged with a Bar humettée

26 A Chief Couped bevelwise. Ar. six muschetors, three, two and one and a Chief couped bevelwise az.
27 — with one indent in chief, or a Chief indent
28 On a Chief a Bar Dancettée, also termed a vivre
29 Chief Couvert
30 — Per-Fess. Bendy of six ar. and gu. A chief per-fesse ar. and erm. in chief three fleur-de-lis sa.
31 — Lowered or Removed
32 — Surmounted, or Surmounte
33 — charged with a Fillet. Sa. a Chief erm. charged with a fillet in the neither part ar. It is also blazoned a Chief supported or surmounted, and a Chief with a fillet in the lower part, also Soustenu, or Souteunée
34 — Vestu, or Revestu
35 — Vestu sinister
36 — Inclave
37 — Arched, convex, or flecked
38 — Double Arched
39 — Charged with a Chapournet, or Shapournett
40 — Chapournated, or a Chapournated-chief. And a Barrulet enfiled with an annulet
41 — Point in Point dented
42 — Pierced by an arrow
43 — Enmancheé, or Chappe. Gu. a chief ar. chappe sa.
44 — Quarterly-Flory counter Flory
45 — Charged with a Bar Nebulee. Gu. three Pheons ar. on a Chief of the last a bar nebulee az.

For Chief Ajouré, and Chausse. See pl. 22, fig. 9 and 8.

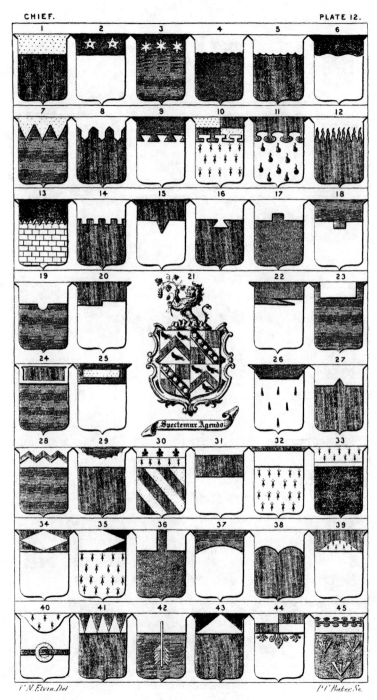

Spectemur Agendo.

C.N.Elvin.Del.   P.C.Baker.Sc.

D

C.N.Elvin.Del   P.C.Baker.Sc

PLATE 13.

1 Bordure. Sa. a Bordure or Border ar.
2 — Engrailed
3 — Invecked
4 — Embattled, or Crenellée
5 — Vair
6 — Nebulée
7 — Compony, or Gobony
8 — Rayonnée
9 — Urdée
10 — Indented
11 — Flory-counter-flory
12 — Potentée
13 — Compony-counter-compony
14 — Point in Point
15 — Dovetailed
16 — Battled, or embattled-grady
17 — Per Border Indented
18 — Indentée
19 — Chequy
20 — Denticules, or Denticles
21 Arms of a Knight Bachelor. Az. a chev. engr., betw. three leopard's faces, ar. Shield ensigned with a Knight's helmet ppr. mantled az. doubled ar., on a wreath of the colours a leopard's face as in the arms. As borne by Sir Peter Eade, Knt., M.D.
22 Bordure Quarterly
23 — Paly of six
24 — Per Saltire a Border counterchanged
25 — Per Fesse
26 — Barry of six
27 Per Bend Border counterchanged. Per Bend ar. and gu., a Border counterchanged
28 — Bendy
29 Bordure Chevronny of six

30 Bordure of England and France
31 — Double counterchanged. Also blazoned Per-Pale ar. and gu. Embordered of the same
32 — Demi
33 Or an Inescutcheon gu. a bordure of the last
34 Bordure Quarterly quartered. Also blazoned as a bordure divided as gyronne of eight
35 — Charged with another, or a Bordure surmounted of another, also blazoned a Border parted per Border
36 — Per-Pale. Per-Pale ar. and gu. a bordure charged with eight escallops all counterchanged
37 — Charged with eight martlets, termed a Bordure Enaluron
38 — On a Bordure eight Lions pass. guard. Also termed a Bordure Enurny of eight Lions, &c.
39 — Verdoy of Trefoils. Sa. on a border or, eight trefoils vert.
40 — Bezantée or Bezanty. Ar. a Lion ramp. gu., ducally crowned or, within a border sa. bezanty. Either Entoyre of eight bezants or garnished with bezants
41 — Billettée
42 — Fretty
43 — as borne when impaled. Gu. a bordure ar., Impaling az. a Fesse ar.
44 — Surmounted of a chief
45 — Engrailed. Sa. three crescents Erm. within a bordure engrailed. Bateman

PLATE 14.

1 Ar. a Pale sa.
2 Ar. a Pallet gu.
3 Ar. an Endorse or Indorse gu.
4 Ar. a Pale endorsed az, or a Pale betw. two Indorses
5 Per Pale, a Pale counterchanged
6 Pale Between two Eagles displayed wings inverted
7 — Surmounted of another
8 — Voided. Or a pale gu. voided of the field
9 — Fimbriated, or bordered engrailed
10 — Engrailed betw. two pallets
11 — Invecked, or invected
12 — Flory-counter Flory
13 — Raguly
14 — Wavy
15 — Indented
16 — Dancetteé
17 — Bretessed
18 — Radiant. (az. on a Pale-radiant or, a Lion ramp. gu.) also termed Rayonneé
19 — Double arched
20 — Fitchée in the foot
21 Arms of a Baronet. Gu. three garbs and a Bordure engr. or. above the Shield an helmet befitting his degree, mantled gu. doubled ar. on a wreath of the colours the Crest, on a Garb lying fesseways or, a Pelican vulning herself ppr. Kemp. Bart.
22 Pale Champaine
23 — Bevilled
24 — Retracted
25 — Fracted, or removed and overlaid
26 Pale Fracted, or removed
27 — Angled
28 — Lozengy conjoined
29 — Counterchanged. Per Fesse gu. and or, a Pale counterchanged
30 Paly of three parted per Fesse, also termed Paly and Fesse of six
31 Two Pales
32 Three Pales
33 Paly of six per-fesse counterchanged see also P. 22. f. 42
34 Two Pales couped in fesse conjoined to another
35 Pale angled quarter, or a Pale nowy quadrate
36 Or three rose leaves in pale vert. betw. two Pallets az., a chief gu
37 Per Fesse in clave, or per fesse a Pale in base. Per fesse ar. and gu. in base a Pale or.
38 Paly of six Saltiery counterchanged
39 Per-Fesse, the base Per-Pale in chief or, a dexter hand couped at the wrist grasping a sword erect entwined with a serpent ppr. betw. two lions ramp. respecting each other gu.; the dexter base vert, charged with a brick trippant or.; on the sinister base per-pale ar. and sa. a boar pass. counterchanged
40 Per Pale a Pheon counterchanged
41 Five Lozenges in Pale
42 Three Palets wavy
43 Three stirrups with leathers couped in pale
44 Paly of six ar. and gu. a Bend sa.
45 Per-Pale ar. and az. in the first. three pallets sa.

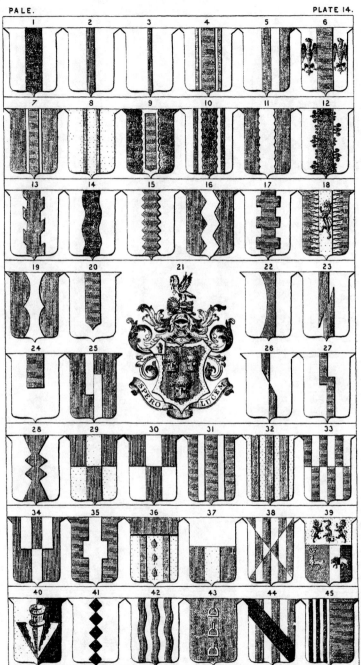

C.N.Elvin.Del.   P.C.Baker.Sc.

C.N. Elvin. Del.   P.C.Baker. Sc.

PLATE 15.

1 Ar. a Chevron gu.
2 Chevronel
3 Couple close
4 Two Couple closes
5 Chevron Engrailed
6 — Invecked
7 — Recoursíe
8 — Bordered, or Fimbriated
9 — Engrailed. Or. a chev. engrailed az. Charged, or surmounted of another ar.
10 — voided of another engrailed
11 — voided. Az. a chev. or voided of the field
12 — Humettée
13 — Embattled
14 — Embattled counter-embattled
15 — Grady
16 — Bretessed
17 — Potent
18 — Potent counter-potent
19 — Urdée, or Champaine
20 — Urdée-Champained
21 Arms of a Baronet of Scotland or Nova Scotia Baronet. See Nova Scotia Baronet
22 Chevron Embattled arondie
23 — Flamant on the upper side
24 — Dovetailed
25 — Indented
26 — Nebulée

27 Chevron Indented embowed, or Hacked and Hewed
28 — Grady on both sides
29 — Griece, or Double escartelée
30 — Embowed
31 — In Point embowed
32 — Enarched
33 — Enarched
34 — Potent, ringed at the top
35 — Pattée at the top, or a Chevron ensigned on the top with a Cross-pattée
36 — Enhansed, or Enhanced
37 — In Base
38 — Cottised. This may be blazoned az. a chev. ar. betw. two couple closes or
39 — Triparted, or Treble-parted
40 Three Chevrons, or chevronels braced, or interlaced
41 Three chevronels
42 Gu. two Chevrons in Fret, or Fretted, the upper one or, the other ar. It may be blazoned ; gu. a chev. ar. interlaced with another reversed or
43 Chevron Reversed
44 — Two Chevrons in counter-point
45 — Two Chevrons couched, dexter and sinister

PLATE 16.

1 Chevron Rompu, or Downset. Ar. a chev. rompu sa.
2 — Debruised, or Fracted
3 — Burst, Eclate, or Split
4 — Disjointed. or Brisse
5 — Removed
6 — Demi
7 — Disjointed and crossed
8 Two Chevrons Palletted, or Two Chevrons and Pale conjoined
9 Chevron supported, or a Chevron with beam and standard
10 Two Chevrons arched and couched from dexter and sinister
11 Two Chevrons arched, couched and fretted
12 Chevron Arched
13 — Couched
14 — Two Chevrons couched, fretted and couped
15 — Pierced with a Barrulet
16 — Pierced with a Bend. (If oppressed the Bend would pass over the chevron)
17 — Pierced with an Arrow, or transfixed with an arrow
18 — Fretted with a Fesse, also termed Debruised and Fretted with a Bar
19 — Oppressed, or surmounted of a Fesse
20 Fesse between Two Chevrons, Sa. on a Fesse betw. two Chevrons ar. three Cornish Choughs ppr.
21 The Arms of a Knight of the Hanoverian Guelphic Order. See arms of a Knight of any Order
22 Chevron Pierced with a Fesse
23 Per-Pale az. and gu., three Chevrons ar. voided per-pale of the second and first
24 On a Chevron. Erm. on a chev. gu. three escallops ar.
25 Quarterly sa. and ar. a chev. perpale or and gu.
26 Chevron Quarterly per chevron. Also blazoned a chevron perpale and per chevron
27 Ar. a chev. sa. a Bordure gu.
28 Chevron with Mascle-head, or chev. with Mascle top
29 — Flory at the top, also termed a chev. ensigned on the top with a fleur-de-lis

30 Per-Chevron ar. and gu. a Crescent counterchanged
31 Per-Chevron, a chevron counterchanged
32 Per-Chevron Crenellée
33 Chevronelly of six
34 A Label with three tags pendent, or double labels. Label of one point, and Label couped with two points
35 Label, or File, of three lambeaux issuing out of chief. Label of three points throughout and Label of three points
36 Labels issuing out of Chief embowed. Label of three points each charged with a Canton Sinister and a Label of four points throughout
37 Label of three points. Label with three bells pendent, or Label Campaned, and Label with three pomegranates pendent enwrapped with a wiure, or ribbon
38 Label issuing out of Chief. Label in Fesse counterposed with another, or Two files in fesse endorsed. This is also blazoned "a Bar gemelles pattée"
39 A Label of three points crossed. A Label of Five points in Fesse, A File of three points fixed
40 Shield of the Prince of Wales is the same as that of the Sovereign with label of three points ar. for difference, and the arms of Saxony en-surtout
41 The Label in Chief is that of the Princess Royal. The one in Base of the Duke of Edinburgh
42 The Label in Chief is that of the Princess Alice. The one in Base of the Duke of Connaught
43 The Label in Chief is that of the Princess Helena. The one in Base of the Duke of Albany
44 The Label in Chief is that of the Princess Louise. The one in Base of the Duke of Cumberland
45 The Label in Chief is that of the Princess Beatrice. The one in Base of the Duke of Cambridge

The Label of His Royal Highness Prince Albert Victor of Wales. P. 25.A f. 1.
     ,,   ,,   ,,   George of Wales.   P. 25.A f. 2.

C.N. Elvin Del.   P.C. Baker Sc.

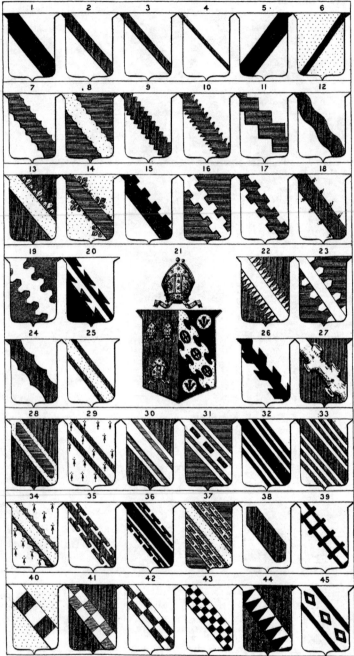

C.N.Elvin.Del.   P.C.Baker.Sc.

PLATE 17.

1 Ar. a Bend sa.
2 Ar. a Bendlet gu.
3 Ar. a Garter gu.
4 Ar. a Cost gu.
5 Ar. a Bend-sinister sa.
6 Or. a Scarpe sa.
7 Bend Engrailed
8 — Invected
9 — Indented
10 — Indented, embowed, or Hacked and Hewed
11 — Dancettée
12 — Wavy
13 — Flory
14 — Flory counter-Flory
15 — Embattled
16 — Bretessed
17 — Embattled counter-embattled
18 — Flamant
19 — Urdée, Urdy, Palisado, Champagne, or Warriated
20 — Dovetail. Per Bend ar. and sa. a Bend Pattée or Dove-tail counterchanged
21 Arms of a Bishop. The arms of the See of Chester gu. three mitres labelled or; Impaled with these the Armorial Bearings of Dr. Stubbs Bp. of Chester, viz. sa. on a Bend Nebulée or, betw. Two Bezants each charged with a Pheon of the field, three oval buckles tongues pendent of the first
22 Bend Radiant, Rayonne, or Radiant rayonne

23 Bend Urdée-Champained
24 — Arondie, nuée, or nuage. Also termed a Bend arondy treble-arched; or gored on both sides
25 — Edged
26 — Raguly
27 — of a limme (limb) of a Tree Raguled and Trunked. Penruddocke
28 — Bordered, or Fimbriated
29 — Voided. Erm. a bend gu. voided of the field
30 — Double edged
31 — Cottised. Az. on a Bend cottised ar. three billets sa.
32 — Double cotised, cottised, or Cotticed
33 — Treble cottised
34 — Surmounted. Erm. a Bend Engrailed az. surmounted of another or.
35 — Potentée
36 — Cottised potentée
37 — Double cottised potent counter-potent, also blazoned, Az. a Bend. betw. four cottises potent on the inner sides or.
38 — Humette, or couped
39 — Bretessed parted
40 — Gobony or Compony
41 — Compony counter-compony
42 — Billettée counter-billettée
43 — Chequy, or Checkie
44 — Indented point in point
45 In Bend. Ar. in bend three mascles betw. two cottises sa.

PLATE 18.

1 Bend Lozengy, or Lozenge. Az. a bend lozengy ar. and gu.
2 In Bend. Five Lozenges in Bend
3 Bend Fusily, or Fusele
4 Five Fusils in Bend
5 Five Mascles in Bend
6 Bend Masculy, or Masculée
7 — Papellonnée
8 — Double Beviled
9 — Traverse counterpoint
10 — Escartele grady, or grady embattled
11 — Double downsett
12 — Rectangled
13 — Escartele, or Escloppe
14 — Debruised, fracted, or removed, also termed double downsett
15 — Grice, or Grady of three, also termed double escartelée
16 — Nowy quadrate
17 — Nowy lozengy
18 — Nowy champaine, or Urdée
19 — Beviled, or Acute-angled
20 — Nowy, or Tranchée
21 Arms of a Baron. Barry of six ar. and az. in chief three annulets gu. Shield surmounted by a Barons coronet. Crest on a wreath of the colours a wyvern's head couped ppr. Supporters two wyverns reguardant, Wings endorsed ar., collared az. and chained reflexed or. each charged on the breast with three annulets in fesse gu. De Grey. Baron Walsingham. Motto Excitari non hebescere
22 Bend Double Nowed.
23 — Eradicated
24 — Demi
25 — Arched, or Bowed, also termed Shapourne
26 — Hemisphere, or Zodiac
27 — Bend Sinister Engoule
28 — Archy Coronetteé, or Coronated
29 — Bretessed nuée
30 — Cottised Dancettée
31 — Cottised Indented
32 Bendy Fusilly
33 Bendy Masculy
34 Two Bendlets
35 Three Bendlets
36 Three Bendlets enhanced
37 Bendy of six
38 Bendy of eight
39 Bendy sinister of six
40 Bendy sinister of six per-Bendy counterchanged, or Counter-bendy
41 Bendy sinister-paly. For Bendy Paly see P. 2. f. 32.
42 Bendy of six angled
43 A wall embattled in Bend-Sinister
44 Bendy-Barried
45 Per-Bend indented bowed points pommettée

C.N.Elvin.Del.   P.C.Baker.Sc.

PLATE 19.

1 Per-Bend ar. and gu. two Bendlets counterchanged
2 — Crenellé
3 — Urdée
4 — Embattled Urdée
5 — Embattled arondie
6 — Indented
7 — Nebuly, or Nebulée
8 — In Point *Urdé*
9 — with one embattlement arondie
10 — In point to Sinister, or Per-Bend Escartelée pointed
11 — Nuée, Double gored
12 — Pointed with ball
13 — Treble arched, or gored to the sinister
14 — Sinister in Aile
15 — Arched
16 — Dancettée
17 — Two Piles, triple pointed, bowed and counter-posed
18 — Sinister, in form of lions' mouths
19 — Indented into three points trefoiled
20 — Waved and counter-trefoiled
21 Arms of an Earl. Erm. a Fer-de-mouline betw. two martlets in pale sa., on a chief engrailed az., two marlions' wings conjoined and expanded or. Shield surmounted by an Earl's coronet. Crest a Lion ramp. Erminois holding a fer-de-mouline as in the arms. Supporters. Dexter a griffin wings endorsed ar., gorged with a marquiss coronet. Sinister a Bear ppr. gorged with a belt ar. buckled and charged with two cresents or. motto Esto quod esse videris. Mills, Earl Sondes
22 Per Bend waved, with two foils, or leaves, contrary posed
23 Per Bend waved with foils of leaves

24 On a Bend, per-bend gu. and az. betw. two cottises engr. sa. three fleur-de-lis or.
25 Per Bend counter-pommettée
26 A Bend-Braced
27 A Batton, or Batune. Also termed the Bar of bastardy
28 Ar. a bentlet gu. betwn. two Greyhounds courant in bend sa., enclosed by as many bendlets of the second
29 Erm. on a Bend sa. two hands and arms issuing out of clouds all ppr. rending a horse shoe or.
30 Gu. a Bend or, a chief ar.
31 Az. four costs or.
32 Ar. a Bend and Bordure gu.
33 Barry of ten or. and sa. a Bend gu.
34 Vair ar. and sa. a Quarter gu.
35 Chequy or. and gu. a Sinister quarter ar.
36 Sa. gutté d' Eau a Canton Erm.
37 Az. on a Canton indented or, a Butterfly of the first
38 Ar. a Brogue, or Shoe sa., on a Canton per- chev. gu. and Erm. Three covered cups or.
39 Ar. a Fritillaria meleagris stalked and leaved ppr. on a Canton gu. a cross pattée or.
40 Ar. a Canton in dexter-base vert.
41 Gyronny or Gyronne of eight ar. and az., within a border Erm. over all a Canton gu. changed with a fleur-de-lis or.
42 Ar. a Gyron gu.
43 Ar. Two Gyrons az. also termed Mi-Taillé. (Gyronny of six, eight, twelve and sixteen see P. 2.)
44 Az. three bars or, on an Escutcheon ar., three nails points in base sa., on a chief of the first two pallets betw. as many gyrons of the second. See P. 21. f. 42.
45 Gyronny of three Arondia gu. or and sa.

PLATE 20.

1 Saltier. Ar. a Saltier az.
2 — Voided. Az. a saltier or voided of the field
3 — Surmounted of another)
4 — Fimbriated, or edged)
These are distinguished by the shading
5 — Quarterly Quartered
6 — Counterchanged. Per Saltire ar. and gu., a Saltier counterchanged
7 — Checky, or Chequy
8 — Compony counter-compony
9 — Compony
10 — Lozengy, or Lozengée
11 — Fusily
12 — Masculy
13 — of Nine Lozenges
14 — of Eight Fusils
15 — of mascles
16 Ar. a mascle fretted with four others in Saltier gu.
17 Saltier Indented
18 — Triparted and fretted, or Three bendlets and three bendlets-sinister interlaced
19 — Raguly
20 — Potentée, or Potented
21 Arms of a Commoner and Lady. The Armorial Bearings of Benjamin Disraeli, and Mary Anne Viscountess Beaconsfield. See Arms of Commoner and Lady
22 Saltier Couped
23 — Bretessed
24 — Nowy
25 — Nowy arched
26 — Nowy quadrat pierced lozengy
27 — Nowy Lozengy
28 — Nowy couped
29 — Saltier. saltiered and flory. or a Crosslet flory in Saltire

30 Saltier Saltiered-pattée
31 — Bottonée
32 — Toulouse and pommettée
33 — Saltered and Flory
34 — Invecked and plain cottised
35 — Pierced
36 — Engrailed. Gu. on a Saltier Engr. or, a crescent betw. four roses of the field, barbed and seeded ppr.
37 — Between. Az. a Saltier or, betw. four annulets ar. Or az. a Saltier or, cantoned with four annulets ar.
38 — Cantoned. Ar. a Chief and Saltier gu., cantoned with two Mascles in the collar and base points az. in the flanks a spot of ermine
39 In Saltier. Az. Five Roses in Saltier ar.
40 Counterchanged. Per-pale or and az. A Saltier counterchanged
41 Surmounted, Or a fesse az. surmounted of a Saltier gu.
42 On a Saltier. Ar. on a Saltier sa. within a border of the last, a gem-ring or. Also blazoned Ar. on a Saltier sa. an annulet or stone az. all within a bordure of the second
43 Az. an annulet ensigned with a cross pattée or, interlaced with a Saltier conjoined in base of the second
44 Saltier of Chains
45 A Gordian Knot, Blazoned a double orle of annulets, linked to each other, and to one in the centre, gyronwise. It is also termed The Double Knot of Navarre, or Navarre Knot

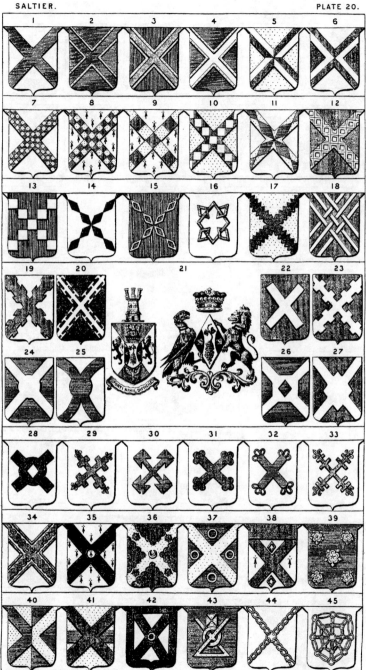

C

C. N. Elvin, Del.

P. C. Baker Sc

PLATE 21.

1 A Point dexter., or Point dexter parted
2 Point pointed
3 — in point reversed
4 — in point, also termed a Graft
5 Plain Point, or a Point in base
6 Point Champaine, Champion, or a Base chausse
7 Vert Two Squires in point from chief on either side, a pale ar. or Points dexter and sinister from the chief on either side of a pale
8 Ar. a Point pointed az. and two points dexter and sinister removed gu.
9 Gu. on a chev. ar., three martlets of the first betw. two points dexter and sinister engrailed and a Point pointed invecked or.
10 Point dexter removed extended to the sinister side
11 Ar. Points pointed to the chief and reversed in base counterchanged gu.
12 Gu. Point sinister removed and extended to dexter fesse point ar. charged with the like point az.
13 Point pointed in point from dexter base to sinister chief
14 — — on the top a pomel, or pomelled
15 — — reversed bottony at end
16 — — fleury, or a Point in Point flory at the top
17 — Escartelled
18 — with one embattlement
19 — dexter and sinister convexed, or champourned
20 — sinister and dexter base indented
21 Arms of Augmentation see Augmentation
22 Points four pointed and Nowy on the top in pale
23 — four, or Lozenge in point. Perfess ar. and vert, four points counterchanged. Hinxley
24 A Base Esquire, or a Point based
25 A Sinister Quarter pointed

26 Per-Pile in base, or Per Chevron reversed
27 A Point dexter and Sinister arched and a Point in point.
28 Urdée in point, or contrary urdée
29 Per-Fesse Varrey in Point, or perfesse ar. urdée in point, paleways of the first and az.
30 Barry point in point, or barry perfret
31 Per-fesse double arched, or gored, or per-fesse point in point reversed
32 A Gore, or Goar sinister
33 Two Gussets, or a dexter and sinister gusset
34 Ente in point ar. az. and gu.
35 Tierce in Pairle gu. az. and ar.
36 — in mantle gu. az. and ar., or parted in three mantle
37 — in Fesse also termed Points three
38 — in Pale
39 — in Bend
40 — in Gyrons bend sinisterways
41 — in Pile from Sinister to Dexter, or Traverse from the sinister
42 Barry of six ar. and az. an inescutcheon of the last; on a chief or, two pallets betw. as many gyrons of the second, sometimes blazoned two based esquires, or Squires base dexter and sinister, instead of gyron's
43 Sa. on a Point wavy ppr. a lion pass. or, in chief three bezants
44 Arms of Hanover. Field divided per-pale and per-chev. enarched 1st. Gu. two lions pass. guard. in pale or, for Brunswick. 2nd. Or, semée of hearts ppr. a lion ramp. az. for Luenburgh. 3rd. Gu. a horse courant ar. for Saxony. In the centre (or En Surcoat) on an inescutcheon gu. the crown of Charlemagne ppr.
45 Ar. a demi lion ramp. az. naissant out of a plain point gu., on a chief indented sa., an estoile betw. two increscents of the first

PLATE 22.

1 Shield of the Trinity
2 Az. an Episcopal Staff in pale or, ensigned with a cross pattée ar. surmounted of a Pall of the last, charged with four crosses formée-fitchée sa., edged and fringed of the second. Archbishop of Canterbury
3 Gu. a Pall ar. edged and fringed or.
4 Holy Dove
5 Spider and Web, also termed "Cobweb"
6 Gurges, or Whirlpool
7 Az. on a mount in base vert, the tree of Paradise environed with the Serpent betw. Adam and Eve all ppr. Fruiterer's Company, London
8 Erm. A Chief ar. Chausse gu.
9 Az. A Chief or, ajoure gu.
10 Ar. on a mount in base vert three pine trees ppr. a dexter side or. Grote
11 Ar. the base vert issuing therefrom three hop poles sustaining their fruit all ppr. Houblon
12 Ar. on a mount vert, a lion ramp. contourne gu. supporting an orange tree-fructed ppr. De la Motte
13 Per-fesse wavy the chief ar., the base representing waves of the sea, in chief a dexter hand couped at the wrist gu., in base a Salmon naiant ppr. O'Neill
14 Ar. two bubbles, and a third rising out of water in base ppr. borne by Aire and Bubbleward
15 Sa. a Fesse ar., in chief three ladies from the waist heads affrontée arranyed and veiled ar. crowned or, in base an ox of the second passing over a ford ppr. See of Oxford
16 Gu., a demi horse ar., hoofed and maned or, issuing out of water in base ppr. Trevelyan. See *Water*
17 Or, Semée of Flowers gentle, in the middle of the chief a sengreen resting upon a book betw. two serpents in pale, their tails knit together all in ppr. colours, resting upon a square stone vert. Caius College Cambridge

18 Per-Pale gu. and az. three lions pass. guard in pale or, Dimidiated with three herrings naiant in pale ar. Gt. Yarmouth. See term Dimidiation
19 Quarterly, 1 and 4 sa. a chev. betw. three fleames ar. 2nd. and 3rd Per-Pale ar. and vert, a Spatula in pale az. surmounted of a Rose gu. charged with another silver, the first rose regally crowned ppr. betw. the four quarters of a cross of St. George charged with a lion pass. guard. or. Barber's Company
20 Gu. on a cross ar., betw. the four ace cards ppr. viz.: the ace of hearts and diamonds in chief, the ace of spades and clubs in base; a lion pass. guard. of the first. Card Maker's Company
21 Arms of a Widow. See Dictionary
22 A Cross Quarterly quartered
23 A Cross Patriarchal
24 Gu. a demi virgin couped below the shoulders, issuing from clouds all ppr. vested or, crowned with an eastern crown of the last, her hair dishevelled, and wreathed round the temples with roses of the second, all within an orle of clouds ppr. Mercer's Company of London
25 Ar. an Orle of three pieces sa.
26 Ar. a Frett bretessed, espined, or crossed sa.
27 Diaper, or Diapre. Quarterly diaper, in the first quarter a mullet or. De Vere
28 De. three cross baskets in pale ar. betw. a prime in chief and an iron in base on the dexter, and a cutting knife in chief and an outsticker in base on the sinister of the second. Basket Maker's Company
29 Az. a Golden Fleece
30 Or, a Buffalo's head cabossed sa. attired ar. through the nostrils an annulet of the last, ducally crowned gu., the attires passing through the crown. Mecklenburg
31 Ar. a Bull's head cabossed ar. armed or. betw. two wings of the last. Hoste

C.N.Elvin, Del.   P.C.Baker, Sc.

PLATE 22 *(Continued.)*

32 Az. Two slaughter axes endorsed in saltire ar. handled or, betw. three Bull's heads couped of the second, armed of the third, viz.: two in fesse, and one in base, on a chief ar. a boar's head couped gu. betw. two block-brushes vert. Butcher's Company

33 Az. on a chev. ar. betw. three Staff-Tree' leaves slipped or, as many Bees volant ppr. Leaf

34 Az. Three Tierce's or. borne by Bourburg and Bernbing. This bearing is Blazoned in Blomfield's His. of Nor., vol. II., p. 469, as sa. three Trimelles or, for the family of Warner

35 Ar. three Viures nebulée, counter-nebulée invected gu.

36 Plaisse, or Plaissa

37 Lattice, Trellise, or Treille

38 Portcullised

39 Barry paly in prospect ar. and sa. Prospect

40 Vert, a fess Cuppa ar. and erminois, betw. three narcissus flowers of the second. White

41 Quarterly, or and az. four lozenges conjoined in cross throughout betw. a mullet in the 1st and 4th quarters and an annulet in the 2nd and 3rd quarters all counterchanged. Peacock

42 Per-fesse paly of six or and gu. counterchanged on a fesse of the last three roses ar. Martineau

43 Ar. a fesse betw. three moles sa. Mitford

44 Ar. Two Crows sa. pendent on an arrow fesseways ppr. Murdock

45 Ar. Three Furisons az. Steel

PLATE 23.

1 A Tower, on the sinister side, avant mur.

2 Castle triple towered

3 — breached, or ruined

4 Triangular Castle with three towers

5 Four square Castle in perspective, also blazoned a Castle with four towers placed two in fesse and two in pale

6 Castle with four towers, also termed square Castle, and a Quadrangular Castle with four towers

7 — also termed a Port between two towers

8 A Tower; and a Tower breached, or ruined

9 Tower with scaling-ladder raised against it in bend

10 — triple-towered

11 — triple-towered chain transverse

12 — domed; and a Tower inflamed, or flammant

13 Castle triple-towered, port displayed of the field

14 Citadel, also blazoned a wall turreted with two towers

15 Arch on three degrees with folding doors open

16 Triple-towered gate, double leaved

17 Embattlements farsoned; and the Turrets, or Embattlements of a Tower

18 Arch; and double arch

19 Bridge of three Arches, with a fane, the streams transfluent

20 Or on a Bridge of three Arches gu. over as many streams transfluent ppr. a tower of the second, thereon a fane ar.

21 Gu. three pears or, on a chief ar. a demi-lion issuant sa. armed and and langued of the first. The Chief surmounted of another with the arms of the order of St. John of Jerusalem viz, gu. a cross ar. The Armorial Bearings of Major Sir Herbert C. Perrott, Bart., Chevalier of Justice of the said order

22 A College

23 Steeple of a Church

24 Church

25 Chapel

26 Antique Temple

27 Ruins of an Old Abbey, or Monastery with ivy and standing on a piece of ground

28 Gu. a chief ar. on the lower part a cloud, the rays of the sun issuing therefrom ppr.

29 The Sun with clouds, distilling drops of rain

30 Rays issuing from dexter chief point

31 The Sun rising, or issuant from clouds. The badge of Prince Napoleon before he was Emperor of France; " The Sun rising from clouds with the motto Emergo"

32 Sun

33 Az. The Sun in Splendour or.

34 Sun in Splendour, each ray illuminated, or inflamed

35 Sun in Splendour, charged with an eye

36 Increscent circled; and a Decrescent circled

37 Moon illuminated, or in her compliment, and a Moon in her Detriment, or Eclipse

38 Crescent; Increscent; and a Decrescent

39 Estoile, issuing out of a Crescent

40 Four Crescents fretted

41 Three Crescents interlaced

42 Estoile, or Etoile

43 Star of six-points; and an Estoile of eight points

44 Star of eight-points; and an Estoile of sixteen-points

45 Blazing Star; or Comet, between the astronomical symbol of Venus as borne by Thoyts. and Uranus-radiated as in the arms of Herschel. Mars ♂ by Wimble and Stockenstrom

PLATE 24.

1 Imperial Crown
2 Coronet of the Prince of Wales
3 Younger sons of Her Majesty
4 Princess Royal and younger Sisters
5 Nephews of the Blood Royal
6 The Garter
7 Collar, Star and Badge of the Order of the Garter
8 Helmet of the Sovereign
9 Helmet of the Nobility
10 Mitre of the Bishop of Durham
11 Helmet of a Baronet and Knight
12 Helmet of an Esquire
13 Mural Crown with three embattlements
14 Mural Crown with four embattlements
15 Mitre of the Archbishops and Bishops except the Bishop of Durham
16 Naval Crown
17 Vallary Crown
18 Collar, Star, and Badge of the Order of the Thistle
19 Jewel of the Order of the Garter
20 Jewel of the Order of St. Patrick
21 Collar, Star, and Badge of the Order of St. Patrick
22 Star of a Knight's Commander of the Bath. K.C.B.
23 Jewel of the Order of the Thistle
24 Order of the Indian Empire, instituted 1st Jan., 1878, revoked 2nd Aug., 1886
25 Order of Victoria and Albert
26 Collar, Star, and Badge of the Order of the Bath
27 Collar, Star, and Badge of the Star of India
28 Civil Badge of the Bath
29 Collar of S.S.
30 Order of the Crown of India
31 Collar, Star, and Badge of St. Michael and St. George
32 Eastern Crown
33 Celestial Crown
34 Triumphal Crown, or Wreath
35 Ducal Coronet, or Crest Coronet of three leaves
36 Ducal, or Crest Coronet of five leaves
37 Palisado Coronet
38 Crown of Edward I.
39 Civic Crown, or Chaplet of Oak
40 Olive Crown
41 Chaplet
42 Coronet of a Duke
43   „   Marquis
44   „   Earl
45   „   Viscount
46   „   Baron

PLATE 25.

1 Crown of Charlemagne, was borne by five Kings of England as Arch-treasures of the Holy Roman Empire. See p. 31. f. 9, and 10
2 A White Rose the Badge of the House of York
3 The Rose and Thistle conjoined. Badge of James I.
4 A Red Rose the Badge of the House of Lancaster
5 Crown of the Elector of the Holy Roman Empire
6 Planta genista. Badge of the Plantagenets
7 Badge of Staunton
8 Badge of Napoleon
9 Badge of Plantagenet also represented as No. 6
10 Gold Medal and Ribbon for Trafalgar
11 Victoria Cross. "Red ribbon if worn by a soldier, and by a blue ribbon if worn by a sailor"
12 Medal and Ribbon for Waterloo
13 Badge and Ribbon, Companion of the Bath. C.B.
14 Star of the Military Knights Grand Cross of the Bath. G.C.B.
15 Collar, Badge and Star of the Royal Hanoverian Guelphic Order. G.C.H.
16 Star, Knights Commanders of the Order of St. Michael, and St. George. K.C.M.G.
17 Badge and Ribbon—Companion of St. Michael, and St. George. C.M.G.
18 Badge and Ribbon for the Crimea, with Clasp for Alma and Balaklava, the same medal and ribbon is also given with Clasps or small Bars, for Inkerman, and Sebastopol
19 The Badge of the Order of the Dooranée Empire
20 Medal or Badge for India, Clasps for Central India and Lucknow; the same medal and ribbon is also borne with Clasps for Relief of Lucknow, Defence of Lucknow, and Delhi
21 Badge of Ogle
22 Badge an ostrich feather erm. quilled or. John of Gaunt
23 Badge of John Beaufort Duke of Somerset. Ostrich feather white, the pen compony ar. and az.
24 Badge of John Duke of Bedford, brother to Henry V. A golden root
25 Hanoverian Crown
26 Badge of Meux. Two wings inverted and endorsed ar. conjoined by a cord with tassels or.
27 A Damask Rose with leaves and thorns, at the bottom of the stalk a beetle all ppr. Crest of Thorndike
28 Badge of Daubeney. Two bats wings endorsed sa. tied by a cord tasselled or.
29 Crown of Scotland

PLATE 25

C.N.Elvin.Del

P.C.Baker Sc

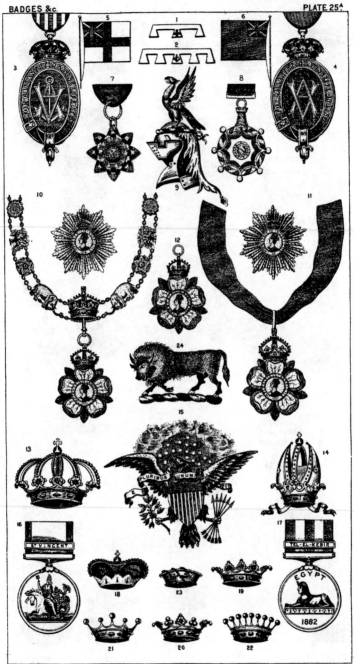

PLATE 25. A.

1 The Label of His Royal Highness Prince Albert Victor of Wales
2 The Label of His Royal Highness Prince George of Wales
3 The Albert Medal for Saving Life at Sea
4 The Albert Medal for Saving Life on Land
5 Ensign of the Royal Navy
6 Ensign of the Naval Reserve
7 Badge and Riband of the Sun and Lion of Persia
8 Badge and Riband of the Royal Portuguese Military Order of the Tower and Sword
9 Helmet with Contoise, or Quintise, with Wreath and Crest an Eagle with wings elevated and endorsed. Crest of Maher
The Most Eminent Order of the Indian Empire
10 The Collar, Star, and Badge of The First Class, or Knights Grand Commanders
11 The Riband and Badge, and Star of The Second Class, or Knights Commanders
12 The Badge of The Third Class, or Companions
13 Crown of Prussia
14 Crown of Austria
15 The American Shield and Eagle, The Badge of the United States
16 Naval Medal. Ribbon White with Blue edges. Medal. Obverse: The Head of the Queen wearing a diadem, with the words "Victoria Regina." Reverse. In waves of the sea, a sea-horse with Britannia seated thereon, holding a trident in her right hand, and an olive branch in her left. A great number of clasps were issued with this medal. Amongst the principal naval engagements for which this medal was issued were; Algiers, Camperdown, Copenhagen, Navarino, Battle of the Nile, St. Vincent, etc.
17 Medal for Egypt. 1882. Ribbon Blue with two white stripes. Medal, obverse, Queen's head with diadem and draped. The inscription "Victoria Regina et Imperatrix." Reverse, a sphinx, the word "Egypt" above and the date 1882 underneath. Clasps for Tel-el-Kebir. The same medal with clasp inscribed "Alexandria, 11th July" was granted to the Navy. The same medal without the date 1882 on the reverse, with clasps for Suakin 1884., El-Teb., Tamaai., Nile 1884-5., Abu Klea., Kirbekan., Suakin 1885., Tofrek granted to those in possession of the Egypt 1882, or Suakin 1884 medal. This Medal also granted for services on the Upper Nile in 1885-86.

FRENCH CORONETS.

18 Prince
19 Duc
20 Marquis
21 Comte
22 Viscomte
23 Baron

24 A Bison. Crest of Fitzjames

PLATE 26.

1 Lion Rampant
2 — Rampant double queued
3 — Ramp. tail forked
4 — Ramp. tail nowed
5 — Morne
6 — Defamed, Defame, or Infamed
7 — Baillone
8 — Coward, or Coue
9 — Double, or Don-headed
10 — Rampant reguardant
11 — Rampant guardant
12 — Bicorporated, or conjoined
13 — Ramp. Collared and Chained
14 — Disjointed
15 — Addorsed, or Endorsed
16 — Combatant
17 — Tricorporated
18 — Sejant Contourne
19 — Sejant-Rampant
20 — Salient
21 — Ramp. Guard. debruised by a fesse
22 — Ramp. jessant and debruised fretways
23 — Passant
24 — Passant Reguardant
25 — Head Erased
26 — Naissant from a Fesse
27 The Crest of the Sovereign of England
28 The Crest of Scotland
29 Lion Issuant from a Chief
30 Lion's Head couped
31 — Demi ramp. gorged with a ducal Coronet
32 — Jessant and debruised with two bendlets
33 — Issuant et Issuant and reversant
34 — Demi ramp.reguard. crowned with a mural Coronet
35 — Passant Guardant
36 — Counter-passant
37 — Antique Ramp.
38 — Antique Head Erased
39 — Statant
40 — Statant tail extended
41 — Sejant
42 — Sejant dexter paw raised
43 — Sejant guardant affrontée
44 — Sejant extendant in full aspect
45 — Couchant
46 — Dormant
47 — Sept-Insular
48 — Statant winged
49 — Demi-passant
50 — Full-faced, or affrontée
51 — of St. Mark
52 — Poisson
53 Sea-Lion
54 Lion Dragon
55 Lampagoe
56 Lion with human face
57 Satyral
58 Chimera

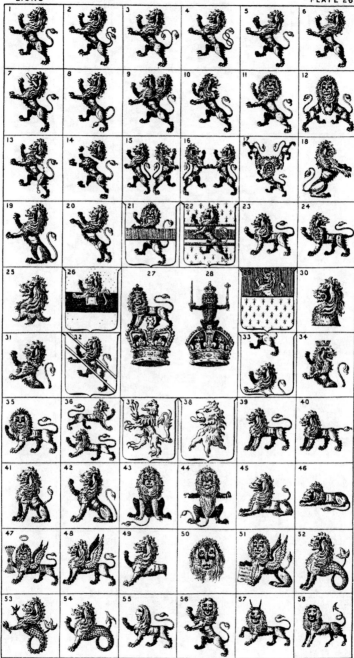

C.N.Elvin.Del.

P.C.Baker.Sc.

E

PLATE 27

PLATE 27.

1 Griffin passant
2 Griffin Segreant
3 Griffin Sejant
4 Demi Griffin Segreant
5 Griffin's head erased
6 Male Griffin
7 Hippogriff passant
8 Opinicus statant
9 Amphisbeme, or Amphister winged
10 Basilisk
11 Wyvern, or Wivern
12 Wyvern-tailed nowed
13 Wyvern sans wings
14 Wyvern sans legs
15 Cockatrice
16 Cockatrice displayed
17 Cockatrice's head, wings endorsed couped
18 Cockatrice's head couped between two wings
19 Dragon statant
20 Demi Dragon ramp.
21 Dragon's head and wings couped
22 Two demi dragons interlaced
23 Dragon sans wings and legs
24 Dragon with two heads vomiting fire at both ends. Crest of Maule
25 Wyvern's head couped
26 Horse forcene
27 Arms of the City of London
28 Elephant statant
29 Dragon's head couped
30 Horse passant
31 Horse spancelled
32 Elephant's head erased
33 Elephant and Castle
34 Horse's head erased
35 Horse's head couped and bridled
36 Unicorn passant
37 Demi Unicorn
38 Unicorn's head erased and gorged with a Ducal-coronet
39 Unicorn's head couped
40 Sagittarius
41 Pegasus passant
42 Demi Pegasus
43 Mule
44 Ass
45 Ass's head couped
46 Allocamelus
47 Dromedary
48 Camel
49 Bagwyn
50 Camelopard
51 Rhinoceros
52 Salamander
53 Badger
54 Manticora, or Man-tiger
55 Porcupine
56 Enfield
57 Musimon

PLATE 28.

1 Leopard statant guardant
2 — Head erased affrontée
3 — Head ppr. erased gu.
4 — Face
5 — Face jessant-de-lis. (sometimes blazoned a Leopard's head swallowing a fleur-de-lis)
6 — Face jessant-de-lis reversed
7 Panther rampant incensed
8 Heraldic Wolf passant. (sometimes horned)
9 Wolf passant
10 — sejant reguardant
11 — head erased
12 — head erased emitting flames
13 Tiger
14 — and Mirror
15 Lynx
16 Hydra
17 Lizard (there is another kind of lizard see p. 39 f. 24)
18 Ounce
19 Heraldic Tiger passant
20 Heraldic Tiger's head couped
21 Ibex passant
22 Antelope passant
23 Heraldic Antelope passant
24 Heraldic Antelope's head erased
25 Genet
26 Cat a mountain sejant
27 Cat a mountain saliant
28 Civet Cat
29 Cow
30 Calf passant
31 Bull-winged; or a flying bull wings indorsed, over the head a circle of glory
32 — passant
33 Bull's head erased
34 — head cabossed
35 Buffalo
36 Elk
37 Reindeer
38 Reindeer's head cabossed
39 Lama
40 Chamois
41 Alpaca
42 Kangaroo
43 Stag Tripping
44 — at Gaze
45 — springing
46 — courant
47 — lodged
48 — browsing, or feeding
49 Stag's head erased
50 Stag's head couped and gorged with a ducal coronet
51 Attires of a stag affixed to the scalp; and Attire
52 Stag's head cabossed
53 Two hinds counter-tripping
54 Out of a mural crown a hind's head
55 A Hart cumbant, or lodged reguardant upon a hill in a park paled
56 Ram passant
57 Ram's head erased
58 Ram's head cabossed
59 Goat passant
60 Goat's head erased

PLATE 29.

1 Indian, or Assyrian Goat, passant
2 Indian Goat's head couped
3 Trogodice's head erased. Lambard
4 Holy, or Paschal Lamb
5 Hare in full course. See Courant
6 Hare sejant playing upon the bag-pipes. Fitz-Ercald
7 Calopus, or Chatloup pass. quarterly or. and sa. horned of the last. Foljambe
8 Fox courant
9 Fox saliant
10 Two Foxes counter-saliant
11 Foxe's head erased
12 Alant statant
13 Talbot statant
14 Demi Talbot, ramp. ar. eared gu., gorged with a ducal coronet or. Southwell
15 Talbot sejant, collared and lined
16 Talbot's head erased
17 Bloodhound on scent
18 Bloodhound statant
19 Rabbit
20 Greyhound courant
21 Greyhound sejant
22 Greyhound's head erased
23 Spring-Bok statant
24 Bull Dog statant
25 Mastaff
26 Beagle courant
27 Spaniel sejant
28 Pointer
29 Newfoundland dog
30 Dog-sleeping. Robertson
31 Boar courant
32 Boar's head couped
   Boar's head erased
33 — head erect and erased. Loftus

34 Boar's head erect in a cup
35 — head erased in a dish
36 — head and neck couped
37 Bear pass. muzzled and chained
38 Bear sejant
39 Demi Bear ramp.
40 Bear's head erased
41 Bear's Gamb erased
42 Bear and ragged-staff
43 Squirrel sejant holding a nut
44 Two Squirrels sejant addorsed
45 Lion's Gamb erect and erased or. Goldingham
46 Lion's Gamb holding a laurel branch fructed ppr. Flint
47 Two Lion's Gambs sa. supporting a Crescent ar. Leche
48 Two Lion's Gambs in saltire gu. Dobson
49 Beaver
50 Beaver's tail Proboscis
   Lion's Tail. Three lions' tails erect, erased borne by the family of Cork
51 Seal
52 Seal's-paw
53 Otter's head couped
54 Otter
55 Sea-Horse
56 Sea-Dog
57 Monkey, or Ape admiring himself in a mirror ppr. also blazoned a monkey sejant enceppe admiring himself in a looking-glass
58 Monkey passant
59 Sea-Monkey
60 Winged-Monkey, or Ape Winged

PLATE 30.

1 Crocodile
2 Sphinx couchant with wings
3 Sphinx couchant sans wings
4 Bat, or Rere-mouse
5 Tortoise
6 Snail, or House Snail
7 Cheese-slip, or wood-louse; Ant; and Asker
8 Grasshopper
9 Cameleon
10 Toad
11 Hedge-hog
12 Guinea-pig; and Rat
13 Martin
14 Weasel
15 Ferret
16 Ermine
17 Polecat
18 War, Weir, or Man-Wolfe
19 Bee
20 Bee-hive with Bees diversely volant
21 Gad Bee, or Fly
22 Harvest Fly
23 Butterfly, or Fly
24 Palmer, or Palm-worm
25 Serpent nowed, nodée, or fretted in the form of a knot
26 — Bowed debruised and counter-embowed debruised
27 — tail erect, embowed, debruised
28 — targent the tail wreathed. Torqued erect in pale, or erect wavy
29 — head and tail elevated and bowed
30 — nowed reversed
31 — wreathed tail embowed debruised. Tail erect and torqued
32 — gliding tail embowed. Reguardant tail embowed. Reversed head reguardant and tail embowed
33 — bowed embowed, or enwrapped debruised
34 — embowed debruised torqued. Reguardant, recurvant, reverted the tail embowed. Reversed bowed, debruised and embowed
35 — embowed, debruised, tail reversed. Head reversed, reguardant tail embowed
36 — double nowed
37 Serpent reversed embowed biting his tail, head to sinister
38 — embowed biting his tail, head to sinister
39 — embowed biting his tail, head to dexter
40 — embowed head debruised
41 — bowed knotted, debruised and torqued
42 — or snake coiled, intortant, wreathed, or wound inwards
43 — stopping his ear with his tail
44 — Trochleated, or enwrapped round in the form of a screw, the head elevated
45 — bowed-embowed debruised with the head
46 — Asp
47 — gliding, or waved in fesse
48 — bowed embowed, the head debruised, or bowed debruised the tail surmounting
49 — bowed embowed, encircled, enwrapped, involved, or voluted
50 — bowed with the tail elevated
51 — two embowed, endorsed and fretted, or two fretted, tail debruised
52 — three embowed and fretted, in triangle
53 — extended, gliding. or creeping also termed a Boa-Serpent. Enarched with head at both ends
54 — interlaced respecting each other
55 — Torqued erect, crowned, devouring an infant
56 Caduceus, or Mercury's Mace also termed Snaky-Staff
57 Rod of Esculapius
58 Serpent torqued, fretted with a long cross, or a cross environed, enwrapped, or entwined with a Serpent; sometimes blazoned the Cross of Christ supporting the Brazen-Serpent
59 Three arrows one in pale and two in saltier points downwards, entwined by a Serpent ppr.
60 Serpent nowed in pale

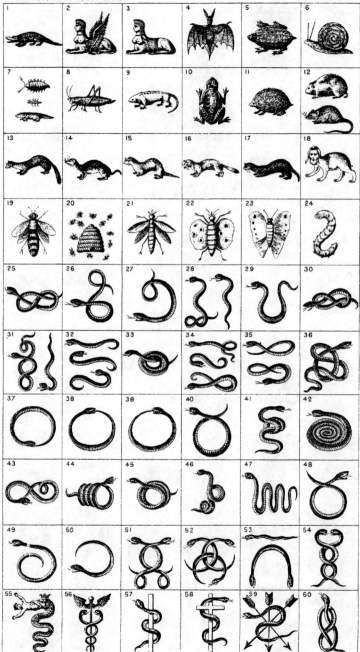

C.N.Elven Del.　　　　　　　　　　　　　　P.C.Baker Sc.

PLATE 31.

1 HOUSE OF NORMANDY: William I., 1066. William II., 1087. Henry I., 1100

2 Stephen, 1135. The shield is also described as Gu. three Sagittarii reguardant in pale or.

3 HOUSE OF PLANTAGENET: Hen. II., 1154. Richard I., 1189. John, 1199. Hen. III., 1216. Edw. I., 1272. Edw. II., 1307 (The same for Edw. III., until 1340. After this date as No. 4.)

4 Edward III., 1327. Richard II., 1377

4 HOUSE OF LANCASTER : Hen. IV., 1399.

5 Henry V., 1413. Henry VI., 1422

5 HOUSE OF YORK : Edw. IV., 1461. Edw. V., proclaimed King 1483, never crowned. Richard III., 1483

5 HOUSE OF TUDOR : Hen. VII., 1485. Hen. VIII., 1509. Edw. VI., 1547. Mary I., 1553. Elizabeth, 1558

6 HOUSE OF STUART: James I., 1603. Charles I., 1625. (Commonwealth declared May 19, 1649, Ensign No. 29). Charles II., 1660. James II., 1685

7 William III. and Mary II., 1689

8 Anne, 1702, as No. 6, before the Union with Scotland. After the Union, May 1, 1707, as No. 8

9 HOUSE OF HANOVER (Guelph) Geo. I., 1714. Geo. II., 1727. The same for Geo. III., until Jan. 1, 1801, after this date as No. 10

10 George III., 1760
The Escutcheon en surtout is ensigned with the Electoral bonnet ; but since June 8, 1816, when the Electorate of Hanover was elevated to the rank of a Kingdom, the Hanoverian regal crown as P. 25, f. 25 was substituted for the Electorate bonnet. George IV., 1820. William IV., 1830

11 Victoria, 1837

12 Badge of Ulster. The Baronet's Badge

13 Badge of Nova-Scotia, or Scotch Baronets

14 Badge and ribbon of the DISTINGUISHED SERVICE ORDER. The ribbon is red, edged blue

15 Scalp of a hare, ears erect ppr. Crest of Dymock

16 A Drinking-cup or, with three fleur-de-lis of the same issuing therefrom, and charged with a rose gu. This is also termed a flower-pot. Crest of Croker

17 Bull's scalp or., horned ar. Crest of Cheney

18 A nest of young ravens ppr. Crest of Drummond; Knevet, etc.

19 Out of a well or., a vine and two columbine branches ppr. Goldwell

20 A Cornish chough hatching in the face of a rock ppr. Cornwall

21 A Lion's gamb. erased erect gu. supporting a shield or. Watts

22 A Bull's leg, embowed couped at the thigh erm. hoof upwards. Vachell

23 An Ox's foot couped sa. Delafield

24 A cup or., inflamed ppr. Lucas

25 A Dove reguardant with olive branch all ppr. Crest of Wiggett, of Guist

26 Ar. a Lion ramp. sa., Queve Renowned, i.e. the tail raised over the head. Buxton

27 Two Doves billing, or respecting ppr. Couran

28 A Tun or., issuing from the bung-hole five roses of the same, stalked and leaved ppr. Cervington

29 The Banner of the Commonwealth containing the Cross of St. George for England. St. Andrew's Cross for Scotland, and the Harp for Ireland, with the Arms of Cromwell Sur-le-tout, viz.: sa. a Lion ramp. ar.

30 Sa. three swords in pile, points downwards ar. hilted and pommelled or. Paulet

31 Gu. three swords in pairle pommels conjoined in fesse point ar. This may be blazoned gu. three swords conjoined at the pommels in centre their points extended to the corners of the Escutcheon. Stapleton

32 Az. three swords one in fesse point to the dexter, surmounted of the other two in saltire points upwards ar. Ewart

33 Gu. three swords barwise in pale,

PLATE 31 *(Continued)*.

their points towards the dexter,
hilted and pommelled or.   Chute

34 Gu. three swords barwise in pale,
points to the sinister hilts and
pommels or.   Rawlyns

35 Sa. three swords paleways ar. two
with their points in base, and the
middle one in chief.   Rawlings.
At p. 9, f. 21.   Az. three swords,
one in pale point upwards, surmounted of the other two in saltire
points downwards ar., hilts and
pommels or.   Norton, of Toftwood,
E. Dereham, Norfolk, and Ricking-
hall, Suffolk

36 Ar. a dexter hand erased fesseways
gu., holding a dagger point downwards az. in chief three crescents
sa.   M'Clure

37 Gu. issuing from the dexter side of
the shield a cubit sinister arm
vested az., cuffed or, in the hand
ppr., a cross-crosslet fitchée in
pale of the third.   O'Donell

38 Ar. an arm sinister in bend issuing
from dexter chief point gu.   Corn-
hill

39 Or. a dexter arm issuing from the
sinister fesse point out of clouds
ppr. in the hand a cross crosslet
fitchée in pale az.   Mac Donnell

40 Az. an armed arm embowed or,
issuing from the sinister, holding
in the hand ppr. a rose gu. stalked
and leaved vert.   Chambre

41 Gu. a balance betw. three garbs or.,
on a chief barry wavy of four ar.
and az., an arm embowed vested
of the first cuff gold, issuing from
clouds affixed to the upper part of
the centre of the chief of the third,
radiated of the second, betw. two
anchors, also of the second.   The
Bakers' Company

42 The Shield of the Duke of Abercorn.
Quarterly 1st and 4th gu., three
cinquefoils pierced erm. for Hamilton. 2nd and 3rd, ar. a lymphad
with sails furled and oars sa. for
Earls of Arran. En surcoat an
inescutcheon az. charged with three
fleur-de-lis or, surmounted by a
French ducal coronet, for the
Duchy of Chatelherault.   See also
term Entoured

43 The Decoration of the Royal Red
Cross

PLATE 32

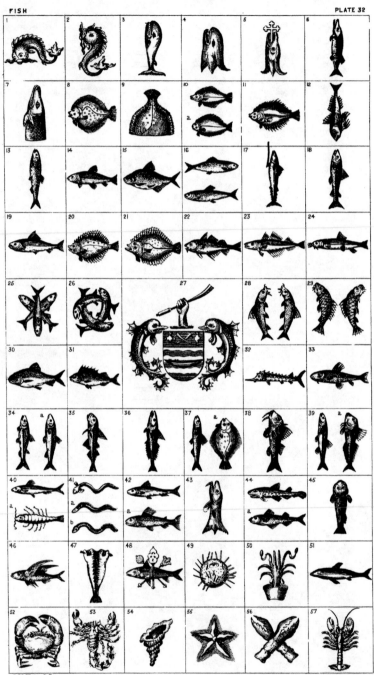

C. N. Elvin. Del.

PLATE 32.

1 Dolphin Naiant embowed
2 Dolphin Hauriant
3 Whale Hauriant
4 Whale's head erased and erect
5 Conger eel's head erased and erect ingulphant of a cross crosslet fitchée, or a conger eels head erased and erect, the jaw pierced with a cross-crosslet fitchy
6 Pike, or Luce hauriant also termed Ged.
7 Demi Luce; or Pike's Head couped
8 Turbot naiant
9 Tail of a Turbot erect, or Demi Turbot tail erect
10 Buttfish, a. Sole naiant
11 Flounder also termed a Fluke, and Butt
12 Gurnet, or Gurnard; Diving or Urinant
13 Herring, Cob-Fish, or Sea-Cob hauriant
14 Tench naiant
15 Bream naiant
16 Two Fish counter-naiant
17 Mackerel hauriant
18 Salmon hauriant
19 Trout naiant
20 Plaice naiant
21 Brill naiant
22 Cod naiant
23 Whiting naiant
24 Loach naiant
25 Three Fish Interchangeably posed. See Teste a la Queve
26 Three Salmons fretted
27 The Watermans Company, London. Barry wavy of six ar. and az. on the middle bar a boat or, on a chief of the second Two oars in Saltire of the third betw. two cushions of the first, tasselled or.

Crest a dexter hand holding an oar or. Supporters Two Dolphins az. finned or.
28 Two Barbels respecting naiant
29 Two Carp hauriant addorsed, or endorsed
30 Roach naiant
31 Perch naiant
32 Sturgeon naiant
33 Gudgeon naiant
34 Smelt, or Sparling hauriant. a. Chub hauriant
35 Haddock hauriant
36 Hake hauriant
37 Pilchard hauriant. (a) Burbot hauriant
38 Mullet hauriant
39 Minnow hauriant. (a) Tubb-Fish hauriant
40 Sprat naiant. (a) shrimp
41 Eel, naiant. (a) Conger Eel naiant b. Lamprey, naiant
42 Sardine naiant. (a) Grayling naiant
43 Ling's head erased and erect
44 Dog Fish naiant. a. Brit naiant also termed a Bret
45 Chabot hauriant
46 Flying Fish
47 Stockfish
48 The Fish of Mogul, per pale or and vert. banded of the last and gu. surmounting a shaft in pale and the Goog and Ullum in Saltire or.
49 Sea-Urchin
50 Cuttle, or Ink-Fish
51 Shark naiant
52 Crab
53 Scorpion
54 Welk
55 Star-Fish
56 Lobster's-claws in Saltire
57 Lobster

PLATE 33.

1 Eagle, sometimes termed an eagle close
2 — wings expanded, also termed eagle wings overture, elevated
3 — rising, or an eagle wings expanded and inverted, also eagle wings overture
4 — reguardent
5 — displayed
6 — displayed with two heads, also termed a spread eagle
7 — displayed wings inverted
8 — demi displayed with two heads, or demi spread eagle
9 — displayed, sans legs
10 — wings surgeant-tergiant
11 — mantling
12 — preying, or trussing
13 — wings endorsed and inverted
14 — degenerate at gaze aloft, wings surgiant, holding up the left foot
15 — displayed foreshortened
16 — volant recursant, descending in bend sinister, wings overture
17 — volant recursant descendant in pale wings overture
18 — displayed recursant, or tergiant
19 — perched
20 Eagle's head erased
21 — leg reversed, or Eagle's talon reversed, and an Eagle's leg erased at the thigh, termed A la quise
22 — leg erased at the thigh conjoined to a sinister wing
23 — leg couped at the thigh conjoined to a plume of Ostrich's feathers
24 The French Imperial Eagle
25 Phœnix
26 Sinister wing, or a demi vol, and two wings endorsed

27 Wings conjoined in base
28 Wings conjoined in lure, or wings inverted
29 An Eagle's head couped betw. two wings
30 Allerion
31 Falcon close
32 Falcon wings endorsed and Inverted
33 Falcon wings expanded and distended
34 Falcon's leg erased at the thigh, belled, jessed and varvelled. Also termed a Falcon's leg a la quise, or Cuisse, etc.
35 Falcon's head erased
36 Vulture
37 Pelican
38 Pelican in her nest, or in her piety
39 Pelican's head erased and vulning
40 Ostrich
41 Ostrich's head couped betw. two ostrich wings
42 Dove with Olive-branch
43 Goldfinch
44 Robin
45 Woodpecker
46 Cock Pheasant
47 Partridge
48 Avocet
49 Bulfinch
50 Starling
51 Sparrow
52 Raven, or Corbie
53 Crow, or Rook
54 Chough, or Cornish chough
55 Lapwing, Pewit, or Terwhitt
56 Bustard
57 Lark, or Sky-lark
58 Kingfisher
59 Razor-bill
60 Kite

PLATE 33

C.N. Elvin. Del.

L. Cully. Sc.

PLATE 34

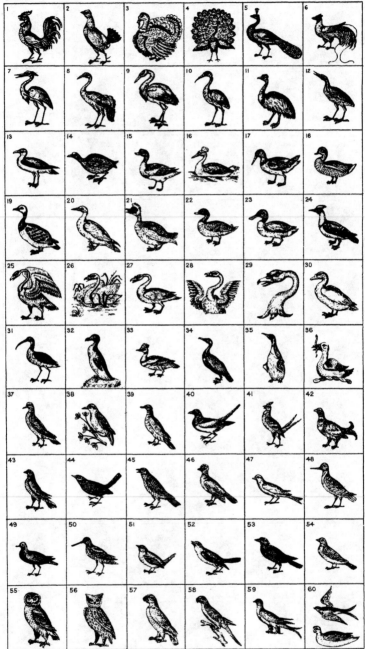

C.N.Elvin.Del.

L.Cully Sc.

PLATE 34.

1 Cock, or Dunghill Cock
2 Game Cock
3 Turkey Cock in his Pride
4 Peacock in his Pride
5 Peacock Close
6 Bird of Paradise
7 Heron
8 Crane
9 Stork
10 Ibis
11 Emeu
12 Bittern
13 Sea Gull
14 Coot
15 Sheldrake
16 Curly Headed Diver
17 Sea Pie, or Oyster Catcher
18 Teal
19 Barnacle Goose
20 Gannet, or Solon Goose
21 Muscovy Duck
22 Drake, Duck, or Mallard
23 Shoveller
24 Didapper
25 Swan, rousant
26 Swan in a Loch
27 Swan, Close
28 Demi Swan wings expanded
29 Swan's head erased
30 Goose
31 Curlew
32 Auk

33 Smew, or White Nun
34 Cormorant
35 Penguin
36 A Morfex, "on a wreath ar and b. a Morfex argent bekyd sa. therin a Cele in p'pur coler." Crest granted to the Town of Newark upon Trent co. Notts 8th Dec., 1561
37 Ring-Dove
38 Nuthatch on a nut branch
39 Wood Pigeon
40 Magpie
41 Heath-Cock, or Moor-Cock
42 Grouse, or Moorfowl
43 Heraldic Bird
44 Blackbird, or Merle
45 Thrush
46 Jay
47 Canary
58 Woodcock
49 Plover
50 Snipe
51 Wren
52 Nightingale
53 Jackdaw
54 Chaffinch
55 Owl
56 Horned Owl, or Eared Owl
57 Parrot, or Popinjay
58 Parrakeet
59 Martlet
60 Martlet Volant ; and Cannet

PLATE 35.

1 Virgin and Child
2 King in his robes of State sitting in a chair
3 Bishop
4 Prester-John
5 Lady Abbess
6 Female figure naked with flowing hair. Crest of Ellis
7 Figure of Justice
8 Figure of Hope
9 Man in Armour, holding in dexter hand a sword in pale
10 Demi-Man in armour ppr. garnished or, his helmet surmounted by a plume of Ostrich feathers az. in his dexter hand a halbert in pale ppr. Crest of Morse
11 Neptune, or Triton
12 Mermaid
13 The Golden Sceptre
14 Septre and Dove. Emblem of Peace
15 Tilting-Spear
16 Mantle. vid. Robe and Mantle in Dictionary
17 St. Edwards-Staff
18 Sceptre of Queen Mary
19 Sceptre
20 Mace of Majesty
21 Sceptre, or Mace of the Lord Mayor of London
22 Mace with Shield of St. George, imperially crowned

23 Tilting Spear with cronel, or Jousting-lance
24 Savage, or wild man, with spiked club over his Shoulder
25 Demi-Savage with club over the shoulder
26 Savage, or Woodman Ambulant, in the dexter hand a club resting on the shoulder, in the sinister hand a Shield ar. charged with a Cros gu.
27 Roman Soldier in Armour, on his head a helmet with three feathers, holding in his dexter hand a Shield thereon a female head, in the sinister a spear
28 A Moor, or Blackamoor wreathed about the temples, habited in short garments, and in buskins, adorned about the waist and shoulders with feathers, holding in dexter hand a string-bow; over the dexter shoulder a sash with quiver of arrows suspended at the sinister side
29 Figure of Time
30 Harpy
31 Harpy with wings expanded and inverted
32 Demi Harpy erased displayed
33 St. John's head in a charger
34 Death's head in a cup
35 Skeleton human

C.N.Elvin.Del   P.C.Baker Sc

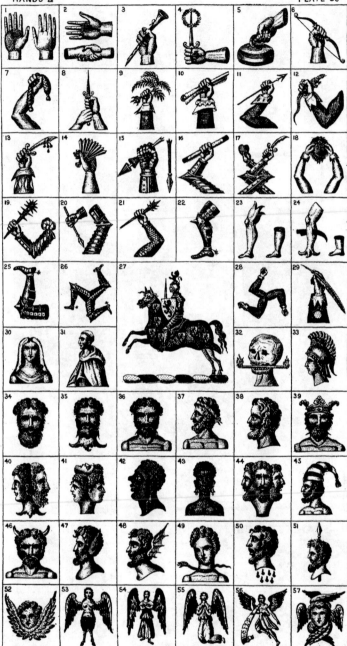

C.N.Elvin Del

R.Rowlandson Sc

PLATE 36.

1 A dexter hand apaumée couped at the wrist, and a dexter hand Aversant.

2 A dexter hand couped in fesse, and two hands conjoined in fesse, also blazoned a dexter and sinister hand couped at the wrist clasped. Le Strange

3 A hand holding a Clarionet. Fell

4 A hand couped in fesse holding a sword in pale supporting on the point a Garland all ppr. Tipper

5 A hand in bend sinister holding a Curling-stone. Bidwell

6 A sinister hand holding a Bow in bend. Grimsby

7 An arm embowed in hand a purse, or a naked dexter arm embowed in the hand a purse all ppr. Baker

8 A dexter and sinister hand couped supporting a sword in pale ppr. Harbour

9 A cubit arm erect vested az. cuffed ar. charged with an acorn or, the hand grasping a fern sapling of New Zealand. Rhodes

10 A cubit arm habited sa. cuffed ar. shirt sleeve turned down and frilled of the last holding in the hand a roll of Parchment ppr. Kellet

11 An arm embowed vested per pale vert and gu. cuffed erm. holding in the hand a spear ppr. Ffolkes

12 An arm embowed resting on the elbow vested gu. cuff indented (Vandyked) ar. holding in the hand a Lizard ppr. Macarthy

13 A cubit arm vested or cuffed and slashed (or puffed) ar. hand ppr. holding a scimitar imbued gu. hilt and pommel gold. Quincy

14 A hand couped ppr. holding a Fan displayed or. Fanmaker's Company

15 A arm in armour gauntleted, grasping a broken tilting spear all ppr. Purfoy

16 An arm in armour embowed holding in the hand ppr. a Baton or, ends sa. Way.

17 Two arms in armour embowed and fretted, or two arms embowed in armour fretted salterways, in the dexter hand a scimitar and in the sinister hand a heart all ppr. O'Donel

18 Two arms dexter and sinister embowed vested ar. holding in the hands a scalp ppr. inside gu. Huddleston

19 An arm in armour couped embowed resting on the elbow ppr. Sash tied at the shoulder gu. and in the hand a Spiked club of the first. Bult

20 An arm in armour counter embowed ppr. couped below the wrist, the hand dropping, therein a spear sa. Daunscourt

21 An Arm in Mail armour counter-embowed holding in the hand ppr. a Spiked club or. Bathurst

22 A leg in armour ppr. couped at the thigh gu. kneecap and spear or. Eyre

23 A human leg erased at the thigh ppr. Rain. and a demi leg couped

24 A leg couped at the thigh, erased at the ancle ppr. pierced through the calf with a coulter sa. and a Foot couped

25 A man's leg couped at the thigh in armour ppr. garnished and spurred or, embowed at the knee, the foot upwards, the toe pointing to the dexter. Haddon

26 Three legs in armour conjoined in the fesse point ppr. spurred and garnished or. See Triquetra

27 On a wreath of the colours, on a horse in full gallop ar. bridled sa. and with mantling gu. semée of escutcheon's or, each charged with a lion ramp. of the third ; a chevalier armed cap-a-pie ; on his helmet his crest viz. a demi lion ramp. gu., in his right hand a sword ppr., on his sinister arm, a shield charged as the escutcheons. Crest of Duff

28 Three arms embowed conjoined in the fesse point ppr. habited az.

PLATE 36 *(Continued.)*

29 A cubit arm erect habited az. charged with a bezant, cuff indented ar. in the hand a pen ppr. Aldridge

30 A Nun's head, face and neck ppr. with a white fall and dress. Daveney

31 A Demi Friar, or Hermit in profile, vested and having a cowl or hood

32 A Dead man's head, or Skeleton's head couped ppr. holding in his mouth a candle or, flammant at both ends ppr. Bolney

33 Minervas Head ppr. Leighton

34 A Man's head affrontée ppr. Frost

35 A Man's head affrontée erased at the neck

36 A Man's Bust, or a man's head affrontée couped below the shoulders

37 A Man's head in profile couped below shoulders, or a Bust in profile wreathed

38 A Man's head in profile couped at the neck

39 A Man's head affrontée couped below the shoulders and ducally crowned

40 Janus's head

41 Three heads conjoined in the neck one looking to the dexter one to the sinister and one upwards. Morrison

42 Moor's or Negro,s Head in profile couped at the neck

43 A Negresses head affrontée couped below the shoulders, with pendants at ears all ppr. Amo

44 Three mens' heads conjoined in one neck, one looking to the dexter, one affrontée, and one looking to the sinister

45 A Man's head in profile couped at the Shoulders ppr. on his head an Infular cap barry ar. and sa. Everard

46 A Whittals Head

47 Man's head in profile with Ass's ears couped at the neck also termed Satyrs head and Midas head

48 Man's head in profile with dragons wings couped at the neck, called Satans or Fiend's head

49 A Child's head enwrapped round the neck with a Snake. Vaughan

50 Savages head couped at the neck in profile distilling blood ppr. Edington

51 A Spear in pale enfiled with a savage's head couped at the neck ppr. Cotton

52 A Cherub, or. Overand

53 A Cherubim

54
55 }See Angel in Dictionary
56

57 Seraph, or Seraphim ppr. Carruthers

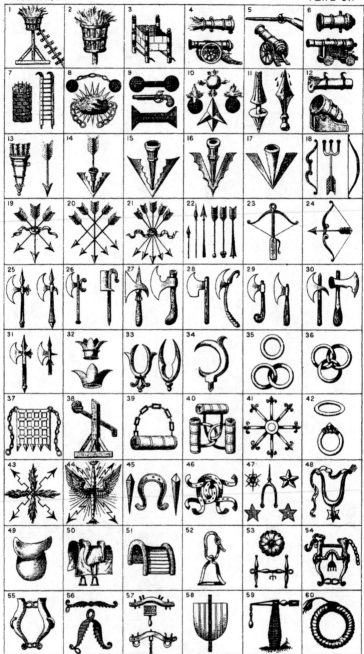

PLATE 37.

1 Beacon-fired
2 Fire-Beacon, also termed Rack-pole-beacon
3 Fire- Chest
4 Chamber-piece fired and a Cannon
5 A musket. Cannon mounted in perspective
6 A Culvering, or Culverin. Ship gun carriage with ordnance mounted
7 A Gabion, and Scaling-ladder
8 Chain Shot, and Chain-Shot as borne by Clifford
9 Bar-Shot; a pistol; and Spar-Shot
10 Ball fired in four places. Two Grenades, or Bomb-Shells; and a Caltrap, also termed Cheval-Trap, or Galtrap
11 Tilting Spear broken; and Spear-head imbrued
12 Battering-ram; and Mortar mounted
13 Quiver filled with arrows. An arrow
14 Pheon mounted on a staff and feathered, or a Pheon shafted and feathered, also termed an arrow Pheoned
15 Pheon
16 Pheon engrailed on the outer side
17 Broad-arrow
18 Two Archers, String, or Long-Bows bent, and a Bird bolt with three heads
19 A Sheaf of arrows
20 Five arrows, two and two paralled in saltire, and one in pale
21 Five arrows banded
22 Half-spear; a spear; a javelin; and three Bird-bolts
23 Arbaleste, or Cross-bow bent
24 Bow with arrow drawn to the head, or Long-bow fully bent
25 Battle axes
26 Lochabar-axes
27 Pole-axe; and Danish axe
28 Broad axe, and Lochabar-axe
29 Axe, or Hatchet
30 Danish Hatchets
31 Halbert and Demi-Halbert, or Curtal-axe
32 Two Cronels of a Tilting spear
33 Crampit, or Crampette, Boteroll, or Bauteroll
34 Match-lock
35 An Annulet; and two annulets conjoined in fesse
36 Three annulets conjoined, or interlaced, also termed Gimble-Rings
37 Portcullis
38 Balista, or Swepe
39 Fetlock
40 Three Fetlocks interlaced
41 Annulet, staffed, or staved flort, or flory
42 Shackle, or Link; and a Gem-ring, also termed annulet stoned
43 A Cross of thunder
44 Thunderbolt, also termed Jupiter's thunderbolt
45 Nail; a Horse shoe; and Passion-nail
46 Three Horse-shoes interlaced
47 Spur-rowel; a Scotch spur; Spur-rowel blemished; and Mullet; and Mullet pierced
48 Spur, leathered
49 Saddle
50 Saddle with stirrups and leathers
51 Pack-saddle
52 Stirrup and leather
53 Boss of a Bit, and a Snaffle bit
54 Manage-Bit
55 Hames
56 Barnacles extended, and Barnacles closed
57 A Curry-comb between Yokes. Two specimens of yokes, or ox-yokes
58 Quintain
59 Quintal
60 Match kindled, i.e. fired

PLATE 38.

1 Morion's
2 Morion
3 Morion's, the bottom one as borne by Blake
4 Basnet, or Basinet, or morion cap as in the Crest of Cecil. Mercury's Cap, or Petasus
5 Burgonet
6 Burgonet
7 Cuirass
8 Brigandine, or Habergon
9 Gorget; and a Brasset, or Vambrace
10 Helmet with vizor raised
11 Dexter and Sinister Close-gauntlets
12 Chamfrain, or armour for head of a horse
13 Armour for the Body
14 Greave
15 Boot sa. spurred or, turned over Erm. or a Boot sa. top turned over Erm. spurred or.
16 Tabard
17 Gauntlet closed; and an open Gauntlet
18 Demi leg in armour
19 A sword; a sword waved, or wavy and a Falchion
20 Two Seax
21 Swords Flamant, or Flaming
22 Cimeter, or Scymetar; and Seax
23 Dagger; and broken sword
24 The Curtana, or Sword of Mercy; and Sword of Estate
25 Galley, or Lymphad
26 Lymphad, also termed ship
27 An ancient ship with oars, three masts, sails furled, colours flying. Crest of Lusk
28 Lymphad
29 Lymphad, or ship with oars
30 Lymphad
31 Stem of a ship. Crest of Nelson
32 Ship in full sail
33 Ship sails furled

34 Magnetic needle; a Boat; and Boat-hook
35 Sail of a Ship; and Round-top of a mast
36 A Demi Hull; and the Hull of a Ship having only one mast, round top and bowsprit or. The Crest of Masters and Mariners
37 Coracle. See Dictionary
38 Mast and Sail of a Ship flotant at top
39 A Mast with a Sail hoisted, Crest of Tennant
40 Two Rudders, or Helms
41 An Anchor, and Anchor with cable
42 Noah's Ark
43 A Boatswain's Whistle; and a Cross, or Fore-Staff
44 Buoy with Cable, the Badge of Nevill, a Lead-line; and a grappling-iron
45 Harpoon and Trident
46 An Astrolabe
47 Sextant, or Quadrant
48 Sistrum
49 Windmill
50 Windmill-sails; and a Mill-clack
51 A Mill-stone charged with a Millrind. Mill or Water-wheel
52 Mill-pick, between two Mill-bills, or picks, the one on Sinister side as borne in the Millers arms
53 Mill-rind, or Fer-de-Mouline
54 Two Fer-de-Moulines, at No. 53 and No. 54 are seven different ways of depicting the Millrind, the first most frequently used
55 Crochet-hook, Fish-Weel; and Fish-hook
56 Fish-Weel with handle
57 Weel, or Fish Weel
58 Fish-Weel with handle
59 Oyster-dredge
60 Three examples of Eel-spears

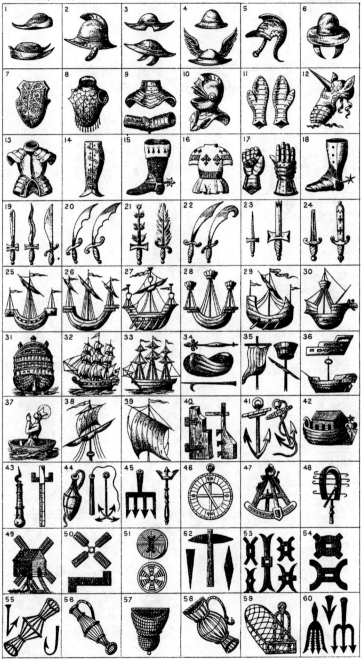

C.N.Elvin Del   P.C.Baker Sc

PLATE 39.

1 Demi Globe, or Northern Hemisphere thereon an Eagle wings expanded
2 Globe Terrestrial in frame environed with a meridian
3 Globe Terrestrial with stand environed with a meridian
4 Armillary sphere
5 A Terrestrial and Celestial Globe
6 A Broken, or fractured Globe under a Rainbow with Clouds at each end all ppr. Crest of Hope. Rainbow. Globe Fractured
7 Two Ploughs
8 Plough paddle 1. Harrow 2
9 Three triangular Harrows conjoined in fesse point with a ring
10 Scythe, or Sithe 1. Coulter 2. Scythe blade 3
11 Rake 1. Flail 2. Shepherd's-crook 3
12 Tillage-rake head 1 and 3. Thatchrake 2
13 Mole-spade 1. Sickles, or Reapinghooks interlaced 2. Dibble 3
14 Dung-fork 1. Sickle with teeth, or Serrated 2. Pitch-fork 3
15 Monogram T.W.N.E.
16 Winnowing-basket, Shruttle, Scruttle, Fruttle, Fan, or Vane
17 Basket with loaves, or a Basket full of Wastel cakes 1. Basket as in the arms of Littlebury 2. Basket as in the arms of Wolston 3
18 Spade 1. Spade irons 2 and 3. Half-spade 4
19 Hay-Fork, or Shake-Fork
20 A Brass. Heaume, or Bascinet 1. Coif de mailles 2. Ailettes 3. Hawberk 4. Surcoat 5. Poleyns 6. Pryck spur 7. Chausses 8. Sir Roger de Trumpington, 1289 Trumpington, Camb.
21 Scoop 1. Hay-hook, also termed a Horsepicker. 2.
22 Pair of Scales 1. Steelyard, or Statera Romana 2

23 On a Saltire, or interlaced by two Amphisbænæ az. langued gu. a rose of the last barbed and seeded ppr. Crest of Gwilt
24 Two scaly Lizards erect on their hind feet combatant ppr. each gorged with a plain collar or, the collars chained together, a chain with a ring at the end pendent between the two lizards of the last
25 Lamp inflamed, borne by Tanner 1. Antique Lamp as borne by the family of Leet 2. Lamp as in Berry's Heraldry 3
26 Roman Lamp 1. Hand, or Burning Lamp 2
27 Taper Candlestick with Candle inflamed 1. Globular, or Ship's Lamp, also termed a Lantern 2. Taper Candlestick 3.
28 Candlestick 1 and 3. Mortcours as in the armorial Bearings of the Wax-Chandlers Company 2
29 Distillatory
30 Still 1. Limbeck, or Alembeck 2
31 Cyphers A.D. Reversed
32 Flaming Brazier
33 Fiery-Furnace
34 Well with frame and handle
35 Bucket, or Well-bucket, also termed a hooped bucket 1. Bucket 2
36 Fire Bucket 1. Cup 2. Dish 3
37 Tun, Barrel, or Cask 1. Bolt and Tun 2
38 Tun erect inflamed 1. Altar inflamed 2
39 Urn 1. Salts, Salt-cellar, or Sprinkling Salt 2
40 Two examples of Turnpikes
41 Turnpike 1. Gate 2
42 Goog 1. Ullum 2. Punja 3
43 Clock as borne by the Clock Makers' Company
44 Sundial 1. Hour-glass, or sandglass 2
45 Hour-glass winged

PLATE 40.

1 Knitting-frame
2 Shuttle, or Wheel Shuttle ; and Spindle threaded
3 Fusil, or Spindle threaded ; a Bottom; and Wharrow Spindle
4 Trundle ; a Quill or Trundle ; and a Quill of Yarn
5 Cotton hank ; a Silk hank ; sometimes depicted as the third figure
6 Silk-Thrower's Mill
7 Stock-Card
8 Floats
9 Preene ; and Empty Quill
10 Wool-Card
11 Hemp Break, or Hackle the Badge of Bray. Second figure is also a Hemp-Break borne by Bree
12 Jersey-comb ; and Rope-hook
13 Ancient Fusil ; and a Fusil
14 Lozenge
15 Lozenge-Flory
16 Rustre ; and a Mascle
17 Seven Mascles conjoined, three, three, and one
18 Four Mascles-fretted
19 Wool Pack
20 Wool-Pack corded
21 Bale of Piedmont Silk ; and a Bag of Madder
22 A Window-grating. Badge of Sutton Baron Dudley
23 Tassel ; and a Ball tasselled
24 Cushion lozengy and tasselled
25 Tent
26 A Tent az. fringed and semée of stars or, ensigned with a pennon gu. Crest of Lindsey
27 Tent
28 Pavilion, or Tabernacle, also termed a Sperver
29 Mantle, or Royal Cloak
30 Parliament-Robe
31 Manche, or Maunch
32 Maunch, as borne in the arms of Lord Hastings

33 Maunch ⎫ antique
34 Maunch ⎬
35 Maunch
36 A hand clenched issuing from a Maunch
37 Purse of State
38 Purse stringed and tasselled
39 Palmer's scrip, or Wallet
40 Palmer's Staff and Scrip
41 Wallet open
42 Powder-horn, or Flask
43 Hatband Nowed ; and a Hatband
44 Circular Hatband
45 Stole
46 Piece of Cloth
47 Head of Hair, or Peruke
48 Comb in a head of hair
49 A Four-cornered and a three-cornered cap
50 A Hat; and a Cap as borne by the name of Wingfield
51 1 Cap as borne by De la Rous. 2 born by Maundefield. 3 Infula, or Long Cap. 4 Cap borne by Drakenford. 5 as borne by Capper
52 Hat worn over the arms of the States General ; and a Hat as in the arms of the Feltmakers' Company
53 Hat turned up and adorned with three Ostrich feathers borne by the name of Balm. A Crown as borne in the arms of the Skinners Company
54 Chapeau, or Cap of Maintenance ; and a Cap, Copped, or Hat
55 Tiara, or Triple-Crown with clouds in base issuing rays, as borne in the arms of the Drapers Company
56 Bonnet Electoral ; and State Cap of the Lord Mayor of London
57 Crown of the King of Arms
58 Cap as in the arms of Robinson
59 The Popes Crown, or Tiara
60 Cardinal's Cap, or Hat

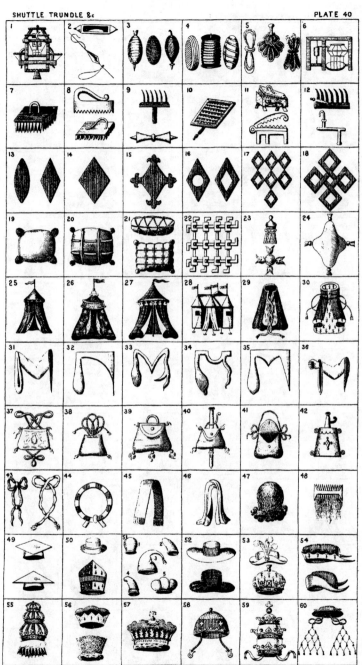

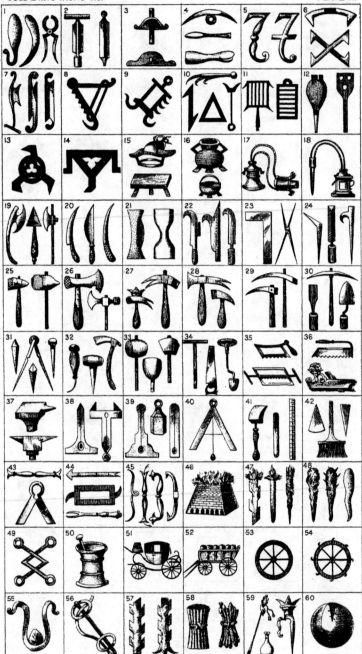

C.N. Elvin. Del.   L. Cully. Sc.

PLATE 41.

1 Two Soldering irons; and Pincers
2 Curriers' Shaves
3 Two examples of the Grose
4 Wolf-trap; a Point; and Burling-iron
5 Fleames
6 A Cramp; and Two Cramps in Saltire
7 Cutting iron; and two examples of Glazier's nippers
8 Hanger
9 Hanger sometimes depicted as this
10 A Flesh-hook; a Kettle-hook; a Triangle iron; and a Flesh-hook
11 Two Gridirons
12 Bellows; and a Peel, or Bakers-shovel
13 Trivet
14 Triangle Trivet
15 Patten; and a Trussel, or Trestle
16 Flesh-Pot; and a Caldron
17 Penner and Ink-horn
18 Another example of a Penner and Ink-horn
19 Plumbers cutting Knife; Plumbers triangular Soldering iron, or Shave-hook; and Slaughter axe
20 Butcher's Knife; a Shredding Knife; and a Knife
21 Brick axe; and Bricklayer's axe
22 A Forest, or Wood Bill; a War-Bill; and Pruning Knife
23 A Square; and Closing Tongs
24 A File, between two Tenter-hooks
25 Hand and Sledge hammer
26 Plasterer's and Lathing hammer
27 A Hammer ducally crowned; and a hammer with claws
28 Hammer with claws; and a Hammer
29 Pavier's Picks
30 Chisel; a Pickaxe; and Trowel
31 A Nail; Compasses; a closing nail; and Passion nail

32 Awl; a Wimble or Winepiercer; and adze
33 Beetle; Mallet, and in the centre a Stone-mason's Mallet
34 Auger; a Saw; and Butteris
35 Frame Saw as in the Arms of the Fanmaker's Company The other as borne by the name of Hamilton
36 A Shaving iron; and a Plane
37 Anvils
38 Level with plummet; and a Level reversed
39 Level with plummet; a Plummet; and a Level
40 A Perpendiculum
41 Bookbinder's polishing iron; a folding stick; and a Rule, or Yard-measure
42 A Cone; a Treble-Flat-Brush; and a Wedge, or Peg
43 A Turret; and Shears
44 Broches; a Merillion; and Broches
45 Four examples of Habicks
46 Brick-Kiln
47 Fire-brand; a Torch; and Hymeneal-torch
48 A Club; a Spiked Club; and an Icicle
49 Angles interlaced
50 Pestle and Mortar
51 Coach
52 A Wagon
53 Cart-Wheel
54 Catherine Wheel
55 A Sling charged with a Stone
56 A Sling
57 A Staff-raguly couped at each end; and a Staff-raguly couped and erased
58 Bundle of Laths; and a Fagot
59 A Trailing-pike, or Leading-Staff; a Stilt, and a Phyal
60 Foot-Ball

PLATE 42.

1 A Heart; and a Hart vulned
2 Heart pierced; a Heart enfiled with ducal coronet
3 Heart flamant; a Heart ensigned and transfixed
4 A Dexter, hand erect betw. two stalks of Wheat flexed in Saltire, issuing from a heart all ppr. in the hand a book shut sa. garnished or. Crest of Higginson
5 Heart winged
6 Heart betw. two wings
7 A Key ensigned; and a Key enfiled
8 A Key; and a Key with double wards
9 Two Keys in Saltire
10 Two Keys endorsed bows interlaced
11 Cross of Keys double claved
12 Two Keys endorsed in bend Sinister bows interlaced with a Sword interposed in bend
13 Two Padlocks and a Door Lock
14 A Staple; a Door joint; Hinge; Two Staples interlaced; and a door Bolt
15 A Demi belt erased betw. four buckles
16 Half-belt and four buckles
                  See Buckle
17 A Garter
18 Demi-Garter, or Perclose
19 Bottle Leathern
20 to 24 Water Bougets. See Dictionary
25 A Covered Cup
26 Chalice; and a Cup, or Goblet
27 Ewer's or Lavér-Pots
28 Tailors bodkin; and a Sledge
29 Penny-yard pence or penny; An Iron Ring. A Peg Top; and Star-pagodas
30 Pentagon
31 A Chain enarched; a circular chain; and Circular chain within another
32 Slay, Slea, or Reed; and a playing Table

33 Copper cake; a Point; and Drawing-iron
34 A Delf; a Billet, and a Billet wavy; and a Flagstone
35 A Gad; and a triangular Gad; this is also termed a Demi lozenge, it is also blazoned a Steel Gad
36 Copper; and Engrossing-block
37 Mound
38 Triangular Fret
39 Swivels, or Manacles
40 Shackbolt; and Double Shackbolt, also termed Handcuffs
41 Rosary; a Patermoster; and Scourge with three lashes
42 Escallop; Escallop reversed; and a Vannet
43 Pilgrims Staffs. The first one is sometimes called a Pike-staff
44 Palmer's Staffs
45 A Priors Staff as in the arms of Malton Priory; and a Crosier
46 A Pastoral Staff. A Crosier-Case, and a Pastoral Staff with Banderole, or Orarium
47 Two Sceptres in Saltire traversed by a Sword in Pale point upwards
48 Papal Staff
49 Block-Brush; and a Broom, or Besom
50 Trepan; and Spatula
51 Scalpel or Lancet; and a Bistoury
52 Fanged Tooth; a Jaw-bone; and Shin-bones
53 Tomb-stone
54 Tomb-stone arraswise
55 Fountain of two basins
56 Rock or Mountain
57 Mountain enflamed. Crest of Grant
58 Three Hills, as in the arms of Brinckman
59 Islands
60 Calamine-Stone; a Mole-hill, Hillock, or Mount; and a Flint-stone

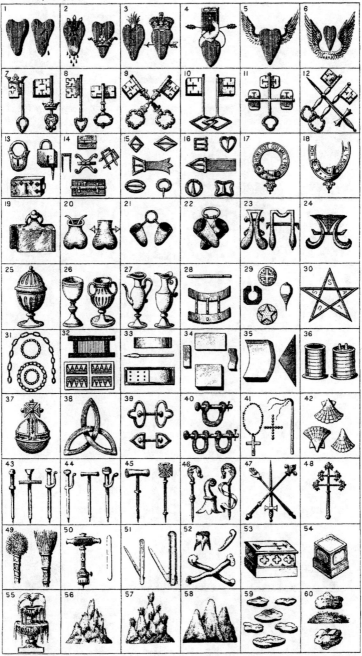

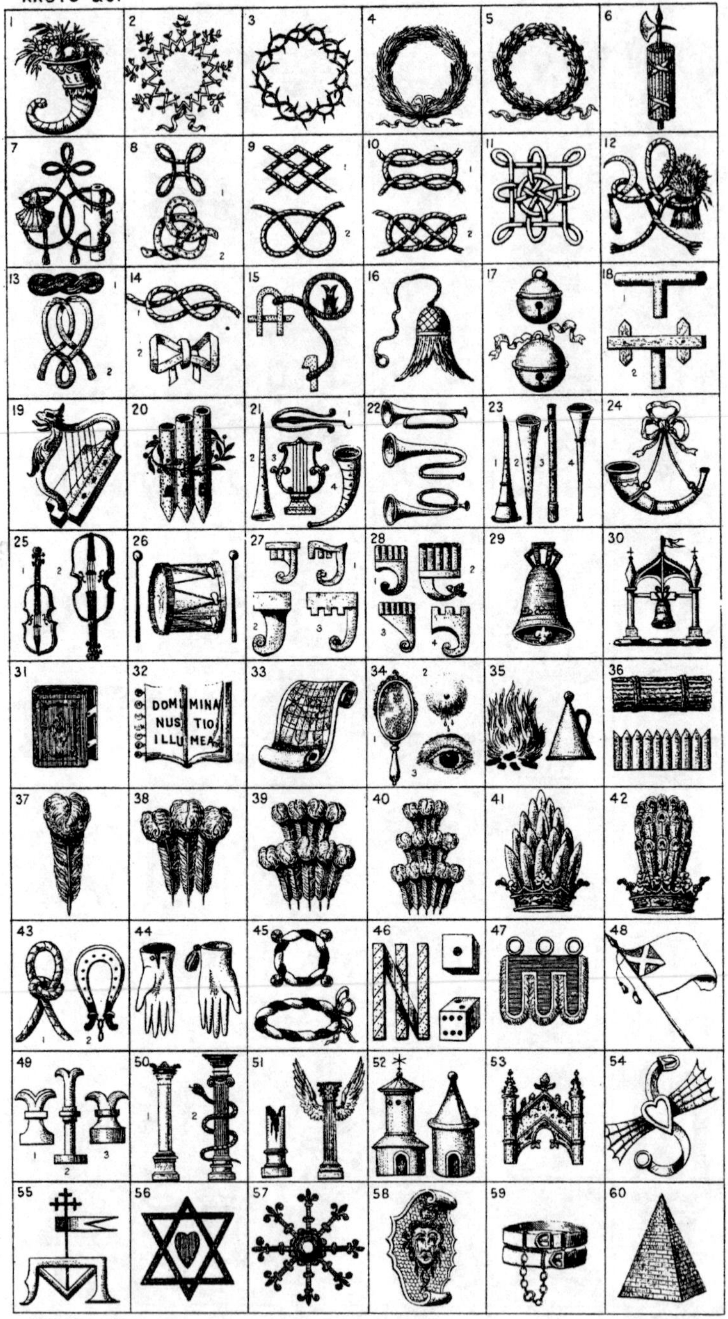

C. N. Elvin. Del. *L. Cully. Sc.*

PLATE 43.

1 Cornucopia
2 Obsidional Crown, or Garland
3 Crown of Thorns
4 Crown Graminee, or Chaplet of Grass
5 Crown Olive, Olive Chaplet, or Civic Wreath
6 Fasces, or Roman-Fasces
7 Dacres Knot. Badge of Dacre an escallop and staff raguly both ar. connected by a Dacre Knot
8 Bowen's Knot. No. 2. Anne of Bohemia
9 Harrington, or Love Knot. No. 2. Stafford Knot
10 Bourchier's Knot. No. 2. Wakes and Ormond Knot
11 Lacy Knot
12 Hungerford Knot. Badge a golden sickle and garb connected by a Hungerford Knot
13 A Coil of flax, as in the Crest of Washbourne, and the Heneage Knot
14 True Lover's Knot. No. 2. A Wedding favour as in arms of Latter
15 A Fetterlock or. to which is attached a rope gu. encircling a fishes tail erect ppr. having a peg at the other end gold. Badge of Lawrence
16 Lure, or Leure
17 Hawk's, or Falcon's bell, and Hawk's bell with jesses
18 Hawk's or Falcon's rests, or perches
19 Harp
20 Three organ pipes enfiled with a laurel branch. Crest of Delapipe
21 Jew's Harp, No. 1. Pipe, No. 2. Lyre, No. 3. Cornet, No. 4.
22 Trumpets
23 Hautboy, No. 1. Horn, No. 2. Flute, No. 3. Trumpet, No. 4.
24 Bugle-horn ; or Hunting Horn stringed
25 Fiddle, or Violin ; a Treble Violin, Violoncello, or Treble Violent
26 Drum and Drum sticks
27 Clarion, Rest, or Sufflue
28 The same, No. 1. Most commonly used
29 Bell, or Church Bell
30 Belfry
31 Book, or Bible closed
32 Book open with seven seals
33 Map, or Chart. The Crest of Holton

34 Mirror, No. 1. Breast distilling drops of milk, No. 2. Eye, No. 3
35 Bonfire; and Extinguisher
36 Fascine; and Park pales
37 Ostrich Feather
38 A Plume of Ostrich Feathers
39 A Double Plume
40 Triple Plume
41 A Panache, or Upright plume of feathers
42 A Panache of Peacock feathers
43 Wrestling Collar ; and a Dog's Collar
44 Falconer's, or Hawking Glove, and a Falconer's glove pendent tasselled
45 Circular wreath ar. and sa. with four hawk's bells joined thereto in quadrature or. borne by Jocelyn. An Oval Wreath
46 Three ingots of Gold, palewise fretted with another in bend. Borne by the name of Wilson Dice charged with an Ace; and a Dice with six spots in front, three on the sinister side, and two on the top. Mathias
47 Gonfanon, or Gonfalone
48 A banner displayed bendways ar. therein a canton az. charged with a saltire of the first, as in the arms of Bannerman
49 Chess-rooks. No. 3. The most common
50 Pillar, or Column (Doric.) Ducally crowned. No. 1. Column (Ionic) enveloped with a Snake. No. 2
51 A Broken Column. A Column (Corinthian) winged, or a Winged Column
52 Dove-cot, or Dove-house. The one on the dexter if without vane, is sometimes blazoned a Castle
53 Canopy, or Stall of Gothic work
54 Gardebras, or Garbraille
55 Weather-cock, or Vane. Badge of Ratcliffe
56 A man s heart gu. within two equilateral triangles interlaced sa. Also blazoned a double Delta. Borne in the arms of Villages
57 Escarbuncle, or Carbuncle
58 The Shield of Pallas
59 Pair of Couples. As borne by Lord Hindlip
60 Pyramid

PLATE 44.

1 Rose Heraldic
2 Rose Branch
3 Garden Rose stalked and leaved
4 Rose and Thistle conjoined
5 Thistle slipped and leaved
6 A Lily; and a Lily stalked and leaved
7 Fleur-de-lis
8 Double Fleur-de-lis
9 Fleur-de-lis seeded
10 Fleur-de-lis of lilies
11 Demi Fleur-de-lis is divided perpale. A Fleur-de-lis couped
12 Antique Fleur-de-lis
13 Caterfoil double and pierced
14 Trefoils No. 1 generally used. 2. Fitched. 3. Slipped raguled and couped. 4. Triple slipped. 5. Double slipped
15 Trefoil double slipped raguled and couped; and a Trefoil the stalk fixed fo a twig lying fesseways
16 1. Quatrefoil, or Quaterfcil. 2. Slipped; sometimes slipped as No. 3. No. 4 Cinquefoil
17 1. Narcissus. 2. Cinquefoil pierced. No. 3. Angenim
18 Eight-foil, or double Quatrefoil
19 Blue-bottle, or Cyanus
20 Gilly Flower; and a Pink, or Carnation
21 Adders tongue; and a Tulip
22 Marygold
23 Columbine; and a Pansy, or Heart's ease
24 Violet stalked and leaved
25 Daisy stalked and leaved
26 Margarette Daisy. Badge of Margaret consort of Hen. VI. (From the Shrewsbury Missal, Brit. Mus.)
27 Bramble, or Wild Rose
28 French Marygold
29 Flower of the Flag
30 Bell flowers, or Blue-bell
31 Tobacco plant
32 Grain tree
33 Sugar cane
34 Tea-plant
35 Cherry Branch fructed
36 Cinnamon
37 Almond slip
38 Date branch fructed
39 Holly sprig, or Sprig of Ilex
40 Laurel sprig; and Laurel branch
41 Watercresses
42 Broom plant; and Broom flower
43 Mallow
44 Bur of Burdock
45 Rue
46 Ash, or Ashen Keys
47 Fir branch
48 Reeds; and a Bull-rush
49 Fern
50 Elder-branch
51 Crequier Plant, or Wild-plum
52 Oak slipped
53 Oak branch
54 Acorn; and a Fir or Pine cone
55 Nut or Hazel branch
56 Pear; a Pine Apple; and Pear slipped
57 Apple; a Pomegranate; and Apple slipped pendant
58 Mulberry, and a Gourd
59 Pea-cod; a Turnip; and Bean-cod, or pod
60 Mandrake

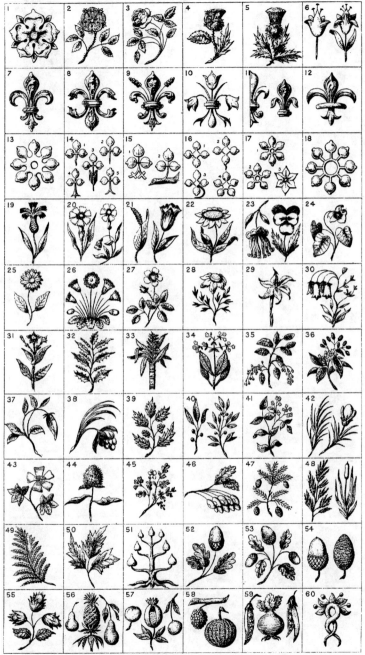

C.N. Elvin, Del.

L. Cully, Sc.

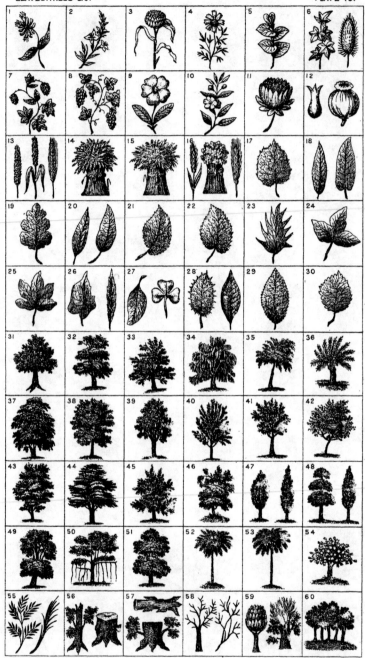

PLATE 45.

1 Honeysuckle, or Woodbine
2 Rosemary
3 Garlic
4 Camomile
5 Barberry
6 Ivy; and a Teazel or Teasel
7 Hop-Plant
8 Vine-Branch
9 Primrose stalked and leaved
10 Myrtle branch with flower and buds
11 Lotus flower
12 A clove; and Poppy-bole
13 Wheat Ear; Wheat stalk-bladed; and a Barley ear
14 Garb, or Wheat-Sheaf
15 Garb of Barley
16 Bladed ear of Wheat; a Garb of Quaterfoils; and an Ear of Rye
17 Hazel-leaf
18 Laurel; and Dock-leaf
19 Oak leaf
20 Bay leaf; and Portugal-laurel
21 Elm leaf
22 Mulberry leaf
23 Holly leaf
24 Maple leaf
25 Fig leaf
26 Burdock; and Betony leaf
27 Woodbine leaf pendant; and Clover
28 Nettle; and Walnut leaf
29 Rose leaf
30 Aspen leaf
31 Oak Tree fructed, and eradicated
32 Ash
33 Beech
34 Birch
35 Willow, or Salix
36 Pollard Willow
37 Linden, or Lime
38 Walnut
39 Pear Tree fructed
40 Cherry
41 Almond
42 Thorn
43 Hawthorn
44 Cedar
45 Alder
46 Asp
47 Yew; and Poplar
48 Box; and Cypress
49 Mahogany
50 Banyan
51 Elm
52 Date-Palm Tree
53 Cocoa-Tree, anciently Coker-Tree
54 Cotton Tree (as engraved in Burke's Heraldic Illustrations)
55 Branch of Southernwood; and Palm-Branch
56 Stem of a Tree erased and sprouting. A stock of a Tree snagged, and erased
57 Stock of a Tree Jacent, eradicated; Stem of a Tree couped, eradicated and sprouting
58 A starved, or Blighted tree couped. A starved, or Blighted branch. See Scrogs
59 A Savin Tree. (From Burke's Heraldic Illustrations). A Burning Bush
60 Oak Trees on a Mount, also blazoned a Hurst, or Wood

PLATE 46.

1 Man and Wife; Baron and Femme. The Husbands arms are quarterly, Impaling a single coat.
When a man marries a second wife the alliance can be shown in three different ways. The Fesse in the engraved examples shewing the position of the man's arms and the Numerals those of the wives. See term Marshalling

2 Man and Two Wives; No. 3, and No. 4

5 Man and Three Wives
6 Man and Four Wives
7 Man and Five Wives
8 Man and Six Wives
9 A Widow
When a Widow marries a second time, her husband impales her paternal arms. If a Peer marries an untitled lady and he die leaving her a widow, and she marry for her second husband an untitled gentleman, there is an absurd fashion of bearing the Heraldic Insignia the same as if she was a Peeress in her own right

10 Widow being an Heiress or Co-Heiress
11 A Woman having had two husbands
12 Pennon of Waleran de Bellomont Earl of Worcester, 1144
13 Gonfanon
14 Pennon as in the Crest of the Duke of Wellington
15 Pennoncell's
16 Triangular Pennon of Ralf Lord Neville, 1386
17 Pennon
18 Banner

19 Pennon
20 Standard of Hastings of Elsing co. Norfolk
21 Guidon
22 Pennon of De Quincey, Earl of Winchester, who died 1219

FUNERAL ACHIEVEMENTS.

Commonly called HATCHMENTS. (See Funeral Achievements.) The engravings, except No. 33, are without the frames

23 Bachelor
24 Maid
25 Husband dead, wife surviving
26 Wife dead, Husband surviving
27 Husband dead, wife an Heiress surviving
28 Wife an Heiress dead, Husband surviving
29 Husband and first wife dead, second surviving
30 Both Wives dead, Husband surviving
31 Widower
32 Widow
33 A Bishop, his Wife dead

DISTINCTION OF HOUSES.

Marks of Cadency or of Filiation, also termed Brisures, are charges placed in the shield to express the differences of descent, e.g. The distinction of the eldest son of the second House is a crescent charged with a label. The eldest son of the third House, a mullet, charged with a label, etc. See also Plate 16, f. 40 to 45, and P. 25a. f. 1 and 2.

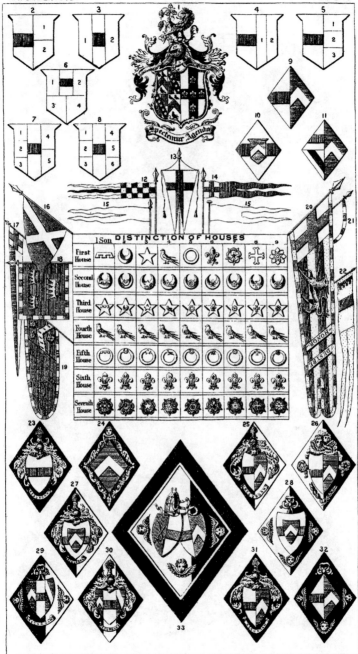

Elvenora Florent Utilis

Spertemur Agendo

Chas. Norton Elvin. M.A. East Dereham

The Dictionary

THE

DICTIONARY OF HERALDRY.

A, or **a**. Abbreviation for Argent; Capital Letters of the Alphabet are used as charges in Heraldry. *See* LETTERS.

AARONS-ROD. A rod entwined with a Serpent. P. 30, f. 57.

ABACOT. An ancient cap of state of the English Kings.

ABAISSE, ABAISE, or **ABASED.** Equivalent to the term "in base" a Cheveron Abaissé. P. 15, f. 37.

ABAISED. A term applied to the wings of eagles when the tips are depressed below the centre of the shield.

ABATEMENT. A mark of disgrace, never used. *See* POINTS.

A'BOUCHE. A Shield was said to be á bouche when it had a carved notch cut out, for the lance to pass through, in the dexter chief, as the shield. P. 31, f. 26.

ABYSS. The centre of an Escutcheon.

ABBESS. A Lady Abbess, as borne in the arms of Abbes. P. 35, f. 5.

ABBEY. *See* MONASTERY.

ABBLAST, ARBALESTE, ARBLAST, or **ARBALIST;** a Cross Bow. P. 37, f. 23.

ABBOT'S PASTORAL STAFF or **PRIOR'S STAFF.** P. 42, f. 45.

ABEYANCE. The expectancy of a title; the right being in existance, but the exercise of it suspended.

On the death of a baron, whose dignity originated in a Writ of Summons, without issue male, the barony becomes vested in his daughters ; if he leaves an only daughter, she succeeds to the dignity, but if there be more daughters than one, the title falls into ABEYANCE amongst them, and continues in that state until all but one of the daughters, or the sole heir of only one daughter survives ; in which case, the barony devolves on the surviving daughter, or on the heir of her body. THE CROWN can, however, at any time, terminate an ABEYANCE in favour of one of the heirs.

ABISME. When the charge, which is between others, is depicted small, so as not to appear as the principal bearing.

ABOUTE. Placed end to end, as four lozenges abouté. P. 8, f. 12.

ABOUTI. Conjoined.

ACCIDENTS OF ARMS. A term sometimes met with which appears to mean nothing else in blazoning than the strictures and marks of difference.

ACCOLES. Two shields in juxta-position. *See* ACCOLLIES.

ACCOLLE, GORGED, or **COLLARED** as P. 18 and 19, f. 21.

ACCOLLIES, or **ACCOLEE.** A term used to express the position of two shields placed side by side and touching each other, and was an early mode of marshalling the arms of a man and his wife.

ACCOMPAGNEE, ACCOMPAGNE, or **ACCOMPANIED.** *See* BETWEEN, and P. 4, f. 31.

ACCORNE. *See* HORNED.

ACCOSTED. Side by side.

The same as counter-tripping. P. 28, f. 49. This term is sometimes used when charges are placed on each side of another charge, but is better expressed by the term "between." P. 14, f. 6.

ACCOUTRED. Same as Caparisoned.

ACCROCHE. One charge hooked into another. P. 39, f. 17.

ACCROUPI. A term sometimes used for Hares, Rabbits, &c., when lodged.

ACCRUED. A tree full-grown.

ACE-CARDS. The four ace-cards are borne in the arms of the Cardmakers Company. P. 22, f. 20.

ACHIEVEMENTS OF ARMS. The armorial bearings with all the exterior ornaments of the Shield. P. 11, f. 21.

ACORN. The seed or fruit of the Oak. When the husk is of a different colour, it must be named, as an Acorn naming the colour, husked and stalked of such a colour. P. 44, f. 54.

ACORN. Slipped and leaved. P. 44, f. 52.

ACORNE. *See* ATTIRED.

ACORNED, or FRUCTED. The Oak Tree so termed when represented with Acorns upon it. P. 45, f. 31.

ACUTE ANGLED, or BEVILED. P. 1.

ADAM, or NAKED FIGURE. P. 22, f. 7. *See* TERM MAN.

ADDER. An Adder obturant his ear, or stopping his ear with his tail. P. 30, f. 43.

ADDERS-TONGUE. A plant whose seeds are produced on a spike resembling a serpent's tongue. P. 44, f. 21.

ADDICE, ADZE. A coopers tool. P. 44, f. 32.

ADDITIONS OF HONOUR. Honourable Augmentations (which see) granted by the Sovereign.

ADDOSSE, or ADDORSY. *See* ADORSED.

ADDOSSE. Same as Adorsed.

ADENTRE. Accosted on the outer side.

ADEXTRE. i.e. on the dexter side.

ADOPTION. Arms of.
Are the arms of another family, borne either singular, or quartered with those of the paternal coat, e.g. If a person by will, adopt a stranger to possess his name and estates, the person so adopted, applies for a special warrant to the Sovereign, to empower him to carry out the will of the Adopter, and thereby assume his name and arms. If however the adopted, be of more noble blood and family than the adopter, he is not obliged to disuse his own name or arms—but, in case he be of an inferior family, he is compelled to assume the name and arms of the adopter.

ADORNED. Decorated as a cap etc., ornamented with feathers etc. P. 40, f. 53.

ADORSED, ADDORSED, ADORSSED, ADORSE, ADOSSE, or ADOSSED. All these terms are better expressed by the word Endorsed.
These terms are all used by different writers to express the same thing, i.e,, when any two bearings are placed back to back. P. 26, f. 15; p. 32, f. 29; p. 42, f. 10 and 12; p. 29, f. 44.

ADVANCERS. The top shoots from the attire of a stag.

ADVENTAIL. A Coat of Arms.

ADUMBRATED. Anything painted in shadow, properly termed IN RELIEF, where the figures are always of the same colour with the ground, and thrown out by the shading.

ADZE. An instrument used by Coopers, Wheelwrights, etc. P. 44, f. 32.

ÆGIS. The shield of Pallas on the boss of which was the head of Medusa. P. 43, f. 58.

ÆSCULAPIUS ROD OF. P. 30, f. 57.
A rod entwined by a snake, which was the form assumed by Esculapius, the God of healing, when he was brought from Greece to Rome in a season of great sickness.

AFRICAN. *See* MOOR.

AFRONTE, AFFRONTEE, AFFRONTED, or AFFRONTANT. When the head of a man, lion, etc., is represented fullface. P. 26, f. 50.

AFFRONTE-SEJANT. P. 26, f. 43.

AGACELLA. The Gazelle, an elegantly formed species of Antelope.

AGNUS DEI. Holy, or Paschal Lamb. P. 29, f. 4.

AIGLON, or AIGLETTE. A small eagle.

AIGUISE, AIGUISEE, or EQUISE. The same as pointed. *See* CROSS-AIGUISE. P. 9, f. 45.

AILES. Wings.

AILETTS. Small escutcheons affixed to the shoulders of an armed Knight. P. 39, f. 20, No. 3.

AINENT. Running; applied to beasts.

AISLE. Winged.

AJOURE. The same as voided, when applied to any of the ordinaries, or parts of them, denoting that the field is seen through, as a Fesse crenellée ajoure of the field. P. 4, f. 16; p. 22, f. 9.

ALAISEE, or ALISEE. Applied to an ordinary, when cut off, so as not to touch the sides of the shield; the common and better term is Humettée. P. 4, f. 1.

ALANT, ALAND, or ALAUNT. A sort of Mastiff. P. 29, f. 12.

A-LA-QUISE, or CUISSE. A term applied to an eagle's leg erased at the thigh. P. 33, f. 21.

ALBERIA. A plain white shield.

ALBERT-MEDAL. *See* MEDAL.

ALBERT. Prince Coronet of. P. 25a, f. 3 and 4.

ALCE. The Male Griffin. P. 27, f. 6.

ALDER. A Tree. P. 45, f. 45.

ALEMBIC, ALEMBICK, LIMBECK, or STILL. A Utensil of the Distillery. P. 39, f. 30, No. 2

ALFEREZ. An ensign.

ALICE, or ALCE. The Male Gryphon. P. 27, f. 6.

ALIECE, or ALAIZE. *See* ALAISEE.

ALLEGORICAL. The representation of anything conveyed by emblem, as the figure of Justice. P. 35, f. 7.

ALLERION, ALERION, or ALLETTE. A fabulous bird represented without beak or legs. P. 33, f. 30.

ALLIANCE ARMS OF. Are those impaled or borne in an escutcheon of pretence to denote alliances formed by marriage, and the arms taken by the issue of an Heiress or Coheiress quartered with those of their Father, thereby shewing their descent from a family of which the male line is extinct. P. 12, f. 21.

ALLIGATOR. A carnivorous amphibious reptile. P. 30, f. 1.

ALLOCAMELUS, or ASS-CAMEL. P. 27, f. 46.

ALLUMEE. The eyes of beasts are so termed when depicted sparkling with red.

ALLUSIVE ARMS, or ARMES PARLANTES, and CANTING ARMS. Are very numerous in English armory, they contain charges hinting at the name, character, office or history of the original bearer, e.g. The arms of Dobell—a Doe betw. three bells, of Colt—three Colts—of Shelly—three shells, etc. *See* REBUS.

ALMOND SLIP. Borne by the name of Almond. P. 44, f. 37.

ALMOND TREE. P. 45, f. 41.

ALPACA, or PACO. Supposed to be a domesticated variety of the Guanaco. P. 28, f. 41.

ALPE. A Bullfinch. A term used by Blomfield in his His. of Nor. in blazoning the arms of Alpe. P. 33, f. 49.

ALPHABET, LETTERS OF THE. Capital letters are sometimes used as charges. *See* LETTERS.

ALTAR. In heraldry, is always drawn inflamed. P. 39, f. 38, No. 2.

ALTERNATE, ALTERNATELY, or ALTERNATIVELY. One after the other.

ALTERNATING. Following by turns. As an Orle of fleur-de-lis and martlets alternating. i.e. four fleur-de-lis and four martlets alternately placed.

AMARANTHAL CROWN. A crown like a garland composed of leaves of the imaginary amaranth that never fades. *See* GARLAND.

AMBULANT. Walking. **AMBULANT-Co.** Walking together. P. 35, f. 26.

AMERICAN EAGLE, and the STARS and STRIPES. P. 25a, f. 15.

AMETHYST. A precious stone. Used by some Heralds to denote purpure, when blazoning the arms of Peers.

AMMENCHE, AMMANCHE, EMANCHE, or CRENEAUX. *See* CRENELLEE.

AMPHIBANES, or AMPHIBENES. P. 39, f. 23.
On a Saltire or, interlaced by two Amphisbænæ az. langued gu. a rose of the last barbed and seeded ppr. Crest of Gwilt.

AMPHISBENE, or AMPHISTA. A beast with dragon's body and wings, the head of a serpent, and the tail ending with a like head. P. 27, f. 9.

AMPHISBONA. A snake with a head at each extremity. (BURKE'S LANDED GENTRY.)

AMPHISIEN-COCKATRICE. *See* BASILISK. P. 27, f. 10.

ANANAS. A Pine Apple. P. 44, f. 56, **ANATOMY OF A MAN.** P. 35, f. 35.

ANCHOR. The emblem of Hope, is always borne as in P. 38, f. 41, unless differently described.
If a cable is attached to it, it is termed an anchor cabled, and the cable is depicted entwined round it. f. 41. When the cross beam is of a different tincture, it is termed an anchor timbered of such a colour. When the barbed part, by which it takes hold of the ground, is of a different tincture from the other part, the anchor is said to be fluked, or flouked.

ANCHORED, ANCHRY, ANCHORRY, ANCHREE, ANCREE, or ANCRED. Terms applied to Crosses whose extremities resemble the flukes of Anchors. P. 10, f. 11.

ANCIENT, or ANSHENT. A small flag, or streamer ending in a point.

ANCREE. *See* ANCHORED.

AND. A Roman, " &." is borne in the arms of And

ANDREW ST. ORDER OF. *See* KNIGHTHOOD ORDERS OF.

ANDREW ST. CROSS OF. Is a silver saltire on an azure field. P. 7, f. 21.

ANELETT. *See* ANNULET.

ANGEL. Variously represented in Heraldry. P. 36, f. 54, 55 and 56.
An Angel wings expanded arms uplifted on the breast, the hands clasped as borne by the family of Crondice. An Angel kneeling wings expanded the hands in a praying position, borne by Hodder, Hynell, etc. An angel volant pointing to heaven with the dexter hand, and to the base with the Sinister, from the mouth a scroll, thereon the letters G.I.E.D. signifying Gloria in Excelsis Deo.

ANGEL'S HEAD. *See* CHERUB.

ANGEMM, ANGENNE. *See* ANGENIN.

ANGENIN. A flower of six leaves, always borne pierced. P. 44, f. 17, No. 3.

ANGLE. Acute or beviled, and rectangled. P. 4, f. 28; P. 12, f. 20.

ANGLE-HOOK. *See* FISH-HOOK.

ANGLED-QUARTER. Also called Nowy-square, or Nowy-quadrant. P. 14, f. 35

ANGLES. Two interlaced saltirewise and having an annulet at each end. P. 41, f. 49.

ANGOLA GOAT. *See* GOAT.

ANILLE. A fer-de-moline, or Mill-rind, to which refer.

ANIMALS. And parts of animals of almost every species, are now to be met within armorial bearings.
In blazoning the teeth, or claws of Lions, Tigers, Wolves and all ravenous beasts, are called their arms; and when of a different tincture to the body must be named, and the animals are said to be armed of such a colour. This term "Armed" also applies to the horns of Bulls, Goats, &c. The tongue of all beasts, if not mentioned is to be gules; except the animal itself is gules, then it must be azure; and when the tongue has to be named, the animal is said to be "langued" e.g. a Lion gu., armed and langued az. But in blazoning Deer, altho' their horns are their weapons, they are said to be "Attired," and when the hoof of the Deer, Horse, Bull, Goat, etc., is of a different tincture it is termed "Unguled." *See* these TERMS.

ANIME. The same as Incensed.

ANJON. A javelin the point of which resemble a fleur-de-lis.

ANNELET. Same as Annulet.

ANNET. A Sea Gull. P. 34, f. 13.

ANNODATED. A term to express anything bent somewhat like an S; as the serpents in the Caduceus of Mercury which may be said to be annodated and entwined about the staff. P. 30, f. 56.

ANNULATED, ANNULY, or ANNULETY. Also termed a Cross ringed. P. 10, f. 35.

ANNULET. A ring. The emblem of strength. P. 37, f. 35.
The Romans represented Liberty by it.

ANNULETS conjoined in fesse. P. 37, f. 35.

ANNULETS interlaced in triangle. P. 37, f. 36.

ANNULET STONED. P. 37, f. 42.

ANNULET STAFFED, or STAVED-FLORT, or FLORY. P. 37, f. 41.

ANNULETTY. *See* ANNULATED and P. 10, f. 35.

ANOMALIES-HERALDIC. Deviations from the general method, or analogy of the science

ANSERATED. *See* CROSS GRINGOLEE. P. 11, f. 36.

ANSHENT, or ANCIENT. A small flag ending in a point

ANTARCTIC-STAR, same as ESTOILE

ANT, or EMMET. Emblematical of patience and forethought; always depicted as in P. 30, f. 7, unless differently named.

ANTE, or ENTE. The same as DOVE-TAIL.

ANTELOPE. An animal of the Deer kind, with two straight horns. P. 28, f. 22.
The Heraldic Antelope is a fabulous animal, and is represented as having the body of a Stag; the tail of a Unicorn; a tusk issuing from the tip of the nose; a row of tufts down the back of the neck, on the chest and thighs. Fig. 23.

ANTHONY ST. CROSS OF. The same as a Cross Tau. P. 9, f. 30.

ANTIC, ANTIENT, ANTIQUE. Ancient, as an antique lion. P. 26, f. 37. Antique Lion's Head, f. 38. Antique style of arms. P. 31, f. 11.

ANTIQUE TEMPLE. As borne in the arms of Temple. P. 23, f. 26.

ANTIQUE CORONET or CROWN. *See* EASTERN CORONET, or CROWN. P. 24, f. 32.

ANTLER. The branch of a stag's horn.

ANVIL. The iron block used by smiths. Two examples. P. 41, f. 37.

APAULMED, or APPALMED. *See* APAUMEE.

APAUMEE, or APPAUMEE. A hand open and extended; showing the palm. P. 36, f. 1.

APE, or MONKEY. An animal well known for its sagacity. P. 29, f. 57. If said to be collared and lined, the collar is put round the loins. f. 58.

APE, or WINGED MONKEY. P. 29, f. 60. A SEA-MONKEY. f. 59.

APEX. The ridge on the top of a helmet to which the crest was attached.

APPLE. Always drawn with a short stalk as P. 44, f. 57.

APPLE TREE. P. 22, f. 7.

APPLE STALKED and LEAVED, and an APPLE SLIPPED PENDANT. P. 44, f. 57.

APPLE OF GRANADA. The Pomegranate, P. 44, f. 57.

APPOINTEE CROSS. *See* CROSS AIGUISE. P. 9, f. 45.

APPOINTED. Armed, accoutred.

APRES, or APREE. An animal like a Bull, with the tail of a bear.

AQUILATED. Adorned with eagles' heads; in the same way a cross is adorned with serpents' heads. P. 11, f. 36

AQUISCE, or EQUISE. A cross equise is couped, voided, and pointed. P. 8, f. 34.

AR. Contraction for Argent.

ARBALESTE, or ARBALIST, A cross-bow. P. 37, f. 23.

ARCH. Borne Single, Double, and Treble, the latter is termed Tri-archée. P. 23, f. 18.

ARCH. On three degrees, with folding doors open. P. 23, f. 15.

ARCHED. Bowed or bent in the form of an arch. See ENARCHED and P. 3, f. 30.

ARCHED-DOUBLE. Having two arches, or bends. P. 12, f. 38.

ARCHBISHOP. The highest Order in the English Church. The Archbishop of Canterbury takes precedency next to the Princes of the Blood Royal.

ARCHBISHOP'S MITRE. P. 24, f. 15.

ARCHEE, or ARCHY. Same as Arched.

ARCHEE CORONETTEE. The bend in the Arms of Saxony is sometimes so termed. P. 16, f. 40 and P. 18, f. 28.

ARCHEE TREBLE, or TRI-ARCHEE. Having three arches.

ARCHER's-Bow. See Bow.

ARCHY. An ordinary so termed when embowed. P. 15, f. 30.

ARCTIC-STAR. Same as Estoile.

ARGENT. Silver. Usually painted white, one of the two metals; when the shield is argent, it is shown in an engraving by being left plain. P. 1. See TINCTURES.

ARK-NOAH's. Is borne by several families. P. 38, f. 42. A Symbol of the Church.

ARM. Variously borne as a Charge, and also for Crest, always understood to be a dexter one, if not mentioned as sinister, and always erect if not stated to the contrary.
A Cubit sinister arm issuing from the dexter side of the shield. P. 31, f. 37.
An Arm sinister in bend. f. 38.
An Arm counter-embowed. P. 36, f. 21.
An Arm embowed issuing from the sinister side of the shield. P. 31, f. 40.
A Cubit Arm. P. 36, f. 9, 10 and 13.
A Cubit Arm in armour gauntleted. f. 15.
Arm erect couped at the elbow. f. 10.
Arm embowed. f. 7.
Arm embowed vested. f. 11.
Arm embowed in armour. f. 16.
Arm embowed fesseways. f. 12 and 19.

Arm in Mail Armour counter-embowed. f. 21.
Two Arms embowed. f. 18.
Two Arms embowed and fretted. f. 17.
Dexter and Sinister arm embowed. f. 18.
Three Arms conjoined at the shoulders f. 28.
For full blazon of Arms and Hands. See P. 36.

ARMED. A term applied to the horns, teeth, and tusks of beasts, also to the beaks and talons of birds, when of a different tincture to the body.
Armed when applied to an arrow, refers to the head.

ARMED at all points. When a man is represented in complete armour. P. 36, f. 27.

ARMES-PARLANTES, or CANTING. See ALLUSIVE ARMS.

ARMES POUR ENQUIRIR. When contrary to the laws of blazon, and in which metal is placed upon metal, or colour upon colour. See INQUIRE ARMS OF.

ARMIGER. An armour-bearer ; an Esquire.

ARMILLARY-SPHERE. P. 39, f. 4.

ARMINED. Ermined.

ARMING BUCKLES. Anciently used for fastening the armour, are in shape like a lozenge. P. 42, f. 15. See BUCKLE.

ARMING-DOUBLET. A SURCOAT.

ARMORIAL-BEARINGS, or COAT OF ARMS. Consists of the Shield and its external ornaments.

ARMORIAL BOOK-PLATES. See BOOK-PLATES.

ARMORIE, or ARMORY. The Science which treats of Coat-Armour. Also a place where arms are kept.

ARMORIST. A person skilled in the knowledge of Armorie.

ARMORY. A List of names with the armorial bearings attached and blazoned.
Armory also defined as an " Art rightly prescribing the true knowledge and use of Arms."—BLOME.

ARMOUR. Defensive clothing of metal. See BRASSARTS, CUISSES, GAUNTLETS GREAVES, VAMBRACES, etc.

ARMOUR coat of. See ARMS.

ARMOUR for a man's body. P. 35, f. 10. P. 38, f. 13.

ARMOUR for a horse's head. See CHAPERON. P. 38, f. 12.

ARMOURER. One who makes armour.

ARMOURIST. One skilled in the science of Coat-armour.

ARMOYE. Charged with coats of Arms. See LAMBREQUIN.

ARMS. Armorial-bearings, or Coat armour; consists of the shield and its external ornaments.

ARMS OF ADOPTION. See ADOPTION ARMS OF.

ARMS OF ALLIANCE. See ALLIANCE ARMS OF.

ARMS OF ASSUMPTION. Such as might be legally assumed by one who had made captive any gentleman of higher degree than himself.

ARMS OF AUGMENTATION. See AUGMENTATION'S.

ARMS OF A BACHELOR. Are simply the paternal coat, unless his mother was an Heiress, or Co-Heiress; then he quarters her arms with the paternal coat. P. 8, f. 21.

ARMS BARON and FEMME. The arms of a man and his wife. See ARMS IMPALED.

ARMS OF A BARON. Are distinguished by the coronet. See P. 18, f. 21. See also term "ROBE" and "CORONET."

ARMS OF A BARONET. Contain the arms of Ulster, placed in the most convenient part of the shield. See BARONET.

ARMS OF A BISHOP. See ARMS OF OFFICE and P. 17, f. 21.

ARMS CANTING, or PUNNING ARMS. See ARMS PARLANTES.

ARMS OF COMMUNITY; those of Bishoprics, Cities, Universities, Corporate-bodies, etc.

ARMS OF A COMMONER AND LADY. When a commoner marries a lady of quality, he impales her arms with his own, and also places the lady's arms in a separate shield by the side of the former. If a Peeress in her own right, the husband bear her arms in an escutcheon of pretence, and also places her arms by the side of his own, as shown at P. 20, f. 21.
If the lady becomes a widow, she bears her own arms as above, and those of her husband, with her own, in a lozenge, omitting the crest.

ARMS OF CONCESSION. Augmentations granted by the Sovereign, of part of his regalia; e.g. Hen. VIII. granted to Thomas Manners, whom he created Earl of Rutland, on account of being descended from a sister of Edw. IV.

The Concession of wearing the Royal Arms upon a Chief. See AUGMENTATIONS.

ARMS DIMIDIATED. It was an ancient custom when impaling arms, to cut off a portion of either coat so impaled; but this being liable to cause great confusion, in fact entirely to destroy the bearing. it has long since ceased to be used in English Heraldry, except in the case of a coat with a bordure, when the bordure is always dimidiated. P. 13, f. 43.
The arms of the Borough of Gt. Yarmouth co. Nor. are Dimidiated. See P. 22, f. 18.

ARMS OF DOMINION. Those which belong to Sovereigns, Princes, and Commonwealths.

ARMS OF A DUKE; known by the Coronet. P. 21, f. 21. See term ROBE

ARMS OF A EARL; known by the Coronet. P. 19, f. 21.

ARMS OF ENGLAND. See ARMS ROYAL, and P. 31, f. 1 to 11.

ARMS FEUDAL. Those annexed to dignified Fees, Dukedoms, Marquisates, Earldoms, etc.

ARMS OF AN HEIRESS, or CO-HEIRESS. The paternal coat borne in a lozenge. If married they are borne on an escutcheon of Pretence, placed in the centre of the husband's shield. P. 11, f. 21. P. 20, f. 21.

ARMS HISTORICAL; such as are given to commemorate any great warlike achievements, or diplomatic services.

ARMS-IMPALED. A term to express the arms of a man and his wife, called Baron and Femme. The Shield is divided by a perpendicular line.—The Husbands arms are placed on the dexter side and the wifes on the sinister as P. 10, f. 21, and P. 46, f. 1.
The arms of office are impaled in the same way. See ARMS OF OFFICE.

ARMS OF A KNIGHT BACHELOR. Are borne in a Shield surmounted by a Knight's Helmet. P. 13, f. 21.

ARMS OF A KNIGHT OF ANY ORDER. Consist of his paternal coat in a shield surrounded with the insignia of the Order of which he is a Knight; and, if married, the arms of his wife must be placed in a distinct shield impaled with his own, as P. 16, f. 21.

ARMS OF A MAID. Are the paternal arms borne in a lozenge. P. 9, f. 21.

ARMS OF A MAN AND HIS WIFE. See ARMS IMPALED.
If the wife dies and the husband marries again, he either places the arms of his first

wife on the dexter side of his shield, and those of the second wife on the sinister, with his own in the centre; or he still divides the shield per-pale, keeping his own on the dexter side, and dividing the sinister side per-fesse places the first wife's arms in chief and the second wife's arms in base. P. 46, f. 3. and 2. For man having married three or more wives. See f. 5, 6, 7 and 8.

ARMS OF OFFICE, or OFFICIAL ARMS. Those borne by Archbishops, Bishops, Deans, Heads of Colleges, etc. The paternal coat is borne impaled with them, the arms of office being placed on the dexter side as P. 17, f. 21. If married the arms are borne as shown on the two shields. P. 46, f. 33.

ARMS PARLANTES. Those having canting charges, which allude to the bearer. See ALLUSIVE ARMS.

ARMS PATERNAL AND HEREDITARY. Such as descend from Father to Son.

ARMS OF PATRONAGE are of two kinds. First they consist of part of the arms of those lords, of whom the persons bearing them held in fee; either adding to the paternal arms of the person assuming such additions; or borne as feudal arms, to show the dependance of the parties bearing them on their particular Lord. Secondly, they are such as Governors of provinces, Lords of Manors, etc. add to their family arms.

ARMS POUR ENQUIRIR. See INQUIRE ARMS OF.

ARMS OF PRETENTION. Are those borne by Sovereigns, who, although they have not possession of certain dominions, claim a right to them. Thus the Sovereigns of England quartered the arms of France from the year 1330 when Edw. iii. laid claim to that kingdom, till the year 1801, although long before this England had laid aside all pretensions to France. P. 31, f. 4 to 9.

ARMS QUARTERED. Show the descent of one family from Heiresses and Co-Heiress of other houses, and is the evidence of maternal descent, and of the extinction of the immediate ancestors of the Mother whose son becomes their heir general, and is entitled at her death to quarter, with his paternal coat, her arms and all the quarterings which she may have inherited. P. 12, f. 21.

ARMS ROYAL. P. 31, f. 1 to 11. William I. to Victoria.

ARMS OF SUCCESSION. Those taken up by such as inherit certain fiefs, or manors etc., by will, entail, or donation, which they quarter with their own arms.

ARMS OF ULSTER. Ar. a sinister hand couped, open and erect gu. This is called the Badge of Ulster, also Baronet's-Badge; as it is borne in the paternal coat of each of the English Baronets. P. 14, f. 21; P. 23, f. 21; P. 31, f. 12.

ARMS OF A VISCOUNT. Known by the Coronet and by the Robe. See term ROBE and CORONET. P. 24, f. 45. See ARMS OF VISCOUNTESS BEACONS-FIELD. P. 20, f. 21.

ARMS OF A WIDOW. Consist of her husband's arms impaled on the dexter side, and her paternal coat on the sinister, in a Lozenge. P. 22, f. 21. If she is an Heiress her arms are to be borne in an escutcheon of Pretence, over those of her husband in a Lozenge. P. 46, f. 10. For Arms of a Widow having had two husbands, and arms of a Widower. See P. 46, f. 11 and 26. The Arms at P. 22, f. 21 are those of Bagge impaling those of Preston.

ARMY, or HARYSYD. A term anciently used to express an arm armed.

ARMYN. See ERMINE.

ARMYS. An old way of spelling Arms.

ARONDA, ARONDIA, ARONDI, or ARRONDI. Anything circular as gyronny arondia. P. 19, f. 45.

ARONDIE, or ARONDY. See BEND ARONDY. P. 17, f. 24.

ARRACHE. Forcibly torn off; the same as erased.

ARRASWAYS, or ARRIS-WISE. A term to express anything of a square form placed with one corner in front showing the top, as P. 42, f. 54.

ARRAYED. Covered, or vested.

ARRIERE. The back. Volant in arriére is a term proper for birds, or insects flying from the spectator, as a Bee volant en arriére. P. 30, f. 19.

ARRONDI, or ARRONDIE. See ARONDA.

ARROW. A missive weapon of offence, is a slender stick, armed at one end and feathered at the other and is termed barbed and flighted, or plumed, i.e. feathered, the point is always downwards unless otherwise expressed. P. 37, f. 13. Arrows when borne in bundles are termed sheaves of arrows, but the sheaf never contains more than three, unless a greater number is named. P. 37, f. 19. Arrows are borne in a variety of positions. which should be described e.g.—Five arrows two and two parallel in saltire, and one in pale. P. 37, f. 20. Three arrows one in pale, and two in saltire, entwined with a serpent. P. 30, f. 59.

ARROW-BROAD. *See* BROAD-ARROW.

ARROW-PHEONED. P. 37, f. 14.

ASCENDANT. The rays of the sun issuing upwards ; the term is also applied to smoke and flames rising.

ASCENDING. Rising.

ASCENTS, or DEGREES. Steps. P. 23, f. 15.

ASEARE, or ASEWRE. An old term for azure.

ASH-KEYS, or ASHEN-KEYS. The seeds which grow in bunches on the Ash Tree. P. 44, f. 46. Also termed Ash-Crops.

ASH-TREE. P. 45, f. 32. An ash sprig is borne by the name of Nash.

ASKER. A reptile. P. 30, f. 7.

ASP. A kind of serpent. P. 30, f. 46.

ASP. The Aspen. P. 45, f. 46.

ASPECT. Full faced, the same as at gaze. P. 28, f. 44, or guardant P. 26, f. 35.

ASPECTANT, or ASPECTING. Face to face. P. 32, f. 28. *See* COMBANT, and RESPECTING.

ASPECT-TRIAN. Showing three parts of the body.

ASPEN-TREE. P. 45, f. 46.

ASPEN LEAVES. Borne by the name of Cogan, Aspmall, etc. P. 45, f. 30.

ASPERSED. Powdered, or strewed, the same as Semée. P. 2, f. 38.

ASS. Properly represents patience. P. 27, f. 44.

ASS's-HEAD. The Crest of Aston, Chamberlain, etc. P. 27, f. 45.

ASSAGAI, or HASSAGAI. A dart. P. 37, f. 22, No. 2.

ASSAILANT, ASSAULTANT, or ASSAULTING. Same as saliant and springing,

ASS-CAMEL, or ALLOCAMELUS. P. 27, f. 46.

ASSEMBLE. Dovetailed.

ASSIS-SEJANT. i.e. sitting. P. 26, f. 41. Same as a Lion sejant.

ASSUMPTIVE ARMS. *See* ARMS OF ASSUMPTION.

ASSURGENT. A term to express anything rising from the sea. P. 22, f. 16.

ASSYRIAN GOAT. P. 29, f. 1.

ASTRICAL. *See* CROSS ASTRICAL.

ASTROID, or ASTEROIDES. *See* STAR.

ASTROLABE. An astro nomical instrument for taking the altitude of the

sun, or stars at sea. P. 38, f. 46.

ASTRONOMICAL CHARACTERS. Are met with in Coat Armour as in the Arms of Herschel, etc. P. 23, f. 45.

ASUR, ASURE. *See* AZURE.

AT-BAY. A term to express the position of a stag standing on his own defence.

AT-GAZE. Applied to animals of the Deer-kind. *See* GAZE and P. 28, f. 44.

AT-LODGE. *See* LODGED.

AT SPEED. Same as Courant. P. 28, f. 46.

ATCHIEVEMENT. *See* ACHIEVEMENT.

ATHELSTAN'S CROSS. A cross botonée placed on a Mound. P. 11, f. 3.

ATTAINDER. Absolute deprivation of every civil right and privilege, and consequent forfeiture of all hereditary claims.

ATTIRE. A single horn of a stag, etc. P. 28, f. 51.

ATTIRED. Is used when speaking of the horns, or antlers of the Stag, Buck, or Hart, etc. ; but Bulls, Goats, Rams, and Unicorns are said to be armed. The term is also applied to the habit, or vest of a man, or woman.

ATTIRES. Both horns of a stag affixed to the scalp, as P. 28, f. 51.

ATTOURNEY. *See* GAUNTLET.

AUGER. A Carpenters' tool. P. 41, f. 34.

AUGMENTATIONS. Are particular marks of honour.

Granted by the Sovereign as additions to the paternal arms; and for the most part are borne upon a Canton, or Inescutcheon, sometimes upon a Chief, and Fesse; and may be derived from acts of valour, or loyalty; from profession; or from any memorable circumstances and events, e.g. The arms of the Duke of Wellington contain the following Augmentation viz. On the honour-point an escutcheon, charged with the Crosses of St. George, St. Andrew, and St. Patrick, conjoined, being the union badge of the United Kingdom of Great Britain and Ireland. Now this badge being the common device of our united opinions, shews that we think the Duke of Wellington was entitled to the highest honours which a united people would desire to confer on the chief defender of their country. P. 21, f. 21. The Augmentation granted to the Duke of Marlborough " in chief an escutcheon ar. charged with the cross of St. George gu. and thereon an escutcheon of the Arms of France." Lord Nelson's is " on a chief wavy ar. waves of the sea from which a Palm tree issuant betw. a disabled ship on the dexter and a battery in ruins on the sinister all ppr." Lord Collingwood " on a chief wavy gu. a lion pass. guard. navally crowned or, with the word TRAFALGAR over the lion of the last."

Pellew Viscount Exmouth. "on a chief of Augmentation wavy ar. a representation of Algiers with a British man of war before it all ppr." Carnegie Earl of Northesk whose arms are, or. an eagle displayed sa. has as an honourable augmentation" a Naval Crown gold on the breast of the eagle and over the eagle the word "Trafalgar" Halford Bart. By Royal warrant of Augmentation, in 1837, a rose ar. was substituted for the centre fleur-de-lis, (arms originally had three fleur-de-lis on a chief), and as further augmentation, on a canton erm. a staff entwined with a serpent ppr, and ensigned by a coronet composed of crosses pattée and fleur-de-lis or. Gull. Bart., for augmentation "a Canton Erm., thereon an ostrich feather ar. quilled or. enfiled by a coronet as in the Badge of the Prince of Wales.

AUGMENTED. Having Augmentations.

AUK, A bird, an inhabitant of the arctic or northern seas. P. 34, f. 32.

AULNED. The aulnes, or awnes, are the beards about the ears of barley, etc., generally termed bearded.

AURE. Drops of gold. *See* GUTTEE.

AU-RENCOUTRE. *See* RENCOUTRE.

AUREOLE. *See* GLORY.

AURIFLAMME, or ORIFLAMME. The ancient banner of St. Denis, carried at the head of the French armies, from the 12th to the 15th century. According to Sir N. H. Nicolas, an oblong red flag, split into five points, described by others as a square banner of flame-coloured silk.

AVANT-BRACES. Armour for the arm. *See* BRASSETS.

AVANT-MUR. Signifies a wall attached to a Tower; e.g. a Tower the sinister side Avant-Mur. P. 23, f. 1.

AVE. Hail! This word "Ave" is borne in the arms of Nadler.

AVELLAINE, AVELLINE, AVILLANE, or AVELANE. *See* CROSS AVELLANE. P. 11, f. 33.

AVELLANE INVECKED, AVELLANED POMMEL, and AVELLANE DOUBLE. *See* CROSS. P. 11, f. 33.

AVERLYE. *See* SEMEE.

AVERDANT. Applied to a mount, when covered with green herbage.

AVERLYE. The same as Semée or powdered.

AVERSANT, or DORSED. A term to express a hand turned so as to shew the back. P. 36, f. 1.

AVOSET. A bird. P. 33, f. 48.

AWL. An instrument to bore holes. P. 41, f. 32.

AWNED. *See* AULNED.

AXE, or HATCHET. Battle, Broad, Chipping, Carpenters, Danish, Fall-ing, or Felling, Pole, Lochabar, Slaughter axe, etc. P. 37, f. 25 to 31. P. 41, f. 19 and 21. P. 22, f. 32.

AYGNISEE, or EQUISE. The same as urdée, or champain, sometimes called mateley, clechée, and verdée. P. 9, f. 45.

AYLET. The same as Cornish-chough. P. 33, f. 54.

AYRANT, or EYRANT. Eagles, or Falcons, are said to be Ayrant when borne in their nests.

AZURE. Blue, contracted az., expressed in engraving by horizontal lines. P. 1. *See* TINCTURES.

B

B. Used as an abbreviation for Blue, i.e. azure.

BACHELORS ARMS. The paternal coat. *See* ARMS OF A BACHELOR.

BACHELOR KNIGHT. *See* ARMS OF A KNIGHT BACHELOR.

BACKGAMMON-BOARD, or PLAYING TABLES. P. 42, f. 32.

BADELAIRES. Curved swords, a Cutlass, P. 38, f. 22.

BADGE. A device, anciently placed on banners, ensigns, caparisons, and liveries; but it fell into disuse in the reign of Queen Elizabeth with the rest of the brilliant relics of the feudal system.

The Badge is never placed on a wreath, and the few families who still use it, have it either depicted below the shield; or if they bear two, one is placed on either side of the crest.

BADGE OF ENGLAND, SCOTLAND, and IRELAND. P. 3, f 21.

BADGE OF WALES. P. 5, f. 21.

BADGE OF THE PRINCE OF WALES. P. 6, f. 21.

Other Badges. See P. 25. P. 25a. P. 31, and P. 43.

BADGES OF KNIGHTHOOD, COMPANIONS, etc. P. 24. P. 25. P. 25a.

BADGER, or BROCK. Sometimes called a "Gray;" an Animal often borne in Heraldry. P. 27, f. 53.

BAG. *See* SCRIP.

BAG OF MADDER. As borne in the Dyers' Arms. P. 40, f. 21.

BAGPIPE. Hopwell of Devon has three Hares sejant playing upon bagpipes. P. 29, f. 6.

BAGRIL. *See* MINNOW. P. 32, f. 39.

BAGWYN. An imaginary animal. P. 27, f. 49.

BAILLONE. A term to express a lion rampant, holding in the mouth a staff or baton. P. 26, f. 7.

BAKER'S-PEAL. As borne in the Arms of Pister. P. 41, f. 12.

BALANCE. An apparatus for weighing bodies; a beam with two opposite scales. P. 39, f. 22.
This is usually, though incorrectly, blazoned a pair of Scales, whereas the scales are the two bowls attached to the end of the beam which together with them makes up the Balance and are said to be equally poised.

BALCANIFER, or BALDAKINIFER. A standard-bearer of the Knights Templars.

BALD-COOT. A Water-fowl. P. 34, f. 14

BALD-HEAD. See DEATH'S HEAD.

BALDRIC, or BAULDRICK. A belt usually worn over the shoulder. See BAUDRICK.

BALE. A package of Merchandize. P. 40, f. 19.

BALE-CORDED. P. 40, f. 20.

BALE OF PIEDMONT. Silk. P. 40, f. 21.

BALISTA, or SWEEP. A machine anciently used for throwing stones. P. 37, f. 38.

BALL, FIRE, or BALL FIRED. i.e., with fire issuing from the top. P. 37, f. 10.
If otherwise it must be named, as a Ball fired in four places. f. 10.

BALL TASSELLED. P. 40, f. 23.

BAND. The fillet or bandage by which a sheaf of corn, arrows etc. are bound together. P. 37, f. 21.

BANDE. The bend dexter.

BANDE-EN. In bend.

BANDED. Anything tied round with a band of a different tincture from itself, is said to be banded, as a Garb, sheaf of arrows, plumes, etc.

BANDEROLE. A streamer tied under the crook of a Pastoral Staff, and folding round the staff. P. 42, f. 46.

BANDERVILLE, or BANNEROLLE. A diminutive of the banner, used at funerals and generally displays the arms of different families with whom the ancestors of the deceased person were connected by marriage.

BANISTER-CROSS. Consists of four staves, fixed crossways to a plate, each crowned at the ends. P. 11, f. 29.

BANNER. Is co-eval with the introduction of Heraldry.
It is a square flag, and on it are exhibited the owner's arms; gentlemen have a right to display their banners on their mansions, but the common practice, when they exhibit any banner, is to hoist the Union-Jack, which might with quite as much propriety be painted on their carriages. See ENSIGN, FLAG and STANDARD.

BANNER OF THE COMMONWEALTH. P. 31, f. 29.

BANNER DISVELOPED. Being open and flying. P. 43, f. 48.

BANNER FUNERAL. A small square flag on which the arms are painted, it is fringed and affixed to a staff, or pike.

BANNER GREAT. The Great Banner is that on which all the quarterings of the deceased are painted.
The size of the several Banner's were originally as follows; viz.
That of an Emperor; six feet square.
King; five feet square.
Prince or Duke; four feet square.
Marquis, Earl, Viscount, Baron, and Knight-baronet; three feet square.

BANNER, THE NATIONAL. Is the Union Jack. P. 7, f. 21.

BANNERET. See KNIGHT BANNERET.

BANNEROLLS, or BANNER-ROLLS. Used at the funeral of either a man or woman, are three feet square composed of silk on which are painted the arms.

BANYAN TREE. Is borne as a Crest by several families. P. 45, f. 50.

BAR, or BARR. One of the sub-ordinaries containing a fifth of the shield, and may be borne in any part of it. P. 5, f. 1.
Two or more bars are frequently borne on the same field, as two bars, P. 5, f. 2, three bars, f. 7. The diminutives of the bar are the Closet, which is half the bar, as f. 3, three Closets, f. 4, and the Barrulet, which is half the Closet; when these diminutives are placed two and two in a Shield they are called Bars-gemel, f. 5 and 6. When one or more Barrulets are placed on each side of a Fesse; the Fesse is said to be Cottised, as P. 5, f. 9, 10, and 11.
These are all subject to the accidental forms of lines as engrailed, embattled, flory, etc. See f. 14, 15, 16, and 17.

BAR-GATE. See GATE.

BAR-GEMEL, BARR-GEMEL, GEMELLE, or GEMELLUS DOUBLE. Are double bars, or two bars placed near and parallel with each other. P. 5, f. 5 and 6.

BAR IN. When two or more charges are placed horizontally they are said to be In-bar.

BAR OF BASTARDY. P. 19, f. 27.

BAR, PER BASE, or BAR MEIRE. A term used by some writers to express potent, or potent counter-potent. It is by Randle Home, termed varry cuppy, or cuppa, and verrey tassa. P. 1, and P. 22, f. 40.

BAR, PER BASE ERASED. P. 4, f. 39. From Gerard Leigh's Accidence of Armory.

BAR, PER AND PILE. More correctly emblazoned per fesse and pile. P. 2, f. 10

BAR, PER AND CANTON, or CANTONED. Better per-fesse cantoned. Is the field divided per-fesse and per-canton.

BARDE, or BARRED. Same as Barry.

BARDINGS. Horse trappings often enriched with Armorial bearings.

BARBED. A term variously applied.

Firstly. To the points that stand back in the head of an arrow or fishing-hook, etc. Secondly. To a Cross when its extremities are like the barbed irons used for striking fish. Thirdly. To the five leaves of the Heraldic-Rose; which always appear on its outside. Fourthly. Sometimes used to express the comb and gills of a cock. Fifthly. To a Horse; when a war-horse is completely accoutred he is termed a Barbed horse, or Steed. Sixthly. To the needles or beard of barley, etc.

BARBEE, or CROIX BARBEE. A Cross-Barbée. P. 9, f. 31.

BARBEL. A fish. Generally depicted embowed. P. 32, f. 28.

BARBERRY. A branch of. P. 45, f. 5.

BARDED. Caparisoned. The Bardings of the Knightly war-horses were commonly charged with heraldic insignia. P. 36, f. 27.

BARDED COURSER. A War-horse caprisoned.

BARKS. Boats. See P. 38.

BARLEY EARS. P. 45, f. 13.

Garb of Barley, f. 15.

BARNACLE-GOOSE, or BARNACLE-FOWL. A large water-fowl. P. 34, f. 19.

BARNACLE-BIRD. Same as Barnacle-goose.

BARNACLES. An instrument used by Farriers, depicted either extended i.e. open as the figure in chief P. 37, f. 56, or closed as the example in base, they are also termed horse-barnacles.

BARON. The lowest rank of the British-Peerage. See Arms of a Baron.

BARONESS. The wife of a Baron. She is styled "My Lady" and is "Right Honourable" her Coronet is the same as her Husband.

BARON and FEMME. Husband and wife.

The Arms are borne impaled, the husband's on the dexter and the wife's on the sinister, as P. 10, f. 21. If the woman is an Heiress, or Co-Heiress, her Arms are borne in an Escutcheon of Pretence; as P. 11, f. 21.

BARONET. The lowest degree of hereditary dignity; rank among themselves according to creation, and follow next to the younger sons of barons, taking precedence of all Knights, except of the Garter.

The order was originally instituted by King James I. in 1611 for the colonization of Ulster, and the Arms of that province were deemed the most appropriate insigna. They are placed on a canton or in an escutcheon on the paternal coat, in the most convenient spot. When the Shield contains many quarterings, it should be borne in the paternal coat, and not as is frequently the case upon the intersection, or partition of the shield. This does not apply where the Baronet has two surnames, bearing arms for each quarterly; then it ought to be placed on the centre division of the four quarterings. Arms of a Baronet, P. 14, f. 21, and P. 23, f. 21.

BARONET'S BADGE. Is on an escutcheon ar. a sinister hand, erect and apaumée, couped at the wrist gu. P. 31, f. 12.

BARON'S CORONET. On a gold circle showing four pearls. P. 24, f. 46. See CORONET.

BARON'S MANTLE. See ROBE.

BARR. See BAR.

BARRALY. Same as Barry.

BARRE, or BARRE-UNE. A Bend Sinister. P. 17, f. 5.

BARRE-WAIES. See BARWISE.

BARREL. A Cask or Tun. P. 31, f. 28. P. 39, f. 37 and 38.

BARRELET, BARRULET, BARRELLET, BARRULA, or BARRULE. A diminutive of the Bar. P. 5, f. 3.

BARRELET. Enfiled with an annulet. P. 12, f. 40.

BARRULET. P. 5, f. 3.

BARRULETTE, BARRULY, or BURELY. Same as Barry. Also termed Barruletty, and Barruled. P. 5, f. 8.

BARRY. A term to express the field or charge when equally divided by horizontal lines.

These division are composed of two tinctures and their number must be named. e.g. Barry of eight, or. and sa. P. 5, f. 8. Barry of ten. P. 19, f. 33. Barry of six, Erm. and gu. P. 2, f. 13.

BARRY OF SIX, PER PALE INDENTED. P. 2, f. 21.

BARRY BENDY. P. 2, f. 35.

BARRY BENDY SINISTER. P. 2, f. 34.

BARRY BENDY COUNTERCHANGED. Same as Barry indented. P. 2, f. 36.

BARRY BENDY LOZENGY, or BARRY LOZENGY. P. 2, f. 35.

BARRY ESSIX. Same as Barry of six. P. 2, f. 13.

BARRY INDENTED. P. 2, f. 36.

BARRY PALY, or BILLETTEE COUNTER-CHANGED. P. 2, f. 42.

BARRY PALY IN PROSPECT. P. 22, f. 39.

BARRY PILY. P. 2, f. 15.

BARRY PER FRET. P. 21, f. 30.

BARRY PER PALE COUNTERCHANGED. P. 5, f. 13.

BARRY POINT IN POINT. Same as Barry indented. P. 2, f. 36.

Barry, is subject to all the accidental forms of lines as Barry Engrailed, Barry Nebule, Urdeé, etc.

BARS-GEMELS. See BAR-GEMEL.

BARS NOWY. P. 2, f. 14.

BAR-SHOT. A bar of iron, having a ball, or shot at each end. P. 37, f. 9.

BARULY, BARRULED. See BARRULETTE.

BARWISE, or BARWAYS. Implies anything placed, in a horizontal line across the field. P. 4, f. 31.

BASCINET, or HEAUME. P. 39, f. 20, No. 1.

BASE. The bottom of the shield.

When a charge is placed at the bottom of the field, it is termed IN BASE, and, if not occupying the middle of the base, it must be expressed as being in the dexter or sinister base point. See CANTON IN DEXTER BASE. P. 19, f. 40. and POINTS OF ESCUTCHEON. P. 1.

BASE-BAR. A portion of the base of the shield equal in width to a Bar, parted off by a horizontal line.

BASE-ESQUIRE. Also termed Base Escuers. P. 21, f. 24 and 42.

BASE-POINT. See P. 1. Dexter, Middle and Sinister base points.

BASED, or BAS'T. A Baste Esquire. P. 21, f. 24. See ESQUIRE.

BASED-ESQUIRES DEXTER AND SINISTER. P. 21, f. 42.

BASILISK. As represented in Heraldry resembles the heraldic wivern, but with the head of a dragon at the end of the tail, and with the comb, wattles, and spurs of a Cock; it is also termed the Amphisien-Cockatrice. P. 27, f. 10.

BASINET. A close-fitting steel helmet.

BASKET. A vessel made of rushes, twigs or splinters, as borne by the family of Littlebury. P. 39, f. 17.

BASKET WITH A HANDLE. Borne by the family of Wolston. P. 39, f. 17, No. 3.

BASKET. As in the arms of the Basket Makers Company, called a cross-basket. P. 22, f. 28.

BASKET OF LOAVES. As borne in the arms of Bethlem Hospital, and Milton Abbey. P. 39, f. 17, No. 1.

BASKET, or SHRUTTLE. Used for winnowing corn; it is also termed a Fan, or Winnowing-basket. P. 39, f. 16.

BASNET, BASSINET, BASSENET, or BACINET. An ancient name for an helmet. P. 38, f. 4.

BAST. See BASED.

BASTARDY-BAR OF. P. 19, f. 27.

BASTE, BASED, BAST, or BASTE. A portion of the base of a shield, same as a plain-point. P. 21, f. 5 and 45.

BASTILE. A double embattlement. See P. 1. Same as Battled-Embattled.

BASTON, or BATUME. See BATON.

BAT, or RERE-MOUSE. P. 30, f. 4.

BAT'S WINGS. P. 25, f. 28.

BATH KING OF ARMS. Is not a member of the Heralds College, but takes precedence next after Garter King of Arms. He has a crown like the other Kings, and a peculiar costume directed by the statutes of the order.

BATH ORDER OF. See KNIGHTHOOD ORDERS OF.

BATON, BATTON. P. 36, f. 16. A truncheon or leading staff given to Field-Marshals, and other high officers, as a token of authority. Two Batons in saltire are borne behind the arms of the Earl Marshal of England. See TITLE-PAGE.

BATON SINISTER, BASTON, BATTON, BATTOON, BATUNE. Also termed a Fissure. A mark of illegitimacy, is a diminutive of the bend sinister, being one fourth its breadth. It does not extend from side to side of the shield; and may be borne either plain or charged. See P. 19, f. 27.

The Baton has been adopted since the fifteenth century, in England, to mark the illegitimate descendants of the Royal Family only; before which time no positive rule prevailed, since the more ancient ways of marking illegitimacy were by the Bend, either placing the Father's arms thereon or debruising them by it; the Border was also used as a mark of bastardy.

BATON CROSS. P. 11, f. 7.

BATTELLE, or BATTELLED. See BATTLED.

BATTERING-RAM. An instrument used by the ancients to breach walls. It had a metal head like that of a ram, whence its name. P. 37, f. 12.

BATTLE-AXE. P. 37, f. 25.

BATTLED, EMBATTLED, or IMBATTLED. When any of the ordinaries are borne in the form of the battlements of a castle, on one side only. P. 3, f. 8. P. 17, f. 15.

BATTLED ARRONDEE. Signifies that the tops of the battlements should be circular. P. 19, f. 5.

BATTLED, COUNTER. Same as Counter-embattled. P. 3, f. 9 ; P. 17, f. 17.

BATTLED-EMBATTLED. One battlement upon another. P. 1.

BATTLED-GRADY, or EMBATTLED-GRADY. So termed because it resembles the form of steps. P. 4, f. 23 ; P. 13, f. 16 ; P. 18, f. 10.

BATTELLY. Same as Battled.

BATTLEMENTS OF A TOWER. The upper works of a castle or fortification. P. 23, f. 17.

BATTON, BATTOON and BATUNE. A staff or truncheon. See BATON.

BAUCEANT, or BEAUSEANT. A banner of the Knights Templers in the thir-teenth century. It was an oblong flag per-fesse. sa. and ar.

BAUDRICK. A sword belt, passing over the right shoulder and under the left arm.

BAUTEROLL. See BOTEROLL.

BAY-AT, or STANDING AT BAY. The po-sition of a stag standing in his own defence, with his head downwards.

BAY-LEAVES. P. 45, f. 20.

BAY-TREE. The Laurel-Tree.

BEACON, or BEACON-FIRE. From the Saxon becnian, to beckon, or call to-gether, denotes a signal-fire; which was usually lighted on a pole erected on some hill or other eminence. P. 37, f. 1.

BEADLE'S STAFF. As borne by the family of Doo of Fincham. P. 42, f. 45. (Prior's staff.)

BEAGLE, or RATCH-HOUND. P. 29, f. 26.

BEAK. See explanation under the term BIRD.

BEAKED. Birds are termed beaked, when the bills are of a different tinc-ture from the bodies. See term BIRD.

BEAKER, or EWER. P. 42, f. 27.

BEAM. A term to express the main horn of a hart, or buck.

BEAMS, or RAYS OF THE SUN. Generally borne issuing from charges, and then termed Radiant, Rayonned, Rayon-nant, or Rayonnée. P. 14, f. 18.

BEAN-CODS, or PODS. P. 44, f. 59.

BEAR. A common bearing in Heraldry as a Bear pass. muzzled, P. 29, f. 37 ; a Bear sejant, f. 38 ; a Demi-Bear ramp, f. 39 ; Bear's Head erased, f. 40 ; Bear and ragged staff, f. 42. The Bear is always to be drawn muzzled if not expressed to the contrary. The fore leg of a Bear which is frequently used in Armoury, is called a GAMB to which term refer and to P. 29, f. 41.

BEARD. The barbs of an arrow, or pheon, blazoned barbed. See BARBED.

BEARDED. A man's head in armoury is always understood to be bearded if not otherwise expressed.

BEARDED, or BLAZING. A term to ex-press the tail of a comet, or blazing star. P. 23, f. 45.

BEARDED. See AULNED.

BEARING. Any charge may be called a bearing; a coat of arms in general.

BEARINGS. A term applied to the entire coat of arms with all its ap-pendages.

BEASTS, AND PARTS OF BEASTS. See P. 26, 27, 28, 29 and 30.

BEAUSEANT. See BAUCEANT.

BEAUTIFIED. See ADORNED.

BEAUVOIR. See BEAVER.

BEAVER, VISOR, or VIZOR. The part of the helmet which protected the face, and which could be raised or lowered at pleasure. P. 38, f. 10.

BEAVER. An Animal. P. 29, f. 49. The emblem of industry and perseverance.

BEAVER'S TAILS. Are found as charges in Armoury. P. 29, f. 50.

BEBALLY. Used by old writers for party-per-pale.

BECQUE. Same as Beak. See BIRD.

BEDEL'S STAFF. See BEADLE'S STAFF.

BEE. Much used in Armoury as the emblem of industry ; generally given to those who have raised themselves by industry and perseverance. P. 30, f. 19.

BEE-GAD. P. 30, f. 21.

BEE-HIVE. Generally depicted as sur-rounded with bees. It is then blazoned, a beehive beset, or re-plenished with bees diversely volant. P. 30, f. 20.

BEECH-TREE. Frequently met with as a bearing. P. 45, f. 33.

BEER-BUTT- A large cask. P. 31, f. 28, and P. 39, f. 37.

BEETLE. A Maul or Mallet. P. 41, f. 33.

BEETLE, or SCARABEE. An insect as borne by the family of Thorndike. P. 25, f. 27.

BELFRY. That part of a building in which a bell is hung. P. 43, f. 30.

BELIC. See GULES.

BELLED. A term applied to Hawks, when bells are affixed to their legs, which is generally the case in coat armour. P. 33, f. 31, and 32. A Falcon's leg a-la-quise, jessed, belled and varvelled. P. 33, f. 34.

BELLFLOWERS. P. 44, f. 30.

BELLFROY. Same as Vair.

BELLOWS. An instrument for propelling air through a tube, as borne in the arms of Skipton. P. 41, f. 12.

BELLS. As borne in armoury are of two kinds, viz., Falcon's bells. P. 43, f. 17, and Church bells. P. 43, f. 29. In blazoning church bells, if the tongues are of a different tincture from the bell itself, the Bell is said to be tongued of such a tincture; or they are sometimes blazoned bells with clappers of such a tincture. The term "Cannoned" is also applied to their tongues. When bells are borne pendant from a file as at P. 16, f. 37; the file is termed campaned.

BELT, or GIRDLE. A strap with a buckle. P. 42, f. 15 and 16.

BEND. One of the honourable ordinaries, is formed by two parallel diagonal lines, drawn from the dexter chief to the sinister base. It contains one third of the field. P. 17, f. 1. If depicted the reverse way, i.e. from sinister chief to dexter base, it is termed a Bend Sinister, which must be so expressed. It may be formed either by straight or crooked lines, in the former case is simply called a Bend. In the latter a Bend Engrailed, Inveck·d, Indented, etc. according to the form of crooked line which it assumes. See P. 17. The Diminutives of the Bend are the Bendlet, Garter, Cost, and Ribbon; of the Bend Sinister the Scarpe and batton. P. 17, f. 2, 3, 4, and 6.

— ANGLED, or RECT-ANGLED. P. 18, f. 12.

— ACUTE ANGLED. P. 18, f. 19.

— ARCHY, ARCHED or BOWED. P. 18, f. 25.

— ARCHY, CORONETTEE, or CORONATED. P. 18, f. 28.

— ARONDY, or NUÉE, gored-tranchée-nuage, or a bend arondie, triple-arched, gored on both sides. P. 17, f. 24.

— BEVILED. P. 18, f. 19.

— BETWEEN. When charges are placed on both sides of any Ordinary, etc., the Ordinary is said to be between. e.g. See P. 17, f. 21.

— BRACED. P. 19, f. 26.

— DOUBLE BEVILED. P. 18, f. 8.

— and BORDER. P. 19, f. 32.

— BORDERED, or FIMBRIATED, P. 17, f. 28.

— BILLETTEE, COUNTER - BILLETTEE. P. 17, f. 42.

— BRETESSED. P. 17, f. 16.

— BRETESSED NUEE. P. 18, f. 29.

BEND BRETESSED PARTED, or DOUBLE PARTED, or a BEND-EMBATTLED-DOUBLE PARTED. P. 17, f. 39.

— and BORDURE. P. 19, f. 32.

— CHARGED. Having anything upon it, generally blazoned " on a bend." P. 17, f. 21 and 31.

— CHAMPAINE, CHAMPIONED, or URDEE. P. 17, f. 19.

— CHEQUY, or CHECKIE. Always consists of three or more rows. P. 17, f. 43.

— and CHIEF. P. 19, f. 30.

— COMPONY, COMPONEE, or GOBONY. P. 17, f. 40.

— COMPONY COUNTER-COMPONY. P. 17, f. 41.

— CORONATED, or CORONETTE. P. 18, f. 28.

— COTTISED. Double and treble cottised. P. 17, f. 31, 32 and 33.

— COTTISED DANCETTEE. P. 18, f. 30. The cottise is subject to the various forms of crooked lines. P. 17, f. 36 and 37; P. 18, f. 30 and 31; P. 19, f. 24.

— COUNTERCHANGED. P. 2, f. 49 and 50.

— COUNTER-EMBATTLED. P. 17, f. 17.

— COUPED, or HUMETTE. P. 17, f. 38.

— CRENELLE. P. 17, f. 15.

— CRENELLE, POINTS POINTED. P. 17, f. 23.

— DANCETTEE. P. 17, f. 11. See term DANCETTEE.

— DEBRUISED, FRACTED, or REMOVED. P. 18, f. 14.

— DEMI. P. 18, f. 24.

— DOUBLE DOWNSETT, also termed ramped, and coupée. P. 18, f. 11.

— DOUBLE EDGED. P. 17, f. 30.

— DOVE-TAIL. P. 17, f. 20.

— EDGED. P. 17, f. 25.

— EMBATTLED. P. 17, f. 15.

— EMBATTLED, COUNTER-EMBATTLED. P. 17, f. 17.

— ENGOULE. So termed when the ends enter the mouths of lions, tigers, dragons, etc. A Bend Sinister Engoule. P. 18, f. 27.

— EN DEVISE. The same as bendlet. P. 17, f. 2.

— ENGRAILED. P. 17, f. 7.

— ENHANCED. i.e. raised higher than its usual place. e.g. three bendlets enhanced. P. 18, f. 36.

— ERADICATED, or ESCLATTE. i.e. rent or splintered. P. 18, f. 23.

— ESCARTELE, or ESCLOPPE. P. 18, f. 13.

— ESCARTELE, GRADY, or EMBATTLED GRADY. P. 18, f. 10.

BEND ESCLATTE. Same as a Bend eradicated.
— FLAMANT. P. 17, f. 18.
— FLORY, or FLORIED. P. 17, f. 13.
— FLORY, COUNTER-FLORY. P. 17, f. 14.
— FUSIL. Bend formed of fusils placed side by side. P. 18, f. 2.
— FUSILY. When the outward shape of the bend is not altered, but its surface is divided so as to form fusils all over it. P. 18, f. 3.
— GOBONY. P. 17, f. 40.
— GRADY EMBATTLED. P. 18, f. 10.
— GRICE, or DOUBLE ESCARTELEE. Sometimes termed grady of three decreasing to base. P. 18, f. 15.
— HACKED. P. 17, f. 10.
— HEMISPHERE, or ZODIAC. P. 18, f. 26.
— HUMET, or HUMETTEE. P. 17, f. 38.
— IN. A term used when charges are placed bendwise e.g. P. 17, f. 45, and P. 19, f. 28.
— INGRAILED, or ENGRAILED. P. 17, f. 7.
— INDENTED. P. 17, f. 9.
— INDENTED, EMBOWED, or HACKED and HEWED. P. 17, f. 10.
— INDENTED POINT IN POINT. P. 17, f. 44.
— INVECKED. P. 17, f. 8.
— OF A LIMB OF A TREE. P. 17, f. 27.
— LOZENGE, or LOZENGY. P. 18, f. 1.
— OF LOZENGES. Are lozenges conjoined in bend. P. 18, f. 2.
— MAILED, or PAPELLONNE. P. 18, f. 7.
— MASCLE, or MASCULY. Also termed masculée. P. 18, f. 6.
— NEBULEE, or NEBULY. P. 17, f. 21.
— NOWY. P. 18, f. 20.
— DOUBLE NOWED. P. 18, f. 22.
— NOWY CHAMPAINE, or URDEE. P. 18, f. 18.
— NOWY LOZENGY. P. 18, f. 17.
— NOWY QUADRATE, or QUADRANGLED. Also termed single- bretessed, and sometimes called a bend with one embattlement on each side. P. 18, f. 16.
— NUEE, or NUAGE. Also termed a bend tranchée nuage, and a bend arondie. P. 17, f. 24.
— ON A BEND, or a BEND SURMOUNTED OF ANOTHER. P. 17, f. 34.
— ON, or CHARGED. As on a Bend three billets. P. 17, f. 31. P. 19, f. 29, Two hands rending a horseshoe.
— PALISADO. P. 17, f. 19.

BEND PAPELLONNE, PAMPELLETEE, or PEPELLOTEE. Also termed a bend mailed. P. 18, f. 7.
— PATTEE. Potentée or dovetail. P. 17, f. 20.
— POTENTEE. P. 17, f. 35.
— RADIANT, RAYONNE, or RAYONNANT. P. 17, f. 22.
— RAGULY, or RAGULED. P. 17, f. 26.
— RECTANGLED. P. 18, f. 12.
— REMOVED. P. 18, f. 14.
— SHAPOURNE. P. 18, f. 25.
— SINISTER. P. 17, f. 5. Not a Mark of Illegitimacy as is frequently asserted.
— SINISTER and DEXTER viz. sa. A bend sinister ar. surmounted of another dexter or. borne by Newton of Essex.
— SURMOUNTED OF ANOTHER. P. 17, f. 34.
— TRANCHEE. The same as nowy. P. 18, f. 20.
— TREFLE. As in the arms of the Prince of Wales. P. 16, f. 40.
— TRAVERSE, COUNTER-POINTED. P. 18, f. 9.
— URDEE. Also termed a bend crenellée points pointed. P. 17, f. 19.
— URDEE-CHAMPAINED, or CHAMPIONED. Differs from the last, the champaines being of a different tincture. P. 17, f. 23.
— VOIDED. P. 17, f. 29.
— WARRIATED ON THE OUTSIDES. Same as urdée. P. 17, f. 19.
— WAVY, or WAVED. Also termed Undée. P. 17, f. 12 ; P. 2, f. 49.
— ZODIAC. P. 18, f. 26.
BEND-PER, or PARTY PER BEND. When the field or charge is divided by a diagonal line from the dexter chief to the sinister base. Observe the first metal or colour named in the blazon should fill the chief part, and the second the base, as P. 2, f. 6.
— — ARCHED. P. 19, f. 15. Also termed enarched, champain, or bowed.
— — BEND. When the bend is divided down the centre by either a straight or crooked line ; as a bend dovetail per bend P. 17, f. 20, and a bend per-bend P. 19, f. 24.
— — CRENELLEE. P. 19, f. 2.
— — DANCETTEE. P. 19, f. 16.
— — EMBATTLED ARONDIE. P. 19, f. 5.
— — EMBATTLED URDEE. P. 19, f. 4.
— — with one EMBATTLEMENT ARONDIE. P. 19, f. 9.
— — INDENTED. P. 19, f. 6.

BEND-PER, INDENTED BOWED, POINTS POMETTEE. P. 18, f. 45.

— — INDENTED INTO THREE POINTS TREFOILED. P. 19, f. 19.

— — NEBULY. P. 19, f. 7.

— — NUEE, DOUBLE GORED, or DOUBLE ARCHED. Also termed tranche en nuage, and arondie dexter-per-bend. P. 19, f. 11.

— — TWO PILES, TRIPLE POINTED BOWED AND COUNTERPOSED. P. 19, f. 17.

— — IN POINT TO SINISTER. P. 19, f. 10.

— — IN POINT URDE. P. 19, f. 8. Also termed per bend champion to the sinister.

— — POINTED WITH A BALL. P. 19, f. 12. Also termed per bend archée, reversed in the middle a pomel.

— — COUNTER POMETTEE. P. 19, f. 25.

— — SINISTER. P. 2, f. 7.

— — SINISTER IN AILE. P. 19, f. 14. Also termed per-bend bande.

— — SINISTER IN FORM OF LIONS' MOUTHS. P. 19, f. 18.

— — TREBLE ARCHED, or GORED TO THE SINISTER. P. 19, f. 13.

— — URDEE. P. 19, f. 3.

— — WAVED AND COUNTER TREFOILED. P. 19, f. 20.

— — WAVED WITH TWO FOILS, or LEAVED COUNTERPOSED. P. 19, f. 22.

— — WAVED WITH FOILS OF LEAVES. P. 19, f. 23.

BENDE, or BENDYS. The old way of spelling bend and bends.

BENDING, REBENDING. The same as bowed, or embowed.

BENDLET, or BENDIL. A diminutive of the bend. P. 17, f. 2.

BENDLETS. Two and three. P. 18, f. 34, 35. and 36. P. 19, f. 28.

BENDWISE, BENDWAYS, or IN BEND. A term to express the position of charges when placed obliquely, resembling a bend either dexter or sinister, as P. 17, f. 45. P. 6, f. 11 and 20.

BENDY. Is when the field is equally divided bendways and may be of any number of parts. P. 18, f. 37, and 38.

— OF SIX and BENDY OF EIGHT. P. 2, f. 11 and 12. P. 18, f. 37 and 38.

— OF SIX,—per bend sinister counter-charged. P. 18, f. 40.

— ANGLED, RECTANGLED, ACUTE or BEVILED ANGLED in the same form as bends. P. 18, f. 42.

— BARRIED. P. 18, f. 44.

— BARRY. P. 2, f. 35.

BENDY BARRY SINISTER. P. 2, f. 34.

— BARRY DEXTER AND SINISTER. P. 2, f. 36. BARRY BENDY LOZENGY. P. 2, f. 35, and barry indented. P. 2, f. 36.

— FUSILY, or FUSILY-BENDY. P. 18, f. 32.

— LOZENGY. Same as Bendy paly. P. 22, f. 21.

— LOZENGY BARRY. P. 2, f. 35.

— MASCULY. P. 18, f. 33.

— PALY, or PALY-BENDY. P. 2, f. 32.

— SINISTER OF SIX. P. 18, f. 39.

— SINISTER PALY, or PALY BENDY SINISTER. P. 18, f. 41. P. 2, f. 33.

— OF SIX ANGLED. P. 18, f. 42.

BENDYS. See BENDE.

BENGAL TIGER. P. 28, f. 13.

BEQUE, or BEAKED. A bird is termed beaked, when its bill is of a different tincture from the body.

BERLY. An ancient term for barry.

BESANTY. See BEZANTEE.

BESAUNTE. A bezant. P. 1.

BESET. Surrounded, as a bee hive beset with bees diversely volant. P. 30, f. 20.

BESOM, or BROOM. P. 42, f. 49.

BETONY-LEAF. P. 45, f. 26.

BETWEEN. A term applied to the principal charge occupying a central position as a cross betw. four roses. P. 7, f. 2; a chev. between three martlets. P. 8, f. 21. P. 14, f. 6. P. 17, f. 21. P. 19, f. 21, etc.

BEVELDED. See BEVILED.

BEVER, or VIZOR. See BEAVER.

BEVIL, BEVEL, or BEVILE. Is a line cut off in its straightness and is termed angled and beviled. P. 1. P. 4, f. 27.

BEVILED, or ACUTE-ANGLED. P. 18, f. 19.

BEVILED-DOUBLE. P. 18, f. 8.

BEVY. A term used to express a company or number of Roses, etc., same as a cluster or bunch.

BEZANT, BESANT, or BESAUNTE. A round flat piece of gold, which was the current coin of Byzantium. Supposed to have been first introduced into coat armour at the time of the Crusades.

It is sometimes called a "Talent," the emblem of Justice, and equal dealing among men. P. 1.

BEZANTEE, BEZANTIE, or BEZANTY. The field, or any charge is said to be bezantée when indiscriminately strewed over with Bezants. Also expressed by the term Semée of Bezants.

BEZANTLIER. The second branch from the main-beam, next above the bow-antler of a buck, etc.

BIBLE. *See* BOOK.

BICAPITATED, or BICAPITED. Having two heads. P. 26, f. 9.

BICORPORATED. Having two bodies. P. 26, f. 12.

BIG-WHEAT. *See* WHEAT.

BILL-FOREST. A Wood Bill. P. 41, f. 22.

BILL.HOOKS. *See* the above.

BILL-STONE. *See* WEDGE.

BILLET. An oblong square with a flat surface. As to what they represent there is a great diversity of opinion; some consider they represent bricks, others billets-doux; but whatever they may be, they are drawn as in P. 42, f. 34, and P. 17, f. 31.

BILLET RAGULED, and TRUNKED IN-FLAMED. Same as Brand. P. 41, f. 47. (A Fire Brand.)

BILLETTY, BILLETTEE, or SEMEE DE BILLETS. Also termed Billete and Billety, represents the Shield, Charge, Crest, or Supporter, as strewed all over with billets.

BILLETTY, COUNTER BILLETTEE. Is a field divided per-pale and per-fesse. The same as Barry Paly, P. 2, f. 42. A Fesse Billettée counter-billettée. P. 4, f. 41.

BILLING. Two birds billing, or respecting. P. 31, f. 27.

BIPARTED. Cut off, so as to leave one angular depression, shewing two projecting pieces and different to erased which shows three jagged pieces.

BIRCH TREE. P. 45, f. 34.

BIRD-BOLT. A short thick arrow without a point, and spreading at the extremity so much as to leave a flat surface; it has sometimes two heads which must be named. P. 37, f. 18 and 22.

BIRDS. Of various kinds are met with armorial bearings. *See* P. 33 and 34.
In blazon, birds of prey whose weapons are their beak and talons, are blazoned armed of such a tincture. But such birds as Swans, Ducks, Herons, etc., who have no talons, in blazoning are said to be beaked and membered, which last term signifies the legs; and when the wings of a bird are of a different tincture from the body, it is said to be winged of such a tincture. When "BIRD" is mentioned in blazon without naming the particular class of bird it is always drawn as P. 34, f. 43.

BIRD'S LEGS. *See* LEGS.

BIRD'S NEST. Is borne by several families. P. 31, f. 18.

BIRD OF PARADISE. P. 34, f. 6.

BIRT. The same as Turbot. P. 32, f. 8.

BISHOPS impale their own Arms with the Arms of their See, the latter being placed on the dexter. P. 17, f. 21.

BISHOP'S MITRE. P. 24, f. 15.

BISHOP. Habited in his pontificals, sitting in a chair of state, leaning on his sinister side, and holding in his left hand a Pastoral staff. P. 35, f. 3.

BISHOP'S CROSIER. P. 42, f. 45.

BISHOP'S CROSS STAFF, or EPISCOPAL STAFF. As borne in the arms of the See of Canterbury. P. 22, f. 2.

BISON. A species of the ox. P. 25a, f. 24.

BISSE. A Snake.

BISTOURI, or BISTOURY. A surgical instrument. P. 42, f. 51.

BIT, and SNAFFLE BIT. P. 37, f. 53.

BIT-MANAGE. P. 37, f. 54.

BITING HIS TAIL. *See* A SERPENT BITING HIS TAIL. P. 30, f. 37.

BITTED. As a horse's head bitted and bridled. P. 27, f. 35.

BITTERN. A bird. P. 34, f. 12.

BL. Abbreviation for Blue. i.e. azure.

BLACKBIRD. Frequently found in Coat Armour. P. 34, f. 44.

BLACK. Sable. *See* TINCTURES.
In engraving is represented by perpendicular and horizontal lines crossing each other.

BLACKAMOOR, or MOOR. P. 35, f. 28.

BLACKAMOOR'S HEAD. P. 36, f. 42.

BLACK-MAN. P. 35, f. 28.

BLADE. Applied to the stalk of grain or corn when of a different tincture from the ear, or fruit, when it is termed "Bladed." P. 45, f. 13 and 16.

BLADES. Are frequently borne without their handles, when their special kind must be named.
The Blade expresses the steel part of any cutting instrument when of a different tincture to the handle. P. 39, f. 10.

BLANCH-LYON. The title of one of the Pursuivants at arms.

BLASTED. Leatless, applied to Trees, same as blighted. P. 45, f. 58.

BLAZING STAR, or COMET. P. 23, f. 45.

BLAZON, or BLASON. A term generally applied to the knowledge and description of armorial bearings according to the rules of Heraldry.
In blazoning a Coat of Arms, i.e. describing

I

it, the Field is always first mentioned noticing the lines wherewith it is divided, and the differences of these lines, whether they be straight or crooked. Then proceed to the charge nearest the centre, and name those charges last which are furthest from the field, i.e. the charges upon the Ordinaries. The principal Ordinary in the coat (with the exception of the Chief) must be named next to the field, e.g. P. 2, f. 45. If the Ordinary itself is charged, such charge to be blazoned next to those between which the Ordinary is placed, e.g. P. 2, f. 3, and P. 22, f. 33. If there is no Ordinary in the arms the central charge is to be first named after the field, then the charge, if any, on the central charge, then the Border; next the Chief or Canton with its charges, e.g. P. 13, f. 40., & P. 22, f. 32. When a bearing is described without naming the point of the Escutcheon where it is to be placed, the centre is always understood; the same is also observed in respect to the charges upon Ordinaries, or one charge upon another. P. 20, f. 42. When there are three charges with or without Ordinary they are borne two in chief and one in base, P. 22, f. 43; but if they are not so placed, or, exceed three, their position must be named, see P. 4, f. 31., P. 22, f. 15 and 18. In Blazoning a coat, repetition of the same word must be avoided, as for example, it would be incorrect to describe the following coat thus; Sa. on a fesse ar. betw. three lions; heads erased ar. three mullets sa. It should be sa. on a fesse betw. three lions' heads erased ar. "as many" mullets "of the first," or "of the field." Of the first, or of the field, is used to prevent repetition of sa. The following rule is now observed by the Heralds, never to place colour on colour, or metal upon metal; and although a few instances of departure from this rule might be produced in some very ancient coats, (Carson, Bissett, Lloyd, White, etc.) yet these exceptions do not destroy the rule.

In Blazoning roundles, or guttée drops, you are not to say a roundle or guttée of such a tincture (unless it be party coloured or counterchanged) for their names vary according to the different tinctures of which they are composed; so that a roundle which is of Gold, is not blazoned a roundle or., but a Bezant, and a guttée drop red, is not to be blazoned a guttée gu., but guttée de sang. When roundles and guttée are borne upon a party coloured field and are of the alternate tinctures, they are blazoned roundles or guttée counterchanged, e.g. Quarterly ar. and sa. six roundles 3, 2, and 1, counterchanged. P. 2, f. 39. A high bonnet, or cap, per pale sa. and ar., banded gu., the cap guttée counterchanged. P. 40, f. 50. In Blazoning animals, a distinction must be particularly observed as to the kind of animal to which the term is to be applied. e.g. The terms Rampant, Saliant, Passant, Couchant, are properly applied to Lions, Tigers, etc. But for Deer the same attitudes are expressed, the first two by the term Springing, the other two by the terms Tripping, and Lodged; and a Lion standing full-faced is termed Guardant, but a Stag would be

termed at Gaze. P. 26 and P. 28. Respecting the blazoning of Men, Animals, Birds, Fish, Trees, etc. see each under its respective term.

After Blazoning the Shield, you proceed to the exterior ornaments viz.: The Helmet, Lambrequin, Crest, Supporters, Badge, and Motto. e.g. P. 8, f. 21 ; P. 18, f. 21.

BLAZONER. One skilled in Blazonry, which is the art of properly describing Coat Armour.

BLAZONRY. See BLAZON.

BLEMISHED, or REBATED. When a charge or bearing is broken, as a Spur-rowel with its points broken. P. 37, f. 47.

BLIAUS. See SURCOAT.

BLIGHTED, BLASTED, or STARVED. P. 45, f. 58.

BLOCK. A Billet, Delf, or Dice so named by Papworth.

BLOCK-BRUSH. As borne in the Arms of the Butchers' Company. P. 22, f. 32, and P. 42, f. 49.

BLODIUS. GULES.

BLOOD-COLOUR. Sanguine.

BLOOD-HOUND. P. 29, f. 18.

BLOOD-HOUND ON SCENT. P. 29, f. 17.

BLOODY. Is used by early Heralds to signify gules.

BLOOM, BLOWN, or BLOSSOM. Flowers, Shrubs, and Plants when bearing blossoms in their proper colours, are blazoned, Bloomed, Flowered, or Blossomed.

BLUDGEON. A club. P. 41, f, 48.

BLUE. Azure.

BLUE-BELL. See BELLFLOWERS.

BLUE-BOTTLE. A Flower. P. 44, f. 19.

BLUE ENSIGN. See ENSIGN.

BLUE-MANTLE. A title of one of the Pursuivants of Arms.

BLUNTED, or ROUNDED. A cross so termed. P. 8, f. 41.

BOA-SERPENT. P. 30, f. 53.

BOAR. Also termed a Sanglier ; always understood to mean a Wild Boar. P. 29, f. 31.
When said to be Bristled, expresses the hair on the neck and back ; Armed, the tusks ; Unguled, the hoofs.

BOAR'S HEAD COUPED. ib. f. 32.

BOAR'S HEAD ERASED. ib.

BOAR'S HEAD ERECT and ERASED. ib. f. 33.

BOAR'S HEAD ERECT IN A CUP. f. 34.

BOAR'S HEAD IN A DISH. f. 35.

BOAR'S HEAD and NECK COUPED. f. 36.

BOARDS. See PLAYING TABLES.

BOATS. Boats of various descriptions are met with in Heraldry. P. 38, f. 34. P. 32, f. 27.

BOAT-HOOK. P. 38, f. 34.

BOATSWAIN'S WHISTLE. P. 38, f. 43.

BOCK. A kind of Deer. P. 29, f. 23.

BODKIN. A Tailors bodkin. P. 42, f. 28.

BODY-ARMOUR. P. 38, f. 13.

BODY-HEART. *See* HEART.

BOILING-POT. *See* FLESH-POT.

BOLE, or HEAD. The seed pods of a plant as a Poppy-bole. P. 45, f. 12.

BOLT. · An arrow. P. 37, f. 22.

BOLT. A door bolt. P. 42, f. 14.

BOOT, and TUN. Is a bird-bolt piercing a tun. P. 39, f. 37, No. 2.

BOLT-HEDYS. An ancient term for a bull's-head.

BOLT-PRISONERS. *See* SHACKBOLT.

BOLTANT, or BOLTING. A term applied to hares and rabbits, when springing forward.

BOMB-SHELL. Two examples of Bombshells inflamed. P. 37, f. 10.

BONES, of various kinds are found in armoury ; Shin-bones, also termed Shankbone. *See* SHINBONES and JAWBONE. P. 42, f. 52.

BONFIRE. Called by Guillim " Firebrands Flamant and Scintillant ppr." P. 43, f. 35.

BONNET. The cap of velvet within a Coronet.

BONNET, or CAP. As borne by the family of Wingfield. P. 40, f. 50.

BONNET ELECTORAL. P. 40, f. 56.

BOOKS. Are variously borne in Coat Armour. e.g. A Book expanded, or open, a Book closed garnished and clasped. P. 43, f. 31.

On a Book open and garnished, on the dexter side seven seales, the words " Sapientia felicitas," sometimes " Dominus illuminatio mea," as in the Arms of the University of Oxford. f. 32.

BOOKBINDER'S POLISHING-IRON. P. 41, f. 41.

BOOKBINDER'S FOLDING STICK. P. 41, f. 41.

BOOK-PLATES HERALDIC. A label on which the Armorial Bearings, name etc. are displayed. P. 47.

BOOT. A covering for the foot and leg. A Boot with Top and Spur. P. 38, f. 15.

BORDER, BORDURE. A Subordinary which surrounds the field, is of equal breadth, and takes up one fifth part of it, and is generally assumed, or granted as a difference ; charged border's may allude to maternal descent, when borne Componée to illegitimacy.

If a coat containing a Border, is impaled with another coat, it extends only to the line of impalement as P, 13, f. 43. If a Border is charged with bezants, plates, billets, or pellets, it is termed a bordure bezantée, platée, billetée, and pellettée ; all other charges must be named with their tinctures. When a border is plain it is thus blazoned ; Sa. a bordure ar. P. 13, f. 1. The Border is subject to all the different forms of lines belonging to the Ordinaries, as the following examples.

BORDER, BARRY. P. 13, f. 26.

— BATTLED-EMBATTLED, or BATTLED GRADY. P. 13, f. 16.

— BENDY. P. 13, f. 28.

— BEZANTY. P. 13, f. 40.

— BILLETTY. P. 13, f. 41.

— charged with another. P. 13, f. 35.

— charged with escallops. P. 13, f. 36.

Other examples of Borders charged f. 37 to 41, and at P. 35, f. 16. is a Border charged with the double tressure of Scotland.

— CHEQUY. P. 13, f. 19.

— CHEVRONNY. P. 13, f. 29.

— COMPONEE, or COMPONY. P. 13, f. 7.

— COUNTER COMPONY. P. 13, f. 13.

— CRENELLEE. P. 13, f. 4.

— DEMI. P. 13, f. 32.

— DENTICLES, or DENTICULES. P. 13, f. 20.

— DOVETAIL. P. 13, f. 15.

— DOUBLE. P. 13, f. 31.

— EMBATTLED. P. 13, f. 4.

— EMBORDERED. P. 13, f. 31.

— ENALURON. P. 13, f. 37.

— OF ENGLAND, and FRANCE. P. 13, f. 30.

— ENGRAILED. P. 13, f. 2 and 45.

— ENURNY. P. 13, f. 38.

— FLORY. P. 13, f. 11.

— FRETTY. P. 13, f. 42.

— GARNISHED. P. 13, f. 40.

— GOBONY. P. 13, f. 7.

— IMPALED. Is cut off at the centre and not continued down the impaled line. P. 13, f. 43.

— INDENTED. P. 13, f. 10.

— INDENTED POINT IN POINT. P. 13, f. 14.

— INDENTEE. P. 13, f. 18.

— and INESCUTCHEON. P. 13, f. 33.

— INVECKED. P. 13, f. 3.

— NEBULEE, or NEBULY. P. 13, f. 6.

— ON. P. 13, f. 38.

— PALY. P. 13, f. 23.

— PARTED-INDENTED. Same as Border indented point in point.

— PER BEND. P. 13, f. 27.

— PER BORDER. P. 13, f. 17 and 35.

— PER FESSE. P. 13, f. 25.

— PER PALE. P. 13, f. 36.

BORDER PER SALTIRE. P. 13, f. 24.
— POINT IN POINT INDENTED. P. 13, f. 14.
— POTENTEE. P. 13, f. 12.
— QUARTERLY. P. 13, f. 22.
— QUARTERLY-QUARTERED. P. 13, f. 34.
— RAYONNEE. P. 13, f. 8.
— SURMOUNTED OF A CHIEF. P. 13, f. 44.
— URDEE. P. 13, f. 9.
— VAIR. P. 13, f. 5.
— VERDOY. P. 13, f. 39.
— WITHIN A BORDER. P. 13, f. 35.
BORDERED, or BORDURED. Edged with another tincture. P. 4, f. 5.
BORDURE. Same as Border.
BORDURE, or BERDER. The old way of spelling bordure.
BORE. See BOAR.
BOSCHAS. A Wild Duck. P. 34, f. 22.
BOSS OF A BIT. As borne in the arms of the Bit-Makers Company, or Loriners. P. 37, f. 53.
BOTEROLL, BOTTEROLL, BAUTEROLL, or CRAMPIT. The steel mounting at the bottom of the scabbard. P. 37, f. 33.
BOTONE, BOTONNEE, BOTTONE, BOTTONY, or BUTTONY Cross. Also termed Cross trefflée. P. 10, f. 20.
BOTONNEE-MASCULED CROSS. P. 8, f. 39.
BOTONED. That which has at its extremities round knots or buds like the trefoil. P. 10, f. 20.
BOTTLE, BLUE. See BLUE-BOTTLE.
BOTTLE, LEATHER, or LEATHERN. A bottle made of leather. P. 42, f. 19.
BOTTOM. A ball of thread. P. 40, f. 3.
BOTTONY. See BOTONE.
BOUCHIERS-KNOT. Is a knot of silk tied as P. 43, f. 10.
BOUCKYS. The ancient orthography for bucks.
BOUGET. See WATER-BOUGET.
BOUJON. An arrow with a broad head. A Bird-bolt. P. 37, f. 22.
BOULT. See BOLT.
BOURDON-STAVES, or BOURDERIS. See PALMER'S STAFF.
BOURCHIER'S KNOT. P. 43, f. 10.
BOURDONNE CROSS. The same as a Cross Pommettée, or pommelle. P. 10, f. 28.
BOURDURE. See BORDER.
BOUSE. A Water-bouget. P. 42, f. 20.
BOW. Bows are of various descriptions, and in blazon must be named, as an Archers, String-bow, or Long-bow; it must also be expressed whether they are bent, or unbent. If charged with an arrow and bent, they are blazoned as, a bow and arrow in full draught, also termed a drawn bow. P. 37, f. 18 and 24. A Cross bow bent, f. 23. When the string is of a different colour, the bow is said to be stringed, or strung. See ARBALESTE.
BOWED, or EMBOWED. Bent like a bow, or otherwise curved or curled. See EMBOWED. For Arms embowed see BLAZON OF ARMS, at P. 36. For Serpents Bowed and Embowed, see BLAZON P. 30.
BOWEN'S KNOT. A Knot of silk tied, as P. 43, f. 8.
BOWGET. See WATER-BOUGET.
BOWL. A deep dish; thereon a Boar's head couped. P. 29, f. 35.
BOY. A naked boy is borne by several families, and a demi boy is the crest of Hayley.
BOY'S-HEAD; or Infant's head couped having a snake enwrapped about the neck. P. 36, f. 49.
BOX-TREE. P. 45, f. 48.
BRACED. The same as interlaced. P. 15, f. 40.
BRACELET. An ornament for the arms. The barrulet is by some writers termed a bracelet.
BRACKET. See REST.
BRAMBLE-WREATH. A crown of Thorns. P. 43, f. 3.
BRAMBLE, BRAMBLINGS, or WILD ROSE. P. 44, f. 27.
BRANCH. A branch if fructed, should consist of four leaves. P. 44, f. 53, if unfructed of nine. A slip of three leaves. f. 52. A sprig of five leaves. f. 39. Branch of Fir-Tree, f. 47.
BRANCHED. Spread like branches.
BRANCHES OF HOLLY, Laurel, Southernwood, Withered etc. see P. 44.
BRAND, FIRE-BRAND. P. 41, f. 47, this is also called a Billet raguled and trunked inflamed on the top.
BRASSARTS, or BRASSETS. Armour for the elbow. See GARDEBRAS.
BRASED, or BRAZED. See BRACED.
BRASIER. A utensil to hold live coals. See BRAZIER-INFLAMED.
BRASSES, Sepulchral, monumental plates anciently called latten, often found in churches, and represent in their outline, or by engraving upon them the figure, and armorial bearings of the deceased. P. 39, f. 20.

BRASSETS. VAMBRACES, or AVANT-BRACES. Pieces of armour for the arms. P. 38, f. 9. *See* VAMBRACED.

BRAZIER-INFLAMED. P. 39, f. 32.

BREAM. A fish. P. 32. f. 15.

BREAST. A woman's breast. P. 43, f. 34.

BREAST-PLATE. *See* CUIRASS. P. 38, f. 7.

BREATHING. A term applied to a stag at gaze.

BRECTESCHES. Parapets, or battlements.

BRET. *See* BRIT.

BRETESSE, BRETESSED, BRETTESSED, or BRETTESSEE. A term used when a charge has battlements on each side, directly opposite each other. P. 3, f. 10; P. 14, f. 17.

BRETTEPEE. The same as Bretesse.

BREYS. *See* BARNACLES.

BRICK, or BRIQUE. Similar to the billet but showing its thickness in perspective.

BRICK-AXE, or BRICKLAYER'S AXE. P. 41, f. 21.

BRICK-KILN. P. 41, f. 46.

BRIDLED. Having a bridle on; as a horse's head bridled. P. 27, f. 35.

BRIDGE. Bridges in coat armour are of various forms, with one, two, or three arches, in blazon the number must be named, as a bridge of three arches, &c., P. 23, f. 19 and 20.

BRIGANDINE. P. 38, f. 8. *See* HABERGON.

BRILL. A fish. P. 32, f. 21.

BRIMSEY. The same as Gad-bee. P. 30, f. 21.

BRINDED, or BREENDED. Spotted. Applied only to animals.

BRINDLED. Same as Brinded.

BRISE, or BRISEE. Broken. *See* ROMPU.

BRISTLED. A term to express the hair on the neck and back of a boar, when of a different tincture from the body.

BRISURE, BRIZURE, or BRISURES. equivalent to the term Difference in marks of Cadency. P. 46.

BRIT, BRET, or BURT. A fish of the herring kind. P. 32, f. 44a.

BROAD-ARROW. Similar to the Pheon, but having the insides of the barbs plain. P. 37, f. 17.
The Broad arrow is the Royal mark on all Government stores &c. It was the regal badge of Richard I.

BROAD-AXE. P. 37, f. 28.

BROACH, or BROCHE. An instrument used by embroiders. P. 41, f. 44.

BROCHANT SUR LE TOUT. When one charge rests upon any other as the Fesse at P. 3, f. 31.

BROCK. *See* BADGER.

BROCKET. A young stag so blazoned in the arms of Hanney.

BROGUE, or IRISH-BROGUE. A kind of shoe. P. 19, f. 38.

BROKEN, SPLINTERED, SHIVERED, or FRACTED. P. 4, f. 31; P. 37, f. 11.

BRONCHANT. A term used by some authors to denote the situation of any beast, when placed on a field strewed with fleur-de-lis; by others it is considered equivalent to "over-all."

BROOM, or BESOM. P. 42, f. 49.

BROOM-PLANT, or PLANTA-GENISTA. P. 25, f. 6 & 9. The Badge of Plantagenet.

BROOM-PLANT, Broom-sprig, Broom-branch, and Broom-flower. P. 44, f. 42.

BROW-ANTLER, or BROWANTLIER. The first branch of the horn of a buck.

BROWSING. The mode of eating of a Graminiverous animal. P. 28, f. 48.

BRUISED. The same as Debruised.

BRUMSEY. A Gad-Fly. P. 30, f. 21.

BRUSH. *See* BLOCK-BRUSH, P. 42, f. 49. Treble-flat-Brush, P. 41, f. 42.

BRUSK. The same as Tenne.

BUBBLE, WATER-BUBBLES. Borne by the name of Aire, and Bubbleward. P. 22, f. 14.

BUCK. *See* STAG.

BUCKET. Is variously depicted. *See* P. 39, f. 35 and 36.

BUCKLE, also termed Fermaile, or Femaille. The emblem of Fidelity and Firmness.
In Armoury these are of various shapes; In blazoning them this must be named; as a lozengy-buckle tongue-fessways. P. 42, f. 15. An oval-buckle and round-buckle tongue pendent. f. 15. A mail, or square-buckle, a buckle of an heart shape tongue pendent, a round-buckle tongue erect, and a belt-buckle. P. 42, f. 16. The last example at f. 16 is also termed a gar-buckle.

BUCKLED. When a belt, band, or collar, etc. is depicted as fastened with a buckle, it is said to be buckled, as a garter-buckled. P. 42, f. 17.

BUCKLER, TARGET, TARGE, or SHIELD. A piece of defensive armour, is depicted in various shapes. P. 1, P. 43, f. 58.

BUD. Flowers in the bud, or budding, occur in arms. P. 45, f. 10.

BUDGET. *See* WATER-BOUGET.

BUFFALO. A Wild ox. P. 28, f. 35. In old blazon, Bulls heads are frequently termed Buffaloes heads.

BUFFALO'S HEAD CABOSSED. P. 22, f. 30.

BUGLE-HORN, or HUNTING-HORN, also termed Hanchet. P. 43, f. 21, No. 4. When said to be strung and garnished it is represented as f. 24. The Garnishing consists of verolls round the horn, and is sometimes termed verolled, when there is no string it is sometimes blazoned a Buglehorn sans strings.

BULL. Of very frequent use in Armoury A Bull pass. P. 28, f. 32.

BULL, WINGED. Also termed a Flying-Bull. P. 28, f. 31.

BULL'S HEAD CABOSSED. P. 22, f. 31, and P. 28, f. 34.

BULL'S HEAD ERASED. P. 28, f. 33. Bull's head couped. P. 22, f. 32.

BULL'S LEG and BULL'S FOOT. P. 31, f. 22 and 23.

BULL'S SCALP. P. 31, f. 17.

BULL-DOG. P. 29, f. 24.

BULL-FINCH. A singing-bird. P. 33, f. 49.

BULLET. The same as Pellet, and Ogress. P. 1. Termed by ancient heralds, Gunstones; they are sometimes blazoned Copper-cakes as in the arms of Chambers, I think when so blazoned ought to be painted Copper-colour.

BULLRUSH. An aquatic plant. P. 44, f. 48.

BUNCH, or CLUSTER. Fruits, flowers, etc. are frequently borne in bunches, or clusters.

BUNDLE OF LATHS. As borne in the arms of the Bricklayers Company. P. 41, f. 58.

BUNTING BIRD, or CHAFFINCH. P. 34, f. 54.

BUOY. A floating body employed to point out the particular situation of anything under water. P. 38, f. 44.

BUR, or BURR. A broad ring of iron behind the place made for the hand on the tilting spear.

BURBOT, or CONEY-FISH. P. 32, f. 37.

BURDOCK, or BUR-LEAF. P. 45, f. 26.

BUR OF BURDOCK. P. 44, f. 44.

BURDON. A Pilgrim's staff. P. 42, f. 43.

BURELLE. A term to express barry.

BURGANDINE. See HABERGEON.

BURGANET, or BURGONET. A steel cap or helmet. P. 38, f. 6.

BURLING-IRON. An instrument used by Weavers. P. 41, f. 4.

BURNING-BUSH, also called Moses' bush, and a Flaming-bush. P. 45, f. 59.

BURNING-LAMP. P. 39, f. 26, No. 2.

BURR. A rough prickly covering of the seed of certain plants. P. 44, f. 44. A Burr proper as borne by the name of Jason.

BURS OF BURDOCK. P. 44, f. 44.

BURST, SPLIT, or OPEN. Also termed disjointed, fracted, or severed. P. 16, f. 7.

BRUSH, or BRUSH OF A FOX. The tail.

BUSH. A Burning-bush. P. 45, f. 59.

BUSKINS, or GAMASHES. A kind of hose, or stocking, either laced, buttoned, or buckled; they reach from half way up the leg, to the instep. See GREAVE, P. 38, f. 14.

BUST. The head to the breast. P. 36, f. 36.

BUSTARD. A bird. P. 33, f. 56.

BUTCHER'S AXE, or SLAUGHTER AXE. P. 22, f. 32.

BUTCHER'S KNIFE. P. 41, f. 20.

BUTT. A fish. P. 32, f. 11.

BUTT. See BARREL.

BUTTERFLY. As in the arms of Beeston, Butterfield, Door, Foster, Papillion, etc. P. 30, f. 23.

BUTTERIS. An instrument used by Farriers. P. 41, f. 34.

BUTTFISH. P. 32, f. 10.

BUTTONED. Ornamented buckles in armoury are said to be buttoned, garnished, or studded.

BUTTON TASSELLED. The same as a Ball tasselled. P. 40, f. 23.

BUTTONY, BOTTONY FLORY, or BOTON-NEE FLORY. See CROSS. P. 10, f. 20.

BUZZARD. Same as Kite. P. 33, f. 60.

C

CABLE. The rope affixed to an anchor as P. 38, f. 41.

CABLE, or CABLEE. As a Cross Cablée or Corded. P. 7, f. 18.

CABOSHED, CABOCHED, CABOSSED, or CABOSED. Terms to express the heads of Deer, Bulls, Goats, etc., when cut off and set full faced, without any part of the neck being left. P. 28, f. 34, 38, and 58. Cabossed does not apply to a Leopard's face. P. 28, f. 4.

CABRE, EFFRAY, or FORCENE. Terms applied to a horse rising on its hind legs. P. 27, f. 26.

CADENCY, or DIFFERENCING. Marks of Distinction by which different members and branches of a family are distinguished. See P. 16, f. 40 to 45, and Distinction of Houses at P. 46.

Cadency, or Differencing effected in the early days of Coat Armour; By changing the tincture of the field—By changing the tincture of the charges—By dividing the shield by different lines of partition—By diminishing the number of the principal figures (very rare)—By altering their position—By surrounding the original charges with a bordure—all these modes have fallen into disuse. See the term LABEL.

CADET. A junior member or branch of a family.

CADUCEUS, or MERCURY'S Mace, or WAND; termed sometimes Snaky-staff, and Mercury's Soporiferous rod. The emblem of peace, depicted as P. 30, f. 56.
It is frequently borne with a cap (called the Petasus P. 38, f. 4.) on the top of the staff.

CAFFAR. Negro, Moor, etc. in Heraldry are depicted in the same way.

CALAMINE-STONE. Forms part of the Crest of the Mineral Company. P. 42, f. 60.

CALDRON. A metal kettle, or boiler. P. 41, f. 16.

CALOPUS. " une Calopus autrement dit Chatloup d'or et de sable esquartelé les cornes aussi esquartelées." The Badge of Folejambe of Walton co. Derby, Esquire of the King's Body 9 June 1513. P. 29, f. 7.

CALF. P. 28, f. 30.

CALTHROP. See GALTRAP.

CALTRAP, CALTROP, CHEVAL-TRAP, or Galtrap. Refer to this last term.

CALVARY CROSS. P. 8, f. 33.

CAMAIL. A small kind of Mantle, it hung down from the Basinet and covered the Mail to the neck and shoulders. Same as Contoise. P. 25a, f. 9.

CAMEL. A Camel and Camel's head are borne by many families. P. 27, f. 48.

CAMELEON. Is depicted as P. 30, f. 9; and when blazoned ppr. is coloured pale green.
The Cameleon is the emblem of inconstancy.

CAMELOPARD. May appropriately be borne by those who have distinguished themselves in Africa. P. 27, f. 50.

CAMELOPARDEL. Is like the Camelopard but with two long horns curved backwards.

CAMOMILE. A plant. P. 45, f. 4.

CAMP, COMPON, or CAMPONE. The same as Componée, or Gobony.

CAMPANED, or CAMPANES. Bells pendent from a fesse, bar, or file are termed CAMPANED ; the number must be named. P. 16, f. 37.

CANARY. Bird. P. 34, f. 47.

CANCER. See CRAB,

CANDLE-EXTINGUISHER. A hollow conical utensil to put on a candle to extinguish it. P. 43, f. 35, borne by the family of Brown, of Great Yarmouth.

CANDLESTICKS. Also termed Taper Candlestick. A utensil to hold a candle. P. 39, f. 27 and 28.

CANELLE. The same as invecked, or invected. P. 1.

CANNET. A duck without feet or beak. P. 34, f. 60. borne by the name of Kennoway.

CANNON. Is always understood to be mounted. P. 37, f. 4.

CANNON MOUNTED IN PERSPECTIVE. P. 37, f. 5. See CULVERIN and a Ship Gun carriage with ordnance mounted.

CANNONED. Bells are said to be cannoned when the tongues are of a different tincture to the bell. See BELLS.

CANOPY, or STALL. As in the arms of the See of Tuam. P. 43, f. 53.

CANTING ARMS. See ALLUSIVE ARMS.

CANTON. One of the Sub-Ordinaries, and is always understood to occupy the dexter-chief of the escutcheon, unless termed a Sinister Canton, and to possess only the third part of the Chief. P. 19, f. 36, P. 2, f. 44.

CANTON, INDENTED. P. 19, f. 37. Canton per-chevron, f. 38. On a Canton, f. 39. Canton in dexter base, f. 40.

CANTON OF ST. GEORGE. Is a silver canton charged with a red-cross. This is sometimes blazoned a Canton of the Red Cross.

CANTONED, or CANTONNEE. The same as between. P. 20, f. 38.

CANTONED-BAR. That is a bar cantoned in the same manner as a Cantoned-Fesse.

CANTONED-FESSE, or FESSE CANTONED. Is a fesse joined to a canton. P. 4, f. 40.
When borne of the same metal or colour, should be united without any division.

CANTONED-LAMBEAUX, or LAMBEAUX CANTONED. A term to express one or more of the feet of the label when charged with a canton. P. 16, f. 44.

CAP-A-PIE. i.e. completely armed from head to foot.
A Chevalier armed Cap-a-pie P. 36, f. 27.

CAP. Various descriptions of Caps are found in Armoury. P. 40, f. 49 to 60. Also the cap of velvet which covers the head within the rim, or circle of the crown, as that of Peers. P. 24, f. 1 to 5, and f. 42 to 46.

CAP OF DIGNITY, or MAINTENANCE. Also termed a Ducipher. See CHAPEAU

CAP of the Lord Mayor of London. P. 40, f. 56.

CAPARISONED. A term to express a War-horse completely accoutred, or armed for the field.

CAPITAL. The head of a column. P. 43, f. 50.

CAPITAL CROSS. P. 10, f. 22.

CAPPELINE. See LAMBREQUIN.

CAPON. A cock without wattles, etc.

CARBUNCLE. See ESCARBUNCLE.

CARD. The four ace cards. P. 22, f. 20. Borne in the arms of the Card Makers' Company.

CARD. A Wool-card. P. 40, f. 10.

CARDINAL'S CAP, or HAT. P. 40, f. 60.
A Cardinal's Hat is red, The Archbishops of France bear a hat of this description over their arms, but its colour is vert, and it has only four rows of tassels; Abbots bear the same sable with three rows of tassels.

CAREERING, or CARIERING. Applied to a horse in a position of a lion saliant.

CARNAT. Flesh coloured.

CARNATION, or PINK. A flower. P. 44, f. 20.

CARP. A fish, P. 32, f. 29.

CARPENTER'S-COMPASSES. An instrument consisting of two pointed legs or branches joined at the top. P. 41, f. 31.

CARPENTER'S-SQUARE. P. 41, f. 23.

CARTOUCHE. An oval shield.

CART-WHEEL. P. 41, f. 53.

CASK, BARREL, or TUN. P. 39, f. 37.

CASQUE. A helmet, generally without a visor.

CASSOWARY. See EMU.

CASTERENSE CROWN. See CROWN PALISADO.

CASTLE. The emblem of safety. Castles are of different forms in armoury, when mentioned as Castles are always borne as at P. 23, f. 7.
If the cement is of a different tincture from the Castle itself, it must be named, and the castle is said to be masoned of such a tincture. The Windows and Ports, when of a

different colour, must be expressed; when supposed to be open, they should be described "voided of the field." When the port is defended by a portcullis it must be named in the blazon. Examples of Castles. See P. 23.

CAT. The domestic Cat occurs as an Heraldic bearing, borne by Catton, etc.

CAT-A-MOUNTAIN, or WILD-CAT. The emblem of vigilance and courage. P. 28, f. 26 and f. 27.

CAT, CIVET. See CIVET-CAT. P. 28, f. 28.

CATERFOIL, or QUATERFOIL. Four leaved grass. P. 44, f. 16. Double Caterfoil. f. 13.

CATERFOIL, or QUARTERFOIL SLIPPED. P. 44, f. 16, No. 2 and 3.

CATHERINE-WHEEL. So called from St. Catherine whom the pagans attempted to put to death by a wheel of this kind. P. 41, f. 54.

CATOOSE, or SCROLL. Anciently written scrowle; a Cross Catoose, or Catoosed. P. 11, f. 31.

CAUDE. See COWARD.

CAUL, or COWL. A Monk's-hood. P. 36, f. 31.

CAVE. Wild animals are sometimes met with in Coat Armour, represented as issuing from a Cave. P. 2, f. 51.

CECKKO, or CHECCHE. An ancient term for Chequy.

CEDAR. An evergreen tree. P. 45, f. 44.

CELESTIAL CROWN. P. 24, f. 33.

CELESTIAL GLOBE, or SPHERE. P. 39, f. 5.

CENTAUR. An imaginary creature representing half a man and half a horse. P. 27, f. 40.

CENTRE, or CENTRE-POINT. The middle or fesse point.

CERCELE, CERCELEE, or RECERCELEE. Applied to a Cross curling at the ends. P. 11, f. 32.

CERCLE. Within a circle or diadem, or having a diadem.

CERES. The Goddess of Corn, represented holding a garb of corn in dexter arm and sickle in the sinister hand.

CERISE. A Torteau.

CHABOT. A fish. P. 32, f. 45.

CHAD. St. Cross of. P. 11, f. 13.

CHAFANT. Enraged applied to the wild boar.

CHAFFINCH. A bird. P. 34, f. 54.

CHAINS are frequently borne in the shield as a charge, or are attached to the Crest or Supporters as P. 21, f. 21; P. 18, f. 21.

A Cross of four chains square linked, fixed to an annulet in fesse P. 8, f. 11. A Saltire of Chains P. 20, f. 44. A Chain enarched, or in arch P. 42, f. 31. A Circular Chain and a circular chain within another. P. 42, f. 31.

CHAINED and COLLARED. Animals having a collar with a chain attached are said to be collared and chained. P. 21, f. 21.

CHAIN-SHOT. Bullets united with a chain. P. 37, f. 8.

The other example is an Heraldic chain shot, and by old authors called a Murthering Chain shot, borne by Clifford.

CHALICE. A cup. P. 42, f. 26.

CHAMBER-PIECE. A piece of ordnance without the carriage. P. 37, f. 4 and f. 6.

CHAME. An annulet with a sharp rising point on one side.

CHAMELION. See CAMELION.

CHAMFRAIN, or CHAMFRON. Armour for the head of a horse. P. 38, f. 12.

CHAMOIS. An animal which inhabits the Alpine mountains. P. 28, f. 40.

CHAMPAGNE, CHAMPAIGNE, CHAMPAIN, or CHAMPION. Same as Urdée, or Warriated. P. 4, f. 22; P. 17, f. 19; P. 15, f. 19.

CHAMPION. A Knight, or Chevalier, who challenges the combat to avenge the cause of another.

CHAPE, BOTEROLL, or BOUTEROLLE. The mounting at the bottom of the scabbard. P. 37, f. 33.

CHAPEAU. A cap. Also termed a Ducipher; and cap of maintenance. P. 40, f. 54.

CHAPEAU-DE-FER. A MORION. P. 38, f. 2.

CHAPEL. As in the arms of Chapel, Lerrier, etc. P. 23, f. 25.

CHAPERON, CHAPOURN, or SHAFFEROON. A term applied to the small shields which contain either the Crest, deaths-head, or other device.

These are placed on the foreheads of the horses drawing the hearse at funerals, and are so called because they were fastened to the Chaperon, or hood, worn over the heads of the horses, with other state coverings.

CHAPERONNE, that is HOODED. A Chief Chaperonne. P. 12, f. 39.

CHAPLET. Garland, or wreath of flowers, laurel, oak, olive, etc.

A Chaplet of Roses, in Heraldry, is always composed of four roses and the rest leaves as P. 24, f. 41.

CHAPOURNET, or CHAPERONNET. A chief divided by a curved line, as ar. a chief gu. charged with a Chapournet, or Shapournett erm. P. 12. f. 39.

CHAPOURNET REVERSED IN CHIEF, or a CHAPOURNATED-CHIEF. P. 12, f. 40.

CHAPPE. To express the field when divided the same as Tierce-in-Mantle. P. 21, f. 36.

CHAPPE. A cross chape, or chappe, is the same as double fitchée. P. 8, f. 42.

CHAPPEAU. See Chapeau.

CHARBONCLE. See Escarbuncle.

CHARGE. In this term is included all kinds of figures whatever they may be, which are in the field of the Escutcheon.

CHARGED. A term applied to either the shield, or any bearing whatever when any device is placed on it. P. 2, f. 45.

CHARGER. A dish. See St. John the Baptist's head in a charger. P. 35, f. 33.

CHARLEMAGNE CROWN OF. P. 25, f. 1, and P. 31, f. 9 and 10, borne in the arms of five kings of England as archtreasures of the Holy Roman Empire.

CHARNELL. Flesh coloured, or ppr.

CHART. See map.

CHATLOUP. See Calopus.

CHATTER, or CHATTERER. The same as Lark. P. 33, f. 57.

CHAUSSE. Shod and denotes a section in base. P. 22, f. 8.

CHAUSSE-TRAP. See Galtrap.

CHAUSSES. Armour for the legs and feet, sometimes of two pieces joined at the knee by garters. P. 39, f. 20. No. 8.

CHECKY, CHECKIE, CHEQUY, CHECKERED, CHEQUERED, CHEQUE, CHEQUEE or CHECQUY. A term to express the field, or any bearing, when divided into small squares of alternate tinctures, and must consist of three or more rows. P. 2, f. 37. P. 4, f. 44. P. 7, f. 15. P. 19, f. 35.

CHEECHE. Same as Checky.

CHEESE-SLIP, or WOOD-LOUSE. P. 30, f. 7.

CHECKERS. Same as Checky.

CHEF, or CHEFE. See Chief.

CHEKERE. See Checky.

CHENE. An oak. P. 45, f. 31.

CHEQUE. See Checky.

CHEQUERED, or CHECKERED. Covered with rows of Checkers. P. 20, f. 7.

CHEQUES. Four pieces of Cheques. same as P. 2, f. 19.

CHERRY TREE. P. 45, f. 40.

CHERRY-BRANCH. P. 44, f. 35.

CHERUB, or ANGEL. A child's head betw. two wings. P. 36, f. 52. A Seraph or Seraphim has three pairs of wings. P. 36, f. 57.

CHERUBIM. P. 36, f. 53.

CHESS-ROOK, or CHESSE-ROOK. One of the pieces used in the game of Chess. P. 43, f. 49.

CHEVAL-TRAP. *See* Galtrap.

CHEVALIER. or KNIGHT ON HORSEBACK, completely armed. P. 36, f. 27. The Crest of Duff. Upon a wreath of the colours, on a horse in full gallop ar. bridled sa. and with mantling gu., semée of escutcheons or., each charged with a lion ramp. of the third, a chevalier armed cap-a-pie, on his helmet his crest viz. a demi lion ramp. gu., in his right hand a sword, on his sinister arm, a shield, charged as the escutcheons.

CHEVELEE. Streaming, i.e. the streams of light issuing from a comet. P. 23, f. 45.

CHEVERON, or CHEVRON. One of the honourable ordinaries, and occupies one third of the field, as Ar. a chev. gu. P. 15, f. 1.
Diminutives of the chev., are frequently met with, and, when placed at equal distances from each other, are blazoned Cheveronels, as, or three chevronels gu. f. 41. If borne in pairs they are termed Couple-close. f. 4, and when a chev. is placed between them, it may be blazoned either a chev. betw. two couple-closes, or a chev. cottised. f. 38.

CHEVERON, ABAISSE, or IN BASE. P. 15, f. 37.

CHEVRON, ARCHED. P. 16, f. 12.

— BETWEEN. P. 8, f. 21 ; P. 15, f. 38.

— BORDURED, or FIMBRIATED. P. 15, f. 8.

— and BORDURE. P. 16, f. 27.

— BRASED, or BRACED. The same as Interlaced. P. 15, f. 40.

— BRETTESSED. P. 15, f. 16.

— BRISSE. P. 16, f. 4.

— BURST, or SPLIT AT THE TOP. Also termed disjointed, or fracted. P. 16, f. 3.

— CHAMPAINE, or URDEE. P. 15, f. 20.

— CHARGED WITH ANOTHER. P. 15, f. 9.

— CHARGED WITH THREE ESCALLOPS, or ON A CHEVRON THREE ESCALLOPS. P. 16, f. 24.

— COTTISED. P. 15, f. 38.

CHEVRON, COUCHANT, or COUCHED. Is springing from the dexter, or sinister side. P. 16, f. 13.

— COUCHED. P. 16, f. 13.

— COUNTER-EMBATTLED. P. 15, f. 14.

— COUPED, or HUMETTEE. P. 15, f. 12.

— COUPLED, or PAIRED. Resembles a Fesse dancettée, but has only two dancets. P. 3, f. 45.

— CRENELLEE. P. 15, f. 13.

— DEBRUISED, or FRACTED. Also termed a broken chev. P. 16, f. 2.

— DEMI. May be either dexter, or sinister. P. 16, f. 6.

— DISJOINTED, or BRISSE. i.e. Burst. P. 16, f. 4.

— DISJOINTED and CROSSED. P. 16, f. 7.

— DOUBLE ESCARTELEE. P. 15, f. 29.

— DOVETAILED. P. 15, f. 24.

— EMBATTLED. P. 15, f. 13.

— EMBATTLED ARONDIE. P. 15, f. 22.

— EMBATTLED, COUNTER-EMBATTLED. P. 15, f. 14.

— EMBOWED. P. 15, f. 30.

— ENARCHED. P. 15, f. 32, and 33.

— ENGRAILED. P. 15, f. 5.

— ENHANCED. P. 15, f. 36.

— ENSIGNED. P. 15, f. 35.

— ECLATE. P. 16, f. 3.

— ESCARTELEE-DOUBLE, or GRIECE. P. 15, f. 29.

— and FESSE, or a Chevron surmounted with a fesse. P. 16, f. 19.

— FIMBRIATED, or BORDERED. P. 15, f. 8.

— FLAMANT. P. 15, f. 23.

— FLORY AT THE TOP. P. 16, f. 29.

— FRETTED WITH A FESSE. P. 16, f. 18.

— FRACTED. P. 16, f. 2.

— GRADY. formed of ascents like steps. P. 15, f. 15.

— GRADY ON BOTH SIDES. P. 15, f. 28.

— GRIECE. P. 15, f. 29,

— HACKED and HEWED. P. 15, f. 27.

— HUMETTEE, or COUPED. P. 15, f. 12.

— IN BASE. P. 15, f. 37.

— IN CHIEF. i.e. placed high up in field. P. 15, f. 36.

— IN POINT embowed. P. 15, f. 31.

— INARCHED. P. 15, f. 32, and 33.

— INDENTED. P. 15, f. 25.

— INDENTED EMBOWED. P. 15, f. 27.

— INVECKED. P. 15, f. 6.

— LOZENGY. P. 2, f. 45.

— MASCLE-HEAD. P. 16, f. 28.

— NEBULEE. P. 15, f. 26.

— ON A CHEV. P. 16, f. 24.

CHEVRON OPEN AT THE TOP, or BURST.
P. 16, f. 3.
— OPPRESSED, or SURMOUNTED. P. 16,
f. 19.
— PALETTED, or CHEV. and PALET CON-
JOINED. As two chevrons and palet
conjoined. P. 16, f. 8.
— PATTEE AT THE POINT. P. 15, f. 35.
— IN POINT EMBOWED. P. 15, f. 31.
— PER-PALE. P. 16, f. 25.
— PER-PALE and PER CHEVRON. P. 16,
f. 26.
— PIERCED WITH AN ARROW. P. 16,
f. 17.
— PIERCED WITH A BEND. P. 16, f. 16.
— PIERCED with a barrulet debruised
on the sinister side. P. 16, f. 15.
— PIERCED with a Fesse debruised on
the sinister side. P. 16, f. 22.
— and PILE COUNTERCHANGED. P. 6,
f. 32.
— POTENT. P. 15, f. 17.
— POTENT-COUNTER-POTENT. P. 15,
f. 18.
— POTENT, RINGED AT THE POINT.
More properly a Chev. potent at the
point and ringed. P. 15, f. 34.
— QUARTERLY. P. 16, f. 26.
— REMOVED. P. 16, f. 5.
— RECOURSIE, CLECHEE, or PERCEE.
P. 15, f. 7.
— REVERSED. P. 15, f. 43.
— ROMPU, double-downcet, double-
downsett, or Coppée. P. 16, f. 1.
— SEVERED, or BURST. P. 16, f. 3.
— SPLIT. P. 16, f. 3.
— SUPPORTED with a beam and Stand-
ard. P. 16, f. 9.
— SURMOUNTED. P. 16, f. 19.
— SURMOUNTED OF ANOTHER. P. 15,
f. 9.
— TRIPARTED, or TREBLE-PARTED.
P. 15, f. 39.
— URDEE. P. 15, f. 19.
— URDEE CHAMPAINED. P. 15, f. 20.
— VOIDED OF ANOTHER ENGRAILED.
P. 15, f. 10.
— VOIDED. Cannot be distinguished
from Couple-closes. P. 15, f. 4
and 11.
— PER or PER-CHEVRON, or PARTY PER
CHEVRON. Expresses the field or
any charge when divided by such a
line as helps to make the Chevron.
P. 2, f. 4, and P. 16, f. 30 and 31.
These lines are subject to all the accidental
forms of lines, as Per Chev. Engrailed, In-
vecked, Nebulée, Wavy, etc. Per. chev.
crenellée f. 32.
— PER AND PILE. P. 6, f. 43. Per Pale
and per chevron. P. 2, f. 8.

CHEVRONELLY. See CHEVRONNY.
CHEVRONEL, or CHEVERONEL. A diminutive of the Chevron. P. 15, f. 2.
Three cheveronels f. 41. Three cheveronels
braced f. 40.
CHEVRONELS, or CHEVERONELS BRACED,
or INTERLACED. P. 15, f. 40.
CHEVRONNY, CHEVERONNY, or CHEV-
ERONEE. A term to express the field
or any bearing, when divided into
equal parts by lines in the form of
chevrons, the number of pieces must
be named. P. 16, f. 33.
CHEVRONWAYS, or CHEVERONWISE.
When figures or charges are placed
in the position of the chevron.
CHEVRONS, TWO ARCHED, COUCHED,
springing from the dexter and sinister
sides of the shield. P. 16, f. 10.
CHEVRON'S, TWO ARCHED, COUCHED and
FRETTED. P. 16, f. 11.
CHEVRONS, TWO COUCHED, DEXTER and
SINISTER. P. 15, f. 45.
CHEVRONS, TWO IN COUNTERPOINT.
P. 15, f. 44.
CHEVRONS, TWO IN FRET. P. 15, f. 42.
CHEVRONS, COUCHED, FRETTED and
COUPED. P. 16, f. 14.
CHEVRONS THREE. P. 16, f. 23.
CHEVIN. See CHUB.
CHEWEROND. A Cheveron.
CHEYNE. See CHENE.
CHEYNYD. Same as chained.

CHIEF, FROM THE FRENCH CHEF. Which
means the head or uppermost position
of the shield. It is one of the honourable Ordinaries and occupies one third
of the upper part of the field. P. 12,
f. 1.
Gu. a Chief or. The Arms of Hampstead.
The Chief may be of any of the forms of
lines used in heraldry.
When the Chief is Charged with any figure,
in blazon it is said to be "On a Chief" P. 12,
f. 2. But when any charge is placed in the
upper part of the shield, in the place of the
Chief it is said to be "In Chief" f. 3.
CHIEF AJOURE. P. 22, f. 9.
— ANGLED. P. 12, f. 20.
— ARCHED. f. 37.
— ARCHED DOUBLE. f. 38.
— BEVELED. f. 22.
— BORDERED, or BORDURED. f. 24.
— CHAMPAINE. f. 8.
— CHAMPOURNET. f. 39. Champourn-
ated. f. 40.
— CHAPPE. f. 43.
— CHARGED. f. 25, 28, 33 and 45.
— CHARGED WITH A CHAPOURNET.
f. 39.
— CHAUSSE. P. 22, f. 8.

CHIEF CONVEX. P. 12, f. 37.
— COUPED. f. 23.
— COUPED-BEVELWISE. f. 26.
— COUSU. f. 24. Same as Rempli.
— COUVERT. f. 29.
— CRENELLEE. f. 14.
— DANCETTE. f. 7.
— DOVETAILED. f. 9.
— WITH ONE DOVETAIL. f. 16.
— EMBATTLED. f. 14.
— EMBATTLED-REBATED. f. 8.
— WITH ONE EMBATTLEMENT. f. 18.
— ENMANCHE. f. 43.
— ENGRAILED. f. 4.
— ESCARTELEE, or one Embattlement in a chief. f. 17.
— FLECKED, or ARCHED. f. 37.
— FLORY-COUNTERFLORY. f. 44.
— WITH FILLET. f. 33.
— INCLAVE. f. 36.
— INDENT, or OF ONE INDENT. f. 27.
— INDENTED. f. 13.
— INVECKED, or INVECTED. f. 5.
— LAMBEAUX, or LABLE. f. 16.
— LOWERED, or REMOVED. f. 31.
— NEBULEE, or NEBULY. f. 11.
— NOWED. f. 19.
— PATTEE, or DOVETAIL. f. 9.
— WITH ONE PATTEE, DOVETAIL, or LABLE. f. 16.
— PER-FESSE. f. 30.
— PIERCED. f. 42.
— POINT IN POINT. f. 41.
— POTENT, or COUNTER-POTENT. f. 10.
— QUARTERLY. f. 10.
— QUARTERLY, Flory-counterflory at the bottom. f. 44.
— RAYONNE, RAYED, or RAISIE. f. 12.
— RECT-ANGLED. f. 20.
— REMOVED. f. 31.
— REMPLI. f. 24.
— REVESTU. f. 34.
— SHAPOURNETT. f. 39.
— SOUSTENU, or SOUTENU. f. 33.
— SURMOUNTED. f. 33.
— UNDEE. f. 6.
— URDEE. f. 8.
— VESTU, or REVESTU. f. 34.
— VESTU-SINISTER. f. 35.
— WAVY, or UNDEE. f. 6.

CHIEF POINTS. The Chief, or upper part of the shield contains three points, viz. The Dexter chief point; The middle chief point; and Sinister chief point; as P. 1, marked A.B.C.

CHILD'S HEAD, couped enwrapped about the neck with a snake. P. 36, f. 49.

CHIMERA. A fabulous beast. P. 26, f. 58.

CHIMERICAL. A term applied to any imaginary figure.

CHINA COCOA-TREE. P. 45, f. 53.

CHINESE-DRAGON. P. 25, f. 7.

CHIPPING AXE. See AXE.

CHISEL, or CHIZZEL. A sharp cutting instrument. P. 41, f. 30.

CHIVES-TIPT. Part of a flower sometimes described in Heraldry like the seeds of a rose.

CHOUGH. See CORNISH CHOUGH.

CHRISTED-IMBATTLED. See IMBATTLED-CHRISTED.

CHRISTIFERUS. The bearer of the Standard in which was displayed the figure of Christ on the Cross.

CHRONEL. See CRONEL.

CHRYSTALS. Used in blazoning the arms of Peers instead of pearl for Argent.

CHUB, or CHEVIN. A Fish. P. 32, f. 34a.

CHURCH, and parts of Churches are met with in Armour. P. 23, f. 24, and f. 23.

CHURCH BELL. See BELLS.

CHURCH-SPIRE, or STEEPLE. P. 32, f. 23.

CIMETER. Same as Scymetar. P. 38, f. 22.

CIMIER. Crest.

CINABAR, or CINABRE. Gules.

CINCTURED. Girt, or encircled.

CINNAMON LEAVES. P. 44, f. 36.

CINOPLE, or SINOPLE. Vert.

CINQUEFOIL, CINQFOIL, or QUINTERFOIL. Five leaved grass. P. 44, f. 16, No. 4. Cinquefoil pierced. f. 17, No. 2.

CINQUE-FOYLE: The same as Cinquefoil.

CIRCELEE, as a CROSS SARCELLY, or SARCELLE. P. 7, f. 20.

CIRCLE OF CHAINS. See CHAINS.

CIRCLE OF GLORY. The nimbus or ring of light placed round, or over the head of Saints, etc.
The Holy Lamb is always represented with a circle of glory as P. 29, f. 4. The Sept-Insular Lion is represented with a Glory as P. 26, f. 47. See also the Bull with a circle of glory ppr., the Crest of the Butchers' Company. P. 28, f. 31. A Circle of Glory also termed radiant or rayonnant as St. John's head, in a charger and represented as P. 35, f. 33.

CIRCLE OF GOLD. See CROWNS.

CIRCLE OF THE ZODIAC, or a FESSE HEMISPHERE. P. 3, f. 29.

CIRCLED, or SURROUNDED WITH RAYS. P. 23, f. 36.

CIRCULAR WREATH, and an OVAL WREATH. P. 43, f. 45.

CIRCULET. Coronet, which see.

CIRCUMFLEXANT. Bent, Bowed round, or about.

CITADEL. A Citadel with two towers, ports shut. P. 23, f. 14.

CITRON-TREE. Same as Apple Tree.

CIVET CAT. P. 28, f. 28.

CIVIC-CAP. The State Cap of the Lord Mayor of London. P. 40, f. 56.

CIVIC CROWN, wreath or garland composed of oak leaves and acorns. P. 24, f. 39.

CLAM. An Escallop.

CLARENCEUX. The title of one of the Kings of Arms.

CLARENDON, CLARICIMBAL, CLAVECIMBAL. See CLARION.

CLARICORD, CLARION, or REST. See CLARION.

CLARINE. A term to express a collar of Bells round the necks of beasts, the same as gorged with a collar of bells.

CLARION, SUFFLUE, CLARICORD, or REST. P. 43, f. 27 and 28.

This is by some supposed to denote the rest for the lance, but this cannot be the case as Clarions are found in armoury before the rest for the lance was invented. In fact the very name sufflue, and clarion, point to some kind of wind instrument.

CLARIONET. A wind instrument. P. 36, f. 3.

CLASPED. See CONJOINED.

CLAVECIMBAL. Same as Clarion.

CLAVED, or CLAVIED. A cross composed of three double-warded keys, with one bow. P. 42, f. 11.

CLAYMORE. A sword, The Highland broadsword.

CLECHE, CLECHEE, CLESCHEE, or CLOCHE. An ordinary so perforated that the chief substance is taken from it, leaving nothing but the edges. P. 7, f. 19.

CLEFT. Split.

CLEG-GOOSE. See BARNACLE GOOSE.

CLENCHED. See CLINCHED.

CLESCHEE. See CLECHE.

CLIMANT. A goat in the same position as rampant, is said to be climbing or climant.

CLINCHED. The hand shut, or grasping anything, is termed clenched. P. 36, f. 9; P. 40, f. 36.

CLIPPING. Equivalent to clasping.

CLOCK. As in the arms of the Clock Makers Company. P. 39, f. 43.

CLOSE. A term applied to all birds of flight, when the wings are closed, as an eagle close. P. 33, f. 1.

It also denotes a helmet with the visor down as P. 24, f. 12.

CLOSE COUPED. Cut off close to the head, no part of the neck being left, as a Boar's head couped close. P. 29, f. 32.

CLOSE-COUPLE, or COUPLE-CLOSE. P. 15, f. 3.

CLOSE-GAUNTLETS. Gauntlets with immoveable fingers. P. 38, f. 11.

CLOSE-GIRT. Said of figures habited, whose clothes are tied about the middle.

CLOSE-SEJANT. Setting together.

CLOSET. A diminutive of the bar, being one half its size. P. 5, f. 4.

CLOSETTED. The same as cottised. P. 5, f. 9.

CLOSETTY. Barry of many pieces, the number must be named.

CLOSING-NAIL. P. 41, f. 31.

CLOSING-TONGS. A tool used by Founders, and is part of their Crest. P. 41, f. 23.

CLOSS, or CLOSSE. See CLOSE.

CLOTH, a piece of. P. 40, f. 46.

CLOTHED. See VESTED.

CLONE. Nailed. See LATTISED.

CLOVE. A spice, as borne in the Grocer's Arms. P. 45, f. 12.

CLOVER. A genus of trefoil. P. 45, f. 27.

CLOUDS. Very common bearing in Coat Armour, particularly with devices issuing therefrom. P. 23, f. 28 and 31.

CLUB, and SPIKED CLUB. Frequently borne in the hand of savages. P. 35, f. 24, 25 and 26; also P. 41, f. 48.

ar. a club erect in pale sa. Smith of Surrey.

CLUSTER. Applied to fruits and flowers growing naturally in clusters.

CLYMANT. See CLIMANT.

COACH. As borne in the Arms of the Coach Makers Company. P. 41, f. 51.

CO-AMBULANT. Passant, or walking together.

COAT OP ARMS, or ARMORIAL BEARINGS. Consist in the shield and its external ornaments. The term Coat of Arms is however more applicable to the surcoat or mantle upon which the armorial bearings were formerly depicted.

COB-FISH, or SEA COB. P. 32, f. 13.

COBWEB and SPIDER. P. 22, f. 5.

Cock. The emblem of vigilance, virility, and bravery. Is always depicted as a Dunghill Cock, if not expressed to the contrary.

When the legs, spurs, comb and wattles are of a different tincture from the Cock, or from each other, they must each be expressed. And the Cock is said to be armed, spurred, crested or combed, jelloped, or wattled of such a colour. P. 3½, f. 1. A Game Cock. f. 2.

Cockatrice, or Cockatryce. An imaginary monster, which is depicted with the head, comb, wattles, and legs of the Cock, and the body, wings, and tail of a Dragon. P. 27, f. 15. A Cockatrice displayed. f. 16. Cockatrice's head wings endorsed couped. f. 17. A Cockatrice's head couped betw. two wings. f. 18.

A Cockatrice in Christian art is the emblem of sin.

Cocke. A Chess-rook.

Cockers. High shoes. See Brogue.

Cockle-shell. See Escallop.

Cocquel. An Escallop.

Cocoa Tree. P. 45, f. 53.

Co-Erected. Set up together, or erected side by side.

Cod. A Fish. P. 32, f. 22.

Codded. Beans, Pease, etc. borne in the Cod, or Pod. P. 44, f. 59.

Cœur. The heart. For Semée of hearts the term Semée de Cœur is sometimes used.

Cœur-Point. The Fesse-point.

Cœur, Party in Cœur. An irregular partition, formed by a short line of partition in pale in the centre of the escutcheon, which extends but a little way, much short of the top and bottom, and is there met by other lines.

Cognisance, Cognizance, or Cognicanze. See Badge.

Coif de mailles. A hood which wraps round the neck and head. P. 39, f. 20, No. 2.

Coil. A Coil of Flax. P. 43, f. 13. as borne in the Crest of Washbourne.

Coins. The Heraldry that may be learned from British and Foreign Coins is of the utmost value, since it is always historically correct.

Coiled. Turned round, or twisted; as an Adder coiled. P. 30, f. 42.

Cointise. A covering for the helmet. P. 25a, f. 9. See Contoise.

Cokke. Ancient orthography for Cock.

Collar. An ornament for the neck, worn by Knights, such as the Collar of the Garter etc. P. 24, f. 7.

Collar of, S.S. P. 24, f. 29.

The collar of S, or " of Esses," as it is written in many records, was a Lancastrian livery, and of the institution of Henry of Bolingbroke. This Collar is still worn by the Heralds, by the Lord Mayor of London, and by the Lord Chief Justices, and some others of the Judges. f. 29.

Collared. A term applied to animals, when they have a plain collar round the neck; if a line or chain is attached to the collar, it is termed collared and lined, or chained. P. 18, f. 21.

If any animal has any kind of Coronet round its neck, it is termed " Gorged," as a Demi lion ramp. gorged with a ducal coronet. P. 26, f. 31 ; P. 19, f. 21.

Collar-point. The position of a charge when placed betw. the upper portions of a saltire. P. 20, f. 38.

Collateral-position, or side by side. The earliest way of placing the arms of a husband and wife was in two separate shields placed by the side of each other.

Collaterally disposed. Things set side by side; and if erect are termed Co-erectant, or Co-erected.

College. P. 23, f. 22. As borne in the arms of the College of Williamsburg.

College of Arms, or Herald's College. An ancient Royal Corporation, endowed with certain priviliges by the Kings of this Realm.

The Corporation consists of Three Kings of Arms, Six Heralds, and Four Pursuivants. See Herald's College. Arms of the College ar. a cross gu. betw. four doves, the dexter wings expanded and inverted az. See Title Page.

Collying. A term used by Falconers to denote the motion of the head made by an eagle or hawk when about to take flight.

Colombs. Doves.

Colorys. See Colours.

Colours. Naval and Military Flags. The colours of the Cavalry are styled " Standards."

Colours. There are seven used in Coat Armour, viz. Gules, Azure, Vert, Sable, Purpure, Sanguine, and Tenne. See Tinctures, and P. 1.

Colt. A young horse. See Horse. P. 27, f. 30.

Columbine. A flower, depicted in Heraldry as P. 44, f. 23. (P. 31, f. 19 Branches of Columbine.)

COLUMN, or PILLAR. *See* P. 43, f. 50.
A Column ducally crowned and a Column envel/oped with a snake. A broken Column and a Winged Column. f. 51. This last is sometimes, though not correctly, called a flying column.

COMB. An instrument with teeth. *See* P. 4, f. 31, and P. 40, f. 48.

COMB IN A HEAD OF HAIR. P. 40, f. 48. A Comb in the hand of a Mermaid. P. 35, f. 12.

COMB. *See* JERSEY-COMB. P. 40, f. 12.

COMB. A Curry-comb. P. 37, f. 57.

COMB AND WATTLES OF A COCK. *See* COCK.

COMBATANT. Fighting, or Ramp. face to face. P. 26, f. 16.

COMBEL. *See* FILLET.

COMET, or BLAZING-STAR. P. 23, f. 45.

COMMISSE CROSS. A Cross Tan. P. 9, f. 30.

COMMIXT. Placed indiscriminately, same as Semée.

COMMONWEALTH. Banner of. P. 31, f. 29.

COMMUNION CUP, or CHALICE. P. 42, f. 26.

COMMUNITY ARMS OF. *See* ARMS OF COMMUNITY.

COMPARTMENT. A kind of carved ornament, upon which the supporters stand.
It is known to Herald-Painters by the term "PEDESTAL." The Label with motto is generally suspended from it. P. 21, f. 21.

COMPASSES. As in the joiners Arms. P. 41, f. 31.

COMPASSED, or ENCOMPASSED. Surrounded.

COMPLEMENT. A term used to signify the full moon as P. 23, f. 37. The moon in her complement.

COMPLEXED. The serpents in the Caduceus. P. 30, f. 56. are sometimes so termed.

COMPON. *See* CAMP.

COMPONED. Same as Gobony.

COMPONEE, COMPONY, GOBONY, or GOBONE. Said of an Ordinary composed of squares in one row of two tinctures alternately placed. P. 4, f. 42; P. 20, f. 9. If there be two rows it is called Counter-Compony, or Company counter-company. P. 4, f. 43. If there are more than two rows it is termed Checky. f. 44.

COMPOUNDED ARMS. Arms formed by the Combination of two or more distinct coats, in such a manner as to produce a single composition.

CONCAVED. Same as Arched. P. 12, f. 37.

CONCESSION ARMS OF. *See* ARMS OF CONCESSION.

CONE. A solid body tapering to a point from a circular base. P. 41, f. 42. See also FIR-CONE. P. 44, f. 54.

CONEY. *See* RABBIT.

CONFRONTE. Facing each other, Combatant, or Respecting each other. P. 26, f. 16, and P. 31, f. 27.

CONGER-EEL. *See* P. 32, f. 5, and f. 41.

CONJOINED. Linked together. P. 37, f. 35 and 36 ; P. 26, f. 12.

CONJOINED IN LURE. A term applied to wings, joined together, with the tips downwards. P. 33, f. 28.

CONJUNCT. Same as Conjoined, or Connected.

CONSPICUOUS, or CONSPICTIANT. Terms anciently used to express any bearing or charge conspicuously placed over another.

CONTOISE. A scarf, worn loose and flowing, attached to the helm with the crest, but discontinued after the middle of the fourteenth century. P. 25a, f. 9.

CONTOURNE. A term applied to animals turned towards the sinister. P. 22, f. 12; P. 26, f. 18.

CONTRA. Contrary. *See* CONTRE.

CONTRA-NUAGE. Same as Counter-Scallopée, or Papellonnée. P. 18, f. 7.

CONTRARY COONYED. An ancient term for Gyronny.

CONTRARY BOWED. Bending in a contrary direction. P. 30, f. 26.

CONTRARY COMPOSED. Contrary placed, or opposite each other.

CONTRARY DEBRUISED. Is the bowing and embowing of serpents, when the head or tail turns under in a contrary direction one to the other. P. 30, f. 35.

CONTRARY FLEXED. Bent in opposite directions.

CONTRARY IMBOWED, or EMBOWED. *See* COUNTER EMBOWED. P. 11, f. 22.

CONTRARY INVECKED. When the upper and under parts are both invecked. P. 3, f. 3.

CONTRARY POSED. Placed opposite, or opposed to each other. P. 26, f. 16.

CONTRARY REFLEXED. Turning in a contrary direction.

CONTRARY URDEE. When the upper and under parts are both Urdée. P. 17, f. 19.

CONTRE, or COUNTER. Applied to animals as Counter· passant. P. 26, f. 36. Also to ordinaries when the upper and under parts are the same, as counter embattled. P. 3, f. 9.

CONTRE BANDE, or CONTRE BANE. Same as P. 18, f. 40.

CONTRE-BRETESSE. Embattled.

CONTRE-CHANGED. Same as Counterchanged.

CONTRE-COMPONE. Same as Compony counter-compony. P. 17, f. 41.

CONTRE-ERMINE. Same as Ermines.

CONTRE-ESCARTELE. Same as counter quartered.

CONTRE-FACE. Same as barre per pale counterchanged. P. 5, f. 13.

CONTRE-PALE. Same as paly of six per-fesse counterchanged. P. 14, f. 33.

CONTRE-POINTE. When two chev. meet in fesse point. P. 15, f. 44.

CONTRE-POSE. Counterplaced, or opposite each other.

CONTRE-POTENT. Same as counter potent.

CONTRE-TREVIS. An ancient term for party per fesse.

CONTRE-VAIRE. Same as counter vair. P. 1.

CONVEX, or CONVEXED. Bowed, or arched. P. 19, f. 15.

COOPED. See COUPED.

COORLET, See CUIRASS.

COOT. A water-fowl. P. 34, f. 14.

COPPEE, COPPED, or COPPEDEE. See chev. double downset, coppée, or Rompu. P. 16, f. 1.

COPPER. An instrument used by wire-drawers, and borne in the arms of their Company. P. 42, f. 36.

COPPER CAKE. A Pellet, or roundle depicted copper colour.

CORACLE. A boat made of a wicker frame covered with the hide of a beast. P. 38, f. 37. The arms of the " See of the Isles " is az. in base waves of the Sea St. Columba praying in a Coracle, ppr. ; in dexter chief a star ar.

CORBIE, CORBEAU, or CORBIE-CROW. A Raven. P. 33, f. 52.

CORDED. Banded with cords. P. 40, f. 20.

CORDED CROSS. P. 7, f. 18.

CORDON. Cords or strings with tassels.

CORLED. See COILED.

CORMORANT. A bird. P. 34, f. 34.

CORN, EARS OF. P. 45, f. 13.

CORNER CAPS. See CAP.

CORNET. A musical instrument. P. 43, f. 21, No. 4.

CORNISH CHOUGH. A species of Crow with red legs. P. 33, f. 54.

CORNISH CHOUGH, HATCHING. P. 31, f. 20.

CORNISHED, or CORNICED. A Cross Cornished. P. 10, f. 23.

CORNUCOPIA. The horn of Plenty represented as overflowing with corn, fruit, etc. P. 43, f. 1.

CORONAL. See CRONEL.

CORONATED. Adorned with a Coronet, as a Fesse Coronated. P. 3, f. 27.

CORONET. A species of velvet cap, turned up with ermine, and surrounded by a circle of gold, by the various forms of which latter the degree of the wearer is denoted. P. 24, f. 2 to 5, and 42 to 46. Coronet of Prince Albert. P. 25a, f. 3 and 4.

I. Coronet of the Prince of Wales, is composed of a circle of gold richly chased; on the edge four crosses pattée between as many fleur-de-lis ; from the two centre crosses an arch, surmounted with a mound and cross, the whole adorned with pearls ; within the coronet, a crimson cap, turned up ermine. P. 24, f. 2.

II. Younger Sons of Her Majesty, a circle of gold richly chased having upon its upper edge, four crosses pattée and fleur-de-lis, a crimson cap, turned up ermine with a gold tassel at top. f. 3.

III. The Princess Royal, and Younger Sisters ; the same as the last, but with two crosses pattée, four fleur-de-lis, and two strawberry leaves. f. 4.

IV. Nephews of the Blood Royal ; differs from the Young Sons by having crosses pattée and strawberry leaves placed alternately. f. 5.

V. Duke, is composed of a circle of gold richly chased (not jewelled), with eight strawberry leaves of equal height, above the rim, a cap of crimson velvet, turned up ermine ; on the top a gold tassel. f. 42.

VI. Marquess ; like the preceding, but with four strawberry leaves and as many pearls, upon short points all of equal height, with cap and tassel as before. f. 43.

VII. Earl ; is the same, heightened up with eight long points ; on the top of which are as many pearls, the interstices being adorned with strawberry leaves, whose apices do not raise so high as the points. f. 44.

VIII. Viscount ; is a circle of gold richly chased with cap etc. as above, having sixteen pearls on the rim, seven of which only appear in the representation. f. 45

IX. Baron; is composed of a plain circle of gold, supporting six pearls, four of which are seen in the drawing; cap, etc. f. 46. This coronet, first granted by Charles ii, before whose time the Barons wore a scarlet cap turned up ermine and on the top a tassel of gold.

CORONET DUCAL. *See* DUCAL CORONET.

CORONET EASTERN, MURAL, and NAVAL, etc. *See* CROWNS.

CORONETS OF THE FRENCH NOBILITY. *See* FRANCE CORONETS OF.

CORONETTE. Adorned with a coronet, as a bend coronette. P. 18, f. 28.

CORPORATE BODIES ARMS OF. *See* ARMS OF COMMUNITY.

COST. A diminutive of the bend, one fourth of its breadth. P. 17, f. 4. When borne in pairs are called cottises. f. 31. Four costs. P. 19, f. 31.

COTE-ARMURE. The coat or vesture on which the arms were exhibited.

COTE-HARDIE. A Surcoat.

COTICE, or COUSTE. A diminutive of the bend; also a French term to express an escutcheon divided bendways into many equal parts; the same as bendy.

COTICED, COTISED, COTTISED, or COT-IZED. A term to express the diminutives of the Bend, Chevron, Fesse, and Pale. When one of these diminutives is borne on each side its proper Ordinary, that Ordinary is blazoned Cottised. *See* P. 5, f. 9; P. 15, f. 38; P. 17, f. 31. If two are borne on each side, it is termed double cottised. P. 5, f. 10. If three, treble cottised. f. 11. If Cottises are borne without the ordinary, their number must be named, and they are blazoned by the terms Barrulet, Couple-close, Endorse, etc.

COTOYE. Same as Cottised.

COTTISE. *See* COST, and COTICED.

COTTISED, COTTICED, or COTIZED. *See* COTICED, and P. 5, f. 9.

COTTISED DOUBLE, and TREBLE. P. 5, f. 10 and 11.

COTTIZE. Same as Cost.

COTTON HANKS, or BUNDLES OF COTTON. P. 40, f. 5.

COTTON TREE. As borne in the Arms of Arkwright. P. 45, f. 54.

COUCHANT, COUCHE, or COUCHED. Lying down, applied to Lions, Tigers, etc. P. 26, f. 45.

COUE, or COUEE. Coward; a Lion or other beast having his tail between his hind legs. P. 26, f. 8.

COULOMBS. Doves.

COULTER OF A PLOUGH. P. 39, f. 10, No. 2.

COULTER. Run through the calf of a man's leg, is borne in the arms of Ball. P. 36, f. 24.

COUNTER. When applied to two animals it signifies that they are turned in contrary directions, as two lions counter passant. P. 26, f. 36. When applied to ordinaries it denotes that the upper and under parts are the same, as a bend embattled counter embattled. P. 17, f. 17.

COUNTER-BARRE. A term to express bend sinister per bend counterchanged. P. 18, f. 40.

COUNTER-BARRY, or CONTREFASCE. The same as Barry per pale counterchanged. P. 5, f. 13.

COUNTER-BATTLED. Embattled on both sides. P. 15, f. 14; P. 3, f. 9.

COUNTER-BENDY. Same as Contrebande. P. 18, f. 40.

COUNTER-BILLETTEE. A division of the field, ordinary, or charge, by lines crossing each other, so as to form the compartments into the shape of billets, as a Bend billettée counterbillettée. P. 17, f. 42.

COUNTER-CAMP, or CAMPEE. The same as Counter-gobony. P. 17, f. 41.

COUNTERCHANGED. When the shield or any bearing is divided into two or more parts, each part having some charge upon it, which is of the alternate tincture. P. 2, f. 39, 49 and 50. P. 5, f. 44. P. 14, f. 29.

COUNTER-CARTELE, or CONTRECARTELE. Also termed contraquadripartitus; The same as counter-quartered, or quarterly quartered; that is, when the grand quarters are quartered.

COUNTER-CHEVERONNY. A division cheveronways. P. 16, f. 33.

COUNTER-COLERYS, or GOLORYS. The same as counterchanged.

COUNTER-COLOURED. *See* COUNTER-CHANGED.

COUNTER-COMPONEE, or GOBONY. Consists of two rows of chequers. P. 4, f. 43.

COUNTER-COUCHANT. When animals are lying with their heads in contrary directions.

COUNTER-CROSSED. P. 22, f. 22.

COUNTER-COURRANT. Animals running in contrary directions.

COUNTER-DEBRUISED. When either the head or tail of a serpent, in the bowing, or embowing, is turned under, in a contrary direction one to the other. P. 30, f. 26.

K

COUNTER-EMBATTLED, IMBATTLED, or BATTLED. When both top and bottom are embattled. P. 3, f. 9.

— EMBOWED. When the arm is bent with the elbow towards the sinister. P. 36, f. 20 and 21.

— EMBOWED. Bent contrary ways one to another. P. 36, f. 18.

— ERMINE. Ermines. P. 1.

— ESCARTELE. See COUNTER-CARTELE.

— FACED, or CONTREFACE. Same as barry per pale counterchanged. P. 5, f. 13.

— FESSY, or BARRY PER PALE COUNTERCHANGED. P. 5, f. 13.

— FLEURY, or COUNTER-FLEURIE. See COUNTER-FLORY.

— FLORY, COUNTER-FLEURY, CONTREFLEURE, or CONTREFLEURONNE. When the edges of anything are charged with fleur-de-lis, alternately placed, as the tressure flory counter-flory. P. 35, f. 16. See P. 3, f. 20. P. 17, f. 14. A Fesse and Bend Flory Counter-flory.

— FLOWERED, or FLURTY. Same as Counter-flory, or floretty.

— GOBONY. Same as Counter-Compony. P. 4, f. 43.

— NAIANT. Fishes swimming in opposite directions. P. 32, f. 16.

— NEBULEE. When both edges of a Fesse, Bend, etc., are nebuled. P. 3, f. 4; P. 15, f. 26.

— NUAGE. P. 18, f. 7.

— PALE, or PALY OF SIX COUNTERCHANGED. P. 22, f. 42.

— PALED. Is when the escutcheon is divided into pales parted per-fesse, the two colours being counterchanged so that the upper and lower are of different colours. P. 22, f. 42.

— PASSANT. Walking in contrary directions, as two lions passant counter-passant. P. 26, f. 36.

— PENDANT. Hanging on each side.

— POINTED. Same as counter-point. P. 15, f. 44.

— POTENT. One of the Furs. P. 1. Also termed Cuppa. P. 22, f. 40.

— POTENTE QUARTERED, or QUARTERLY QUARTERED. Also termed Contre-cartele. Same as counter-escartele. See COUNTER-CARTELE.

— QUARTERED. As Quarterly, quartered. P. 7, f. 11.

— RAGULED. Raguled on both sides. P. 17, f. 26.

COUNTER-SALIENT, or CONTRE SAILLANT. When two animals are borne, leaping contraryways from each other, as Two Foxes counter-salient in saltier. P. 29, f. 10.

COUNTER-SCALLOPEE, or SCALLOPED. Covered with escallop-shells, laid like the scales of fish. P. 18, f. 7.

COUNTER-TRIANGLE. Same as barry indented. P. 2, f. 36.

COUNTER-TRIPPANT, or TRIPPING. A term applied to all animals of the deer kind when walking in opposite directions. P. 28, f. 53.

COUNTER-VAIR, VAIRY, or VERRY. One of the Furs, depicted as at P. 1.

COUNTERLY. A term used by some authors to express the field divided into two equal parts; the same as party per pale, or per-pale.

COUNTESS. The title and rank of the wife of an Earl, she is styled "My Lady" is "Right Honourable" and her Coronet the same as her husband's.

COUPE. The same as Couped.

COUPEE-CLOSE. Same as Couple-close.

COUPE PARTED, or COUPED BIPARTED. When anything is cut off, or notched, shewing two projecting pieces; but contrary to what is called erased, which is jagged by being torn off.

COUPED, or COUPY. A term to express the head or limbs of men, animals, or any charge when evenly cut off, as P. 20, f. 22; P. 26, f. 30; P. 27, f. 39.

COUPED AT THE SHOULDERS. P. 36, f. 45.

COUPED BELOW THE SHOULDERS. P. 36, f. 37.

COUPED CLOSE. Cut off close to the head. P. 29, f. 32.

COUPED FITCHED. P. 9, f. 15.

COUPE, or COUPEE. Couped.

COUPLE. Used instead of pair.

COUPLE-CLOSE. A diminutive of the cheveron P. 15, f. 3 and always borne in pairs. f. 4, and f. 38.

COUPLED. A term applied to charges borne in pairs, joined or linked together as two annulets coupled, or conjoined. P. 37, f. 35.

COUPLES. As borne on the Supporters of Lord Hindlip. P. 43, f. 59.

COUPY. Couped.

COURANT, CURSANT, or CURRENT. Terms for a horse, buck, greyhound, etc. borne running, they are also said to be in full course. P. 19, f. 28; P. 21, f. 44; P. 28, f. 46; P. 29, f. 5.

COURBE. Embowed.

COURLETT. Same as Cuirass.

COURONE, or COURONNE. Crowned.

COURSANT. Same as Courant.

COURSE, IN HIS, or IN COURSE. See COURANT.

COURSIE, or RECOURSIE. P. 7, f. 19.

COURTESY, TITLE OF. A nominal degree of Rank, conceeded by Royal Grace and sanctioned by usage to some of the children of the Peers. The term is especially applicable to the "Second Titles" of their Fathers, that are thus borne by "Courtesy" by the eldest sons of Dukes, Marquesses, and Earls.

COURVUNE. Ducally crowned.

COUSU, or COUSUE. According to Edmondson the same as rempli. By others used to express any of the ordinaries when borne of metal with metal, or colour with colour. P. 7, f. 32.

COUTEAU-SWORD. A Knife sword.

COUTEL. A military implement which served both for a knife and a dagger.

COUTERE. A piece of armour which covered the elbow.

COUVERT. Shadowed, or partly covered with the foot of hangings or tapestry. P. 12, f. 29.

COVERED. A term applicable to any bearing with a cover, as a covered cup. P. 42, f. 25.

COVERT. Partly covered.

COVERTANT. When charges are borne side by side, so that part of one is seen projecting before the other; they are termed Covertant, or Coerectant.

COW. Borne by the name of Cowell, Vach, etc. P. 28, f. 29.

COWD. See COWARD.

COWARD, COWARDISED, or COWARDLY. Applied to lions, etc., when the tail is represented hanging down and passing between the hind legs. P. 26, f. 8.

COWL. A Monk's hood. P. 36, f. 31.

CRAB. A shell-fish. P. 32, f. 52.

CRABS, or WILD APPLES. Borne by Crabb. M.D. Norwich 1664.

CRABBET. See HABICK.

CRAMP, or CRAMPOON. An iron bent at each extremity used for the purpose of strengthening buildings, and are generally borne in pairs. P. 41, f. 6.

CRAMPETTE, CRAMPIT, CHAPE, or BOTEROLL. The steel mounting at the bottom of the scabbard. P. 37, f. 33.

CRAMPONEE, and TOURNEE. P. 11, f. 39.

CRAMPOON. See CRAMP.

CRANCELIN. The chaplet that crosses the shield of Saxony, as in the arms of the Prince of Wales. P. 16, f. 40.

CRANE. A bird with long neck and legs. P. 34, f. 8.

CRAWLING, GLIDING, or CREEPING. As a serpent gliding. P. 30, f. 47. Extended Crawling, etc. f. 53.

CRAWFISH, CREFISH, or CREVICE. A fish represented like a shrimp as P. 32, f. 40a. Not to be blazoned hauriant as fish that have fins but upright.

CRENEAUX, or EMMANCHE. Terms for Embattled, or Crenellée.

CRENELLA, or CRENELLEE. Embattled, or Kernelled. P. 3, f. 8.

CRENELLATED. Same as Embattled.

CREQUER PLANT, or CREQUIER. The wild plum. P. 44, f. 51. By some it is termed "seven-branched candlestick of the temple." Crequer plant of seven branches eradicated, as borne by the family of Girflet.

CREQUIER. See CREQUER.

CRESCENT. A half-moon with the horns turned upwards. P. 23, f. 38. If the horns are turned towards the dexter, it is termed an INCRESCENT. If the horns are to the sinister, a DECRESCENT. P. 23, f. 38. When the horns are turned down it is termed a CRESCENT REVERSED. Three Crescents interlaced are borne by the name of Munnings. f. 41. Four Crescents interlaced. f. 40. A Decrescent and Increscent circled. f. 36.

CRESCENTED. A cross having a crescent at each end. P. 10, f. 31 and 32.

CRESSET, or CRESSI. A Fire-Beacon. P. 37, f. 2.

CREST. Named by the French Cimier, from Cime, the top or apex; by the Italians Cimiero; by the Latins, Crista, the comb of a cock. A figure set upon a wreath, coronet, or chapeau, placed above the Helmet. The manner of placing the Crest differs according to the rank of the bearer. By all below the Peerage, it is placed above the Helmet, the latter rests on the shield. Peers carry the coronet on the shield, and the Helmet and Crest above; but in both cases the Helmet very frequently is altogether omitted. See examples of Crests, Helmets, etc. P. 11, f. 21; P. 12, f. 21; P. 13, f. 21; P. 15, f. 21; P. 18, f. 21. Ladies are not entitled to wear Crests. But as an appendage to sepulchral monuments Crests are placed beneath the head of the armed effigy; are attached to the helmet, or are carved as the feet of the recumbent figures.

CREST-CORONET. See DUCAL-CORONET.

CRESTED. A term used for the comb of a Cock, Cockatrice, etc.

CREVICE. *See* CRAWFISH.

CRI-DE-GUERRE. War-cry; termed by the Scots slughorn, or Slogan; any sentence, or word becoming a general cry throughout the army on its approach to battle.

CRIMEAN MEDAL is silver, the ribbon blue with yellow edges; separate clasps for Alma, Balaklava, Inkerman, Sebastopol. P. 25, f. 18. *See* MEDAL.

CRINED. When the hair of a man, or woman, or the mane of a horse, Unicorn, etc., are borne of a different tincture, from the other part, they are termed Crined of such a metal, or colour.

CRIPPING IRONS, or GLAZIER'S CRIPPING IRONS. Same as Glazier's nippers. P. 41, f. 7.

CROCODILE. A genus of the saurian animals. P. 30, f. 1.

CROCHES. Little knobs about the tops of a Deer's horn.

CROCHET-HOOK. Used in a kind of netting. P. 38, f. 55.

CROISADE. *See* CRUSADE.

CROISSANS. Crescents.

CROISSANT CONTOURNE. The decrescent. P. 23, f. 38.

CROISSANTEE CROSS. P. 10, f. 32.

CROIX DE TOULOUZE. P. 8, f. 39.

CROIX RECROISEE. A Cross Crosslet. P. 8, f. 18.

CRONEL, CRONET, CORONET, or CORONAL. The iron end of a jousting lance, terminating in three points. P. 35, f. 23, and P. 37, f. 32.

CROOK. A Shepherd's staff. P. 39, f. 11.

CROSE, or GROSE. A drawing board, an instrument used by coopers, and is borne as part of their armorial ensign. Two examples. P. 41, f. 3.

CROSIER, or BISHOP'S STAFF. Also termed Croysée. P. 42, f. 45. (the figure on the sinister side.)
The Pastoral Staff erroneously called a Crosier is similar to a Shepherd's Crook. P. 42, f. 46.

CROSIER CASE. P. 42, f. 46.

CROSS. One of the honourable ordinaries, occupying a third of the shield. P. 7, f. 1.
The Cross is subject to all the accidental forms of lines, as Indented, Engrailed, Raguly, etc.

CROSS, AIGUISEE, ARGAISE, or URDEE. P. 9, f. 45.

CROSS ALISLEE, or alisée pattée. P. 9, f. 23.

— ALLISE, or alisée. P. 8, f. 41.

— ANCHORED, anchorie, anchory, ancree, or ancred. P. 10, f. 9 and 11.

— ANCHORED and double parted. P. 10, f. 10.

— ANDREW ST. P. 7. f. 21.

— ANILLE. P. 10, f. 1.

— ANNULATED, annuled, or annuletty. P. 10, f. 35.

— ANNULATED REBATED. Also termed a Cross the ends tenatée, or tenanted and annuled. P. 10, f. 36.

— ANNULY, or annuletty, each fretted with a ring. P. 10, f. 37.

— OF ANNULETS INTERLACED. P. 8, f. 10.

— AT EACH END a Demi Annulet inverted. P. 11, f. 19. (or Cross demi anuled inverted.)

— ANSERATED, or Gringolée. P. 11, f. 36.

— ANTHONY ST. A Cross Tau. P. 9, f. 30.

— APPOINTEE. Same as Aiguise. P. 9, f. 45.

— ASTRICAL, adorned, or cornished. P. 10, f. 23.

— ATHELSTAN'S ST. P. 11, f. 3.

— AVELANE, avellane, or aveline. P. 11, f. 33.

— AVELLANED-POMELL, or avelanepomette. P. 11, f. 33.

— AVELLANED, double-pomettée. P. 10, f. 30.

— AYGUISEE. P. 9, f. 45.

— BANISTER. P. 11, f. 29.

— BARBED, barbée, cramponée, and tournée. P. 9, f. 31.

— BATON, battoon, batune, or potent. P. 11, f. 7.

— OF FOUR BATONS FRETTED. Also termed a cross couped double parted and fretted. P. 11, f. 38.

— BEZANTEE. Properly a Cross of bezants conjoined. P. 8, f. 8.
A Cross bezantee would be a plain cross strewed over with bezants.

— BLUNTED, or rounded at the ends. P. 8, f. 41.

— BORDERED, or fimbriated. P. 7, f. 24.

— BORDERED COUPED. P. 8, f. 29.

— BOTONE-MASCULED. P. 8, f. 36.

— BOTONNEE, bottony, botoned, or trefflée. P. 10, f. 20.

— BOTONNEE PATTEE. P. 8, f. 36.

— BOURDONNEE. Same as a Cross Pommelled. P. 10, f. 28.

Cross bourdonnee, or pommettée flory. P. 10, f. 27.
— bretessed. P, 8, f. 17.
— buck-axed. *See* Cross capital.
— buttony, or buttonee. P. 10, f. 20.
— cable, or cablée. P. 7, f. 41.
— calvary, or cross of the Passion. P. 8, f. 33.
— capital. P. 11, f. 45.
— of the capitals of four pillars flurty, and a leopard's face issuant. P. 10, f. 22.
— caterfoil, quatrefoil, quarterfoil, or four leaves conjoined in Cross. P. 11, f. 17.
— with caterfoils in the centre, and at each end, the extremities issuant trefoils. P. 11, f. 34.
— catoosed, adorned with scrolls at the extremities, also termed modilions. P. 11, f. 31.
— cercelee, cercelle, or recerceled. P. 11, f. 32.
— Chad S. P. 11, f. 13.
— of Chains, or four chains square linked in cross fixed to an annulet in fesse point. P. 8. f. 11.
— champagne, or Champaine. P. 9, f. 45.
— chappe, or double fitchée of four. P. 8, f. 42.
— charged ; i.e. with figures thereon. P. 7, f. 3.
— checky, chequy, or chequered. P. 7, f. 15.
— of Christ. P. 8, f. 33.
— clechee, or recoursie. P. 7, f. 19.
— clechee, cleschée, or cloche. P. 11, f. 44.
— clechee, voided and pommettée. P. 8, f. 39.
— Cleschee, or cloche cross. P. 11, f. 44.
— commisse. The cross Tau. P. 9, f. 30. used as a token of absolution. Malefactors were stamped on the hand with it.
— componee, compony, or Gobony. P. 7, f. 13.
— componee, counter-componée. P. 7, f. 14.
— corded, or cordee. P. 7. f. 18.
— cornished. P. 11, f. 45.
— cornished flurt. P. 10, f. 23.
— coronetted, or crowned. P. 11, f. 28.
— cottised. P. 7, f. 22.
— cottised with demi fleur-de-lis bottoms in fesse point. P. 7, f. 42.
— counter-quartered, any cross may

be so termed when the field is quarterly, and the cross counterchanged. P. 7, f. 11.
Cross couped, or humettée. P. 8, f. 28.
— couped, at each end an annulet. P. 10, f. 35. Also termed a Cross annulated.
— couped bordered, bordured, boardered, or fimbriated. P. 8, f. 29.
— couped crescented. P. 10, f. 32.
— couped fimbriated. P. 8, f. 29.
— couped and fitchée at all points. P. 8, f. 43.
— couped fitchee of four at each end. P. 9, f. 37.
— couped flory, or fleurettée. P. 10, f. 18.
— couped and pierced. P. 8, f. 31.
— couped pointed and voided. P. 8, f. 34.
— couped and voided. P. 8, f. 30.
— cooped at the top, and flurt. P. 7, f. 40.
— couped treble-fitchee. P. 9, f. 36.
— coursie voided. The same as recoursie. P. 7, f. 19.
— cramponnee. P. 11, f. 39.
— crenellee, or a cross-crossed. P. 8, f. 17.
— crescented. P. 10, f. 32. Also termed croissantée.
— crossed. P. 8, f. 17.
— crossed, bretessed, or crenellée. P. 8, f. 17.
— crossed pattee. Also termed cross crosslet pattée, and cross pattée crossed. P. 8, f. 26.
— crossell, or crosslet. P. 8, f. 18.
— crosset, fimbriated. Is a cross crosslet having a bordure round it. P. 8, f. 29.
— crossie, or crucelett. Same as crosslet.
— crosslet. Also termed crosset. P. 8, f. 18.
— crosslet cantoned with four crosses. P. 8, f. 25.
— crosslet, crossed. P. 8, f. 24.
— crosslet, double crossed. P. 8, f. 22.
— crosslet fitchee, or fitched. P. 8, f. 19.
— crosslet fitchee at the foot. P. 8, f. 20.
— crosslet double-fitched and rebated of all four. P. 10, f. 40.
— crosslet double fitchée of all four, rebated, debruised, or broken off. P. 10, f. 39.
— crosslet fixed. P. 8, f. 17.

Cross CROSSLET FLORY, in saltire. P. 20, f. 29.
— CROSSLET mounted on three grices, or degrees. P. 8, f. 23.
— CROSSLET PATTEE, or cross crossed pattée. When each end terminate in a cross pattée. P. 8, f. 26.
— CROWNED, crownated, or coronetted. P. 11, f. 28.
— CROWNED POMELL. P. 10, f. 28.
— CRUCELETTE, or crossie; a cross crosslet. P. 8, f. 18.
— CUTHBERT ST. P. 11, f. 1.
— DEGRADED, the extremities of which are each fixed in a step or degree. P. 7, f. 35.
— DEGRADED and CONJOINED. P. 7, f. 45. The number of steps should be named.
— DEGRADED NOWED or NOWYED. P. 10, f. 38.
— DEMI ANNULATED, or anuled inverted. P. 11, f. 19.
— DEMI SARCELLED. P. 9, f. 8.
— DENIS ST., a plain cross. P. 7, f. 1.
— DISJOINT, or recercelle voided. P. 11, f. 40.
— DISJOINT fitchée pattée. P. 9, f. 26.
— DOUBLE. P. 9, f. 34. Same as Cross double portante, and anciently only called a Cross double.
— DOUBLE AVELLANE. P. 11, f. 5.
— DOUBLE CLAVED. P. 42, f. 11.
— DOUBLE CROSSED. P. 8, f. 22.
— DOUBLE FITCHEE and rebated of all four. P. 10, f. 40.
— DOUBLE FITCHEE at the four points. P. 8, f. 42.
— DOUBLE FRUITAGEE, or a mascle with four fruitages, or avellanes, joined to the points thereof in cross. P. 11, f. 5.
— DOUBLE PARTED. P. 7, f. 26.
— DOUBLE PARTED and anchored, or a cross double-parted and crescented. P. 10, f. 34.
— DOUBLE PARTED FLORY. P. 10, f. 12.
— DOUBLE PARTED, fretted with four annulets. P. 7, f. 33.
— DOUBLE PARTED, voided flory. P. 10, f. 10. Also termed a cross moline resarcelly disjoined, or disjointed.
— DOUBLE PARTED and fretted, or frettée. P. 7, f. 27.
— DOUBLE PORTANTE. P. 9, f. 34.
— DOUBLE TRIPARTED. P. 11, f. 4.
— EDGED. P. 8, f. 35.
— EGUISEE. P. 9, f. 45.
— ENCREE. P. 10, f. 9.

CROSS OF THREE ENDORSES, surmounted of as many barrulets. P. 7, f. 29.
— ENGRAILED. P. 7, f. 5.
— ENHENDEE, or potence of Saxon F. P. 11, f. 18.
— ENTRAILED. P. 10, f. 41.
— ERMINEE, or a cross of four ermine spots, their tops meeting in the centre point. P. 11, f. 41. A cross ermine is a cross with spots of ermine. P. 7, f. 5.
— ESCARTELLE PATTEE. P. 9, f. 8.
— ESTOILE, ETOILE, or star-cross. P. 8, f. 45.
— FENDUE-EN-PAL, i.e. voided per pale.
— FERRATED. Shod with iron in the form of an horse shoe. P. 10, f. 33.
— FER-DE-FOURCHETTE. P. 11, f. 6.
— FER-DE-MOLINE. Pierced lozengy of the field, also termed a cross moline nowy lozengy pierced, and a cross moline nowy masculy. P. 11, f. 23.
— FILLET. Contains one fourth part of such ordinary. P. 7, f. 31.
— FIMBRIATED, fimbrated, or edged. P. 7, f. 24, and P. 9, f. 3.
— FIMBRIATED pointed at the ends. P. 8, f. 35.
— FITCHEE, or furche. P. 9, f. 43.
— FITCHEE COUPED. At the top a fusil. P. 9, f. 42.
— FITCHEE at all points. P. 8, f. 45.
— FITCHEE at all points, and quarterly pierced. P. 8, f. 37.
— FITCHEE disjoint pattée. P. 9, f. 26.
— FITCHEE double at the four points. P. 8, f. 42.
— FITCHEE TREBLE. Also termed fourchée of three points. P. 9, f. 36.
— FITCHEE of sixteen. P. 9, f. 37.
— FLANKED, urdée, or aiguisée. P. 9, f. 45.
— FLEURY BIPARTED. Same as a cross moline sarcelled. P. 10, f. 10.
— FLEUR-DE-LIS, or fleury. P. 10, f. 18.
— WITH DEMI FLEUR-DE-LIS on each side, the bottoms to fesse point. P. 7, f. 42.
— FLORY. P. 10, f. 17. Cross flory as in old drawings. f. 19.
— FLORY COUPED. P. 10, f. 18.
— FLORY DOUBLE PARTED, or double parted voided flory. P. 10, f. 10.
— FLORY TRIPARTED. P. 10, f. 26.
— FLOWERED. Same as cross-flory. P. 10, f. 19.
— FLURT. Same as flory.
— FORKED, or double fitchée. P. 8, f. 42.

Cross formee. P. 9, f. 1.
— formee flory. P. 9, f. 13.
— fourchee. Also termed a cross miller rebated. P. 9, f. 35.
— fourchee of three points. P. 9, f. 36.
— fourchee ou Kouee. A cross forked or double fitchée. P. 8, f. 42.
— fourchy, or furshe. P. 9, f. 35.
— fretted, or interlaced with annulets. P. 7, f. 32.
— fruitagee with an annulet in the centre, or four fruitages in cross joined to an annulet in the centre. P. 11, f. 30.
— fruitage double, or a cross mascle fruitagée. P. 11, f. 5.
— furchee, or Fourchy. P. 9, f. 35.
— furchee of three. P. 9, f. 36.
— fusil at each end. P. 9, f. 33.
— fusil rebated. i.e. the points cut off. P. 9, f. 32.
— of seven fusils, or seven fusils in cross conjoined. P. 8, f. 3.
— fusily. Properly seven fusils conjoined in cross extending to the edges of the shield. P. 8, f. 3. A cross fusily is a cross covered with fusils of alternate colours in the same way as a cross lozengy. P. 8, f. 2. Although the former is by many called a cross fusily but incorrectly.
— fylfot. See Gammadion.
— gammadion, fylfot, fytfot, or Thorr's hammer. Called Gammadion, from its being formed of four gammas conjoined in the centre, which, as numerals, expressed the Holy Trinity. P. 11, f. 39.
— gemelle. A cross potent crossed. P. 11, f. 8.
— german, or Teutonic. P. 8, f. 36.
— globical-pattee. P. 9, f. 23.
— gobony. P. 7, f. 13.
— of golpes. Is the same as a cross of bezants the colour being purple. P. 8, f. 8.
— grady. Is a cross fixed on steps. P. 7, f. 43, 44 and 45.
— grady-pomelled. P. 11, f. 35.
— grieced. Same as grady. P. 8, f. 33.
— gringolee, or anserated. The extremities terminating in snakes heads. P. 11, f. 36.
— with horse shoes at each end. See Ferrated. P. 10, f. 33.
— hamecon. P. 11, f. 15.

Cross humettee, humetty, or couped. P. 8, f. 28.
— humettee, flurty. P. 10, f. 18.
— indented. P. 7, f. 7.
— ingrailed, or engrailed. P. 7, f. 5.
— interlaced, or fretted. P. 7, f. 32.
— irish. Is a saltire. See Cross of St. Patrick. P. 7, f. 21.
— james st. P. 11, f. 2.
— jerusalem. P. 8, f. 25.
— of the Knights Templars was a cross patriarchial gules fimbriated or.
— lambeaux. Is a cross upon a label, the kind of cross must be named. P. 9, f. 25; P. 10, f. 42.
— lambeaux in all four. P. 8, f. 40.
— lambeaux rebated. P. 11, f. 25.
— latin, the. P. 9, f. 38.
— of leaves, or four leaves conjoined in cross. See Cross bottonée. P. 8, f. 36. The cross caterfoil as at P. 11, f. 17 is termed a cross of four leaves, or four leaves conjoined in cross.
— long, or Cross of the Passion. The stem is much longer than the crosspiece. P. 9, f. 38.
— long, couped, with the felloe of a wheel conjoined at the top. P. 9, f. 39.
— long, on a globe, or ball, the top like a Roman P. P. 11, f. 27.
— long cross, potent pommelled of three, or a long cross pommelled the foot potent. P. 9, f. 40.
— long raguled, or Raguly and trunked. P. 11, f. 37.
— lorrain voided. P. 8, f. 38.
— of Lorrain. Is like a cross lambeaux-rebated. P. 11, f. 25.
— lozengy. P. 8, f. 2.
— of nine lozenges, conjoined extending to the extremities of the shield. P. 8, f. 1.
— of five lozenges, or five lozenges in cross. P. 8, f. 4.
— of four lozenges aboute. P. 8, f. 12.
— lozengy nowed, or a Cross Nowy lozengy. P. 7, f. 34.
— Maltese, or Cross of Malta. P. 11, f. 42.
— mascle, or four mascles conjoined in cross. P. 8, f. 7.
— mascle fruitage. P. 11, f. 5.
— masclee at each point a plate, or a cross masclée and pomettée. P. 8, f. 39.
— of nine mascles. P. 8, f. 5.

Cross MASCULY. Differs from that of mascles, and is properly a cross, the surface of which is formed of mascles, as P. 8, f. 6.
— MASCULY FRUITAGEE. P. 11, f. 5.
— MATELEY. Also termed Urdée and Ayguisée. P. 9, f. 45.
— MILLER, or mill-rind. P. 10, f. 24.
— MILLER, rebated. Same as a cross furchée. P. 9, f. 35.
— MILL-RIND, or miller voided, and disjointed. P. 10, f. 25.
— MOLINE. P. 10, f. 1.
— MOLINE anchored. P. 10, f. 9.
— MOLINE anchory. P. 10, f. 11.
— MOLINE angled with acorns. P. 10, f. 4.
— MOLINE double-parted flory. P. 10, f. 12.
— MOLINE double-rebated. P. 10, f. 8.
— MOLINE per cross, at each end at the centre of the extremities a leaf of three points. P. 10, f. 5.
— MOLINE nowy lozengy pierced. P. 11, f. 23.
— MOLINE in pale, and pattée in fesse. P. 10, f. 6.
— MOLINE invertant. P. 11, f. 32.
— MOLINE, pierced lozengy. P. 10, f. 2.
— MOLINE quarterly pierced. P. 10, f. 3.
— MOLINE pommelled, or pommettée. P. 10, f. 7.
— MOLINE rebated. P. 9, f. 41.
— MOLINE double-rebated. P. 10, f. 8.
— MOLINE nowy lozengy pierced. P. 11, f. 23.
— MOLINE sarcelled. P. 10, f. 10.
Also termed a Moline voided and disposed, and a cross Moline double parted anchored ; by some it is called a cross Moline voided flory.
— MOLINE umbre. P. 10, f. 10. Also termed a cross double parted anchored, or double parted voided flory.
— MONTESE, or mountain. Same as a cross humettée. P. 8, f. 28.
— MOUSUE, moussue, mourned, or blunted. P. 8, f. 41.
— NELLE. P. 10, f. 1.
— NOTCHED. P. 9, f. 8.
— NOWED grady conjoined and fixed. P. 7, f. 43.
— NOWED grady conjoined and fitchée at the foot. P. 7, f. 44.
— NOWY. P. 7, f. 37.
— NOWY couped. P. 8, f. 32.
— NOWY lozengy. P. 7, f. 38.

Cross NOWY quadrant, or square. P. 7, f. 39.
— NOWY quadrat couped. P. 8, f. 32.
— NOWYED, or nowed, degraded. Also called a cross nowed grady. P. 10, f. 38.
— NYLE, anille, nigle, nelle, or nyllée. P. 10, f. 1.
— NYLE, or nylée angled with acorns. P. 10, f. 4.
— PER cross. P. 7, f. 11.
— PER pale. P. 7, f. 10.
— PER fece newe, or a cross triparted and fretted. P. 7, f. 28.
— PALL. P. 8, f. 14.
— PANDALL, pendall, or spindle. P. 11, f. 43.
— PARTED. P. 7, f. 16. Also termed perforated, quarterly pierced, quarterly voided, or quarter pierced.
— DOUBLE parted, or four battunes in cross fretted. P. 11, f. 38.
— DOUBLE parted, or biparted. P. 7, f. 26.
— DOUBLE parted and fretted. P. 7, f. 27.
— DOUBLE parted voided flory. P. 10, f. 10.
— PASSION. P. 9, f. 38.
— PATER-NOSTER. Composed of a number of beads. P. 42, f. 41.
— PATONCE. P. 10, f. 13.
— PATONCE angled with passion nails, or at each angle a passion nail. P. 10, f. 15.
— PATONCE fitchée. P. 10, f. 14.
— PATONCE voided. P. 10, f. 16.
— PATRIARCHAL, or double cross. P. 22, f. 23.
— PATRIARCHAL grieced. P. 8, f. 27.
— PATRIARCHAL pommettée upon three grieces, or steps. P. 10, f. 43.
— PATRIARCHAL thrice crossed potence, the foot lambeaux of three points. P. 10, f. 42.
— PATRIARCHAL, a lambeaux on the dexter side. P. 11, f. 25.
— PATRIARCHAL pattée. P. 9, f. 28.
— PATRIARCHAL pattée conjoined and annulated in the middle of the bottom cross. P. 11, f. 24.
— PATRIARCHAL pattée flory at the foot. P. 9, f. 24.
— PATRIARCHAL voided. P. 8, f. 38.
— PATTEE, or formee. P. 9, f. 1.
— PATTEE ɛlisée. P. 9, f. 23.
— PATTEE bottonée, bottony-mascled, or a cross Teutonic. P. 8, f. 36.

Cross pattee blemished or rebated. P. 9, f. 4. Properly a cross pattée concave or concaved.
— pattee circulated, or circuled. P. 9, f. 23.
— pattee concave. P. 9, f. 4.
— pattee convexed. P. 9. f. 23.
— pattee couped fitched. P. 9, f. 15.
— pattee crenellée. P. 9, f. 22.
— pattee crescentways rebated. P. 9, f. 4.
— pattee crossed, or a cross crossed pattée. Also termed a cross crosslet pattée. P. 8, f. 26.
— patte. An engrail at each point. P. 9, f. 19.
— pattee engrailed. P. 9, f. 6.
— pattee, entire, or throughout. Also termed fixed, or firme. P. 9, f. 7.
— pattee escaitelle. P. 9, f. 8.
— pattee with an engrail in each point. P. 9, f. 19.
— pattee fimbriated. P. 9, f. 3.
— pattee fitchée, or fitched. P. 9, f. 14.
— pattee fitchée rebated. P. 9, f. 15.
— pattee double fitched. P. 9, f. 17.
— pattee fitchée at the foot. P. 9, f. 18.
— pattee fitchée at all points. P. 9, f. 20 and f. 27.
— pattee fitchée disjointed, or disjoint fitchée of all four, or disjoint in the centre. P. 9, f. 26.
— pattee fitchée on a label of three points. P. 9, f. 25.
— pattee double fitchée of all four. P. 10, f. 11.
— pattee, fitchée double. P. 9, f. 17.
— pattee fixed double rebated. P. 7. f. 36.
— pattee fixed escartelled at each end, or notched. P. 9, f. 8.
— pattee fixed and notched. P. 9, f. 8.
— pattee flaunchée, or flanched. P. 9, f. 23. Also termed Convexed.
— pattee flory, fleury, or florettée. P. 9, f. 13.
— pattee flory patriarchal. P. 9, f. 24.
— pattee furche. Same as fitchée. P. 9, f. 23.
— pattee fusily fitchée. P. 9, f. 44.
— pattee globical. P. 9, f. 23.
— pattee intire, or entire. P. 9, f. 7.
— pattee invecked. P. 9, f. 5.
— pattee lambeaux, or fitchée lambeaux. P. 9, f. 25.
— pattee moline. P. 9, f. 9.

Cross pattee pierced of the field. P. 9, f. 2.
— pattee pommettée charged with another formée. P. 9, f. 11.
— pattee quadrat in the centre. P. 11, f. 1.
— pattee quarted. P. 9, f. 10.
— pattee rebated crescentways. P. 9, f. 4.
— pattee throughout. P. 9, f. 7.
— pattee double rebated. P. 9, f. 12.
— pattee sarcelled at bottom. P. 9, f. 16.
— patte demi sarcelled. P. 9, f. 8.
— pendall, or cross spindle. P. 11, f. 43.
— per. Anything divided by a line paleways and fesseways, usually blazoned quarterly. P. 7, f. 11.
— per pale. P. 7, f. 10.
— per-fece-newe, or a cross triparted and fretted. P. 7, f. 28.
— perforated. See Pierced.
— pierced. The piercing is always in the middle, and if not otherwise expressed in circular. P. 8, f. 31. When the piercing is in any other form it must be named as lozenge. P. 10, f. 2. When square, or quarterly as P. 7, f. 16.
— plain. Is always understood to be a cross ar.
— plain waved, also termed a watery cross. P. 7, f. 9.
— platee. When a cross is semée of plates. The term is also used for a cross formed of roundles when argent. See Cross Bezantée.
— point in point. P. 7, f. 12.
— pointed. Same as Aiguisée. P. 9, f. 45
— pointed voided. P. 8, f. 34.
— of sixteen points. When each extremity has four indents. P. 9, f. 37.
— points, pointed fimbriated. P. 8, f. 35.
— pomel, pomelle, pometée, or bourdonée. P. 10, f. 28.
— pomell flory. P. 10, f. 27.
— pommellee, pomelle, or pommy. When each end terminates with a knob, or ball. P. 10, f. 28.
— pommelle, pomelled or pommettée, avellaned, or a cross pommelle flory. P. 10, f. 27.
— pommelle, or pomelle crowned. P. 10, f. 28.
— pommelle voided and removed. P. 10, f. 29.

Cross POMMELLED and crescented. Or a cross couped at each end a crescent fixed to a pommel. P. 10, f. 31.

— POMMELLED, pomelle, or Crowned pomelle. P. 10, f. 28.

— POMMELLED Grady, or a cross degraded pommelle. P. 11, f. 35.

— POMMELLED Moline. P. 10, f. 7.

— OF four pommels. P. 11, f. 16.

— POMMETTEE, or pometty. P. 10, f. 28.

— DOUBLE pommelled. P. 10, f, 30.

— PORTATE. P. 8, f. 15.

— PORTATE, or portrate double and couped. P. 9, f. 34.

— PORTATE, or portante, raguled and trunked. P. 11, f. 37,

— POTENCE of Saxon F. P. 11, f. 18.

— POTENT, or potence. P. 11, f. 7.

— POTENT crossed. P. 11, f. 8.

— POTENT engrailed. P. 11, f. 9.

— POTENT fitchée. P. 11, f. 10.

— POTENT flory, or fleury. P. 11, f. 11.

— POTENT gemell. P. 11, f. 8.

— POTENT pommelled and fitched in the foot. P. 11, f. 12.

— POTENT of all four points, double fitched and rebased. P. 10, f. 39.

— POTENT quadrat in the centre. P. 11, f. 13.

— POTENT rebated, or cross cramponne. P. 11, f. 39.

— POTENT, the ends rounded, surmounted of a cross couped. P. 10, f. 45.

— POTENT, repotent in four points. P. 11, f. 14.

— OF four pruning-hooks contrary embowed. Also called four coulters joined to a ball contrary bowed in the points. P. 11, f. 22.

— QUADRAT. P. 11. f. 13.

— QUARTER, or quarterly pierced. P. 7, f. 16.

— QUARTER voided. Same as quarter pierced. P. 7, f. 16.

— QUARTERLY-QUARTERED. P. 22, f. 22.

— QUARTERLY quartered. When the field is quarterly, and the cross counterchanged as P. 7, f. 11.

— QUARTERLY quartered couped, the ends sarcelled and reverted. P. 10, f. 44.

— QUARTERFOIL, quatrefoil, caterfoil, or four leaves conjoined in cross. P. 11, f. 17.

— QUEUES ermine, or four ermine spots in cross heads in fesse point. P. 11, f. 41.

Cross RAGULED, or raguly. P. 7, f. 6.

— RAGULED and trunked. P. 11, f. 37.

— RAYONATED, rayonnated, rayonned, or rayonnant. P. 7, f. 17.

— REBATED. Is when a part of the cross is cut off. P. 9, f. 32.

— REBATED annuled. P. 10, f. 36.

— REBATED lambeaux. P. 11, f. 25.

— REBATED potent, or Patonce rebated. P. 11, f. 39.

— RECERCELEE, recersile, or resarcelled disjoined. P. 10, f. 10.

— RECERCELEE voided. P. 11, f. 40.

— RECERCELLED of another. Same as a cross cotticed. P. 7, f. 22.

— RECERCELLED with eight demi fleur-de-lis. P. 7, f. 42.

— RECOURSIE. Same as voided. P. 7, f. 20

— RECOURSIE couped. P. 8, f. 30.

— RECROSSETTEE, or recrossie. P. 8, f. 18. Same as Cross crosslet.

— RINGED. P. 10, f. 35.

— OF roundles ends tasselled. P. 8, f. 9.

— THE Royal Red Decorations of. See Royal Red Cross.

— OF the Saints. See each under their respective names.

— OF Saint John of Jerusalem. P. 11, f. 42.

— SALTIER, or saltire. P. 20, f. 1. See Saltier.

— AND saltiers. See Union-Jack.

— SARCELE, sarcelly, sarcell, or sarcelled. P. 7, f. 20.

— SARCELLED demi. P. 9, f. 8.

— SAXON wheel. See Saxon Wheel-Cross.

— IN each stem a Saxon B. P. 11, f. 26.

— WITH eight serpents' heads. P. 11, f. 36.

— SNAGG, or snagged. Is a cross couped shewing its thickness. P. 11, f. 20.

— SPINDLE, pendall, or pandall. P. 11, f. 43.

— STAFF. A rule used by plumbers and borne as part of their armorial ensign. It is also termed a Fore-staff. P. 38, f. 43.

— STAR, or Star-cross. P. 8, f. 45.

— SUR-ANCREE, or sur-anchored. P. 10, f. 34.

— SURMOUNTED of another. P. 7, f. 25.

— SURMOUNTED of a bendlet. P. 7, f. 4.

— TAU, or cross of St. Anthony. P. 9, f. 30. Also termed a cross commisse.

— TAU ends convexed mounted upon three grieces. P. 9, f. 29.

Cross ends tenantée, or tenanted. Also termed annulated rebated. P. 10, f. 36.
— theutons, Teutonick, Tholose, or Thoulouse. P. 8, f. 39.
— Thomas, St. Same as the cross at P. 8, f. 28 with the addition of an escallop shell in the centre.
— Thoulouse. See Theutons, and P. 8, f. 39.
— of Thunder. P. 37, f. 43.
— tourne. Same as Cramponnée. P. 11, f. 39.
— treble, or triparted. P. 7, f. 30.
— trefoil, treflée, or botonnée. P. 10, f. 20.
— of triangles. P. 8, f. 13.
— triparted double. P. 11, f. 4.
— triparted flory. P. 10, f. 26.
— triparted and fretted. P. 7, f. 28.
— tron-onner. P. 8, f. 16. Is a cross cut in pieces, which are removed apart, but still retain the form of the cross.
— trunked. P. 7, f. 6.
— undee. P. 7, f. 8.
— union, or Union-jack. See Union cross.
— urdee, or Urdy. As Aiguisée. P. 9, f. 45
— urdee, recoursie, or voided. P. 8, f. 34. Same as cross pointed and voided.
— vair, or vairy, better to say four escutcheons in cross with bases to the centre.
— verdee. Same as a cross urdée.
— Virgin Mary. A cross pattée. P. 9, f. 1
— voided-sarcelled, or resarcelled. P. 7, f. 23.
— voided of another. P. 7, f. 22.
— voided of the field. P. 7, f. 20.
— voided and couped.. Also termed recercelée. P. 11, f. 40.
— double voided. P. 7, f. 23.
— watery. P. 7, f. 9. (or Plain Cross waved.)
— wavy, or undée. P. 7, f. 8.
— wyverned. When the extremities of the cross, end in wiverns heads, in the same way as a cross ending in serpents heads. P. 11, f. 36.
Cross-per, or Quarterly. P. 2, f. 9.
Crossed. Charges borne crossways, or in the form of a cross.
Crossell. Crossett. See Crosslet.
Crosslet, or Crosseletty. P. 8, f. 18.
Crossys, or Croysys. See Crosses.
Cross Bow. An ancient weapon. Also termed an Arbelete or Arbalist. P. 37, f. 23.

Cross-staff. A rule. P. 38, f. 43.
Crosswise, or in Cross. Charges placed in the form of a cross, five being the usual number. P. 8, f. 4.
Crotchet. A note in music.
Crouch, or Crowche. A cross.
Crow. A bird remarkable for its gregarious and predatory habits. P. 33, f. 53.
Two Crows pendant on an arrow. P. 22, f. 44. Arms of Murdock.
Crow-cornish. See Cornish Chough.
Crown. Crowns were not originally marks of Sovereignty, but were bestowed by the Greeks on those who gained a prize at the public games. At first they were only bands, or fillets, but subsequently assumed various forms according to the peculiar feat of valour the person, to whom they were granted had performed.
Crown. When borne as a charge if not named to the contrary is generally drawn as a Ducal Coronet. P. 24, f. 35.
— of the Sovereign of Great Britain. Is a circle of gold richly chased ornamented with pearls and stones, and heightened up with four crosses pattée, and four fleur-de-lis alternately; from these rise four archdiadems, adorned with pearls, which close under a mound ensigned by a cross pattée, within the coronet a crimson cap, turned up Ermine. P. 24, f. 1.
— of the Prince of Wales, etc. See Coronet, and P. 24, f. 2.
— of Austria. P. 25a, f. 14.
— of Charlemagne. P. 25, f. 1.
— celestial. A gold rim adorned with eight rays surmounted with small stars, five only of the rays are seen in the drawing. P. 24, f. 33.
— civic, or Wreath. A garland composed of oak-leaves and acorns. P. 24, f. 39.
The Corona Civica was among the Romans, the highest military reward, assigned to him who had preserved the life of a citizen. It bore the inscription "Ob civem servatum."
— ducal. See Ducal Coronet. P. 24, f. 35 and 36.
— of Hanover. P. 25, f. 25.
— eastern, or Antique Crown. A gold rim with eight rays, of which five only are seen. P. 24, f. 32.
It is given to British subjects who have distinguished themselves in the East.

CROWNS IMPERIAL. P. 24. f. 1.
— INDIAN Order of. *See* Order of the Crown of India.
— OF a King of Arms. P. 40, f. 57.
— OF Edward I. P. 24, f. 38.
— MURAL, or Mural Coronet. Corona muralis; is a coronet with pinnacles, or battlements erected upon it. P. 24, f. 13 and 14. It is given to those who have assisted in storming a Fortress.
— NAVAL, or Naval Coronet. Corona Navalis, is composed of a rim surmounted with the sterns of ships, and sails alternately, and is given to those who have distinguished themselves in the Navy. P. 24, f. 16.
— OBSIDIONAL, Corona Obsidionalis. A reward given to him who delivered a besieged town, or a blockaded army. It was made of grass; if possible of such as grew on the delivered place and interwoven with twigs of trees. P. 43, f. 2.
— OLIVE, Olive Crown, or Garland. Was a reward given among the Greeks to those who came off victorious at the Olympic games. P. 43, f. 5.
— PALISADO, or Vallary. Also termed Vallairie, Corona castrensis; is depicted differently as shewn at P. 24, f. 17 and 37.
It is given to those who first enter the entrenchment of an enemy.
The term Vallary is derived from the Latin Vallum.
The Crowns Ducal, Eastern, Mural, Naval, and Palisado, may be of any tincture and placed on the Helmet with or without a wreath.
They are also very frequently placed on the heads, or round the necks of Crests and Supporters.
— PAPAL. *See* Tiara. P. 40, f. 59.
— PRUSSIAN. The Imperial Crown of Prussia. P. 25a, f. 13.
— OF the Roman Empire. P. 25, f. 5. *See* Elector of the Holy Roman Empire.
— OF Rue. The bend in the paternal arms of the Prince of Wales is so termed. P. 16, f. 40.
— OF Scotland. P. 25, f. 29.
— OF Thorns. P. 43, f. 3.
— TRIUMPHAL. Corona triumphalis; a wreath of laurel, which was given by the army to the Imperator. He wore it on his head at the celebration of his triumph. P. 24, f. 34.
CROWN VALLARY. *See* P. 24, f. 17, and Crown Palisado.

CROWNS. *See* P. 25, f. 1 and 5, 25 and 29; P. 40, f. 53 and 57; P. 43, f. 2, 3, 4 and 5; P. 25a, f. 3, 13 and 14.
CROWNED. When any animal has a crown or coronet on the head, it is said to be crowned, and if in blazon no particular crown is named it is always understood to be a Ducal Coronet as P. 24, f. 35.
CROWNAL. *See* Cronel.
CROWNET. A coronet.
CROYSYS. Crosses.
CROZIER. *See* Crosier.
CRUCELL, or Crucellett. A cross crosslet.
CRUCILY, Crusuly, or CRUSILLY. *See* Crusily.
CRUCIFIX. A cross with the figure of Christ on it; borne by the family of Le-Poer.
CRUSADES. Expeditions undertaken from the end of the eleventh to the end of the thirteenth century to deliver the Holy Land from the Infidels who prevented the passage of pilgrims to the Holy Sepulchre. There is sufficient evidence that to them, we are indebted for the multitude of Crosses, Escallop shells, Byzants, etc., which are found in Heraldry. Owing to the variously coloured crosses, which the different nations who went on them assumed, they were called Croisades from Crux, or Croix, a Cross.
CRUSILY, Crucily, Crusilly, Crusule, Crusilée, Crusuly, Semée de croix, or Semée of crosses. Terms to express the field or any bearing when strewed or powdered over with crosses, without any regard to number. P. 2, f. 40.
CRUTCH. *See* Pilgrims Staff.
CRUX. A cross.
CRWTH. An ancient term for violin. P. 43, f. 25.
CRYSTAL. A term used by some heralds instead of pearl, to express argent.
CRY of War. *See* Cri-de-guerre.
CUBE. A regular solid body with six equal square sides, same as the dice without the ace. P. 43, f. 46.
CUBIT-ARM. Is the hand and arm couped at the elbow. P. 36, f. 9. *See* Arm.
CUFF. Part of the sleeve. *See* Cubit arms vested and cuffed. P. 36, f. 10, etc.

CUIRASS, cuirasse. A piece of armour. P. 38, f. 7.

CUISSES, Cuissots, or Cuisats. A covering of mail for the front of the thighs and knees. P. 36, f. 22.

CULLIVERS, Cullvers, Cuilliers, or Cubboers. Same as Cuisses.

CULTER, or Coulter of a Plough. P. 39, f. 10, No. 2.

CULVERIN, or Culverling. A short piece of ordinance, the same as Chamber-piece. P. 37, f. 4 and 6.

CUMBENT. Same as Lodged. P. 28, f. 47 and 55.

CUP, or Chalice. P. 42, f. 26.

CUP, covered, or Covered-cup. P. 42, f. 25.

CUP, with fleur-de-lis. Also termed a Flower-pot. P. 31, f. 16.

CUP, inflamed. P. 31, f. 24.

CUP. As in the arms of St. Alban's. P. 39, f. 36, No. 2.

CUP. Out of which is a boar's head erect. P. 29, f. 34.

CUPE. Same as couped.

CUPID. The Heathen God of Love; is represented as a naked winged boy, armed with a bow and quiver.

CUPPA. One of the furs; composed of pieces of potent counter-potent, same as potent counter potent. P. 1; P. 22, f. 40.

CUPPULES. Bars-Gemell are sometimes termed bars-cuppules.

CUPPY, varry cuppa, or cuppy. Same as potent counter-potent. P. 1.

CURLEW. An aquatic bird. P. 34, f. 31.

CURLY-HEADED DIVER. P. 34, f. 16.

CURLING. Same as a snake coiled. P. 30, f. 42.

CURLING-STONE. A flat round stone polished on the bottom, and having a handle in the upper side used in the game of Curling. P. 36, f. 5.

CURRENT, Courant, or Cursant. Terms applied to Deer, Greyhounds, etc., when running. P. 29, f. 20.

CURRIERS' shaves, or Paring knives. As borne in the arms of the Curriers' Company. P. 41, f. 2.

CURRY-COMB. A comb used for combing horses. P. 37, f. 57.

CURTAL-AXE. P. 37, f. 31.

CURTANA. The sword of Mercy. P. 38, f. 24.

CURTELASSE. *See* Cutlass.

CURVAL, or Curvant. Curved, or bowed. P. 30, f. 50.

CURVED, recurved. The same as flexed reflexed, and bowed embowed; bent in the form of the letter S.

CURVI Linear. A curved line, such as a quadrant; the fourth part of a circle.

CUSHAT. The ring-dove. P. 34, f. 37.

CUSHION tasselled. Sometimes of a square form, and sometimes lozenge shaped. P. 40, f. 24.

CUT. The same as sarcelled.

CUTHBERT, St. Cross of. P. 11, f. 1.

CUTLASS. A sword. P. 38, f. 22. No. 1.

CUTTING iron. A tool used by Patten-Makers and borne in their arms. P. 41, f. 7.

CUTTING-KNIFE. P. 22, f. 28.

CUTTLE Fish. Also called Ink-fish. P. 32, f. 50.

CYANUS. The corn-flower. P. 44, f. 19. Also termed a Blue-bottle.

CYCLAS, Surcoat, or Tabard. Was a sleeveless dress, long or short, and open at the sides, back or front, according to the fancy of the wearer. *See* Tabard.

CYGNET. A young swan. A Cygnet Royal; a Swan so termed when gorged with a Coronet and a chain affixed thereto.

CYGNUS. A swan.

CYNKFOIL. *See* Cinquefoil.

CYPHERS. Initial letters variously intertwined.

The Crest is generally placed above them. Cyphers, used at funerals of women, are small escutcheons of silk, or buckram, whereon are painted the initial letters of the deceased, placed within a bordure. Cyphers-reversed. P. 39, f. 31.

CYPRESS. A Tree. P. 45, f. 48.

D

DACRE Knot, or Badge. P. 43, f. 7.

DAGGER. A short sword. P. 38, f. 23.

DAISY. A flower. P. 44, f. 25.

DAISY Margarette. P. 44, f. 26.

DAMASKED, Diapre, or Diapered. *See* Diaper.

DAMASK-ROSE. P. 25, f. 27, and P. 44, f. 3.

DANCETTE, or Dancettée. The largest indenting in Coat-Armour, and its points never exceed three. P. 3, f. 14, and P. 5, f. 18.

DANCETTE couped, or Fesse dancette couped of two pieces. Also termed a Fesse Emaunche couped. P. 3, f. 16.

DANCETTE-DOUBLE. Same as double-downset. P. 18, f. 11.

DANCETTE per long. Same as pily of seven traits. P. 6, f. 24.

DANCHE, and DENTELLE. Same as Indented.

DANCY. See Dancette.

DANISH axe. P. 37, f. 27. Termed Danish-hatchet. P. 37, f. 29.

DANSE. See Dancette.

DANTELLE. Same as Dancette.

DAPPLED. Marked with spots.

DART. See Spear. P. 37, f. 22.

DATE-PALM Tree. P. 45, f. 52.

DATE, slipped. A branch of the Date Tree. P. 44, f. 38.

DAUNCETTE, Dauncy, or Daunse. Same as Dancette.

DAW. A bird. P. 34, f. 37.

DEATH'S-HEAD, Morts head, or Human skull. P. 35, f. 34.

DEATH, or Skeleton. P. 35, f. 35.

DEBASED, Everted, Reversed, Subverted and Subvertant. Terms to express anything turned downwards from its proper position. P. 15, f. 43.

DEBRUISED. A term to express any animal or bird, when an ordinary is placed over it. P. 26, f. 21.
The term also applies to any charge over part of which another is placed. P. 7, f. 4.

DEBRUISED. Applied to serpents in the folding, expresses whether the head or tail is overlaid, or debruised by the other parts. P. 30, f. 27.

DEBRUISED, FRETTED. P. 16, f. 18.

DEBRUISED, FRACTED, or removed. P. 16, f. 2; P. 4, f. 15.

DECAPITE, or Deffait. Signifies couped. P. 27, f. 29.

DECHAUSSE, disjointed, or dismembered. The parts being cut off from the body, and placed at small distances still preserving the original shape. P. 26, f. 14.

DECKED, Adorned, or Ornamented. P. 35, f. 28.

DECKED, or Marguette. Is said of an eagle or other bird, when the feathers are trimmed at the edges with a small line of another colour.

DECLINANT, or Declivant. Also termed pendant, recurvant, and reclinant; applied to the serpent borne with the tail straight downwards. P. 30, f. 28.

DECOLLATED. The head cut off.

DECORATED. Charges may be decorated with heads of different animals; if with those of serpents they are said to be gringolly, or gringolée. P. 11,

f. 36. If with lions, leonced; if eagles, aquilated; if with peacocks, pavonated.

DECORATIONS of Honour. See Knighthood and Medals.

DECOUPLE, or Uncoupled. Parted, or severed. P. 16, f. 4.

DECOURS, or Decrement. See Decrescent.

DECRESCENT. The half-moon looking to the sinister. P. 23, f. 38.

DEER. See Stag.

DEFAMED. Being without a tail. P. 26, f. 6.

DEFENCES. The horns of a stag; the tusks of a boar, etc.

DEFENDEE, defendu, or defendre. Same as armed.

DEFFAIT. Couped.

DEGENERATE. Applied to an eagle at gaze, aloft, wings surgiant, and left foot raised. P. 33, f. 14.

DEGOUTTE. Same as Guttée.

DEGRADATION of Honour. See Abatement.

DEGRADED. A cross degraded, has steps, or degrees; also termed grieced. P. 8, f. 27.

DEGREES. Steps.

DEJECTED. Cast down, as a garb dejected or dejectant. P. 14, f. 21.

DELF, DELPH, or DELFT. Is a square sod of earth, or turf. P. 42, f. 34.
When the colour is tenne, it is the abatement due to the revoker of his challenge. When more than one is borne in a coat, they are called Delves.

DE-LIS. Contraction for Fleur-de-lis.

DELTA-DOUBLE. P. 43, f. 56.

DELVES. See DELF.

DEMEMBRE, Dechausse, Dismembered, Demembred, Derrache, or Disjointed. See Dechausse.

DENCHE. Same as Dancetty.

DEMI, or DEMY. Signifies one half. e.g. See Demi belt. P. 42, f. 15.
Demi bear. P. 29, f. 39.
Demi dragon. P. 27, f. 20.
Demi eagle. P. 33, f. 8.
Demi fesse. P. 4, f. 24. Fleur-de-lis. P. 44, f. 11. Fish. P. 32, f. 7.
Demi griffin. P. 27, f. 4.
Demi lion. P. 26, f. 31.
Demi man. P. 35, f. 25.
Demi talbot. P. 29, f. 14.
Demi unicorn. P. 27, f. 37.
Demi vol. P. 33, f. 26, No. 1.

DENIS, St. Cross of. P. 7, f. 1.

DENTALS, Dented, Dentels, or Dentelle. See Indented.

DENTED. A term sometimes used to express the teeth of an animal.

DENTICULES, Denticles, or Denticulated. Small square pieces. P. 13, f. 20.

DEPENDING. Hanging from.

DEPRESSED. *See* Debruised.

DESCENDANT. *See* Eagle descendant. P. 33, f. 17.

DESCENDANT, displayed. P. 33, f. 17.

DESCENDING. A term used for a lion with its head turned towards the base of the shield.

DESCENT. Is when any beast is borne as if springing from a higher to a lower part, as from chief to base,

DESPECTANT, or Dejectant. Looking downwards.

DESPOUILLE. The whole skin of a beast, with head, feet, tail, etc.

DETRANCHE. A line drawn bendways, either above or below the party per bend line.

DETRIMENT. The moon is said to be in her detriment when depicted as P. 23, f. 37.

DEVELOPED. Unfurled, as colours flying. P. 43, f. 48.

DEVICE. Any representation, emblem, or hieroglyphic; a painted metaphor.

DEVOURING, or GORGING. Applied to animals, fish, etc., in the act of swallowing anything. P. 30, f. 55.

DEWLAPS. Wattles.

DEXTER. The right hand side of the escutcheon. i.e. the left to the spectator.

DEXTER-CHIEF, and Dexter base. *See* Points of the Escutcheon. P. 1.

DEXTER-SIDE. A portion of the shield, one sixth of its breadth, cut off by a perpendicular line. P. 22, f. 10.

DEZ. A die. *See* Dice.

DIADEM. The fillets, or circles of gold, which close on the tops of the Crowns of Sovereigns, and support the mound. The Torse, or Band, on a Blackamoor's head is sometimes termed a Diadem.

DIADEMATEE, or Diademed. A term applied to the imperial double headed eagle, which bears a circlet, or diadem differing from the kingly crown.

DIAMOND. A precious stone; used in blazon to express sable.

DIAL. *See* Sun Dial, and P. 39, f. 44.

DIAPER, Diapre, Diapered, or Diapering. Formerly used, in arms painted on glass. It was covering the field with little squares, and filling them with a variety of figures, or with a running ornament according to the fancy of the painter. P. 22, f. 27.

DIBBLE. A pointed instrument used for making holes for planting seed. P. 39, f. 13, No. 3.

DICE. Pieces of bone, or ivory, of a cubical form marked with dots on each face. P. 43, f. 46.

DIDAPPER. A bird. P. 34, f. 24.

DIE. *See* Dice.

DIFFAME, or Defamed. An amimal, borne without a tail. P. 26, f. 6.

DIFFERENCES, or Brisures. Certain additions to Coat Armour in order to distinguish one branch of a family from another. *See* Cadency, and Distinction of Houses. P. 46.
Royal Differences. P. 16, f. 40 to 45. and P. 25a, f. 1 and 2.

DIFFERENCING is sometimes used in the same sense as Cadency ; but, strictly, it is distinct, having reference to alliance and dependency, without blood relationship, or to the system adopted for distinguishing Coats of Arms.—Boutell.

DIGAMMA. P. 11, f. 18.

DIGGING-IRON. *See* Spade.

DIJRID. A javlin. P. 37, f. 22.

DILATED. Opened widely, or extended. Applied to Barnacles, pair of Compasses, etc. P. 37, f. 56, and P. 41, f. 31.

DIMIDIATION, or Dimidiated. A term used to express anything which has a part cut off, a halving; a method of joining two coats of arms; and was formerly used in joining the arms of a husband and wife.
Three herrings were the ancient arms of Great Yarmouth, at a subsequent period, as a mark of Royal favour, the arms of England were borne in chief, and in base az. three herrings naiant two and one argent ; but when the fashion of Dimidiation was introduced the Royal arms were placed on the dexter side, and those of Yarmouth on the sinister, by which means the fore parts of the lions of England became joined to the hind parts of the herrings of Yarmouth. P. 22, f. 18. A Rose and Thistle dimidiated as P. 25, f. 3. The Badge of James I.

DIMINUTION of Arms. A termed used instead of differences.

DIMINUTIVES. This term is only applied to the modifications of certain of the Ordinaries which resemble them in form, but are inferior to them in breath, and should not be charged.
Diminutives of the Bar. The Closet, Barrulet and Bar-Gemel. P. 5.
  ,, of the Bend. Garter, Cost, and Ribbon. P. 17.
  ,, of the Bend Sinister. Scarpe, and Baton. P. 17.
  ,, of the Bordure. Orle, and Tressure. P. 5 and 35.

Diminutives of the Cheveron. Chevronal and Couple-close. P. 15.
  „ of the Flasque. Voider. P. 5.
  „ of the Pale. Pallet and Endorse. P. 14

DIRK. A Dagger. P. 38, f. 23.

DISARMED. An animal or bird is so termed when depicted without claws, teeth, or beak.

DISCLOSED. A term to express the wings of an eagle, or other bird, spread open on either side of the head, with the points downwards; it is also termed Overt, Flotant, Hovering, and wings displayed inverted. P. 33, f. 3.

DISCLOSED, Elevated, or Rising. It is also termed Rowsant, or wings extended and stretched out. P. 33, f. 2.

DISHEVELLED. The hair flowing loosely. P. 35, f. 6. P. 22, f. 24.

DISH. As borne in the arms of Standish. P. 39, f. 36, No. 3.

DISIPLINE. See Scourge.

DISJOINTED. A Chevron is said to be disjointed when its branches are sawn asunder. P. 16, f. 4. A Lion disjointed. P. 26, f. 14.

DISMEMBERED. An animal depicted without legs or tail; this term is also used in the sense of disjointed or Trononnee as P. 8, f. 16.

DISPLAYED. A term to express the position of the wings of eagles, etc., when expanded, or disclosed. P. 33, f. 5.

DISPLAYED recursant, or Tergiant. The wings crossing each other, sometimes termed backward displayed, the wings crossing. P. 33, f. 18.

DISPLAYED foreshortened. P. 33, f. 15.

DISPLUMING. A plucking of feathers, the same as Preying. P. 33, f. 12.

DISPOSED, or Disponed. Arranged.

DISTENDED. A Falcon wings distended. P. 33, f. 33.

DISTILLATORY, double armed. As in the arms of the Distillers' Company. P. 39, f. 29.

DISTILLING, or Shedding. In Heraldry and in old English is equivalent to "dropping with" or sending forth. P. 23, f. 29. P. 36, f. 50.

DISTINCTION of Houses, Differences, Brizures, or Marks of Cadency. Are used to distinguish the younger from the elder branches of a family, and to show from what line each is descended.
Thus in Modern Heraldry the Eldest son. during his Father's lifetime, bears a Label, the second a Crescent, the third a Mullet, the fourth a Martlet, etc. See P. 46.

These distinctions are placed in the shield at the middle chief, or in a quarterly coat at the fess point. See term Cadency.
In the case of the Royal Family, each member bears the Label, extending across the shield; the points of which are variously charged, and are borne on the crest and supporters. P. 16, f. 40 to 45, and P. 25a, f. 1 and 2.

DISTINGUISHED Service Order. By the Statutes of the Order, which was created by Royal Warrant bearing date 6. Sep., 1886, none but Naval and Military Commissioned Officers are eligible for the distinction, and it is necessary that their services shall have been marked by the special mention of their names in despatches for meritorious or distinguished service in the Field, or before the Enemy. Foreign Officers under certain circumstances are eligible to be honory. members.
Companions of this Order take rank immediately after Companions of the Order of the Indian Empire.
The BADGE to consist of a gold Cross enamelled white, within a wreath of laurel enamelled green, the Imperial Crown in Gold, upon a red enamelled ground, and on the reverse, within a similar wreath and similar red ground the cypher V.R.I. to be worn suspended from the left breast by a red ribbon edged blue of one inch in width. P. 31, f. 14.

DISVELLOPED. Displayed, or open, as a banner displayed. P. 43, f. 48.

DIVER. Curly-Headed. P. 34, f. 16.

DIVERSE. A term used to express the position of three swords when placed in pairle. P. 31, f. 26.

DIVING. or Urinant. Any fish, borne with its head downwards, more commonly blazoned reversed. P. 32, f. 12.

DIVISION. The dividing of the field by any of the partition lines.

DOCK-leaf. P. 45, f. 18.

DOE. The Female deer. Two does, or hinds counter tripping. P. 28, f. 53.

DOG-FISH. A species of shark. P. 32, f. 44.

DOGS. The Dog or Hound is very commonly met with in Heraldry, and when simply blazoned "Dog" is depicted as "hound." P. 29, f. 13.
Those of most frequent use are the Talbot and Greyhound; see also Alant, Bloodhound, Bull-dog, Pointer, Mastiff, etc. P. 29, f. 12 to 30.

DOG, sleeping. P. 29, f. 30.

DOG's Collar. As borne in Armory. P. 43, f. 43, No. 2.

DOLPHIN. Generally drawn naiant embowed, and therefore unnecessary to name it. P. 32, f. 1. But if borne hauriant or torqued, as f. 2, or in any other position, it must be mentioned.

The Dolphin, in Heraldry, seems originally to have conveyed an idea of Sovereignty. The first of the Troubadours was called the Dauphin, or Knight of the Dolphin, from bearing that figure on his shield.

The Dolphin appears to have been employed on early Greek coins as an emblem of the sea.

Vespasian had medals struck with a dolphin entwining an anchor, in token of the naval superiority of Rome.

Dolphin in Archæology the emblem of swiftness, diligence, and love.

DOMED. Having a cupola. P. 23, f. 12.

DOMINION, Arms of. See Arms of Dominion.

DONJONNE, or Dungeoned. Said of a Tower which has an inner tower rising above its battlements.

DOOR-BOLT. P. 42, f. 14.

DOOR-HING. i.d.

DOOR-LOCK. i.d. f. 13.

DOOR-STAPLE. i.d. f. 14.

DOORANEE. Badge of the Order of. P. 25, f. 19.

DORIC-COLUMN. See Column.

DORMANT. Sleeping. P. 26, f. 46; P. 29, f. 30.

DORS, and Dors endorsed. Back to back. P. 26, f. 15.

DOSSERS. See Water-Bouget.

DOUBLE Arched. Having two arches or bends. P. 12, f. 38.

DOUBLE Beveled. P. 4, f. 19.

DOUBLE caterfoil, or Quatrefoil. P. 44, f. 18.

DOUBLE downsett, or Dauncettée. P. 4, f. 25.

DOUBLE eagle. See Spread Eagle. P. 33, f. 6.

DOUBLE escartelled, or Escartellée. P. 4, f. 34.

DOUBLE fitchée. P. 9, f. 17.

DOUBLE fretted, or Fret fretted. P. 5, f. 23.

DOUBLE headed, or Don headed. P. 26, f. 9.

DOUBLE labels, or tags. P. 16, f. 34.

DOUBLE-leaved Gate, triple-towered on an ascent of four degrees. P. 23, f. 16.

DOUBLE nowed, or nowyed. A bend double nowed. P. 18, f. 22.

DOUBLE orle, or Orle of two pieces. P. 5, f. 33.

Double orle, saltier and cross, composed of chains passing from an annulet in the centre. P. 20, f. 45.

DOUBLE parted. Divided into two. P. 7, f. 26.

DOUBLE plume of Ostrich's feathers. P. 43, f. 39.

DOUBLE pointed dart. See Spear.

DOUBLE queued. Having two tails. P. 26, f. 2.

DOUBLE rose. P. 3, f. 21.

DOUBLE slipped. P. 44, No. 5, f. 14.

DOUBLE-TETE. Having two heads. P. 26, f. 9.

DOUBLE topped. Sprigs or branches having two tops from one stem. P. 45, f. 7.

DOUBLE torqued. The folding of a Serpent in the form of two Roman S's, one above the other.

DOUBLE tressure flory counterflory. P. 2, f. 43, and P. 35, f. 16.

DOUBLET. See Traverse. P. 21, f. 41.

DOUBLINGS. The linings of the mantle, or lambrequin. P. 8, f. 21, and P. 35, f. 16.

DOVE. The emblem of Peace and Chastity. As an Heraldic crest generally depicted with the olive branch in its beak. P. 33, f. 42.

Dove reguardant and Doves billing. See P. 31, f. 25 and 27.

DOVE, with dexter wing expanded and inverted.

See Title Page. The Arms of, the College of Arms.

DOVE, displayed in glory, or in the glory of the sun. P. 22, f. 4. Termed the Holy Dove.

DOVE-COT, or Dove-house. P. 43, f. 52.

DOVETAIL. A tenon made by letting one piece, in the form of a dove's tail into a corresponding cavity in another. P. 1; P. 3, f. 5; P. 15, f. 24.

DOVETAILED. In the form of Dovetails. P. 12, f. 9.

DOWNSETT. P. 18, f. 14.

DRAGON. A Fabulous creature, represented as a strong and fierce animal, and depicted as P. 27, f. 19.

On the same plate will be found, a Demi Dragon, Dragon's head couped, Dragon sans wings, legs, etc.

DRAGON with two heads vomiting fire. P. 27, f. 24.

DRAGON's head couped. P. 27, f. 29.

DRAGON's head. When arms are blazoned by the planets, Dragon's head implies Tawney. P. 1.

DRAGON's head and wings endorsed. P. 27, f. 21.

DRAGONS interlaced. P. 27, f. 22.

DRAGON's tail. In blazon implies Murrey colour, or Sanguine. P. 1.

DRAGONY, or Dragonne. A term applied to a Wivern whose head and tail are of a different tincture from its body.

DRAKE, or Duck. P. 34, f. 22.

DRAPEAU. An ensign, or standard.

DRAWING-BOARD. Same as Grose. P. 41, f. 3.

DRAWING-IRON. An instrument used by wire-drawers. P. 42, f. 33.

DRINKING-CUP. P. 31, f. 16.

DROMEDARY. P. 27, f. 47.

DROPED. Same as Guttée.

DROPPING, or Shedding. See Distilling, and P. 36, f. 50.

DROPS. See Guttée.

DRUM and Drum Sticks. P. 43, f. 26.

DUCAL Coronet. Is depicted with three strawberry leaves as P. 24, f. 35. If with more, they must be named as a Ducal Coronet of five leaves. f. 36. The Ducal coronet has recently received the name of Crest-Coronet.

DUCHESS. The wife of a Duke, her Coronet the same as that of her husband. She is styled " Your Grace," and is " Most Noble."

DUCIPER. A Chapeau. P. 40, f. 54.

DUCK. A Water-fowl. P. 34, f. 22. When represented without either beak or feet is termed Cannet.

DUCK-MUSCOVY. P. 34, f. 21.

DUFOIL, or Twyfoil. Having only two leaves.

DUG, or Woman's breast. P. 43, f. 34. See Woman's breast.

DUKE. The highest order of the English Nobility.
The first Duke of England, properly so called, was Edward the Black Prince, who was called Duke of Cornwall in 1337, and the first born son of the Sovereign of England is Duke of Cornwall from his birth. The title is hereditary, and a Duke's eldest son is by courtesy styled Marquess, and the younger sons Lords, with the addition of their christian name. The daughters of a Duke are styled Ladies.

DUKE's Coronet, or Crown. P. 24, f. 42.

DUKE's Mantle. Is distinguished by having four guards or rows of fur on the dexter side. The engraved example of a mantle at P. 35, f. 16, is that of a Marquess, shewing three rows and half of fur. See Robe.

DUNG-FORK. P. 39, f. 14, No. 1.

DUNG-HILL Cock. See Cock. P. 34, f. 1.

DUPARTED. The same as biparted.

DUN-FLY. The same as Gad-Fly. P. 30, f. 21.

DWAL. An herb ; also called nightshade, and in blazon signifies sable.

DYKE. A wall fesswise broken down in some places, is blazoned a " Dyke" and borne by the name of Graham.

E

EAGLE. Emblematical of fortitude and magnaminity of mind. The Romans used the figure of an eagle for their ensign, and their example has been often followed. It is the Device of Russia, Austria, Germany, and the United States of America, P. 25a, f. 15; and the Emperors of France, P. 33, f. 24.
In Blazon, when the talons, or claws and beak, are of a different tincture to the other part, it is said to be armed of such a colour. When the claws or talons are borne in arms, they should be turned towards the dexter side of the escutcheon, unless expressed to the contrary. P. 33, f. 21.

EAGLE. P. 33, f. 1.

EAGLE descending, or descendant. f. 16.

EAGLE descendant displayed. f. 17.

EAGLE displayed. f. 5.

EAGLE displayed, recursant. f. 18.

EAGLE displayed foreshortened. f. 15.

EAGLE displayed wings inverted. f. 7, and P. 14, f. 6.

EAGLE displayed sans legs. f. 9.

EAGLE displayed with two heads, commonly called a Spread Eagle. f. 6.
Symbolical of the Eastern and Western Roman Empire.

EAGLE at gaze aloft. f. 14.

EAGLE Imperial of France. f. 24.

EAGLE imperial. f. 6.

EAGLE mantling. f. 11.

EAGLE perched. P. 33, f. 19.

EAGLE preying. P. 33, f. 12.

EAGLE reguardant. f. 4.

EAGLE rising, or rousant. f. 2.

EAGLE Royal. f. 6.

EAGLE spread. f. 6,

EAGLE statant. f. 1.

EAGLE surgeant tergiant. f. 10.

EAGLE volant. P. 33, f. 16 and 17.

EAGLE wings endorsed and inverted. f. 13.

EAGLE wings endorsed and elevated, P. 25a, f. 9.

EAGLE wings expanded and inverted. P. 33, f. 3.

EAGLE demi displayed with two heads. f. 8.

EAGLE demi displayed erased sans legs. f. 9.

EAGLE's head erased. P. 33, f. 20.

EAGLE's head couped between two wings. f. 29.

EAGLE's wing, or Eagle's sinister wing. f. 26, No. 1.

EAGLE's wings endorsed. f. 26, No. 2. For other examples of the Blazon of Eagles see P. 33.

EAGLE's wings conjoined in base. f. 27, and P. 22, f. 31.

EAGLE's wings conjoined in lure. P. 33, f. 28.

EAGLE's leg erased at the thigh, termed à la quise. f. 21.

EAGLE's leg erased, conjoined at the thigh to a sinister wing. f. 22.

EAGLE's leg couped, conjoined at the thigh to a plume of Ostrich's feathers. f. 23.

EAGLE's talon, or claw. f. 21.

EAGLET. A term used by some Heralds to express small eagles when several are borne in a coat.

EARED. When the ears of animals differ in tincture from the body, they are blazoned eared of such a tincture. P. 29, f. 14. This term also applies to corn, when the stalk or blade differs from the ear in tincture.

EARL. A title next below a Marquess. The Earl is distinguished by his Coronet and Mantle. See Coronet and Robe. The wife of an Earl is called Countess. The eldest son of an Earl is by courtesy a Viscount, his other sons are " Honourable," and all the daughters Ladies.

EARL's Coronet. P. 24, f. 44.

EARL Marshal of England. A great officer, who had, anciently, several courts under his jurisdiction, as the Court of Chivalry and the Courts of Honour. Under him is the Herald's office, or College of Arms. The office of Earl Marshal belongs by hereditary right to the Duke of Norfolk.

EARS of Corn. Wheat, Barley, and Rye ; all are borne in Coat Armour. P. 45, f. 13 and 16.

EASTERN Crown, or Coronet. Also termed Antique Crown. P. 24, f. 32.

EAU. See Guttée d'eau. P. 1.

ECAILLE. Scaled.

ECARTELE. Quartering.

ECARTELE en sautoir. Party per Saltire.

ECHIQUETE, Echiquette, and Echiquier. Terms for Chequy.

ECLIPSED. Is said of the Sun and Moon when either partially or wholly obscured, the face and rays being sable. P. 23, f. 37.

ECUSSON. An inescutcheon.

ECUSSON a bouche. See à bouche.

EDGED. See Fesse Edged. P. 4, f. 3.

EDGED double. See Bend double edged. P. 17, f. 30.

EDOCK-LEAF. P. 45, f. 26.

EDMUND St. Banner of. Az. three Crowns or. P. 46, f. 18.

EEL. A fish. P. 32, f. 41.

EEL-CONGER naiant. P. 32, f. 41a.

EEL-SPEAR. An instrument for catching eels. P. 38, f. 60.

EFFEARE, or Effare. Salient, or springing.

EFFELLONIE. Said of a lion when drawn as salient, but in a perfect upright position.

EFFETT. A lizard. P. 36, f. 12.

EFFRAYE. Rampant.

EFT. A lizard. P. 39, f. 24.

EGUISCE, Eguisée, or Aiguisée. Same as pointed, or urdée. P. 9, f. 45.

EIGHTFOIL. A double Quaterfoil. P. 44, f. 18.

ELDER-LEAF and Branch. P. 44, f. 50.

ELECTOR of the Holy Roman Empire. Crown of. P. 25, f. 5.

ELECTORAL-BONNET, or Crown. P. 40, f. 56.

ELEPHANT. A Quadruped. P, 27, f. 28. A very appropriate bearing for those who have distinguished themselves in the East, and is of common use in Armory. Elephants are borne in Coat Armour with and without Castles on their backs. P. 27, f. 33. The trunk is also frequently met with as a bearing, and is always blazoned a Proboscis. P. 29, f. 50.

ELEVATED. Raised applied to the wings of birds when open and upright. P. 33, f. 2.

ELEVATED and endorsed. P. 25A, f. 9.

ELIPTIC circle. P. 3, f. 30.

ELK. A large quadruped of the Stag-kind. P. 28, f. 36.

ELLES. See Ailes.

ELM-LEAF. P. 45, f. 21.

ELM-TREE. P. 45, f. 51.

ELVERS, Elves, Griggs, or Eels. P. 32, f. 41.

EMANCHE, Maunch, Manche, or Maunche. A sleeve. P. 40, f. 31.

EMAUNCHEE. A term used by Ferne for Dacette of two pieces. P. 3, f. 16.

EMAUX de l'Escu. The metal and colour of the shield.

EMBATALID. See Crenelle.

EMBATTLED, or Imbattled. Also termed Crenelle. When the Ordinary, or Lines of partition are formed like the battlements of a Castle. P. 3, f. 8. P. 19, f. 2.

EMBATTLED counter-embattled. When both sides of an ordinary have embattlements. P. 3, f. 9, and P. 17, f. 17.

EMBATTLED-GRADY. P. 1, P. 4, f. 23.

EMBLEM. An illusive picture, a painted enigma.

EMBLEM of the Sacrament. Shield. Gu. three cups or., at the top of each a plate (wafer).

EMBLEMS of the Passion. See Instruments of the Passion.

EMBLEM of the Crucifixion. Shield. Ar. a heart wounded betw. a dexter and sinister hand in chief, and a dexter and sinister foot pierced in base gu.

EMBLEM of St. Paul. Shield. Gu. two swords in saltire ppr.

EMBLEM of St. Peter. Shield. Gu. two keys in saltire or.

EMBLEM of the Trinity. The Shield is either gu. or az. The device four plates, two in chief, one in the middle point, and one in base, conjoined to each other by an Orle, and a pall ar. with the words as at P. 22, f, 1. See Trinity.

EMBORDURED, or Embordered. Said of a Bordure when of the tincture as the field.

EMBOWED. When the arm is bent back, with the elbow to the dexter. P. 36, f. 16.

EMBOWED contrary, or counter embowed. Bowed to the sinister side. P. 36, f. 21.

EMBOWED debruised. The tail of a serpent is termed Embowed debruised when turned round, the end overlaid by the fold, and projecting underneath. P. 30, f. 27.

EMBOWED-DEJECTED. i.e. bowed with the extremity turned downwards.

EMBRACED. Braced together, tied, or bound. Also used to express a dexter and sinister arm embowed as P. 36, f. 18.

EMBRACING. The serpents in the Caduceus as P. 30, f. 56, are sometimes so termed.

EMBRASURE. The interval between the cop's of a battlement.

EMBRUED. Any weapon depicted with blood on it. P. 37, f. 11.

EMEAUX de l'escu. Tinctures of the shield.

EMERALD. A precious stone, and in blazoning signifies green. P. 1.

EMERASSES. Small escutcheons fixed to the shoulders of an armed Knight.

EMET, See Emmet.

EMEW, or Emeu. See Emu. P. 34, f. 11.

EMITTING. Sending forth fire, rays, etc. P. 27, f. 24. P. 28, f. 12.

EMMANCEE, Viurée, and Serrated. Indented.

EMMANCHE. Dancettée of two. P. 3, f. 16. See Emaunchée.

EMMANCHE, Creneaux, Embattled or Crennellée. P. 17, f. 15.

EMMET, Ant, or Pismire. P. 30, centre figure, f. 7.

EMMUSELLEE. Muzzled. P. 29, f. 37.

EMU, or Cassowary. An Australian bird. P. 34, f. 11.

ENALURON. A term to express a bordure charged with birds, the number must be named. P. 13, f. 37.

ENARCHED, or Inarched. P. 15, f. 32.

ENARCHEE. Arched, or Enarched.

ENARMED. See Attired.

EN ARRIERE. i.e. going forward, anything with its back in view. P, 33, f. 17.

ENCEPPE. Fettered, Chained, or Girt, about the middle as the Monkey. P. 29, f. 57 and 58.

ENCIRCLED. Surrounded with anything. See Enfiled.

ENCLAVE, or Inclave. Anything jointed or let one into the other. P. 12, f. 36.

ENCLOSED. The same as Between.

ENCOUNTERING. Opposed to each other. P. 26, f. 16.

ENCOUPLED. Joined together. See Interlaced.

ENDENCHEE, or Endentée, Indented. See Indentee.

ENDORCE, Endorse, or Indorse. A diminutive of the Pale of which it is one eighth part. P. 14, f. 3.

ENDORSE. As the preceding. Seldom borne but when a pale is between two of them. P. 14, f. 4.

ENDORSED, Indorsed, or Addorsed. Placed back to back. P. 26, f. 15. P. 33, f. 26.

ENFIELD. A fictitious animal having the head of a Fox, chest of a Greyhound, fore claws, or talons of an Eagle, body of a Lion, hind legs and tail of a Wolf. P. 27, f. 56.

ENFILADED. See Enfiled.

ENFILED. Sometimes expressed by the term pierced through, or transfixed. When the blade of a sword, shaft of a spear, etc., is passed through any charge, such as the head of a man, boar, etc.; it is said to be enfiled with that charge as P. 36, f. 51.

Any other bearing may be similarly enfiled, e.g. The Badge of the Prince of Wales is three Ostrich feathers, enfiled with a Prince's coronet. P. 6, f. 21. A barrulet enfiled with an annulet. P. 12, f. 40; P. 43, f. 20.

ENGLAND, Badge of. P. 3, f. 21. Crest of England. P. 26, f. 27.

ENGLANTE. Term for an Oak tree fructed.

ENGLISHMAN's head. See Head.

ENGLISLET. An escutcheon of Pretence.

ENGOULED, Engoulant, Devouring, Gorging, Ingullant, or Swallowing. Applied to animals, fish, etc., in the act of swallowing anything. P. 30, f. 55, and P. 32, f. 5.

ENGOULEE. A term for crosses, saltires, etc., when their extremities enter the mouths of lions, leopards, etc. P. 18, f. 27.

ENGRAILED. A term to express the edge of any ordinary when composed of semicircular indents. P. 1; P. 3, f. 2; P. 7, f. 5.

ENGRESLE. See Engrailed.

ENGROSSING-BLOCK. A tool used by wire-drawers. P. 42, f. 36.

ENGUICHE. A term used to describe the great mouth of a hunting horn, when the rim is of a different tincture from the horn itself.

ENHANCED. Removed above its proper place. P. 15, f. 36.

ENHENDEE. A Cross so called the same as a Cross potence.

ENLEVE. See Enhanced.

ENMANCHE. When the chief has lines drawn from the centre to the upper edge to the sides as P. 12, f. 43.

EN pied. A bear erect on its hind feet is said to be en pied. The term is also used for Statant.

ENQUIRIR Arms, or Armes pour enquirir. Arms which, being contrary to the general rule, excite enquiry why the grantor should have placed metal upon metal, or colour upon colour, as in the Arms of Jerusalem, viz. ar. a cross-crosslet cantoned with four plain crosses or. said to symbolize the five wounds of Christ. See Inquire Arms of.

ENRASED. The same as Indented.

ENSIGN. A Flag. See also Banner, Flag, and Standard.

The ensign of the Royal Navy is white with St. George's cross cantoned with the Union Jack. The Naval Reserve is blue with the Union Jack in the dexter chief. That of the Merchant Service is a red flag with the Union Jack as the last. P. 25a, f. 5 and 6.

ENSIGNED. A shield, or charge, having a Crown, Coronet, Mitre, or Helmet, placed above it, is said to be ensigned with such a Crown, etc. P. 8, f. 21; P. 42, f. 3; P. 43, f. 50.

EN Surcoat, Surtout, or Sur-le-tout. An escutcheon placed upon the centre of the Shield of Arms. P. 31, f. 7, 10, 29, and 42.

ENTANGLED. Fretted.

ENTE. Engrafted. See the following.

ENTE in point. Grafted in point. P. 21, f. 34.

ENTE en rond. Differs from Indented, inasmuch that the cuts are made round in and out.

ENTE. A partition of the field like nebulée.

ENTIRE. Throughout; also termed fixed, or firm, being attached to the sides of the shield as a Cross pattée entire. P. 9, f. 7.

ENTOIRE, Entoyer, or Entoyre. A term used when the bordure is charged with inanimate things as a bordure entoyre of escallops. P. 13, f. 36.

ENTOURED. A term to express a shield externally decorated with branches, or ornaments not heraldic. P. 31, f. 42.

ENTRAILED. An outline only, as a cross entrailed. P. 10, f. 41.

ENTWINED. Anything twisted round something else; as a snake entwined round a rod, etc. P. 30, f. 58.

ENTWISTED or Annodated. The same as Entwined, the folds being more open. P. 30, f. 56.

ENURNY. Said of a bordure when charged with animals. P. 13, f. 38.

ENVECKED. See Invecked.

ENVELOPED, Enwrapped, or Inwrapped. See Entwined.

ENVIRONED, or Environnée bound round, or about, the same as wreathed. P. 36, f. 37.

ENWRAPED. The same as Enveloped.

ENWRAPT, or Enwrapped. Same as Entwined. P. 36, f. 49.

EPAULIER. The armour on the shoulder.

EPIMACUS. See Opinicus.

EPISCOPAL, or Bishop's staff. P. 22, f. 2; P. 42, f. 45.

EPLOYE. Displayed.

EQUILATERAL-TRIANGLE. P. 43, f. 56.

EQUIPPE. Armed at all points. P. 36, f. 27.

EQUIPPED. Applied to a horse when furnished with all his trappings.

EQUIRE, Esquire, or Squire. Similar to the Gyron; it is also termed Base Esquire. P. 21, f. 24, and f. 42.

EQUISE. Same as Aiguise.

EQUITES aurati; Golden horsemen, i.e. Knights with golden spurs.

ERADICATED. Torn up by the roots. P. 45, f. 31, and f. 57.

ERASED, or Erazed. Torn off, having a jagged edge as a Lion's head erased. P. 26, f. 25 and 38.
It also expresses the lower part of the neck when of a different colour from the rest. P. 28, f. 3. Observe if the head were perfesse the partition line would be in the centre.

ERECT. Upright, as a boar's head erect and erased. P. 29, f. 33.

ERECT. Applied to wings when extending outwards. P. 32, f. 2. Inverted when downwards. P. 33, f. 7.

ERECTED endorsed. Two things borne upright, back to back. P. 42, f. 10.

ERM. Contraction for Ermine.

ERMEYN. See Ermine.

ERMINE. A little animal about the size of a squirrel, and borne by several families as their Crest. P. 30, f. 16.

ERMINE. A white fur with black tufts. P. 1.

ERMINES; also a fur, being black, with white tufts. ib.

ERMINOIS. A fur of gold and black tufts. i.b.
The opposite fur to this i.e. black with gold tufts is termed Pean ib.

ERMINETES, or Erminites. Another fur with black tuft, having a red hair on each side of it.

ERMYN. Same as Ermine.

ERNE. An eagle.

ERRANT. An old term for haurient.

ESCALLOP-SHELL. A badge much used by Pilgrims, and is a common bearing in Coat Armour. P. 42, f. 42.

ESCALLOPEE, or Counter scallopée. Also termed Papellonne. P. 18, f. 7. P. 2, f. 22.

ESCARF. i.e. a scarf, or band. As a sheaf of arrows bound with an escarf. P. 37, f. 21.

ESCARBUNCLE. Is always depicted with eight points as P. 43, f. 57, if not named to the contrary.
In the Arms of Pherpowe is an escarbuncle of six points or rays, and in those of Ruthfio

one of twelve points. Sometimes blazoned an escarbuncle pomete and florety, or pomette and florette.
The Carbuncles, or Escarbuncles, were originally merely ornamental points of the shield. It is said from the Boss was developed the endless varieties of the Crosses which are abundant in armoury, and from the other strengthening bands of the shield were derived the ordinaries of the armorial system.

ESCARPE. Same as Scarpe.

ESCARRONED. Same as chequy.

ESCARTELEE. When the straight line is cut off in the middle, with a perfect square, into an ordinary or partition. P. 1. P. 21, f. 17. It is also a French term for quartered or quarterly.

ESCARTELEE GRADY. P. 4, f. 23 and 34.

ESCARTELEE pointed. P. 19, f. 8.

ESCARTELLED. Cut, or notched in a square form ; a Pattée escartelle. P. 9, f. 8.

ESCARTELLED-COUNTER, or Double. The same as per bend, two piles triple-pointed, bowed and counterposed, bend sinisterwise counterchanged. P. 19, f. 17.

ESCATTLE grady. Same as escartele grady, or embattled grady. P. 4, f. 34.

ESCHECQUE. Same as checquy.

ESCLATTE. A shiver, or splinter, anything violently broken off. P. 4, f. 7.

ESCALOPPE. See Escallopée.

ESCOCHEON. See Escutcheon.

ESCROLL, Escrol, Scroll, or Slip. A ribbon, on which the motto is placed. P. 18, f. 21.

ESCULAPIUS-ROD. A rod entwined by a snake, which was the form assumed by Esculapius the God of healing, when he was brought from Greece to Rome in a season of great sickness. P. 30, f. 57.

ESCUTCHEON, Escusson, Escocheon, or Escu. The shield with the arms painted on it, in opposition to the Ecu which was a shield without device. The shield may be of any shape, but the oldest escutcheons are like a Gothic arch reversed, and are called the Roman or Heater shield. P. 8, f. 21.
The surface of the escutcheon or shield is termed the Field, because it contains those marks of honour which were formerly acquired in the Field. These shields are of every imaginable shape, according to the fancy of the bearer, the only restriction now being that Ladies must bear their Arms in a Lozenge. P. 9, f. 21; and P. 22, f. 21. The Escutcheon has certain Points, distin-

guished for the place of the charges which the field contains. (*See* Points of Escutcheon. P. 1) It is also frequently divided by *Lines*, called either Partition lines, or Crooked lines, the former are known by the term *Party*, and of these there are seven, viz.: Party per Chevron, Party per Fesse, Party per Pale, Party per Cross, Party per Saltire, Party per Bend, and Party per Bend Sinister, usually blazoned Per Chevron, Per Fesse, etc. *See* P. 2.

The *Crooked Lines* most commonly met with are nine, called Engrailed, Invecked, Wavy, Nebule, Imbattled, or Embattled, Raguly, Indented, Dancettée, and Dovetail; there are, however, many more used in Heraldry, but which are of rare occurrence. *See* P. 1.

ESCUTCHEON of Pretence. Is a shield on which a man carries the arms of his wife, when she is an Heiress, or Co-Heiress. It is placed in the centre of his own shield, and usually depicted of the same shape. P. 11, f. 21.

ESCUTCHEON, Points of. *See* Points of the Escutcheon.

ESCUTCHEONS. Are sometimes borne as charges. *See* P. 13, f. 33, and P. 19, f. 44.

ESQUIRE. A gentleman ranking next below a Knight, formerly a Knight's shield-bearer; Escuyer.

The following persons are properly termed Esquires:—The eldest sons of Knights and their eldest sons; the eldest sons of the younger sons of Noblemen. Those to whom the Sovereign has granted collars of S.S., or Gold or Silver spurs; also the eldest sons of the latter. Esquires attendant on Knights of the Bath at their installation, and their eldest sons, Sheriffs of Counties (for life); Justices of the Peace (while in commission); Special Officers of the Royal household; and all, under the degree of Knight near the Royal person. Such officers of the Navy and Army as are addressed as such in their patents of commission, with their eldest sons, Counsellors of Law, Bachelors of Divinity, Law, and Physic. Mayors of Towns are only Esquires by Courtesy. No property whatever conveys the title.

ESQUIRE's Helmet. P. 24, f. 12.

ESQUIRE, Equire, or Squire. Is similar to the Gyron it may extend across the shield; termed also a Base Esquire. P. 21, f. 24 and 42.

ESSONIER. A diminutive of the Orle.

ESSORANT. An Eagle standing on the ground, with the wings somewhat lifted up, is said to be Essorant.

ESTENDANT. A standard.

ESTOILE. A Star of six waved points. P. 23, f. 42.

When the Estoile has more than six points, the number should be expressed. When of eight or more points half should be straight and half waved. f. 44.

ESTOILE issuing out of a Crescent. P. 23, f. 39.

ESTOILE of sixteen points. f. 44.

ESTOYLE. Same as Estoile.

ETETE. A term used to signify a beast headless.

ETOYLE. *See* Estoile.

ETOILE. *See* Estoile.

ETOILEE Cross, or Cross Estoilée. A star with only four long rays, in the form of a cross; as a Cross Etoilée. P. 8, f. 45.

EWER. A pot, or cream-ewer. P. 42, f. 27.

EXASPERATED. Depicted in a furious attitude.

EXPANDED, and Expansed. Same as displayed.

EXTENDANT. Laid open in full aspect; i.e.

When any beast stands up, and stretches out the fore-legs on each side the body, so that the full face, breast, belly, and inner parts of the thighs are seen, it is blazoned extendant. P. 26, f. 44.

EXTENDED. The same as displayed.

EXTENDING, as three nails conjoined in base, extending themselves in chief. P. 19, f. 44.

EXTINGUISHER. *See* Candle Extinguisher.

EYE. The emblem of Providence.

EYED. A term used in speaking of the variegated spots in the peacock's tail. P. 34, f. 4.

EYES. Are borne in Armory, and are emblems of vigilance and vivacity. P. 43, f. 34.

The family of Peploe bears an eye shedding tears.

EYRANT. Applied to birds in their nests.

EYRY. The nest of a bird of prey.

F

FACE. A Fesse.

FASCE. Same as barry.

FACED, or Faced-lined. That part of the lining of anything which turns outward. *See* Doubling.

FAGOT. A bundle of wood. P. 41, f. 58.

FAILLIS. The fracture in an ordinary as if a splinter had been taken from it. P. 16, f. 2.

FAITH. A hand in hand clasped, is so termed. P. 36, f. 2.

FALCHION, or Faulchion. A broad sword. P. 38, f. 19.

FALCON, or Hawk. In Heraldry is always represented close as P. 33, f. 31, if not mentioned to the contrary, and usually borne with bells on its legs, when it is termed a Falcon belled.

If represented with hood, virols, or rings, and leashes, then it is said to be hooded, jessed, and leashed, and the colours must be named. For examples of Falcons see P. 33, f. 31 to 35.

FALCONERS, or Hawking Gloves. P. 43, f. 44.

FALCON'S Bells. P. 43, f. 17.

FALCON'S leg erased at the thigh, belled, jessed and varvelled. P. 33, f. 34.

FALCON'S Lure. P. 43, f. 16. See Hawk's lure.

FALCON'S Perch, or Rest. P. 43, f. 18.

FALSE. Voided. An Orle is blazoned as a "false escutcheon" by the early Heralds. An Annulet, as a False Roundle. A Cross voided, as a False Cross.

FALSE Heraldry. That which is contrary to the rules of the science.

FAN. A well-known hand ornament used by ladies to cool themselves by agitating the air. As in the armorial bearings of the Fan-Makers' Company. P. 36, f. 14.

FAN, Winnowing Basket, Shruttle, or Fruttle. A Fan by which the chaff is blown away. P. 39, f. 16.

FANG-TOOTH. P. 42, f. 52.

FARSONED. The projecting, or coping stone of a battlement. P. 23, f. 17.

FASCE, or Fasicle. The same as faggot.

FASCIS. The Roman-Fasces, or Lictors rods. A bundle of polished rods, in the middle of which was an axe, to express the power of life and death.

It was carried before the Roman Consuls, by the lictors. as an ensign of the superior magistrates. The Fasces are now frequently given to those who have held magisterial offices. P. 43, f. 6.

FASCIA. A Fesse.

FASCINES. Fagots of small wood bound by withes, used in military operations. P. 43, f. 36.

FASCIOLÆ Gemellæ, and Fasciolæ Duplices. Is the same as Bar-gemel. P. 5, f. 5.

FAUX-ROUNDLETS. Roundlets voided of the field. i.e. an annulet.

FAWCON. See Falcon.

FAWN. A young deer. See Two Hinds counter tripping. P. 28, f. 53.

FEATHERS of Birds, but more particularly of the Ostrich, are borne in Coat Armour. See Plumes and Ostrich-Feathers. P. 6, f. 21. P. 43, f. 37 to 40.

FEATHERS, Panache of. P. 43, f. 41 and 42.

FEATHERED, flighted, or plumed. As an arrow-flighted. P. 37, f. 13.

FEEDING. The same as Preying. P. 33, f. 12.

FEEDING. See Browsing.

FEERS. Horse-shoes. P. 37, f. 45.

FELLING AXE, or Slaughter-axe. P. 41, f. 19.

FEMALE-FIGURE. P. 35, f. 6.

FEMAU. See Fermaile.

FEMME. See Baron and Femme.

FENCOCK. See Heathcock.

FENDUE-EN-PAL. The same as voided per-pale.

FENYX. See Phœnix.

FER DE FOURCHETTE. All crosses so termed when the extremities end with a forked iron. P. 11, f. 6.

FER DE MOLINE, Mouline, Millrind, or Mill-ink. An iron affixed to the centre of the Mill-stone usually drawn as the first figure at P. 38, f. 53.

The six following are different forms of the millrind sometimes met with.

FERDUMOLIN. Same as Fer de moline.

FERMAILE, Fermaulx, Fermeau, or Fermeux. The buckle of a military belt. For examples. See P. 42, f. 15, and 16, and term Buckle.

FERN. A plant. P. 44, f. 49.

FERN-SAPLING of New Zealand. P. 36, f. 9.

FERR. A horse-shoe.

FERRATED, adorned with horse-shoes as a Cross Ferrated. P. 10, f. 33.

FERRET. An animal. P. 30, f. 15.

FERRULE, Ferral, or Verule. A metal ring on the handle of a tool, or end of a baton. See Veruled.

These terms are sometimes applied to the annulet.

FESS, or Fesse. One of the honourable ordinaries, formed by two horizontal lines drawn across the field. P. 3, f. 1.

The Fesse occupies the third of the field, and like the other ordinaries, is subject to all the accidental lines as Engrailed, Wavy, etc. When the Fesse is placed higher than the centre, it is said to be transposed; and when below the centre, it is termed abaisse. The diminutives of the Fesse are the Bar, P. 5, f. 1. Closet, f. 4, and Barrulet, f. 3. These are also subject to the accidental lines; e g. Three Bars Nowy, P. 2, f. 14; two Closets, or Cottises Fleury, P. 5, f. 14.

FESSE, Ajouré. P. 4, f. 16.

FESSE Angled acute. P. 4, f. 27.

FESSE Angled, or rect-angled. P. 4, f. 28.

FESSE, Arched, Archy, or Bowed. P. 3, f. 30.

— ARCHY coronettée on the top. P. 3, f. 27.

— ARONDY, Nuée goared. P. 4, f. 6.

— BATTLED embattled, or grady embattled. P. 4, f. 23.

— BETWEEN. As a Fesse between two Greyhounds. P. 4, f. 29.

— BETWEEN two bars gemelle. Same as Double Cottised.

— BETWEEN two barrulets, same as cottised. P. 5, f. 9.

— BETWEEN two chevrons. P. 16, f. 20.

— BEVILED. P. 4, f. 27.

— BEVILED double. P. 4, f. 19.

— BILLETTEE counter-billettée. P. 4, f. 41.

— BORDERED, or Bordured. P. 4, f. 5.

— BOTTONY. P. 4, f. 14.

— BRETESSED. P. 3, f. 10.

— BRETESSED embattled parted, or double parted. P. 4, f. 20.

— AND Canton conjoined. P. 4, f. 40.

— CHAMPAINE, or urdée. P. 4, f. 22.

— CHAPOURNE. Same as Arched.

— CHARGED with five music bars. P. 5, f. 12.

— CHEQUY. P. 4, f. 44.

— COMPONY. P. 4, f. 42.

— COMPONY counter compony. P. 4, f. 43.

— OF Chevrons conjoined. P. 3, f. 45.

— CONJOINED in Fesse. P. 3, f. 34, 35, 37, 40, and 41.

— COPPEE, or coupé. P. 4, f. 25.

— CORONATED. P. 3, f. 27.

— COTTISED. P. 5, f. 9.

— COTTISED double. P. 5, f. 10.

— COTTISED treble. P. 5, f. 11.

— COTTISED dancettée. P. 5, f. 18.

— COTTISED flory, or a Fesse between two barrulets flory. Flory means only the top of the fleur-de-lis. Flory counter flory is the top and bottom of the fleur-de-lis placed alternately as P. 5, f. 14.
See Fesse Flory and Fess Flory counter-flory. P. 3, f. 19 and 20.

— COTTISED potent. P. 5, f. 15.

— COTTISED potent, counter-potent. P. 5, f. 16.

— COUNTERCHANGED. P. 2, f. 50.

— COUPED, or Humettée. Also termed a Fesse Carnelle, and a humet, or a hawned Fesse. P. 4, f. 1.

— CRENELLEE. P. 3, f. 8.

FESSE CUPPA. P. 22, f. 40.

— DANCETTEE. P. 3, f. 14.
The indents of the dancettée may be engrailed, invecked, wavy, etc.

— DANCETTE-FLEURY-COUNTER-fleury on the points. P. 3, f. 15.

— DANCETTEE gobony. P. 3, f. 17.

— DANCETTEE of two pieces couped in the form of a Roman W. P. 3, f. 16.

— DEBRUISED, fracted, removed, or double downsett. P. 4, f. 15.

— DANCETTEE of two-pieces couped, blazoned by Ferne, a Fesse emaunchée couped. P. 3, f. 16.

— DEMI. P. 4, f. 24.

— OF Demi Belt, or a demi belt fixed in fesse buckled, edged and garnished. It is the waist-belt from which the fesse originated. P. 4, f. 18.

— DOUBLE-BEVILED. P. 4, f. 19.

— DOUBLE cottised. P. 5, f. 10.

— DOUBLE downsett, Rompu, or fracted. P. 4, f. 25.

— DOUBLE parted. P. 4, f. 20.

— DOVETAIL. P. 3, f. 5.

— EDGED. Has a rim along the top and bottom. P. 4, f. 3.

— EMAUNCHEE. The same as dancettée of two pieces. P. 3, f. 16.

— EMBATTLED. The same as Crenellée. P. 3, f. 8.

— EMBATTLED counter-embattled. P. 3, f. 9.

— EMBATTLED, with one embattlement on the top; Counter.embattled, with two in the bottom. P. 3, f. 12.

— EMBATTLED grady. P. 4, f. 23.

— EMBATTLED masoned. P. 3, f. 11.

— ENGRAILED. P. 3, f. 2.

— ENHANCED. P. 3, f. 6.

— ERADICATED. P. 4, f. 7.

— ESCARTELEE, or Escloppe. P. 4, f. 8.

— ESCARTELEE grady. P. 4, f. 23.

— ESCLATTE. P. 4, f. 7.

— FEUILLE de scie. P. 3, f. 23.

— FIMBRIATED. P. 4, f. 5.

— FLAMANT. P. 3, f. 24.

— FLORY, or Fleury. P. 3, f. 19.

— FLORY counter-flory. P. 3, f. 20.

— FRETTY. P. 3, f. 43.

— FUSILY. P. 3, f. 36.
Observe that a Fesse Fusily preserves the outward shape of the fesse, the surface being divided into fusils of alternate colours.

— GOBONY. P. 4, f. 42.

— GOARED. P. 4, f. 6.

— GRADY embattled. P. 4, f. 23.

— GRIECE, or Grady of three. P. 4, f. 9.

FESSE HEMISPHERE. P. 3, f. 29.
— HUMETTEE, or Humet. P. 4, f. 1.
— INDENTEE. P. 4, f. 11.
— INDENTED. P. 3, f. 13.
— INDENTED on the top. P. 3, f. 23.
— INDENTED point in point. P. 3, f. 26.
— INVECKED, or Invected. P. 3, f. 3.
— LOZENGY. P. 3, f. 42.
  This, as with a Fesse Fusily, preserves the
  outward shape of the Fesse.
— OF Five Lozenges, or Five Lozenges
  in Fesse. P. 3, f. 41.
— MASCULEE, or Masculy. P. 3, f. 39.
— MASCLES on a Fess. P. 3, f. 38. In
  Fesse. f. 37.
— NEBULEE, or Nebuly. P. 3, f. 4.
— NEBULY on the top, and Invecked
  on the bottom. P. 4, f. 26.
— NOWY. P. 4, f. 14.
— Nowy champaine. P. 4, f. 12.
— Nowy lozengy. P. 4, f. 10.
— Nowy quadrate. P. 4, f. 13.
— NUEE, or Nuagée. P. 4, f. 6.
— PATTEE, or Dovetail. P. 3, f. 5.
— PER Fesse crenellée. P. 3, f. 32.
— POMETTY. P. 4, f. 14.
— POTENT counter-potent, or Potentée.
  P. 3, f. 7.
— QUARTERLY. P. 4, f. 45.
— RADIANT. P. 3, f. 25.
— RAGULY counter-raguly. P. 3, f, 18.
— RAMPED, or coupé. P. 4, f. 25.
— RAYONEE, or Rayonnant. P. 3, f. 25.
— RECOURSE, or Recoursie. P. 4, f. 2.
— RECTANGLED. P. 4, f. 28.
— RECTANGLED at both ends. P 3,
  f. 44.
— ROMPU, coppée, coupé, or double
  downset. P. 4, f. 25.
— SARCELLE. P. 4, f. 2.
— SHAPOURNE. See Fesse Arched.
— SUPPORTED with two stays cheveron-
  wise. P. 3, f. 33.
— SURMOUNTED of another. P. 4, f. 4.
— SURMOUNTED of a Saltire. P. 20,
  f. 41.
— TORTILE. P. 3, f. 28.
— TRANCHEE. P. 4, f. 14.
— TRANCHEE Nuage. Same as Fesse
  Arondy Nuée Goared.
— TREFLEE. P. 3, f. 22.
— URDEE. P. 4, f. 22.
— VOIDED. P. 4, f. 2.
— WARRIATED. Same as Urdée.
— WAVED, Wavy, or Undée. P. 3,
  f. 31.
— WEIR. P. 2, f. 47.
— WIURE, nebulée counter nebulée.
  P. 4, f. 17.
— WREATHED. P. 3, f. 28.

FESSE ZODIAC, with three signs on it, viz.
  Libra, Leo and Scorpio. P. 3, f. 99.
— BETWEEN. P. 2, f. 3; P. 4, f. 22;
  P. 22, f. 43.
FESSE. IN FESSE a term to express the
  position of charges when they occupy
  the position assigned to that ordinary. P. 3, f. 37, 40, and 41.
FESSE. ON A FESSE as P. 2, f. 3; P. 4,
  f. 30.
FESSE per, Party per Fesse. Divides
  the field horizontally through the
  middle; it was anciently called
  Fessely.
  Observe that Per-Fesse is quite sufficient
  in blazon. See P. 2, f. 2 and 3. This per-
  fesse line is subject to all the accidental
  forms of crooked lines, as Per-Fesse engrailed, wavy, etc. e.g. Per Fesse Crenelle.
  P. 4, f. 38. Per Fesse Dovetail. f. 37. Per-
  Fesse Dancettée. f. 36; and Per Fesse In-
  dented. f. 35. Per-Fesse Wavy. P. 22, f. 13.
  P. 4, etc.
FESSE-EN-DEVISE. A term for a Bar.
FESSE Point. See Points of the Es-
  cutcheon.
FESSE-TARGET. An old term for Es-
  cutcheon of Pretence.
FESSEWISE, Fesseways, or in Fesse.
  Implies any charge placed or borne
  in Fesse; i.e. in a horizontal line
  across the shield. e.g. P. 4, f. 31.
FESSELY. Party per fesse.
FESWE. A fusil.
FETLOCK, or Fetterlock. A horse-fet-
  lock. P. 37, f. 39.
  Three Fetlocks interlaced. f. 40. See also
  P. 43, f. 15.
FETTER, or Shackbolt. P. 42, f. 40.
FETTERED, or Spancelled. P. 27, f. 31.
FEUDAL Arms. See Arms Feudal.
FEUILLE-DE-SCIE. A Fesse, or Pale
  indented on one side with small teeth
  like the edge of a saw. P. 3, f. 23.
FICHE. See Fitchée.
FIDDLE, or Violin. P. 43, f. 25.
FIELD of a Coat of Arms. The surface
  of the escutcheon, or shield.
FIELD-PIECES on their carriages, are
  met with in Coat Armour. P. 37,
  f. 4 and 5.
FIEND, or Fury's Head. Also termed
  Satan's Head. The head of a man
  couped at the neck in profile, and
  having ears like the wings of a
  Dragon. P. 36, f. 48.
FIERY Furnace. A furnace with a
  melting pot thereon, as in the arms
  of the Founders' Company. P. 39,
  f. 33.

FIFE. A small pipe used as a wind instrument, and borne by the name of Pipe. P. 43, f. 23, No. 3.

FIG-LEAF. P. 45, f. 25.

FIGETIVE. *See* Fitched.

FIGURE. A character denoting a number. Three figures of 7 are borne in the Arms of Bernard.

FIGURED. Charges on which human faces are depicted, are blazoned Figured, as the Sun, Crescents, etc. P. 23, f. 34 and 36.

FILBERTS. *See* Nut, and P. 44, f. 55.

FILDE. *See* Field.

FILE. An instrument used by Smiths. P. 41, f. 24.

FILE, or Label. A mark of Cadency. *See* Label.

FILE of three points fixed, or extending to the base; also termed a chief removed and three pales conjoined. P. 16, f. 39.

FILIERE, or Filet de bâtardise. Fillet of Bastardy. *See* Baton Sinister.

FILLET. A diminutive of the chief, being one fourth of that ordinary. P. 12, f. 33.

FILLET of Bastardy. A baton in bend sinister. P. 19, f. 27.

FIMBRIATED. An ordinary, or charge, having an edge or Bordure all round it, is called " Fimbriated." P. 4, f. 5.

FINCH. A bird. P. 34, f. 54; P. 33, f. 43 and 49.

FINNED. Applied to fishes when their fins are of a different tincture to their bodies.

FINYX. *See* Phœnix.

FIR-BRANCH. P. 44, f. 47.

FIR-CONE. P. 44, f. 54.

FIR-PINE, or Fir Tree. P. 22, f. 10.

Fire. *See* also Bonfire. P. 43, f. 35.

FIRE-BALL. A grenade. P. 37, f. 10.

FIRE Beacon. *See* Beacon. P. 37, f. 2.

FIRE-BRAND. Generally represented raguly. P. 41, f. 47.

FIRE Bucket. P. 39, f. 36, No. 1.

FIRE-CHEST, or Fire-pan. A large iron box. P. 37, f. 3.

FIRE, flames of. P. 42, f. 57. *See* Inflamed, or Enflamed.

FIRED. Same as Inflamed.

FIREY furnace. *See* Fiery Furnace.

FIRME. A term used for a cross pattée, when it extends to each side of the shield; the same as a cross pattée throughout, or entire. P. 9, f. 7.

FISH. In great variety, are met with

in Coat Armour. e.g. The 'Whale, Salmon, Pike, etc., *see* P. 32. When a Fish is borne in fesse, i.e. as if swimming, it is termed *Naiant* ; if with the head erect, it is termed *Haurient*; if with the head downwards, *Urinant.* In blazoning Fish, when the fins are of a different colour to the body, they are said to be finned of such a tincture. If with their mouths open they are termed *Paume*, or *Pame.*

In the early church a fish was generally used by Christians as a symbol of their faith, the Greek word ιχθυς (a fish) forming the initials of the most important titles of our blessed Lord Ι·Χ·Θ·Υ·Σ· Ιησους Χριστος, Θεου Υιος, Σωτηρ.

In blazon when no particular kind is mentioned it should be drawn as f. 16.

FISH-HOOK. P. 38, f. 55.

FISH of Mogul. P. 32, f. 48.

FISH-NET, or Fish-Weel, as in the arms of Colland. P. 38, f. 55.

FISH-POT. *See* Fish-Weel. P. 38, f. 57.

FISH-WEEL with handle, as borne by Wheeler. P. 38, f. 56, f. 58, by Williams of Thame.

FISH-WEEL, as borne by Wylley. i.d. f. 57.

FISH-WEIR. *See* Weir, and P. 2.

FISH-WHEEL. *See* Fish-weel.

FISSURE. The fourth part of the Bend. Sinister. P. 17, f. 6.

FITCHE, Fitchée, Fiche, Fitched, or Fitchy. From the Latin figo to fix or fasten; a term applied to a cross, the lower extremity of which is sharpened to a point, to enable those Primitive Christians who originally carried them on their pilgrimages to easily fix them in the ground. P. 8, f. 19.

FITCHEE at all points. P. 8, f. 43.

FITCHEE of four. P. 9, f. 37.

FITCHED double. P. 8, f. 42.

FIVE leaved grass. *See* Cinquefoil. P. 44, f. 16, No. 4.

FIXED. Crosses, when attached to the side of the escutcheon, are said to be fixed, throughout, or entire. P. 9, f. 7.

FLAG. An Ensign or Colour. The depth from chief to base is termed the " *hoist*," and the length is called the " *Fly.*" *See* term Banner, Standard, and Ensign.

FLAG of England. The Union Jack. P. 7, f. 21.

FLAG of St. George. A white Flag with a red cross. P. 7, f. 21.

FLAG. An aquatic plant. P. 44, f. 29.

FLAGELET. A wind instrument. P. 43, f. 23, No. 1.

FLAGGED. i.e. decorated with a flag, as a castle flagged. P. 23, f. 3.

FLAGON. Generally depicted as a covered cup. P. 42, f. 25.

FLAGON, with spout. i.d. f. 27.

FLAG-STONE. P. 42, f. 34.

FLAIL. Two long staves connected by a leather thong, by which grain is beaten out of the ear. P. 39, f. 11, No. 2.

FLAME of fire, or Bonfire. P. 43, f. 35.

FLAMBEAU. See Fire-brand.

FLAMES of fire issuing out of a rock. The crest of Grant. P. 42, f. 57.

FLAMANT, Flammant, Flambant, Flaming, or Burning. As a Fire-brand. P. 41, f. 47. A Flaming, or Burning Bush. P. 45, f. 59.

FLAMING-BUSH. P. 45, f. 59.

FLAMING-BRAZIER. P. 39, f. 32.

FLAMING-HEART. See Heart Flamant. P. 42, f. 3.

FLAMING-SWORD. Is depicted in two ways. P. 38, f. 21.

FLANCH, Flanque, Flasque, or Flaunche. Is an ordinary made by an arched line that swells towards the centre, and is always borne in couples. P. 5, f. 40.
The diminutive of the flanch is the *Voider*; it resembles a Flanch, but is not so circular towards the centre of the field, and it should be depicted much less in breadth. P. 5, f. 41.
Examples of Flanches, viz.:
Between Two Flanches. f. 42, and f. 43.
Flanches Charged. f. 44.
Square Flanches. f. 45.

FLANCHED. Glover gives as the arms of a natural son of one of the Fitz-Alans, Ralph de Arundel, a shield of Fitz-Alan, flanched ar.; that is, a shield ar., having flanches of Fitz-Alan and Warrenne quarterly. P. 2, f. 48.

FLANK. See In Flank. P. 20, f. 38.

FLANKED, or Flanque. See Flanch.

FLANQUE point of the escutcheon. The same as base point. P. 21, f. 5.

FLASK. See Powder-horn.

FLASQUE. See Flanch.

FLAX-BREAKER, Hemp-Hackle, or Hemp-Breaker. P. 40, f. 11.

FLAX, a Coil of. P. 43, f. 13.

FLEAM. A surgical instrument. P. 41, f. 5; P. 22, f. 19.

FLEAM. An instrument used by farriers, represented by ancient heralds as P. 41, f. 5.
Some w.iters call them Crampoons; but properly Cramp. P. 41, f. 6.

FLECHAS. Arrows.

FLECT, Flectant, and Flected. Bowed, or bent in contrary directions. See Reflected.

FLEECE. The skin of a Ram with the wool on, commonly called the Golden Fleece, always represented as P. 22, f. 29.

FLEGME. See Fleam.

FLESH-HOOK. An instrument used for taking meat out of a seething-pot, or caldron. P. 41, f. 10. In chief, and on the sinister side.

FLESH-POT. A three-legged iron pot. i.d. f. 16.

FLETCHED. Feathered as an arrow.

FLEUR-DE-LIS, contracted de-lis. Also termed Flower-de-luce; is variously depicted, but most commonly as P. 44, f. 7. Antique as f. 12.
As to its origin antiquaries are at variance, some supposing it to be the flower of the iris, others that of the common lily, whose name "lys" has a certain resemblance to that of Loys, or Louis, a common name of the Kings of France, while a third party, with perhaps more probability, suppose it to be the head of a partizan, or halbert.
When the field, or any charge, is promiscuously scattered over with de-li·, it is termed strewed, powdered, or replenished with fleur-de-lis; or it is said to be Semée-de-iis. P. 2, f. 38.

FLEUR-DE-LIS double. P. 44, f. 8.

FLEUR-DE-LIS seeded. i.d. f. 9.

FLEUR-DE-LIS, formed of three lilies. i.d. f. 10.

FLEUR-DE-LIS couped. i.d. f. 11.

FLEUR-DE-LIS demi. Is divided per pale. i.d. f. 11.

FLEURONEE, and Fleur-de-lisse. Is the same as botonnée, buttony and budded florettée, or flurty. See Cross Botonée. P. 10, f. 20.

FLEURY, Fleurty, Floretty, Flurt, or Flury. Said of anything ending with a fleur-de-lis, sometimes termed Fleurette. P. 9, f. 13.
Differenced from the cross-flory, by having a line between the ends of the cross and the flowers. P. 10, f. 18.

FLEURY-BIPARTED. See Cross Moline Sarcelled. P. 10, f. 10.

FLEURY contre fleury. See Flory counter-flory.

FLEXED. Bent, or bowed. P. 42, f. 4.

FLEXED in Triangle. P. 32, f. 26.

FLIES. Are borne by the family of Muschamp, no doubt in allusion to the name; Musca is the Latin for Fly. *See* Harvest Fly. P. 30, f. 22.

FLIGHTED. Applied to an arrow denotes that it is feathered as P. 37, f. 13.

FLINT-STONE. As in the Arms of Flint. P. 42, f. 60.

FLINTSTONE. A gunstone, or Pellet. P. 1.

FLINT-STONE chained. Called also a murdering chain-shot. *See* Chain Shot. P. 37, f. 8.

FLOAT. An instrument used by Bowyers, and borne as part of their armorial ensign. P. 40, f. 8.

FLOOK, or Flounder. A small fish. P. 32, f. 11.

FLORETTE-DE-LIS. Same as Semée-de-lis. *See* Semée.

FLORETTY. *See* FLEURY.

FLORY, or Florée. An ordinary is said to be flory when the edge is ornamented with fleur-de-lis as a Bend Flory. P. 17, f. 13.

FLORY, counter-flory counter-flowered, fleury, flurty, or floretty. Terms to express an ordinary, when the edges are charged with fleur-de-lis, the tops of the fleur-de-lis being shewn on one edge, and the bottom of the fleur-de-lis directly on the opposite edge, and so reversed alternately, as a Tressure flory connter-flory, P. 35, f. 16; and a Bend Flory counter-flory, P. 17, f. 14.

FLORY-CROSS. P. 10, f. 17 and 19.

FLORY-DE-LIS. Same as Semée-de-lis.

FLOTANT. Any thing flying in the air, as a banner displayed, or Flotant. P. 7, f. 21. It is also applicable to any thing swimming.

FLOUKE. *See* Fluke.

FLOUNDER. A fish. P. 32, f. 11.

FLOURETTE, and Flourished. Adorned with Fleur-de-lis, Trefoils, etc.

FLOWERS. Are of common use in Heraldry. *See* Rose, Lily, Pansy, Daisy, Primrose, etc. P. 44 and 45.

FLOWER-DE-LICES.
FLOWER-DE-LUCES. } *See* Fleur-de-lis.
FLOWER-DE-LYSES.

FLOWER of the Flag. P. 44, f. 29. The Fleur-de-lis is sometimes called the Flower of the Flag.

FLOWER gentle. P. 22, f. 17.

FLOWER of the French. The Fleur-de-lis.

FLOWER-POT. P. 31, f. 16.

FLOWERED, and Counter Flowered. Same as Flory, counter-flory.

FLUKE. A flounder. P. 32, f. 11.

FLUKE, or Flouke of an anchor. The semicircular barbed part, by which it takes hold of the ground. P. 38, f. 41.

FLURES. The fleur-de-lis.

FLURY, or Flurry. Same as Flory.

FLURT. Same as Fleury.

FLUTE. A wind instrument. P. 43, f. 23, No. 3.

FLUTING. The furrows in a column. P. 43, f. 50, No. 2.

FLY of a Flag. The length, outside, or extremity.

FLY. *See* Butterfly, Gad Fly, and Harvest Fly. P. 30, f. 21, 22 and 23.

FLYING Ape. P. 29, f. 60.

FLYING-COLUMN; or, more properly, a column with wings, or winged. P. 43, f. 51.

FLYING Fish. P. 32, f. 46.

FOILS. *See* Cinquefoils, Trefoils, etc.

FOLDING-STICK. *See* Bookbinder's Folding-stick.

FOLIAGE. The leaves of a tree, or branch.

FOLIATED. Leaved.

FONDANT. Stooping for prey.

FOOT BALL. P. 41, f. 60.

FOOT Human. P. 36, f. 24.

FORCENE. Said of a horse rearing. P. 27, f. 26.

FORCHE, or Fourchée. Divided into two parts towards the extremity. P. 9, f. 35 and 41.

FORERIGHT. Same as Affrontée.

FORE-SHORTENED. Animals, or birds, so borne that their whole length is not seen, by either turning towards or from you. P. 33, f. 15.

FORE-STAFF, or Cross-staff, marked with the degrees of latitude. P. 38, f. 43.

FOREST-BILL; also termed a Wood-Bill. An instrument used for lopping trees, etc. P. 41, f. 22.

FOREST of Trees. P. 45, f. 60.

FORK. An instrument with handle and metal blade divided into two or more points, as a Pitch-fork. P. 39, f. 14, No. 3. A Dung-fork. f. 14, No. 1.

FORK. Hay, or Shake-fork. P. 39, f. 19.

FORKED. Branching into two parts. *See* Fourchey. P. 9, f. 35.

FORM, or Seat. The resting place of a hare.

FORMEE-FLORY. Same as Cross Pattée flory. P. 9, f. 13.

FORME. Same as pattée. P. 9, f. 1.

FORMY. A cross pattée. P. 9, f. 1.

FORT. A square Fort with four towers, P. 23, f. 6.

FORTIFIED. Applied to a wall fortified with towers. P. 23, f. 14.

FOUNTAIN, Syke, or Well. Terms which are always applied to a roundle barry wavy of six ar. and az. as at P. 1. These should now be blazoned " Heraldic-Fountains," in order to distinguish them from Modern Fountains, which have been introduced into Coat Armour, and which are generally borne playing. In the latter, the number of basins should be named; in a modern grant a fountain is depicted. P. 42, f. 55.

FOURCHEE, or Fourchi. The same as Furche. P. 9, f. 35.

Fox. A wild animal. P. 29, f. 8.

Fox. Salient. i.d. f. 9.

FOXES, counter-salient. .i.d f. 10.

FOXE's head, erased. i.d. f. 11.

FRACTED. Broken. P. 37, f. 11 ; P. 39, f. 6.

FRAME-SAW. P. 41, f. 35.

FRANCE, Coronets of. A Prince. P. 25a, f. 18. Duc. f. 19. Marquis. f. 20. Comte. f. 21. Vicomte. f. 22. Baron. f. 23.

FRANCE, emblem of. See Tricolore.

FRANCE, imperial eagle of. P. 33, f. 24.

FRANCE, label of. A label az., charged with fleur-de-lis.

FRASIER, Frases, or Fraze. The same as Cinquefoil ; sometimes termed a primrose. P. 44, f. 16, No. 4.

FRENCH-MARYGOLD. P. 44, f. 28.

FRESNE. Said of a horse rearing, or standing on his hind legs. P. 27, f. 26.

FRET. Consists of two long pieces in saltire, extending to the extremities of the field, and interlaced within a mascle. P. 5, f. 19. It is sometimes termed a true-lovers knot, and sometimes a Harrington Knot.

FRET, Couped, Engrailed, Fleury, Charged, Double Fretted, Interlaced, Throughout, etc. P. 5, f. 19 to 28.

FRET, Bretessed, Espined, or Crossed. P. 22, f. 26.

FRET-KNOT. See Lacy Knot. P. 43, f. 11.

FRET-PER, or Parted per fret ; also termed barry per-fret. P. 21, f. 30.

FRETTED, or Frettée, interlaced one with the other. P. 30, f, 52 ; P. 32, f. 26.

FRETTED in saltire. P. 36, f. 17.

FRETTED in triangle. P. 32. f. 26.

FRETTING each other. i.e. interlacing each other. P. 37, f. 40 and 46.

FRETTY. An even number of pieces crossing bendways, dexter and sinister, and interlacing each other. P. 5, f. 29, and f. 30.

FRIAR, or Grayfriar. A member of a religious order is met with in Heraldry. P. 36, f. 31.

FRIGHTED. Same as Fresne, applied to a horse rearing.

FRILL. An edging. P. 36, f. 10.

FRINGED. Edged with fringe.

FRITILLARIA Meleagris. A flower. P. 19, f. 39, borne by the name of Turnley.

FROG. Erect borne by the name of Trevioneck. P. 30, f. 10. The arms of Overend. Ar. on a chev. gu. betw. three pheons sa., as many frogs or.

FRONT, or Frontal. The front of any thing, as a cap ; also applied to ornaments which adorn the head of men and women.

FRONTAL. A piece of armour put upon the forehead of a horse. P. 38, f. 12.

FRONTLET. A fore-head band.

FRUITS. Much used in armoury, and when stalked or leaved must be mentioned. See terms Grapes, Pine-Apple, Apples, Pears, Cherries, etc. P. 44, f. 56, 57 and 58.

FRUCTED. Bearing Fruit. The tincture of the fruit must be named, as an Oak Tree ppr. fructed or. P. 45, f. 31.

FRUTTLE. A winnowing-fan. P. 39, f. 16.

FULGENT. Having rays.

FULL-COURSE. Same as courant.

FUMENT, Fumant, or Fumid. Emitting smoke.

FUNERAL Achievements, or Hatchment. Is the Coat of Arms painted and framed. The frame is lozenge shaped, and covered with black cloth. It is placed on the front of the house on the morning of interment, where it generally remains for twelve months, and thence is removed and frequently put up in the Church.—The arms on a Hatchment are always painted as borne by the party when living, so that the Hatchment of a Peer is known by his Coronet, Mantle, etc. A Baronet by his Badge; a Knight by his Helmet, or Badge and Motto of his Order; a Bishop by the Mitre, etc.; a Bachelor's by his Shield; and a Maid, or Widow's by her Lozenge; the only difference is, that when a married woman dies before her husband the Crest is omitted. To distinguish what party is dead, the ground on which the arms are painted, is represented either Black or White, or one side White, the other Black. Thus the Arms of a Bachelor, Maid, Widow, and Widower, are painted upon a Black ground. When a married woman dies, her husband still surviving, the sinister half of the ground is painted Black, the dexter White. If a married man dies, and his wife survives, the ground is painted the reverse.

In many instances, instead of the family motto, the words "In cœlo quies" or "Resurgam" are placed on the Hatchment.

THE HATCHMENT OF A

Bachelor. P. 46, f. 23.
Bishop. f. 33.
Husband dead, wife surviving. f. 25.
Husband dead, wife an Heiress surviving. f. 27.
Husband dead, first wife dead, second surviving. f. 29.
Husband both wives dead f. 30.
Maid. f. 24.
Widow. f. 32.
Widower. f. 31.
Wife dead, husband surviving. f. 26.
Wife an Heiress dead, husband surviving. f. 28.

FURCHE, Furchée, Furchy, Forché and Fourchée. P. 9, f. 35.

FURISONS. The steel used for striking fire from a flint. P. 22, f. 45.

FURNACE. See Fiery-Furnace.

FURNISHED. A Horse is said to be furnished when completely caparisoned.

It also applies to a stag furnished with (giving the number) antlers.

FURS. Used for the linings of robes of state, and the linings of mantles. They are also borne on the shield and charges, and are as follows :—

Ermine, Ermines, Erminites, Erminois, Pean, Vair, Counter Vair, Potent, Counter-Potent, or Cuppa, Vair in point, Vaire, and Vaire-Ancient. See each under its respective term ; also under the term Tincture, and P. 1. Metals and colours may be placed on them.

FUSEE. The same as Fusil.

FUSIL. A kind of spindle used in spinning. P. 40, f. 13. Formerly depicted as f. 3.

FUSIL on a Spindle, termed also a Fusil, or quill of yarn. P. 40, f. 4.

FUSILY, or Fusilly. Covered with fusils. P. 2, f. 28.

FUSILLEE. Same as Fusily.

FUSILY-BENDY, or Bendy-fusily. P. 18, f. 32.

FYLFOT, or Mystic fylfot. See Gammadion. P. 11, f. 39.

G

GABIONS. Baskets of Willow filled with earth to make a parapet, or cover. P. 37, f. 7.

GAD. A plate of steel, or iron. P. 42, f. 35.

GAD-BEE, or Dung-fly. P. 30, f. 21.

GAD-FLY, or Brimsey. See Gad-bee.

GADLYNGS. Small spikes projecting from the knuckles of mediæval gauntlets.

GALLY, Gallie, or Galley. A vessel with oars. See Lymphad.

GALTHRAP, Galtrap, Cheval-trap, Caltrap, Chausse-trap, or Gal-trap. P. 37, f. 10.

Termed Galtraps from their application to the purpose of galling horses ; they are iron instruments, used in war to prevent or retard the advance of cavalry, and consist of four points so formed that whichever way they are placed one point is always erect.

GAMASHES. See Buskin.

GAMB, Gambe, or Jambe. The whole fore leg of a beast. If couped, or erased near the middle joint, it is called a paw. See Seal's Paw. P. 29, f. 52.

Bear's gamb erased. P. 29, f. 41.
Lion's gamb erect and erased. f. 45.
Lion's gamb erased, holding a laurel branch fructed. f. 46.
Two Lions' gambs, supporting a crescent. f. 47.
Two Lions' gambs in saltire. f. 48.
Lion's gamb erased and erect, supporting a shield. P. 31, f. 21.

GAME COCK. P. 34, f. 2.

GAMMADION. A Cross potent rebated. P. 11, f. 39. See Cross Gammadion.

GANNAPES. See Turkey Cock.

GANNET, or Solon Goose. P. 34, f. 20.

GANTLET, or Gauntlop. See Gauntlet.

GARB. A sheaf of Wheat. P. 45, f. 14. If the sheaf is of any other grain, the particular grain must be named, and when the straw is of a different tincture to the ears, it must be mentioned ; as a Garb or. Eared ppr. A Garb fesseways. P. 14, f. 21. Gu. three Garbs ar. a bordure sa. bezantée. The arms of Clement of Lincolnshire and Norfolk.

GARB of Barley. P. 45, f. 15.

GARB of Quaterfoils. i.b. f. 16.

GARDANT, or GUARDANT. Signifies full-faced, when applied to the Lion. Tiger, etc. P. 26, f. 35. This term does not apply to the Deer-Kind ; they are said to be at Gaze.

GARDE-DE-BRAS, or Garbraille. The elbow piece, with buckles and straps as worn toward the end of the fifteenth century. P. 43, f. 54. The Badge of Sir John Ratcliffe, time of Edward IV.

GARDEN-PALES, or Park-Pales. Are depicted with pointed tops and conjoined as P. 43, f. 36.

The pales in the Arms of the Town of Derby are depicted as at P. 28, f. 55.

GARDE-VISURE. The vizor of a helmet, which is a safeguard and defence for the face. *See* Helmet with vizor up. P. 38, f. 10, and an Esquire's Helmet which has the vizor down. P. 24, f. 12.

GARDEN spades. *See* Spade. P. 39, f. 18.

GARLAND, Chaplet, or Wreath of flowers, or leaves. A Garland of Roses, is always composed of four flowers and the rest leaves. P. 24, f. 41, and P. 36, f. 4.

GARLICK. A plant. P. 45, f. 3.

GARNISHED. Ornamented. Sometimes used for Semée. A leg in armour ppr. garnished or. P. 36, f. 22.

GARTER, Order of. *See* Knighthood Orders of.

GARTER. Generally borne in the form of a circle buckled and nowed, with ornamented end pendent, P. 42, f. 17; and the Garter surrounding the Royal Arms. P. 31, f. 11.
The Garter is sometimes divided and called a Demi Garter, or Perclose. P. 42, f. 18.
A Garter, with Motto, is now very frequently met with surrounding the Arms, Crest, or Cyphers, of persons who are not members of any Order of Knighthood, and who, therefore, have in reality no right whatever to it.

GARTER, King of Arms. The principal officer of the Order of the Garter, and principal King of Arms in the Corporation of the Heralds' College, or College of Arms.

GARTER, as represented around the shield of a Knight of that order. P. 31, f. 11.

GARTER, or Gartier. A diminutive of the bend. P. 17, f. 3.

GARTER-PLATE. *See* Stall-Plate.

GATE; also termed Yate. P. 39, f. 41, No. 2. Sometimes blazoned a Bar-Gate, the number of bars being named.

GAULES. Gules.

GAUNTLET; also termed Gantlet. An iron glove ; it must in blazon be named whether a dexter, or sinister gauntlet. *See* Examples. P. 38, f. 11 and 17.

GAUNTLETED. Being armed with a Gauntlet. P. 36, f. 15.

GAZE. All the Deer-kind when borne full faced, or looking affrontée, are said to be at Gaze. P. 28, f. 44. All other beasts in this attitude are called Guardant.

GAZON. A sod, or tuft of grass.

GED. A Pike, or Lucy. P. 32, f. 6.

GEMEL, or Gemew. *See* Bar-Gemel.

GEM-RING. A ring set with some precious stone. P. 37, f. 42.

GEMEL-RING. *See* Gimmal-Ring.

GEMMEL, Gimble, or Gimbal-Ring. Also termed a Gemmow-Ring. *See* Gimmal Ring.

GEMULATE. A Bar Gemelle.

GENEALOGY. The systematical account of the origin and alliances of Families, vid. Pedigree.

Abbreviations and Marks met with in Genealogies.

Æ. or Æt. age.
b. born.
bap., or bapt. baptized.
bd., bu., bur., burd., or burᵈ. Buried.
coh., or cohr. coheir.
co., or com. in the county of.
d. died.
da., or dau. daughter.
da., or dau. & coh. daughter and heiress.
fil. et. hær. son and heir.
h. heir.
hr. ap., or appart. heir apparent.
m., md., or mar. married.
na., or nat. born.
ob., or obt. died.
ob. inf. died an infant.
ob. juv. died in youth.
ob. inf. æt. died a minor.
ob. cœl. died a bachelor.
ob. inn. died a spinster.
ob. s.p. died without issue.
ob. s.p. leg. died without lawful issue.
ob. s.p. mas. died without male issue.
ob. s.p.s. died without surviving issue.
ob. v.p. died in the lifetime of his or her Father.
s. son.
s. & h. son and heir.
sp. or sepult. buried.
temp. in the time of.
unmar. unmarried.
viv. or vix. was living, or lived in the time of.
wid. widow.
= signifies married.
⌐ or ⌐ when placed under a name signifies that he or she had children.
X signifies extinction of that branch of the family.

GENET. A small animal. P. 28, f. 25.

GENOVILLIER. A piece of armour that covers the knee.

GENTLE. Well-born, of a good family.

GENTLE-FLOWER, or Flower-Gentle. A semée of which is borne in the arms of Caius College, Cambridge. P. 22, f. 17.

GENTLEMAN. Under this term are comprised all that are above yeomen and artificers.

A Gentleman has either inherited Coat Armour from his ancestors, or has received a patent for a new coat from the King of Arms. His achievement is the same as that of an Esquire.

GENTRY. The lesser nobility, gentlemen, descended from ancient families that have borne Coat Armour.

GENUANT. In a kneeling posture as an angel genuant, or kneeling. P. 36, f. 55.

GEORGE, St. The patron Saint of England. The Cross of St. George is red on a white field. P. 7, f. 21.

GEORGE. The George is the pendant to the collar of the order of the garter. P. 24, f. 7.

GERATTIE. An ancient term for powdering or semée.

GERATTYNG. The ancient practice of powdering shields for difference is described under this term in the "Book of St. Alban's."

GERBE. A garb.

GEROUNE, or Geronny. See Gyronnée.

GILLY-FLOWER, or July-flower. A species of carnation of a red colour. P. 44, f. 20.

GIMBAL, or Gimble-Rings. See Annulets conjoined in triangle. P. 37, f. 36.

GIMLET. See Wine-Piercer. P. 41, f. 32.

GIMMAL-RING. A double ring. P. 37, f. 35.

Gimmal-rings are also borne triple and quadruple. f. 35 and 36.

GIRAFFE, or Camelopard. P. 27, f. 50.

GIRON. See Gyron.

GIRONNE, Girony, or Gyronny. See Gyronne.

GIRONETTE. A term for towers, when topped with spears.

GIRT, Girded, or Cinctured. Bound round with a girdle, or band.

GIVES, or Gyves. Fetters.

GLAIVE, or Gleave. A javelin. P. 37, f. 22.

GLAYMORE. See Claymore.

GLAZIERS' Nippers, or Grater. A tool used by glaziers, and borne by them as part of their armorial ensign. P. 41, f. 7.

GLIDING, or Glissant. A term used to blazon serpents, snakes, etc., when moving forwards in Fesse. P. 30, f. 47.

GLOBE. P. 39, f. 5.

GLOBE-BROKEN, or Fractured. The Crest of Hope is a broken globe under a rainbow, with clouds at each end. P. 39, f. 6.

GLOBE-DEMI. i.d. f. 1.

GLOBE-CELESTIAL. i.d. f. 5.

GLOBE-FRACTURED. i.d. f. 6.

GLOBE-TERRESTRIAL. i.d. f. 5.

GLOBE in a Frame, environed with a meridian. i.d. f. 2.

GLOBE with a stand. i.d. f. 3.

GLOBICAL, or Convex. Circular on the outside. P. 9, f. 23.

GLOBULAR Lamp. P. 39, f. 27, No. 2.

GLORY. A Nimbus, or circle of glory. P. 28, f. 31.

The Christian attribute of Sanctity.

GLOVE. A Falconer's glove pendent, and a like glove with a tassel. P. 43, f. 44.

GLOVED. The hand covered with a glove.

GLOW-WORM. The Palmer worm. P. 30, f. 24.

GOARE. See Gore.

GOAT. A quadruped. The Heraldic Goat is always of the kind as P. 28, f. 59. Goat's head erased. f. 60.

If the bearing is an Assyrian, Indian, or Angola, Goat, it must be blazoned as such. P. 29, f. 1 and 2.

GOBLET. As borne by the name of Candish. P. 42, f. 26.

GOBBONE. See Gobone.

GOBONE, Gobony, or Gobonated. Is composed of two tinctures in equal divisions, as a Bend Gobony. P. 17, f. 40. If it consists of two rows of chequers, it is termed Counter-Gobony, or Counter-Componée, for Componée is the same as Gobony. P. 17, f. 41.

GOBON. An old term for a Whiting. P. 32, f. 23.

GOBONY. See Gobone.

GOLD. One of the metals termed or. in engraving is expressed by dots. P. 1.

GOLDEN Fleece. See Fleece.

GOLDEN Orb. See Mound.

GOLDFINCH. A beautiful bird. P. 33, f. 43.

GOLPES, or Golps. Roundles of a purple colour. P. 1.

GONFALON, Gonfannon. P. 43, f. 47. Gonfannon; a banner, standard, or ensign. P. 46, f. 13.

GONNE. A cannon, same as Culvering. P. 37, f. 6.

M

GOOG. As borne in the Arms of Lake. P. 39, f. 42, No. 1.

GOOSE. A well-known aquatic fowl. P. 34, f. 30. *See* also Barnacle Goose. f. 19.

GORDIAN-KNOT. A double orle of annulets, linked to each other, and to one in the centre. It is sometimes called the double knot of Navarre, being the arms of that kingdom. P. 20, f. 45.

GORE. Either dexter, or sinister, the former is honourable, the latter being tenne dishonourable as an abatement for cowardice in battle. P. 21, f. 32.

GORED, or Gorée. Cut into large arched indents; the same as Per-bend Nuée Double Arched. P. 19, f. 11.

GORGED. A term to express any animal or bird, having its neck encircled with a crown, coronet, collar, or wreath, as a demi lion ramp. gorged with a ducal coronet. P. 26, f. 31.

GORGE. A term used by Leigh for Water-bouget.

GORGES. *See* Gurges. P. 22, f. 6.

GORGET. Armour worn round the neck. P. 38, f. 9.

GORGING, or Devouring. P. 32, f. 5.

GORY. Red, the hand of the Baronet's badge is sometimes called a gory-hand.

GOSHAWK. A Falcon without bells.

GOULIS, Gowles, or Gowlys. Gules.

GOURD. A many seeded fruit. P. 44, f. 58.

GOURNET, or Gurnet. A fish. P. 32, f. 12.

GOUSSES. Same as bean pods. P. 44, f. 59.

GOUTS, Gouttée, or Gutty. *See* Guttée.

GOWLYS. Gules.

GRADIANT. A term applied to a Tortoise supposed walking. P. 30, f. 5.

GRADY. Represents steps, or degrees. P. 15, f. 15.

GRAFT. A point in point. P. 21, f. 4.

GRAFTED. Inserted and fixed.

GRAIN TREE. P. 44, f. 32.

GRAMINE. A chaplet of grass, is the same as a Crown Graminée. P. 43, f. 4.

GRANADA, Apple of. A Pomegranate. P. 44, f. 57.

GRAND-QUARTERINGS. *See* Marshalling.

GRANNAPYE. Same as Shoveller. P. 34, f. 23.

GRAPES. Grapes on the vine branch are frequently met with in Coat Armour. *See* Vine Branch Fructed. P. 45, f. 8, and P. 47. A Slip of Vine Fructed. P. 20, f. 21.

GRAPPLE. *See* Cramp.

GRAPPLING-IRON. An instrument used in the navy. P. 38, f. 44.

GRASPING. Holding. P. 36, f. 10, 11, and 12.

GRASSHOPPER. The crest of Gresham. P. 30, f. 8.

GRATER, Grazier, Grosing-iron, or Glaziers' nippers. P. 41, f. 7.

GRAY. A Badge, or Brock. P. 27, f. 53.

GRAYLED. Same as Engrailed.

GRAYLING. A fish. P. 32, f. 42a.

GRAZIER, or Glaziers' nippers q.v.

GRAZING. *See* Browsing.

GREAVE. That part of the armour which covers the leg from the knee to the foot. P. 38, f. 14.

GREEK Cross. Has its four limbs all of equal length.

GRECES, steps. A cross on three greces. P. 8, f. 33. *See* Grieces.

GREEN. Vert. q.v.

GREEN, or Wild-man. A savage. P. 35, f. 24.

GREEZE. *See* Grieces.

GRELL. Same as Engrailed.

GRENADE. A hollow ball; a kind of bomb filled with powder, and fired by means of a fuse. P. 37, f. 10.

GREYHOUND. A slender dog fitted for running; a Greyhound Courant. P. 29, f. 20.
Greyhound sejant. i.d. f. 21. Greyhound's head erased. f. 22.

GREYHOUND's Collar. *See* Dog's Collar. P. 43, f. 43, No. 2.

GRICES. Young wild boars.

GRIDIRON. P. 41, f. 11, as in the arms of Laurence.
The other example on the sinister is an antique gridiron. A gridiron is the emblem of St. Lawrence.

GRIECES, Greeces, Greces, Grees, Greezes, or Griezes. Steps; a cross on three grieces. P. 8, f. 33. A Fesse Griece. P. 4, f. 9.

GRIFFIN, Griffon, or Gryphon. A Fabulous animal. P. 27, f. 1.
It has the wings, fore feet and head of an Eagle with the addition of ears; the body, hind legs, and tail of a Lion. When the Griffin is in the position of Rampant it is not to be so blazoned, but is said to be *segreant*. P. 27, f. 2.
Griffin passant. f. 1.
Griffin sejant. f. 3.
Demi Griffin segreant. f. 4.
Griffin's head erased. f. 5.

GRIFFIN Male. Is represented without wings, having tufts issuing from various parts of the body. It is also termed *Alce*, or *Alice*. P. 27, f. 6.

GRIGGS, or Elvers. Young eels. P. 32, f. 41.

GRINGALEE, Gringole, or Guivré; Any bearing so termed when its extremities end with the heads of Serpents. P. 11, f. 36.

GRIPE. Medieval name for Griffin.

GRIPHON. *See* Griffin.

GRIPPING. When hands, paws, or talons, are represented grasping anything. P. 29, f. 46. P. 36, f. 16.

GRISE. *See* Grieces.

GRITTIE. A term for a field composed equally of metal and colour.

GROSE. Or Drawing board. P. 41, f. 3.

GROSING IRON, or Glazier's-nippers. P. 41, f. 7.

GROUSE, or Moorfowl. P. 34, f. 42.

GROVE OF TREES. Also termed a Wood or Hurst. P. 45, f. 60.

GRYCE. *See* Grice.

GRYPE, or Gryphon. *See* Griffin.

GUARDANT, or Gardant. Said of Lions, Tigers, etc., when full faced. P. 26, f. 11, 27, and 35.

GUARDS. Rows of Fur upon the dexter side of Peer's Mantles and denote the rank, viz. Four guards for a Duke, Three and half for a Marquis. *See* P. 35, f. 16. Three for an Earl. Two and a half for a Viscount. And Two for a Baron.

GUARDED. Applied to Mantles when trimmed with rows of Fur, etc.

GUAY, or Cheval Guay. A horse rearing

GUDGEON. A fish. P. 32, f. 33.

GUELPHIC, or Hanoverian Order. *See* Knighthood Orders of.

GUIDON, Guidhomme, or Pennon. P. 46, 12 and 14.

GUIGE. A Shield-belt worn over the right shoulder.

GUINEA PIG. A small quadruped. P. 30, f. 12.

GUINEA-WHEAT. *See* Wheat.

GUIRON. *See* Gyron.

GUISARME. The same as Halbert.

GUIVRE. *See* Gringalee.

GULES. Red. Iu engraving is represented by perpendicular lines, and is expressed sometimes in Blazon by the precious stone Ruby, or the planet Mars, etc. *See* P. 1.

GULL, or Sea-Gull. P. 34, f. 13.

GULY. *See* Gules.

GUN-SHOT, or Gun-Stone. An old name for Pellet, or Ogress. P. 1.

GURGES, or Whirlpool. P. 22, f. 6.

GURNARD, GOURNET, or GURNET. A fish. P. 32, f. 12.

GURNET. A fish. P. 32, f. 12.

GUSSET. Dexter and sinister. P. 21, f. 33. When sanguine both are abatements.

GUTTÆ, or Gouttes. *See* Guttée.

GUTTEE, or Gutty, from the Latin gutta a drop. Guttée is a term which expresses the field, or any charge strewed over with drops. P. 12, f. 11. In blazon, be it observed, you are not to say guttée of such a colour, for the name expresses the colour; e.g. Gold drops are termed Guttee d'or; drops of water guttee d'eau; drops of blood guttee de sang. &c. P. 1. Az. Guttee d'eau. P. 2, f. 41. P. 19, f. 36.

GUYDON, or Guydhomme. *See* Guidon.

GUZE. Roundle of a Sanguine or Murry colour. P. 1.

GYPSY's head. *See* Head.

GYRATION. A winding.

GYRON. A gore in a Robe, Gown or Coat, formed by two straight lines, drawn from the dexter fesse and chief points, meeting in an acute angle in the fesse point. P. 19, f. 42. If the gyron issues from any other part of the shield it must be mentioned. Two Gyrons. P. 19, f. 43, and 44, The Gyron is subject to the accidental forms of lines, as engrailed, invecked, wavy, &c.

GYRONNE, Gyronny, or Gyrony. The field is said to be Gyronny when divided into several Gyrons as gyronne of six, of eight, of twelve, of sixteen. P. 2, f. 25, 26, 29 and 30. Gyronny of eight within a bordure. P. 19, f. 41.

GYRONNY, or Gyronne of three Arondia. P. 19, f. 45.

GYRONWAYS. Anything disposed in the form of a Gyron.

GYTON. A pennon, or flag with pointed ends.

H

HABERGEON, Haubergeon, or Hauberk. A shirt of mail without sleeves. P. 38, f. 8.

HABICK, or Habeck. A tool used in the process of dressing cloth, and borne in the arms of the Clothiers' Company. P. 41, f. 45.

HABITED. Clothed, or vested. P. 35, f. 28, and P. 36, f. 10, etc.

HACHE, or HACKE. An axe.

HACKED, or Hewed. When the indents are embowed. P. 15, f. 27.

HACKETT. Plumbers' cutting knife, or iron. P. 41, f. 7.

HACKLE. A Hemp-Break. P. 40, f. 11.

HADDOCK. A fish. P. 32, f. 35

HAFT, a handle. As a knife ar. haft, or hafted or. P. 41, f. 20.

HAIE. *See* Weir.

HAIR. *See* Head of Hair. P. 40, f. 47.

HAKE-FISH, or Hakot. P. 32, f. 36.

HALBERT, Halbard, or Halberde. A battle axe. P. 37, f. 31.

HALCYON. *See* Kingfisher.

HALF. *See* Demi.

HALF-SPADE. P. 39, f. 18, No. 4.

HALF-SPEAR. P. 37, f. 22.

HALO, or Circle of Glory. P. 28, f. 31.

HAMECON-CROSS. P. 11, f. 15.

HAMES, or Heames. Pieces of wood or metal, by which the traces and body harness of a horse are attached to the collar. P. 37, f. 55.

HAMMERS in great variety are found in Coat Armour. P. 41, f. 25 to 28.

HANCHET. *See* Bugle-horn.

HAND. Borne variously in Coat Armour.
The Hand is always understood to be a dexter one, if not mentioned as sinister, and when no other position is named it is understood to be Apaumée. P. 36, f. 1.

HAND aversant. The back of the hand. f. 1.

HAND couped at the wrist. f. 1.

HAND couped in fesse. f. 2.

HAND couped. f. 3 and 14.

HAND couped in bend sinister. f. 5.

HAND sinister couped. f. 6.

HAND dexter and sinister couped, supporting a sword in pale. f. 8.

HANDS, two, conjoined in fesse. f. 2.

HANDS, two, rending a horse-shoe. P. 19, f. 29.

HAND erased fesseways. P. 31, f. 36.

HAND erect. Out of a human heart a hand erect betw. two stalks of Wheat flexed in saltire all ppr., in the hand a closed book sa. garnished or. P. 42, f. 4.
For full blazon of Hands and Arms *see* P. 31, and P. 36.

HAND-CUFFS. *See* Manacles.

HAND-LAMP. P. 39, f. 26, No. 2.

HAND-RED, or bloody. *See* Baronet's Badge. P. 31, f. 12.

HANGER. A short curved sword.

HANGERS, or Kettle-irons, as borne by the name of Kettler. P. 41, f. 8. The Hanger at f. 9, borne by Tecke.

HANK of Cotton. P. 40, f. 5.

HANOVERIAN Crown. P. 25, f. 25.

HANOVERIAN Guelphic Order. *See* Knighthood.

HARBOURED. The same as lodged.

HARE. A swift timid animal. P. 29, f. 5.

HARE playing on the Bagpipes. id. f. 6. Borne by Fitz-Ercald.

HARE, scalp of. P. 31, f. 15. The Crest of Dymoke.

HARIANT. *See* Haurient.

HARNYSED. Clad in armour.

HARP. A stringed instrument with triangular frame, the cords of which are distended in parallel directions from the upper part to one of its sides. It is the well-known ensign of the kingdom of Ireland. P. 3, f. 21. For other examples *see* P. 43, f. 19, and P. 31, f. 6.

HARP-JEWS. P. 43, f. 21.

HARPOON, Harpoon-head, Harping-iron, or Salmon spear. P. 38, f. 45.

HARPY. A fabulous monster, represented as a vulture with the head and breast of a woman. P. 35, f. 30. A Harpy with wings expanded and inverted. f. 31. A Demi Harpy displayed. f. 32.

HARRINGTON Knot. The badge of that family. P. 43, f. 9.

HARROW. A frame of timbers crossing each other, and set with teeth. P. 39, f. 8, No. 2.
Three triangular harrows conjoined in the fesse point with an annulet. i.d. f. 9.

HART. *See* Stag.

HART, Royal. A stag who has escaped when hunted by a King, or Queen.

HARVEST Fly. P. 30, f. 22.

HARYANT. Same as Haurient.

HASEL-SPRIG. Same as a nut-branch only with three leaves. P. 44, f. 55.

HAT. A cover for the head. P. 40, f. 50.
A Hat as worn over the arms of the States General. f. 52. Hat as borne in the arms of the Felt Makers' Company. i.d. Hat turned up and adorned with three ostrich's feathers, borne by the name of Huth. f. 53. Hat of a Cardinal. P. 40, f. 60.

HAT-BAND. P. 40, f. 43.
The dexter one as borne by the families of Bury, Magnes, etc.; the other as borne in the Arms of the Felt Makers' Company.

HATCHET, and Danish-hatchet. P. 37, f. 29 and 30.

HATCHING. A bird hatching. P. 31, f. 20.

HATCHMENT. A corrupted term applied to denote a Family Funeral Achievement. *See* Funeral Achievement.

HAUBERK, or Hauberg. *See* Habergeon

HAUETTE. *See* Habick.

HAUMETTY. *See* Humettée.

HAURIANT, or Haurient. A term applied to Fish when placed erect. P. 32, f. 6, 13, 17, and 18.

HAURIENT embowed. Borne paleways, but bowed. P. 32, f. 2.

HAURIENT torqued, or targant. Borne paleways, but in the form of an S.

HAUSSE. or Hause. *See* Enhanced.

HAUTBOY. A musical wind instrument. P. 43, f. 23, No. 1.

HAWBERK. A shirt of mail. P. 39, f. 20, No. 4.

HAWK, or Falcon. A very common bearing in Coat Armour. A Hawk, or Falcon, blazoned ppr. is represented with a bell tied to each leg. *See* Falcon.

HAWK's leure, or lure. As depicted in Armory are two wings conjoined with their tips downwards, fastened with a line and ring. P. 43, f. 16.

HAWK'S-BELLS. P. 43, f. 17.

HAWK'S-BELL and Jesses. The jesses are leather thongs with which the bells are tied to the hawk's legs. P. 43, f. 17.

HAWKS, Perch, or Rest. i.d. f. 18.

HAWKING, or Falconer's gloves. P. 43, f. 44.

HAWMED. *See* Humettée.

HAWTHORN Tree, or Bush. P. 45, f. 43.

HAYDODDES. *See* Cyanus.

HAY-FORK, or Shake-Fork. Depicted as P. 39, f. 19.

HAY-HOOK. As borne in the arms of Metringham. i.d. f. 21.

HAY-RAKE. *See* Rake.

HAZEL. There are two varieties, the common hazel nut and the filbert, met with in Coat Armour; a branch of the common hazel fructed. P. 44, f. 55.

HAZEL leaves. P. 45, f. 17.

HEAD. Heads of Men and Women, Beasts, Birds, Fish, etc., are of frequent occurrence in Coat Armour. They are in profile (termed side long, or side faced), front faced, i.e. affrontée, or guardant, and reguardant, which is looking back.

In blazon, all heads are understood to be in profile, if not expressed to the contrary.

The terms, Man's Head, Savage's Head, Saxon's Head, Englishman's Head, and Gipsy's Head, are used to describe heads of exactly the same kind. *See* Man's Head.

Blazon of Heads.
Bear's. P. 29.
Bird's. P. 33.
Boar's. P. 29.
Bull's. P. 22 and 28.
Dragon's. P. 27.
Fish's. P. 32.
Fox's. P. 29.
Greyhound's. P. 29.
Griffin's. P. 27.
Goat's. P. 28 and 29.
Horse's. P. 27.
Leopard's. P. 28.
Lion's. P. 26.
Man's P. 36.
Ram's. P. 28.
Stag's. P. 28.
Talbot's. P. 29.
Tiger's. P. 28.
Unicorn's. P. 27.
Wolf's. P. 28.
Wivern's. P. 27.

HEAD of hair. P. 40, f. 47.

HEADPIECE. A helmet.

HEALME, or Casque. A Helmet.

HEAMES. *See* Hames.

HEART. In blazon, the heart is termed a human or body heart. P. 42, f. 1.

Heart. *Enfiled, Ensigned, Flamant, Pierced, Transfixed, Vulned, Winged*, etc. i.d. f. 1 to 5, f. 4 is a dexter hand erect, betw. two stalks of wheat flexed in saltire, issuing from a heart all ppr., in the hand a book shut sa. garnished or.

HEART'S-EASE, or Pansy-flower. P. 44, f. 23.

HEATER-SHIELD. *See* Escutcheon.

HEATH-COCK. P. 34, f. 41.

HEAUME, Heawme, Heaulme, or Casque. *See* Helmet.

HEAVENLY bodies. *See* Planets.

HEDGEHOG, or Urchin. A small animal, the upper part of its body is covered with prickles. P. 30, f. 11.

HEDGEHOG-FISH, or Sea-Urchin. P. 32, f. 49.

HEINUSE. Signifies a young roe, in the third year.

HEIR Apparent. Is a person so called in the lifetime of the present possessor at whose death he is heir at law.

HELM. An instrument by which a ship is steered. P. 38, f. 40.

HELMET, Helme, Heaulme, or Casque. Was also termed Heaume, Basinet, Cask, Salet, etc.

Although these were all terms to denote coverings for the head in time of war, still they differed not only in name, but in shape. Our custom of bearing the Crest on the Helmet is borrowed from the ancient fashion of adorning it with some kind of device, to make it appear terrible to the enemy.

Helmets are now used as the distinctive marks of Nobility, and are differently depicted. They are frequently met with as charges in Coat Armour, and are also borne singly as Crests.

The Helmet of a King, or Prince, is full faced, with six bars, all of gold, and lined inside with crimson. P. 24, f. 8.

The Helmet of a Duke, Marquis, Earl, Viscount, and Baron, is of steel, garnished with gold, placed in profile with five bars, lined with crimson. f. 9.

The Helmet of a Baronet, or Knight, is of steel, ornamented with gold, and is shewn full-faced, with beaver open, lined with crimson. f. 11.

The Helmet of an Esquire, or Gentleman, is a steel profile Helmet, ornamented with gold, the beaver close, f. 12; Helmet with Vizor raised, P. 36, f. 10.

If two Helmets are placed on one shield to support two different crests, they are usually set face to face. P. 2, f. 24.

HELVED. A term to express the handle of an axe, adze, hammer, etc., when of a different tincture. *See* Haft.

HEMISPHERE - NORTHERN, or Demi-Globe. P. 39, f. 1.

HEMP-BREAK, or Hackle. An instrument formerly used to break or bruise hemp. P. 40, f. 11.

Borne by the family of Bray. The bottom example as borne by Bree.

HENEAGE-KNOT. P. 43, f. 13.

HERALD. An officer of Arms. The duties of a Herald were originally of a military and deplomatic character, but have for centuries been confined to matters relating to Armorial Bearings, Genealogy, and the Superintendence of Public Ceremonies.

HERALDIC-ANTELOPE. A fabulous animal represented with two straight horns, the body of a Stag, the tail of a Unicorn, a tusk issuing from the tip of its nose, a row of tufts down the back of the neck, on the chest and thighs. P. 28, f. 23.

HERALDIC Antelope's head erased. P. 28, f. 24.

HERALDIC-TIGER. A fictitious beast, depicted with a hooked tusk at the nose, and with a mane formed of tufts. P. 28, f. 19.

HERALDIC-TIGER's head couped. i.d. f. 20.

HERALDS College, or College of Arms. A Royal Corporation instituted in the reign of Rich. III.

It's head is the hereditary Earl Marshal of England, the Duke of Norfolk, and its officers are divided into three classes, viz., Kings, Heralds, and Pursuivants of Arms, whose precedence is regulated by seniority of appointment. The King's of Arms are three; the first, or chief, is termed *Garter* principal King of Arms, the second *Clarenceux*, and the third *Norroy*. (*See* Bath King of Arms.) The number of Heralds is six,

viz., *Windsor, Chester, Lancaster, Richmond, Somerset,* and *York*. There have been, at different periods, other Heralds whose titles are now laid aside. Heralds extraordinary have also been occasionally created. The Pursuivants are four, viz., *Rouge Croix, Blue Mantle, Rouge Dragon,* and *Portcullis*.

Besides the Heralds College of London, there is Lyon Office, Edinburgh, and the Office of Arms, Dublin. These have cognizance of the Heraldry of Scotland and Ireland respectively; each has one King of Arms, *Lord Lyon* and *Ulster*.

HERALDRY. Intimately connected with the early history of Europe, its chivalry, and its conquests. Is the science of armorial bearings; how to blazon or describe them in proper terms, and to Marshal or dispose the different arms in an escutcheon or shield.

HERAND and Herault. A Herald.

HERCE. *See* Harrow.

HERCULES. Called by the Greeks Heracles and Alcides, the most celebrated hero of the Mythological age of Greece. Hercules is depicted as a naked man holding a club, and his shoulders are enwrapped with a Lion's skin.

Hercules in his second labour, i.e. in close engagement with the Lernean Hydra, is borne in the coat of Herklots.

HEREDITARY. That has descended from an ancestor to an heir. *See* Arms Paternal.

HERISSE. Set with long sharp points, as a hedgehog.

HERISSON. The hedgehog.

HERMINES. Ermine represented by Ermines; i.e. white ermine spots on black. P. 1.

HERMIT. One who retires from society to contemplation and devotion, and frequently in blazon is termed a Monk or Friar. P. 36, f. 31.

HERN, or Herne. *See* Heron.

HERON, or Heronshaw. A large bird with long slender legs, neck and bill. P. 34, f. 7.

HERRING. A small sea-fish. P. 32, f. 13.

This is also blazoned a Cob-Fish, or Sea-Cob.

HERSE. Same as Portcullis.

HEURT. *See* Hurt.

HIEROGLYPHICS. Symbolical figures.

HILL, or Hillock; also termed Mole-hill. P. 42, f. 60.

Three Hills, as in the arms of Brinckman. f. 58.

HILT. The handle of a sword, which is termed Hilted when the tincture has to be named.

HIND. The female of the stag. Hinds counter-tripping, and a Hind's head couped. P. 28, f. 53 and 54.

HINGE. A joint on which a door, gate, etc., turns. P. 42, f. 14.

HIPPOCAMPUS. A sea horse. P. 29, f. 55. Sometimes represented having the entire fore part of a horse, ending in the tail of a dolphin.

HIPPOCENTAUR. *See* Centaur.

HIPPOGRIFF. A fabulous animal, with a Griffin's body, terminating in that of a horse. P. 27, f. 7.

HIRONDELLE. A swallow.

HIRUNDO. A swallow.

HOBY. A Falcon.

HOGSHEAD. *See* Tun.

HOIST. The depth of any flag from chief to base; also its head or upper side.

HOLLEN. *See* Holly.

HOLLY, or Ilex. The sprig, branch, and leaf, are all met with in armoury. P. 44, f. 39; P. 45, f. 23.

HOLY Bible. *See* Book.

HOLY-DOVE. P. 22, f. 4.

HOLY, or Paschal Lamb. Represented passant with a cross-staff, banner argent, thereon a cross gules, over the head a glory or. P. 29, f. 4.

HONEYSUCKLE, or Woodbine. P. 45, f. 1.

HONOUR Point. *See* Points of the Shield. P. 1, and P. 21, f. 21.

HONOURED. Crowned.

HONOURABLE Ordinaries. *See* Ordinaries.

HOOD. The caul, coif, or cowl of a hermet. *See* Hermet's head with cowl. P. 36, f. 31.

HOODED. Said of a hawk, when borne with its hood on.

HOODED-CROW. *See* Crow.

HOOFED. *See* Unguled.

HOOK. *See* Fish-hook, Flesh-hook, Hay-hook, Pruning-hook, Reaping-hook, Shave-hook, and Tenter-hook.

HOOPED-BUCKET. P. 39, f. 35, No. 1.

HOP ; also termed Houblon. A plant. P. 45, f. 7.

HOP-POLES, sustaining their fruit. P. 22, f. 11.

HOPE, the emblem of. P. 35, f. 8.

HORN. P. 43, f. 23, No. 2. The Trumpet, f. 23, No. 4, is sometimes called a horn.

In Heraldry the term Horn is used to denote. I. The horns of an animal; *see* term ARMED. II. A Musical Instrument, blazoned a Cornet. P. 43, f. 21, No. 4. III. A Bugle, or Hunting Horn. f. 24. IV. The extremities

of a Crescent which are called its horns, and anything placed within them, is said to be between the Horns ; when anything is placed between and above the horns, it is said to be Issuant, or Out of. As an Estoile issuant of a Crescent. P. 23, f. 39.

HORNED. When the horns are of a different tincture from the animal it is said to be horned, or armed. A Stag is said to be *Attired.*

HORNED Owl. *See* Owl.

HOROLOGIUM. An hour-glass. P. 39, f. 44

HORSE. A Draught-horse, distinguished by having a collar and traces. The Badge of the Earl of Pembroke.

HORSE. Much used in armory. A horse passant. P. 27, f. 30.

HORSE, courant. P. 21, f. 44.

HORSE, forcene. P. 27, f. 26.

HORSE, in full gallop. P. 36, f. 27.

HORSE, spancelled. P. 27, f. 31.

HORSE'S Head, couped and bridled. i.d. f. 35.

HORSE'S Head, erased. i.d. f. 34.

HORSE-DEMI. P. 22, f. 16.

HORSE-BARNACLES. *See* Barnacles.

HORSE-FLY. *See* Gad-Fly.

HORSE-HEAMES. *See* Hames.

HORSE-PICKER. P. 39, f. 21, No. 2.

HORSE-SHOE. P. 37, f. 45.

HORSE-SHOES, three interlaced. i.d. f. 46.

HORSE-SHOE, two hands rending a horse-shoe. P. 19, f. 29.

HOSPITALLARS, Knights of St. John of Jerusalem, instituted about A.D. 1092. They wore over their armour a black robe, having a white linen cross of eight points fastened to the left breast. P. 11, f. 42. Between the year 1278 and 1289, when engaged in military duties, they assumed a red surcoat bearing a silver cross. P. 23, f. 21. *See* Knights Templers. Order of the Hospital of St. John of Jerusalem in England.

On the 14th May, 1888, *Her Majesty the Queen* was graciously pleased to grant a *Charter of Incorporation* to "The Grand Priory of the Order of the Hospital of St. John of Jerusalem in England," and to "declare that *Her Majesty the Queen* is the Sovereign Head and Patron of the Order, and that on the Eve of St. John the Baptist next following *His Royal Highness the Prince of Wales* shall become the Grand Prior of the Order."

In consequence of the above Charter a Lion passant guardant and a Unicorn passant placed alternately or, was added to the angles of the Cross in the arms.

HOUBLON. *See* Hop.

HOUCE des armes. *See* Surcoat.

HOUND. *See* Dog. P. 29, f. 12.

HOURGLASS, or Sandglass. P. 39, f. 44, No. 2.

HOURGLASS, winged. i.d. f. 45.

HOUSELEEK. *See* Sengreen. P. 22, f. 17.

HOUSE-SNAIL. P. 30, f. 6.

HOUSING. The embroidered caparison of a horse.

HOVERING. As an eagle with wings displayed. *See* also Disclosed, and Flotant.

HUERT. *See* Hurt.

HUIT-FOIL. Eight-foil, or double quaterfoil. P. 44, f. 18. The mark of cadency for the ninth son.

HULK. The body of a ship. *See* Hull. P. 38, f. 36.

HULL. As in the arms of Masters and Mariners. i.d.

HUMAN figure. See Man.

HUMAN skull. See Death's-head.

HUMET. A fesse couped is so termed. P. 4, f. 1. See Humettée.

HUMETTEE, Humetty, couped, or coppée. An ordinary which is cut off so that the extremities do not touch the sides of the shield. P. 8, f. 28; P. 15, f. 12.

HUNGERFORD Knot. P. 43, f. 12.

HUNTER'S, or Hunting-horn, or Cornet. See Bugle Horn and Cornet.

HURCHIN. A hedgehog. P. 30, f. 11.

HURE. A term for the head of a wild boar, bear, wolf, and other such like animals, but not for those of lions.

HURST. A wood, or thicket of trees. P. 45, f. 60.

HURT, Heurts, or Huerts. Blue roundles. P. 1.

HURTEE. Semée of Hurts.

HURTY, or Semée of Hurts, Anything is so termed when powdered, or strewed over promiscuously with Hurts.

HUSBAND and Wife, arms of. *See* Arms Impaled.

HUSBAND with two or more wives. *See* P. 46.

HUSK. The term Husk in heraldry is applied to the cup of the acorn. When the acorn and cup are of different tinctures, the former is said to be husked. *See* Acorn.

HYACINTH. A precious stone, used in blazon to express the colour tenne.

HYDRA. A fabulous monster with seven heads. P. 28, f. 16.

HYMENEAL-TORCH. A torch bound with ribbons, flames issuant. P. 41, f. 47.

HYRST. *See* Hurst.

I

IBEX. In armory, an imaginary animal, it has two straight horns projecting from the forehead, serrated. P. 28, f. 21.

IBIS. An Egyptian-bird. P. 34, f. 10.

ICICLE. A pendent conical mass of ice. P. 41, f. 48.

I.H.S. Iota, Eta, and Sigma of Jesus, also abbreviation for Jesus, or Jesus Hominum Salvator.

ILEX. See Holly.

IMBATTLED, or Embattled. Same as Crenellée. P. 3, f. 8.

IMBATTLED Christed. A chief imbattled christed. Same as a Chief Urdée, or Champagne. P. 12, f. 8.

IMBORDURED. *See* Bordered.

IMBORDERING. A term to express a field bordered with the same tincture as the field.

IMBOWED, or Embowed. Bent. P. 36, f. 11.

IMBRUED, Imbued, or Embrued. Stained with blood. P. 37, f. 11, and P. 36, f. 13.

IMPALE-TO. Is to join two coats of arms palewise. *See* Arms Impaled.

IMPALED. United by impalement. P. 46, f. 1.

IMPALING. Dividing the shield perpale. P. 1.
In impaling a coat with a border, the border is not continued down the centre line. *See* P. 13, f. 43.

IMPERIAL Crown. Properly that which is worn by an Emperor; the Crowns of Kings are, however, often termed imperial, and any bearing that is crowned with a regal crown is said to be *Imperially Crowned.* P. 26, f. 27.

IMPERIAL Eagle. An eagle with two heads. P. 33, f. 6.

IMPRESE, or Impress. A device on a shield. A painted metaphor.

IN. Added to the Ordinary, is used to express the position of charges when they occupy that position of the shield assigned to the ordinary; e.g.
Five Roses *in Saltire;* P. 20, f. 39. *In Pale;* P. 14, f. 36. *In Bend;* P. 17, f. 45. Three lozenges *in Fesse;* P. 3, f. 40. Two combs *in Fesse;* P. 4, f. 31. *In Orle* eight estciles; P. 5, f. 36. Five lozenges *in Cross;* P. 8, f. 4. *In Chief* three estoiles; P. 12, f. 3, etc. Observe it is correct to use the following terms instead of "In," viz: Bendways, Paleways, Fesse, or Barways, Cheveronways, Saltireways.

INARCHED. *See* Chevron Enarched. P, 15, f. 32.

INCENSED, Incensan, or Anime. Terms for animals when borne with fire issuing from their mouths and ears. P. 28, f. 7.

INCLAVE. The same as pattée, or dovetailed. P. 12, f. 9.

INCONTRANT. Meeting. The same as Respectant.

INCREMENT. Used to express the moon in her increase ; the same as the next term.

INCRESCENT. A crescent with horns towards the dexter. P. 23, f. 38.

INDE. Azure.

INDENTED. Notched. P. 3, f. 13.

INDENTED-EMBOWED. A chev. Indented-embowed. P. 15, f. 27.

INDENTED, point in point. P. 3, f. 26.

INDENTEE. Having indents not joined. P. 13, f. 18.

INDENTELLY. Indented Perlong, with notches much deeper than usual.

INDIAN Empire, Order of. *See* Knighthood Orders of.

INDIAN Goat. P. 29, f. 1.

INDIAN Goat's head couped. P. 29, f. 2.

INDIAN Palm. P. 45, f. 52.

INDORCE. *See* Endorse.

INDORSED, or Endorsed. Placed back to back. P. 26, f. 15.

INESCUTCHEON, Inescochen, or Escochen. A small escutcheon borne as a charge, or on the centre of a shield, but much smaller than what is termed an escutcheon of Pretence. P. 19, f. 44, and P. 21, f. 44.

INFAMED. *See* Defamed. P. 26, f. 6.

INFANT's Head. P. 36, f. 49.

INFLAMED, or Flamant. Any thing burning. P. 42, f. 57; P. 45, f. 59.

INFULA. A long cap. P. 40, f. 51, No. 3.

INFULÆ. Ribands hanging from a Bishop's Mitre. P. 24, f. 10.

INFULATED. Adorned.

INFULED. Having a long cap embowed, at the end a tassel. P. 36, f. 45.

IN-FLANK. P. 20, f. 38.

IN-FULL course. Same as Current.

IN Glory, or In Splendour. The sun surrounded by rays. P. 23, f. 32.

IN-LURE. Two wings conjoined and inverted are said to be in lure. P. 33, f. 28.

IN-PRETENCE. Placed upon, and in front of. P. 11, f. 21.

IN-PRIDE. Said of the Peacock and Turkeycock when depicted with tail extended. P. 34, f. 3 and 4.

IN-SURCOAT. *See* Surtout.

INGOTS OF GOLD. P. 43, f. 46.

INGRAILED. *See* Engrailed.

INGULFANT, or Engoulant. *See* Ingullant.

INGULLANT. Swallowing. P. 32, f. 5.

INGULPHANT The same.

INHANCED. Same as Enhanced.

INK-FISH. *See* Cuttle-Fish. P. 32, f. 50.

INK-HORN. Anciently termed " penner and ink-horn. P. 41, f. 17 and 18.

INK-MOLINE, Ink-de-Moline, or Mill-Rind. Which *see*.

INQUIRE, arms of, an Heraldic anomaly. Is when a Coat contains charges so contrary to the general rules of Heraldry, that persons are led to ask why they have been granted. *See* Enquirir Arms of.

INRACED, or Racée. The same as indented.

INSECTS. Of different kinds are borne in Coat Armour, viz.: Bees, Ants, Butterflies, etc. P. 30, f. 7, and f. 19 to 23.

INSIGNA. Badges of distinction.

INSIGNED, or Ensigned. Crowned.

INSTRUMENTS of the Passion. Displayed on shields in ecclesiastical decorations are the Pitcher, the Towel, Sword, Scourge, Crown of Thorns, Reed and Sponge, Spear, Nails, Ladder, Pincers, and a Heart pierced with five wounds, arranged in different ways.

INTER. Between.

INTERCHANGEABLY-POSED. As fish lying across each other, the heads and tails interchangeably posed, the head of each appearing between the tails of the others. This might be blazoned three fish, two in saltire heads upwards, one in pale head downwards. P. 32, f. 25.

INTERCHANGED. The same as counterchanged.

INTERFRETTED, Interlaced, or Interlinked. Linked together, as three crescents interlaced. P. 23, f. 40. Three annulets interlaced. P. 37, f. 36. Three horse shoes interlaced. f. 46.

INTERLACED. As three chevronals interlaced. P. 15, f. 40.

INTERPOSED. Alternately disposed.

INTERSICANTS, or Intersectants. Per-transient lines which cross each other.

INTERSTICE. The narrow space between two or more bodies, as Ar. fretty Sa. in each interstice a crescent of the last. P. 5, f. 30.

INVECKEE AND GOAREE. The same as Double Arching, or Archée, Nuée, and Undée. P. 19, f. 11.

INVECKED, Invected, or Invecqued. The reverse of engrailed. P. 1, and P. 3, f. 3.

INVELLOPED, or Involved. Surrounded by, or issuing from clouds, etc.

INVERTANT, Inverted, or Reversed. Any thing turned the wrong way. P. 15, f. 43 ; P. 33, f. 28.

INVEXED. Arched, as a chief arched. P. 12, f. 37.

INVOLVED. See a Serpent Involved. P. 30, f. 49.

IONIC-PILLAR. P. 43, f. 50.

IRELAND, Arms of. Az. a Harp or, stringed ar. See Title-page.

IRELAND, Badge of. P. 3, f. 21.

IRELAND, Crest of. P. 4, f. 21.

IRISH Brogue. See Brogue.

IRISH Crown. P. 24, f. 38.

IRISH-CUPS. See Covered-cups.

IRON. See Cutting, Drawing, Soldering, and Spade Iron.

IRON Ring. A tool used by wire-drawers, and borne as part of their arms. P. 42, f. 29.

IRRADIATED. Surrounded by rays.

ISANT. See Issuant.

ISLANDS. Depicted as P. 42, f. 59.

ISLE-OF-MAN arms. A shield gu. three legs as described at P. 36, f. 26.

ISSUANT, or Issuing. Terms which signify proceeding from, or coming out of, as a Lion issuing out of a fesse. P. 26, f. 26, and f. 29. An Estoile issuant out of a Crescent. P. 23, f. 39. Rays issuing. f. 30.

ISSUANT et Issuant, or Issuant-Revert-ant. Terms to express an aninal as if he were issuing or coming into the field in base, and going out again in chief. P. 26, f. 33.

IVY. A plant that runs up trees, walls, etc. An Ivy branch. P. 45, f. 6. A wreath of ivy is round the temples of the Negresses head borne by the family of Norton. (Lord Grantley.) "Ivy is the symbol of eternal life." The arms of the Town of St. Ives. ar. an Ivy branch overspreading the whole field vert.

J

JACENT. Lying along, as a stock of a Tree jacent eradicated. P. 45, f. 57.

JACKDAW. A bird of the genus Crows. P. 34, f. 53.

JACK-UNION. See Union Jack.

JACOB's Staff. See Pilgrim's staff.

JACYNTHE. See Hyacinth.

JAGGED. Notched, uneven. P. 18, f. 23.

JAGUAR. See Ounce.

JAMBE. See Gamb.

JAMBEUX. Armour for the leg. P. 36, f. 22.

JAMES, St. Cross of. P. 11, f. 2.

JANUS' Head. Is represented with two faces, an old and a youthful one, of which one looks forward and the other backward. P. 36, f. 40.

JASHAWK. A Hawk.

JAUNE. Yellow, or gold.

JAVELIN. A spear with a barbed point. P. 37, f. 22.

JAWBONE. P. 42, f. 52.

JAY. A bird. P. 34, f. 46.

JELLOP, or Jowlop. The comb of a cock, cockatrice, etc., and when of a different tincture from the head, the cock, etc., is said to be Jelloped. See Wattled.

JELLOPED. See Jellop.

JERSEY-COMB. A tool used by wool-combers. P. 40, f. 12.

JERUSALEM Cross. A cross crosslet cantoned with four crosses. P. 8, f. 25.

JESSANT. Throwing out, or shooting forth as a lion rising, or issuing from the middle of the fesse. P. 26, f. 26. A Lion jessant of a fesse, also termed a Lion naissant of a fesse.

JESSANT and Debruised. i.d. f. 32.

JESSANT-DE-LIS, or Jessant-de-lys. When a fleur-de-lis issues from any object. As a Leopard's face jessant-de-lis. P. 28, f. 5.
In old writings the word vorant is used to express a leopard's face jessant-de-lis.

JESSAMINE. In blazoning arms by flowers represents argent.

JESSES. Short straps to tie the bells on the legs of a hawk, in which were fixed the varvels, or little rings, and to these was fastened the leash, or long strap by which the Falconer held her on his hand.
See a Falcon's leg belled, jessed and varvelled. P. 33, f. 34.

JEWELS. The tinctures of the arms of Peers are blazoned by some writers by the names of precious stones. See P. 1.

JEWELLED. Adorned with Jewels, as the Coronets. P. 24, f. 42 to 45.

JEWS-HARP. P. 43, f. 21, No. 1.

JOHN, St. of Jerusalem. See St. John of Jerusalem.

JOHN, St., Head of S. John the Baptist in a charger. P. 35, f. 33.

JOHN, Prester. See Prester-John.

JOINANT. Same as conjoined.

JOUSTS. See Justs.

JOUSTING-LANCE. P. 35, f. 23.

JOWLOPPED. See Jellop.

JUDDOCK. A Snipe. P. 34, f· 50.

JUGARIÆ Fasciolæ. See Bar-Gemel.

JUG. A drinking vessel See Ewer.

JULIAN, St. Cross of. A cross crosslet placed saltireways.

JULY-FLOWER. See Gilly-flower.

JUMEL, or Jumelle. See Gemel.

JUPITER. Azure is expressed by this planet in blazon. P. 1.

JUPITER's thunderbolt. P. 37, f. 44.

JUPON, or Just-corps. A surcoat without sleeves, worn over their armour by the Nobles and Knights of the Middle Ages from about A.D. 1360 to A.D. 1405. The Jupon was emblazoned with the insignia of the wearer.

JUSTICE, the emblem of. P. 35, f. 7.

JUSTS. Military exercises in former times, for the display of martial prowess, conducted with great pomp and ceremony. See Tournaments.

K

K. Three Roman K's ar. on a field az. are the arms of Knocks.

KAARE. A cat. P. 28, f. 26.

KAE-CORNWALL. A Cornish chough. P. 33, f. 54.

KANGAROO. An animal found in Australia. P. 28, f. 42.

KATHERINE Wheel. See Catherine Wheel.

KELWAY-PEARS, (See Pear) borne by the name of Kelloway.

KERNELLED, or Kernellated. Same as Crenelle.

KETTLE-HOOK. P. 41, f. 10. on the dexter side.

KEYS. Are variously borne in Coat-Armour ; for examples see P. 42, f. 7 to 12.

Two Keys in Saltire. f. 9. The Emblem of St. Peter.

KID. A young goat.

KILN. See Brick-kiln. P. 41, f. 46.

KING in his robes of state sitting in a chair. P. 35, f. 2.

KING of Arms. See Heralds College, and Bath King of Arms.

KING of Arms, Crown of. P. 40, f. 57.

KING-FISHER. The Halcyon of the ancients; a bird with beautiful plumage. P. 33, f. 58.

KITE. A bird of prey. P. 33, f. 60.

KNIFE. Knives of various kinds are met with in Heraldry, as a Cutting Knife, Butcher's, Pruning, Shredding, etc. P. 22, f. 28; and P. 41, f. 20 and 22.

Ar. three Shoemakers Knives gu. borne by Hacklet.

KNIGHT. A Title of Honour next to that of a Baronet, not hereditary. Knights may be divided into two classes. First ; those who are invested with some Order, and bear their Arms as P. 16, f. 21. Secondly ; Those who are not so invested, termed Knight Bachelors. The arms of a Knight Bachelor is distinguished by the Helmet. P. 13, f. 21.

KNIGHT-BANNERET. A Knight who, for good service under the Royal Banner, was advanced by the King to a higher Order of Knighthood on the Field of Battle.

KNIGHT-ERRANT. One who wanders in quest of adventure.

KNIGHT of St. John of Jerusalem. See Hospitallers.

KNIGHTHOOD. The character, or dignity of a Knight.

KNIGHTHOOD, Orders of.

THE MOST NOBLE ORDER OF THE GARTER.

This Order was instituted by King Edward iii., A.D. 1350. The Original statutes of the Order are lost. By a Statute passed 17th July, 1805, the Order was to consist of the Sovereign and twenty-five Knight's Companions, together with such lineal descendants of King George the First as may be elected, but exclusive of the Prince of Wales, who is a part of the original institution. Foreign Sovereigns, and Princes and Extra Knights, have since been added by special statutes. The latter, however, become merged in the twenty-five Companions as vacancies occur.

THE GARTER is of dark blue velvet, edged with gold, bearing the motto " Honi soit qui mal y pense" in letters of gold, with buckle and pendant of richly chased gold. It is worn on the left leg below the knee.

THE GEORGE. An enamelled figure of St. George on horseback, encountering the Dragon. It is worn as a pendant to the collar.

THE COLLAR is of gold, composed of twenty-six pieces (in allusion to the original number of Knights) in the form of Garters and Gold Knots. The Garters are enamelled azure, within the Garters alternately placed is a Red and White rose, barbed and seeded ppr. surmounting each other.

THE STAR of eight points silver, in the centre of which is the Cross of St. George, gules, encircled with the Garter and Motto.

THE MANTLE of blue velvet lined with white taffeta, on the left breast the star embroidered.

THE HOOD of crimson velvet.

THE SURCOAT of crimson velvet lined with white taffeta.

THE HAT of black velvet lined with white taffeta, to which is fastened by a band of diamonds, a plume of white ostrich feathers, in the centre of which a tuft of black heron's feathers.

RIBBON of the Order. Blue.

MOTTO. Honi soit qui mal y pense. " Dishonoured be he who thinks ill of it." See Elvin's Hand-Book of Mottoes.

THE COLLAR, Star, Badge, etc. P. 24, f. 6, 7 and 19.

THE MOST ANCIENT AND MOST NOBLE ORDER OF THE THISTLE.

It is said this Order was instituted by James V. of Scotland, A.D. 1540. It was revived by King James II. of England, 29th May, 1687, subsequently by Queen Anne, 31st Dec., 1703, and by a statute passed in May, 1827, the Order is to consist of the Sovereign and Sixteen Knights.

THE BADGE, worn pendant to the Collar, or to a dark-green ribbon over the left shoulder and tied under the arm, consists of a radiant star or, charged with the figure of St. Andrew ppr. of gold enamelled, with his gown green, and the surcoat purple, bearing before him the cross Saltire argent, standing upon a mount vert, upon which the cross is resting.

THE COLLAR is of golden thistles, intermingled with sprigs of rue enamelled ppr.

THE JEWEL, worn attached to a green ribbon, consists of an oval plate ar. charged with the same figure as the Badge, within a border vert, fimbriated (both internally and externally) or, and inscribed in letters of the same, " Nemo me impune lacessit."

THE STAR is worn on the left side of the Coat, or Cloak, and consists of St. Andrew's Cross of silver embroidery, with rays emanating from each angle; in the centre is a Thistle of green, heightened with gold, upon a field of gold, surrounded by a circle of green, bearing the motto of the Order in golden characters.

RIBBON of the Order. Green.

MOTTO. Nemo me impune lacessit. No one provokes me with impunity.

Collar, Star, Badge, etc. P. 24, f. 18 and 23.

THE MOST ILLUSTRIOUS ORDER OF ST. PATRICK.

This Order was instituted by King George III., 5th February, 1783, and consists of the Sovereign, a Grand Master, and Twenty-two Knights. The Lord Lieutenant of Ireland' pro. tempore, being Grand Master.

THE BADGE, pendant from the Collar, is of gold, surrounded with a wreath of Shamrock or trefoil, within which is a circle of Blue Enamel containing the Motto of the said Order in letters of gold, viz., Quis Separabit, with the date MDCCLXXXIII, being the year in which the Order was founded, and encircling the Cross of Saint Patrick Gules, surmounted with a trefoil slipped vert, each leaf charged with an Imperia crown or, upon a field argent.

THE COLLAR, of gold, is composed of six harps and five roses, three alternately, joined together by twelve golden knots; the roses are enamelled alternately by white leaves within red and red leaves within white, and in the centre of the Collar is an Imperial crown surmounting a harp of gold.

THE MANTLE made of rich sky-blue tabiret lined with white silk, and fastened by a cordon of blue silk and gold with tassels.

THE STAR consists of the Cross of Saint Patrick Gules, on a field argent, charged with a trefoil as on the Badge, surrounded by a sky-blue enamelled circle, containing the motto and date, and is encircled by four greater, and two lesser rays of silver.

Ribbon of the Order. Sky-blue.

MOTTO Quis Separabit. Who shall separate us.

Collar, Star, Badge, etc. P. 24, f. 20 and 21.

THE MOST HONOURABLE ORDER OF THE BATH.

The Order of the Bath was probably instituted by King Henry IV., 1399, although Selden and Ashmole are of opinion that the said King did not institute, but rather revive it. After the coronation of Charles II., the Order was neglected until the year 1725, when George I. revived and remodelled it. However, several alterations have since been made, and on the second day of January, 1815, it was enlarged and divided into three classes, in commemoration of " the auspicious termination of the long and arduous contest in which this empire has been engaged." On the 14th April, 1847, it was further increased by the addition of Civil Divisions of the second and third classes, when new Statutes were made for the Government of the Order, which have since been revised and the Order now consists of the following members, viz. :—

1st Class—*Knight's Grand Cross*—for the military service, fifty, exclusive of the Sovereign and princes of the blood royal, and such distinguished foreigners as may be nominated Honorary Knights Grand Cross, and twenty-five for the Civil Service. By Royal Warrant, 2nd June, 1725, all Knights Grand Cross are entitled to a grant of supporters.

2nd Class—*Knight's Commanders*—for the military service, one hundred and twenty-three, and for the civil service eighty, exclusive of foreign officers, who may be admitted as Honorary Knights Commanders. In the event of actions of signal distinction, or of future wars, the numbers of this, as well as of the third class, may be increased. The members of the second class are entitled to the distinctive appellation of Knighthood, after having been invested with the Insignia. 3rd Class—*Companions of the Order*—six hundred and ninety, and for the Civil Service two hundred and fifty; they take precedence of Esquires, but are not entitled to the appellation or style of Knights. No officer can be nominated to the military division of the third class of the Order, unless his services have been marked by special mention of his name as having distinguished himself in action against the enemy. This class has never been conferred upon any officer below the rank of Major in the Army, and Commander in the Navy.

THE BADGE for the Military Classes of the Order is a gold Maltese cross, of eight points, enamelled argent; in each angle a lion passant-guardant or ; in the centre, the rose, thistle and shamrock, issuant from a sceptre between three imperial crowns or, within a circle gules, thereon the motto of the Order, surrounded by two branches of laurel, proper, issuing from an escrol azure, inscribed ICH DIEN (I serve) in letters of gold. It is worn by the Knights Grand Cross pendent from a red ribbon across the right shoulder, by the Knights Commanders around the neck, and by the Companions suspended from the left breast.

THE COLLAR is of gold (weight 30oz. Troy), is composed of nine imperial crowns, and eight roses, thistles and shamrocks, issuing from a sceptre, enamelled in their proper colours, tied or linked together with seventeen gold knots, enamelled white, having the Badge of the Order pendent therefrom.

THE STAR of the Grand Cross of the Military Division is formed of rays or flames of silver, thereon a gold Maltese cross, and in the centre, within the motto, branches of laurel, issuant as in the Badge.

THE BADGE AND STAR of the Knights Grand Cross of the Civil Division are the old badge and star of the Order. The Star is of silver, formed with eight points or rays, charged with three imperial crowns, proper upon a glory of silver rays, surrounded with a red circle, upon which is the motto of the Order. *The Badge* is of gold, composed of a rose, thistle, and shamrock, issuing from a sceptre between three imperial crowns, encircled by the motto. *The Knights Commanders of the Civil Division* wear the like badge, of a smaller size, round the neck by a red ribbon, and the Companions of the same division the same, but of a still smaller size, from the left breast, pendent from a red ribbon.

The Star is a cross-pattée silver, charged with three imperial crowns proper upon a glory of silver rays, surrounded with a red circle, upon which is the motto of the Order. The Star of the *Knights Commanders Civil Division* is of the same form and size, omitting the laurel wreath and the escroll, and is worn embroidered on the left side.

RIBBON of the Order—pale red.

MOTTO—TRIA JUNCTA IN UNO. Three joined in one.

Collar, Stars, Badges, etc. P. 24, f. 22, 26 and 28 ; and P. 25, f. 13 and 14.

THE MOST EXALTED ORDER OF THE STAR OF INDIA.

This Order was instituted by Her Majesty Queen Victoria, 23rd February, 1861, and enlarged 28th March, 1866, and in 1875, and 1876.

The Order consists of the Sovereign, the Grand Master, and 205 Ordinary Companions or Members, together with such Extra and Honorary Members as Her Majesty, her heirs and successors, shall from time to time appoint. The 205 Ordinary Members are divided into three classes. The first Class are styled *Knights Grand Commanders*, and consists of thirty members (eighteen Natives and twelve Europeans); the second class of seventy-two members, styled *Knights Commanders*; the third class of one hundred and forty-four members, styled *Companions*. Her Majesty's Viceroy and Governor-General of India is Grand Master.

The Statutes enable the Sovereign to confer the dignity of Knight Grand Commander of the Order upon such of Her Majesty's British subjects as have, by important and loyal services rendered by them to the Indian Empire, merited the Royal favour; and the second and third classes upon persons who, by their conduct or services in the Indian Empire, have merited the Royal favour.

THE BADGE—an onyx cameo of Her Majesty's effigy, set in a perforated and ornamented oval, containing the motto of the Order "HEAVEN'S LIGHT OUR GUIDE," surmounted by a Star all in diamonds. *The Ribbon* of the Order is sky-blue, having a narrow white stripe towards either edge, and is worn from the right shoulder to the left side.

THE COLLAR is composed of the Lotus of India, of Palm branches, tied together in saltire, and of the united Red and White Rose. In the centre is an imperial crown; all richly enamelled on gold, in their proper colours.

THE STAR is composed of rays of gold issuing from the centre, having thereon a Star in diamonds, resting upon a light blue enamelled circular riband, tied at the ends, inscribed with the motto of the Order, viz. : "HEAVEN'S LIGHT OUR GUIDE," also in diamonds.

THE MANTLE—Light blue satin, lined with white, and fastened with a cordon of white silk, with blue and silver tassels, on the left side a representation of the Star of the Order.

Collar, Badge, and Star. P. 24, f. 27.

THE MOTTO, "Heaven's light our guide."

THE MOST DISTINGUISHED ORDER OF ST. MICHAEL AND ST. GEORGE.

Instituted by King George IV., when Prince Regent, 27th April, 1818, by Letters Patent, under the Great Seal of Great Britain, in commemoration of the Republic of the Ionian Islands being placed under the protection of Great Britain. The Order was enlarged and extended 4th December, 1868, and 30th May, 1877, for the natural born subjects of the United Kingdom as may have held, or shall hold, high and confidential offices within Her Majesty's colonial possessions; and again, 1879, by the admission of persons rendering good service to the Crown in relation to the Foreign Affairs of the British Empire.

The Members of the Order take rank and precedency immediately after the corresponding classes of the Order of the Star of India, that is to say, the Knights Grand Cross, after Knight Grand Commanders of the Star of India; the Knights Commanders, after the Knights Commanders of the Star of India; and the Companions, after the Companions of the Star of India. The Grand Master is the First and Principal Knight Grand Cross. The Knights Grand Cross are entitled to bear supporters, and to encircle their arms with the collar, ribbon, and motto, of the Order. The Knights Commanders also encircle their arms with the ribbon and motto, and the Companions suspend the Badge of the Order from their escutcheon.

The Order is to consist of not more than fifty Knights Grand Cross, exclusive of Extra and Honorary Members, one hundred and fifty Knights Commanders, and two hundred and sixty Companions.

THE BADGE is a gold cross of fourteen points of white enamel, edged with gold, having in the centre, on one side, the Archangel St. Michael, encountering Satan, and on the other St. George on horseback, encountering a dragon, within a blue circle, on which the motto of the Order is inscribed. The Cross is surmounted by the Imperial Crown, and worn by the *Knights Grand Cross* attached to the Collar, or to a wide Saxon-Blue-Ribbon, with a scarlet stripe from the right shoulder to the left.

KNIGHTS COMMANDERS wear the badge suspended to a narrow ribbon from the neck.

THE COMPANIONS wear the small cross of the Order from a still narrower ribbon at the button-hole of their coats.

THE STAR OF A KNIGHT GRAND CROSS is composed of seven rays of silver, having a small ray of gold between each of them, and over all the Cross of St. George, gules. In the centre is a representation of the Archangel St. Michael encountering Satan, within a blue circle, inscribed with the motto, AUSPICIUM MELIORIS ÆVI.

THE COLLAR is formed alternately of lions of England, of Maltese crosses, and of the cyphers S.M. and S.G., having in the centre the imperial crown, over two winged lions, passant guardant, each holding a book and seven arrows. At the opposite end of the collar are two similar lions. The whole is of gold except the crosses, which are of white enamel, and it is linked together by small gold chains.

THE MANTLE is of Saxon-blue satin, lined with scarlet silk, tied with cordons of blue and scarlet silk and gold, and has on the left side the Star of a Knight Grand Cross.

THE CHAPEAU is of blue satin, lined with scarlet, and surmounted with white and black ostrich feathers.

THE RIBBON of the Order—Saxon—blue with a scarlet strip.

MOTTO. AUSPICIUM MELIORIS ÆVI. A pledge of better times.

Collar, Star, Badges, etc. P. 24, f. 31, and P. 25, f. 16 and 17.

THE ORDER OF THE INDIAN EMPIRE.

By Royal warrant, dated India Office, 15th Sept., 1887:—The Queen taking unto her Royal consideration the expediency of making certain changes in the constitution of the *Order of the Indian Empire*, as well by altering the designation of the Order as by adding thereto additional Classes, so as to enable her Majesty, her Heirs and Successors, to reward a greater number of persons who, by their services, official or other, to her Majesty's Indian Empire, have merited the Royal favour, has been graciously pleased by Letters Patent under the Great Seal of the United Kingdom of Great Britain and Ireland, bearing date the second day of August, 1886, to revoke and abrogate so much of the Royal Warrant bearing date the thirty-first day of December, one thousand eight hundred and seventy-seven, by which the said Order was instituted, as limits the same to the Sovereign, a Grand Master and one class of Members or Companions, and as is inconsistent with or contrary to the provisions of the now recited Letters Patent. And to ordain, direct, and appoint that the said Order of Knighthood shall henceforth be styled and designated in all acts, proceedings and pleadings as "The Most Eminent Order of the Indian Empire."

"THE MOST EMINENT ORDER OF THE INDIAN EMPIRE."

Instituted 1st January, 1887. Enlarged 1st June, 1887.

The Order consists of the Sovereign, Grand Master, and three Classes.

The First Class, or Knights Grand Commanders, who have place and precedency next to and immediately after Knights Grand Cross of St. Michael and St. George.

The Second Class, or Knights Commanders, who have precedency next to Knights Commanders of St. Michael and St. George.

The Third Class, or Companions, who have precedency next to Companions of St. Michael and St. George.

THE BADGE. A Rose gold enamelled gules, barbed and seeded vert, having in the centre Her Majesty's Royal Effigy within a purple circle edged with gold, inscribed with the Motto of the Order, surmounted by an Imperial Crown both gold.

THE COLLAR is composed of Elephants, Lotus-flowers, Peacocks in their pride, and Indian roses, in the centre the Imperial Crown from which The Badge is pendant, the whole linked together by chains of gold.

THE STAR of The First Class or Knights Grand Commanders (G.C.I.E.) is composed of five rays of Gold and Silver, issuing from a Gold centre thereon Her Majesty's Royal Effigy, within a purple circle inscribed with the motto of the Order, the circle surmounted by the Imperial Crown both gold.

THE STAR of the Second Class or Knights Commanders (K.C.I.E.) is composed of rays alternately bright and chipped, issuing from a gold centre, having thereon Her Majesty's

Effigy within a purple circle inscribed with the Motto of the Order in letters of gold, the circle surmounted by the Imperial Crown also gold.

THE MANTLE.—Imperial purple satin, lined with, and fastened by, a cordon of white silk, with purple silk, and gold tassels attached, on the left side a representation of the Star of the first-class of the Order.

THE RIBBON of the Order is blue. For the second-class, is two inches in breadth.

THE MOTTO. "Imperatricis Auspiciis."

COLLAR, STAR AND BADGE of the first class, or Knights Grand Commanders. P. 25a, f. 10.

RIBBON AND BADGE, AND STAR of the second-class, or Knight Commanders. f. 11.

THE BADGE of the third class, or Companions. f. 12.

THE ROYAL HANOVERIAN GUELPHIC ORDER.

This Order was instituted by King George IV., when Prince Regent, 12th August, 1815, and has not been conferred by the British Crown since the death of William IV., when the British Sovereign ceased to be Monarch of Hanover.

The Collar, Star, and Badge. Military Grand Cross. P. 25, f. 15.

The Badge and Riband. Military Knight Commander. P. 16, f. 21.

The Collar, Star and Badge, is the same for a Civil Knight omitting the swords which are crossing each other over the Badge.

The Ribbon is light blue, watered.

Motto Nec aspera terrent. Difficulties do not daunt.

KNIGHT Templers (soldiers of the pilgrims). The Order of the Knights Templers was founded about A.D. 1117 by Hugh de Paynes. vide Mardment's Templaria. They agreed in profession with the Hospitallers in vowing poverty, chastitie, and obedience, and to defend Pilgrims to the Holy Sepulchre.

These soldiers wore a white mantle over their armour, as their peculiar habit, to which was afterwards added a red cross, emblazoned on the left breast, identical with the white cross of the Hospitallers. P. 11, f. 42. Their helmet had no crest, their great banner was oblong in form and per-fesse sable and argent, ornamented with the Cross of the Order, and the old French word "Beau-Seant," by which name it was commonly known, was also their War-Cry. The Badge was the Agnus Dei.

KNITTING-FRAME, as borne in the arms of the Framework Knitters Company. P. 40, f. 1.

KNOTS. Entwined cords, used as Badges. For the different Knots, see P. 43, f. 7 to 15.

Knots are mostly distinguished by the name of the family who bear them, as the Knot borne by the Family of Bourchier is termed a Bourchier Knot. See Bowen, Dacre, Harrington, Heneage, Hungerford, Lacy, Ormond, Stafford, and Wake Knots.

The Bow-Knot is depicted as the knot and bow. f. 24. The Wedding Knot, or Bow. f. 14, No. 2.

KNOTTED. See Raguly. A limb of a tree knotted. P. 17, f. 27.

L

LABEL, Lambeaux, or File. A Mark of CADENCY used to distinguish the arms of the eldest son. See *Distinction of Houses.* P. 46.

All the Members of the Royal Family use the Label extending across the shield, each being charged with different figures, except that of the Prince of Wales, which is plain. P. 16, f. 40 to 45.

Label of H.R.H. Prince Albert Victor of Wales. P. 25a, f. 1.

Label of H.R.H. Prince George of Wales. i.d. f. 2.

Label of H.R.H. the late Prince Albert extending across the shield, charged on the centre with the cross of St. George.

LABEL of one point. P. 16, f. 34.

LABEL of two points. P. 16, f. 34.

LABEL of three points. P. 16, f. 35.

LABEL of three points issuing out of chief. f. 35.

LABEL of three points crossed. f. 39.

LABEL of four points. f. 36.

LABEL of five points. f. 39.

LABEL with three bells pendent, or of three campanes, or points campaned. f. 37.

LABEL with three tags pendent, or double labels. f. 34.

LABEL with three pomegranates pendent, enwrapped with a wiure or ribbon. f. 37.

LABEL in fesse of three points, each charged with a canton sinister. f. 36.

LABEL in fesse, counter-posed with another, the points erect, or two files in fesse, endorsed, sometimes called a bar gemel, or fesse voided pattée. f. 38.

LABEL of three points fixed. f. 39

LABEL. A name given to the ribbons that hang down from a mitre or coronet; the Escroll on which the motto is placed is also termed a Label, Scroll, or Slip.

LABENT. See Gliding.

LACED. Adorned, or fastened with a lace.

LACS d' amour. True love knot. P. 43, f. 14.

LACY Knot. See Knots. P. 43, f. 11.

LADDER-SCALING. P. 37, f. 7.

LADY. A title properly belonging to the daughters of all Peers above the rank of Viscount; it is, however, by courtesy, now invariably extended to the wives of Baronets, and Knights of every degree.

LADY. As a Crest and Supporter, is frequently met with in Coat-Armour, and is blazoned either as a Lady, Female figure, or Woman. P. 35, f. 6.

Three Ladies from the waist as in the Arms of the See of Oxford. P. 22, f. 15.

LA-FLEUR-DU Maistre. See Marygcll.

LAMA. An animal. P. 28, f. 39.

LAMB. Frequently used as a bearing in Heraldry, as P. 29, f. 4, without the banner.

LAMB-HOLY, or Paschal Lamb. Also termed the Lamb of God. Is a Lamb passant, holding a banner argent, charged with a cross gules (the cross of St. George), and circle of glory over the head. P. 29, f. 4.

LAMBEAUX. See Label.

LAMBEAUX Cross. P. 9, f. 25; P. 10, f. 42.

LAMBEAUX Cross rebated. P. 11, f. 25.

LAMBEAUX per long. So termed when the points fall to the fesse point.

LAMBEAUXED. The same as Dovetailed. P. 12, f. 9.

LAMBEL. See Label.

LAMBENT. See Gliding.

LAMBREQUIN, or Lamequin. The mantle or hood, intervening between the helmet and Crest, always represented flotant. P. 2, f. 24; P. 8, f. 21; P. 13, f. 21; P. 16, f. 21. If charged with the Arms it is termed a Lambrequin Armoyées.

LAMBREQUIN. A term anciently applied to the points which hang from the straight lines of the label.

LAMINATED, or Scaled. Having scales.

LAMPAGOE, or Lampargoe. See Limpago.

LAMPREY$. A fish. P. 32, f. 41b.

LAMPS of various shapes are borne in Coat-Armour. P. 39, f. 25 to 27.

Antique Lamp, as borne by the family of Leet. f. 25.
Globular, or Ship's Lamp; also termed a Lantern. f. 27.
Hand, or Burning Lamp. f. 26.
Lamp Inflamed. f. 25.
Roman Lamp. f. 26.

LAMPARGOE. See Limpago.

LAMPASSE. The same as langued.

LANCASTER Rose. A Red Rose. P. 25, f. 4.

LANCE. A spear. P. 35, f. 15.

LANCET. A sharp pointed, two-edged surgical instrument. P. 42, f. 51.

LANDSCAPES, or Landskips, are sometimes granted in Modern Coats. They are False Heraldry, inasmuch as it is impossible so to blazon them in heraldic terms that a person can paint or engrave them without having seen the original grant.

LAND-TORTOISE. See Tortoise.

LANGUED. A term to express the tongue of beasts when of a different tincture to that of the body.

The tongue, when red, need not be expressed, as it is always understood to be of that colour. if not named to the contrary, unless the thing depicted is gules, when it will be azure, if not named of some other tincture.

LANTERN. A ship's lamp, or lantern. P. 39, f. 27, No. 2.

LAPPED. The same as wreathed.

LAPWING, or Pewit. A bird. P. 33, f. 55.

LA-QUISE. See A-la-Quise.

LARK. A bird. P. 33, f. 57.

LARMES, or Larmettes, Guttée de. Liquid drops representing tears. See P. 1, and the term Guttée.

LASH. See Scourge.

LATHING hammer. P. 41, f. 26.

LATHS, Bundle of. P. 41, f. 58.

LATIN Cross. P. 9, f. 38.

LATTICE, Tirlace, or Treilée. Consists of bars crossing one another at right angles, which do not interlace, but are nailed together at the crossings sometimes termed Fret-cloué. P. 22, f. 37.

LAUNCE. A tilting spear.

LAUREL. The leaves, sprigs and branches of which are of common use in Coat Armour.

A Laurel-leaf. P. 45, f. 18. A Laurel-sprig and Branch. P. 44, f. 40. The Triumphal Crown is composed of laurel; it is sometimes blazoned a Chaplet of laurel. P. 24, f. 34.

LAVENDER. A plant. A chaplet of Lavender is borne by the name of Lavender, and a Garb of Lavender by Ducket.

LAVER, or Laver-cutter. See Coulter.

LAVER-POT, or Ewer. P. 42, f. 27.

LAYER. At Layer, the same as lodged. P. 28, f. 47.

LEADING-STAFF, or Trailing-pike. P. 41, f. 59.

LEAD-LINE. A plummet and line. P. 38, f. 44. Used by Mariners to sound the depth of the sea.

LEAF. See Leaves.

LEAPING, or Skipping. A term applied to beasts of the chase when in the position of courant; also to the Crocodile, Salamander, Cameleon,

Newte, Asker, Spider, Ant, etc., when borne erect.

LEASH. A band wherewith to bind anything; also a leather thong with a button at the end, by which Falconers (having run it through the varvels) hold the Hawk fast upon the hand. P. 33, f.·34. The term is also applied to the line which passes from the collar of one greyhound to another.

LEASH. A term used for three birds, bucks, foxes, hares, etc.

LEASHED. Having a leash, or thong.

LEATHER Bottle, as borne in the arms of the Bottle-Makers and Horners Companies. P. 42, f. 19.

LEAVES of all kinds are born in Heraldry. e.g. The *Aspen, Bay, Elm, Elder, Hazel, Holly, Laurel, Mulberry, Oak, Vine,* etc. P. 45, f. 17 to 30. A *Staff-Tree Leaf.* P. 22, f. 33. Leaves are always erect if not otherwise named. A leaf pendant. P. 45, f. 27.

LEAVED. Said of any plant when its leaves are of a different tincture to the stem.

LE Bourlet. The Wreath, or Torse.

LEGS of Men, Animals, and Birds, are of common use in Heraldry. Animals legs are termed Gambs which see. Birds legs, when erased, are termed A-la-Quise to which refer. Men's legs are borne in various ways in Coat-Armour, and each form should be particularly expressed in blazon; but it is always to be understood that when a man's leg is blazoned couped, or erased at the thigh, it is to be bent at the knee, whether clad in armour or not, as a leg in armour, couped at the thigh. P. 36, f. 22, and f. 23. A leg erased at the thigh, and other examples. Same plate, and P. 38, f. 18.

LEGS in Armour. As borne in the Arms of the Isle of Man. P. 36, f. 26.

LEGGED, or Membered. See Bird.

LEISH. See Leash.

LENTALLY. The same as Indented.

LEONCED. See Decorated.

LEOPARD. The positions of the Leopard are blazoned by the same terms as those of Lions. A Leopard's head, i.e. when depicted with the neck is always blazoned a Leopard's Head. When no part of the neck appears it is blazoned a Leopard's-face, and is always guardant. A Leopard's-face jessant-de-lis, is depicted with a fleur-de-lis in its mouth, the top shewing above the head, for examples see P. 28, f. 1 to 6.

LEOPARDY, or Leopardé. A French term for a Lion passant guardant.

LE TOUT DE TOUT. When an inescutcheon is surmounted of another it is said to be Le tout de tout. P. 31, f. 10.

LETTERS of the Greek, Hebrew, Roman, Text, and other Alphabets are borne in Coat Armour, either singly, or in words. e.g. The Greek Alpha A and Ω Omega form part of the arms of the Regius Professor of Greek at Cambridge; and the Professor of Hebrew has the Hebrew letter Hhet ח. See Upsilon, etc.

" The text ע pierced through with a dash in the centre in the arms of Battle Abbey." " Now though I have read letters to be little honourable in arms, this cannot be disgraceful, partly because Church-Heraldry moveth in a sphere by itself, partly because this was the letter of letters, as the received character to signify CHRISTUS." Fuller's Church History, vol. ii. p. 227.

LEURE. See Lure.

LEVANT. Rising, a term applied to birds.

LEVEL. An instrument used by Masons. P. 41, f. 38.

LEVEL-REVERSED. i.d.

LEVER. A name sometimes given to the Cormorant. P. 34, f. 34.

LEVERET. A young hare. Borne by the name of Leverington.

LEVYD. Leaved.

LEWRE. See Lure.

LEZARD. See Lizard.

LIBARDE, or Libbarde. A Leopard.

LICTOR'S-ROD. See Fasces.

LIE. French-Heralds use this term to express strings.

LIGHTER. A heavy boat. P. 38, f. 34.

LILY of the Flag. A Fleur-de-lis.

LILY of the Garden, or White Lily. P. 44, f. 6. The emblem of purity.

LIMB of a Tree. A bend of the limb of a tree raguled and trunked. P. 17, f. 27.

LIMBECK, Alembic, or Still. Is the vessel through which distilled liquors pass into the recipient. It is borne as part of the Arms of the Pewterers Company. P. 39, f. 30, No. 2.

LIME Tree. P. 45, f. 37.

LINIME of a Tree. See Limb of a Tree.

LIMPAGO. The engraving, P. 26, f. 55, is a copy of a Limpago given in Burke's Heraldic Illustrations. Viz: a Lion's body with human face and flowing hair. It is generally represented as a Lion's body, the face of a man with the scalp and horns of a Bull. P. 27, f. 54.

LINDEN, or Lime-Tree. P. 45, f. 37.

LINED, or Doubled. A term applied to the inner covering, or lining of a mantle, robe, cap, etc.

LINED. When a line is affixed to a collar, which enriches the neck of any animal, it is termed collared and lined. P. 29, f. 15.

LINES of Partition. P. 1. See also Party lines. P. 2. Also Dancette, Dovetailed, Engrailed, Embattled, Indented, Invecked, Nebule, Potent, Raguly, Wavy, etc.

LING. A fish. P. 32, f. 43.

LINGUED. See Langued.

LINK, or Shackle. P. 37, f. 42.

LINKED, or Conjoined. As annulets. P. 37, f. 36.
Two triangles linked, or interlaced. P. 43, f. 56.

LINKS, or Fetters. See Shackbolt.

LINNET. A bird. P. 34, f. 54.

LION. The noblest of all wild beasts, which is made to be the emblem of strength and valour, and is on that account the most frequently borne in Coat-Armour, as a Charge, Crest, and Supporter. The Heraldic Lion is always armed and langued gules unless such be the tincture of the field, when, if not named to the contrary, it is azure. See Langued.

LION of England. A term used when speaking of an augmentation of arms, such as a Canton Gules charged with a Lion passant-guardant or. which may be blazoned on a Canton a Lion of England.

LION ADDORSED. P. 26, f. 15.

— AFFRONTEE. f. 28.

— ANTIQUE rampant. f. 37.

— ANTIQUE head erased. f. 38.

— ASSIS. Same as Sejant. f. 41.

— BAILLONE. f. 7.

— BICORPORATED. f. 12.

— COLLARED and chained. f. 13.

— COLLARED, or gorged. f. 31.

— COMBATANT. f. 16.

— CONJOINED. f. 12.

— CONTOURNE. f. 18.

— COUCHANT. f. 45.

— COUEE. f. 8

— COUNTER-PASSANT. f. 36.

— COUPED. f. 30.

— COWARD. f. 8.

— CROWNED. f. 27 and 34.

— DEBRUISED. f. 21. A lion ramp. guard. debruised by a fesse.

— DECHAUSSE. f. 14.

— DEFAMED, or Diffame. f. 6.

LION DEMI-PASSANT. f. 49.

— DEMI-RAMPANT, gorged with a ducal coronet. f. 31.

— DEMI-RAMP. reguardant, crowned with a mural coronet. f. 34.

— DISJOINTED. f. 14.

— DISMEMBERED. f. 14.

— DON-HEADED. f. 9.

— DON-TAILED. f. 2.

— DORMANT. f. 46.

— DOUBLE-HEADED. f. 9.

— DOUBLE queued. f. 2.

— DRAGON. f. 54.

— ENDORSED, or Addorsed. f. 15.

— FULL-FACED. f. 50.

— GORGED with a ducal coronet. f. 31.

— GUARDANT. f. 11, 27 and 35.

— GUARDANT-CONJOINED, or Bicorporated. f. 12.

— ISSUANT et issuant, and revertant. f. 33.

— ISSUANT from a Chief. f. 29.

— JESSANT and debruised with two bendlets. f. 32.

— JESSANT and débruised fretways, with a fesse and two barrulets. f. 22.

— LEOPARDE. See Leopardy.

— MARINE, or Sea-Lion. f. 53.

— MORNE. f. 5.

— NAISSANT from a fesse. f. 26.

— PASSANT. f. 23.

— PASSANT guardant. f. 35.

— PASSANT reguardant. f. 24.

— POISSON. f. 52.

— RAMPANT. f. 1 and 37.

— RAMPANT, collared and chained. f. 13.

— RAMPANT guardant. f. 11.

— RAMPANT reguardant. f. 10.

— RAMPANT tail nowed. f. 4.

— OF St. Mark. f. 51.

— SALIENT; sometimes termed springing. f. 20.

— SEA, or Marine Lion. f. 53.

— SEJANT. f. 41.

— SEJANT-CONTOURNE. f. 18.

— SEJANT DEXTER. Paw raised. f. 42.

— SEJANT-EXTENDED. f. 44.

— SEJANT-GUARDANT, affrontée. f. 43.

— SEJANT-RAMPANT. f. 19.

— SEPT-INSULAR. f. 47.

— STATANT. f. 39.

— STATANT guardant. f. 27.

— STATANT tail extended. f. 40.

— STATANT winged. f. 48.

— TRICORPORATED. f. 17.

— TAIL nowed. f. 4.

— TAIL forked. f. 3.

— WINGED. f. 48.

— WITH Human-face. f. 56.

Lion's-Gambe; the whole fore leg. P. 29, f. 45. The Paw is the foot couped or erased near the middle joint.

Lion's Head Affrontée. P. 26, f. 50.

Lion's Head Couped. f. 30.

Lion's Head Erased. f. 25 and 38.

Lion's Tail. P. 29, f. 50.

Lionced. Adorned with lion's heads. When the limbs of a cross terminate in the heads of lions, it is termed a Cross Lionced, or Leonced.

Lioncel, Lionel, or Lionceau. A name given to Lion's when more than three are borne in a shield.

Lionne. A term applied to the leopard when rampant.

Lis. A contraction of Fleur-de-lis.

Liston. The scroll or ribbon upon which the motto or device is inscribed.

Lists. Enclosed spaces for holding Tournaments.

Litre. A French term for a funeral girdle, depicted on the wall of a church, with the arms of the Lord of the Manor.

Litvit's Skin. A pure white fur.

Livery-Colours frequently correspond with the first two tinctures named in blazoning the coat of arms.

Lizard or Lezard. An animal of the Lynx, or wild cat kind, of a dark brown colour, spotted black, with short ears and tail, borne by the Skinners' Company, London, and the Russian Merchants' Company. P. 28, f. 17.

Lizard, or Eft. A small animal of the crocodile species, borne by the Ironmongers' Company, London. P. 39, f. 24, and P. 36, f. 12, properly Scaly Lizard.

Lizare, or Lisere. Bordered, edged, or fimbriated.

Loach. A fish. P. 32, f. 24.

Lobster. A crustaceous animal, sometimes used in Coat Armour, and is borne by the name Banester, Dikes, etc. P. 32, f. 57. Lobsters-claws in Saltire, f. 56, borne by the name of Tregarthick, Kerne, etc.

Loch. A lake, represented as P. 34, f. 26, without the rushes.

Lochabar-axe. P. 37, f. 28.

Lock. Pad-lock and Quadranglar-lock. P. 42, f. 13.

Lockets. See Manacles.

Lodged. A term applied to beasts of chase when lying at rest. P. 28, f. 47. and f. 55. Beasts of prey are couchant.

Log-line. A line used for ascertaining the speed of a vessel. P. 38, f. 44.

Lolling. Expresses the position of an eagle in the act of feeding upon its prey when the wings hang down.

London, Lord-Mayor Collar of. See Collar of S.S.

Long-Bow. See Bow.

Long-Cross. P. 9, f. 38.

Long-per. When the fitched part of a cross is longer than the other limbs it is said to be per-long.

Looking back. When a lion is rampant towards the sinister, with the head turned, looking backwards.

Looking-glass. See Mirror.

Loop-holes. Long and square are often borne in battlements, castles, towers, etc. P. 23, f. 11.

Looring-tonges. See Closing-tongs.

Lopped, or Snagged. Couped, shewing the thickness. P. 45, f. 56.

Lord. A title of three-fold application. First: To Peers of the Realm, or Lords of Parliament, below the rank of Duke. Secondly: It is bestowed on several high offices, and belongs to the office, as the Lord Chancellor, Lord Chamberlain, etc. The Mayor's of London, York, and Dublin, have also this title during the Mayoralty. Thirdly: To those persons who, without being Peers, enjoy the title of Lord by courtesy, such as the sons of Dukes, Marquesses, and the eldest sons of Earls.

Lorrain Cross. P. 8, f. 38.

Lotus flower. P. 45, f. 11; P. 24, f. 27.

Lou, Loup, or Loupe. A wolf.

Loup-Cervier. A large kind of wolf.

Love Knot. P. 43, f. 9.

Lowered. The same as Abaisse. P. 15, f. 37.

Lozenge. The Lozenge is a rhomboidal figure that has equal sides, and unequal angles as P. 40, f. 14. The arms of all Maidens and Widows are borne in a Lozenge. See P. 9, f. 21, P. 22, f. 21, and P. 46, f. 9, 10, 11, 24, and 32.

Lozenges conjoined, as three lozenges conjoined in fesse. P. 3, f. 40. Five lozenges conjoined in fesse. f. 41. Five lozenges conjoined in bend. P. 18, f. 2. Four lozenges conjoined in Cross throughout. P. 22, f. 41.

Lozenge fleury, or flory. P. 40, f. 15. Lozenge-grand. When the lozenge reaches every way to the centre of the escutcheon it is called a Grand Lozenge, or a Lozenge throughout.

Lozenge in Point, or extending itself to all points of the escutcheon. P. 21, f. 23.

Lozenges in Cross. P. 8, f. 12.

Lozenges. A cross of five lozenges. P. 8, f. 4.

LOZENGRE, or Lozengy. Terms to express the field when covered with lozenges of alternate tinctures. P. 2, f. 31. See also Chevron Lozenge. P. 2, f. 45.

LOZENGIE. A shield, or charge, divided or parted Lozengeways.

LOZENGY-CROSS. P. 8, f. 2.

LOZENGY-BARRY, Barry-lozengy, or Barry-indented. Is formed by bend lines, dexter and sinister, crossed by lines barways. See Barry Indented. P. 2, f. 36.

LOZENGY-BARRY bendy, or Barry-bendy. P. 2, f. 35.

LOZENGY-MASCULY, formed like lozenges but every alternate one is perforated, and forms a mascle, through which the field is seen. See P. 2, f. 23, Masculy-conjoined.

LOZENGY-PALY-BENDY. P. 2, f. 32, and P. 22, f. 21.

LOZENGEWAYS. Any thing placed in the form of a lozenge.

LUCE, or Lucy. A fish, the Pike. P. 32, f. 6.

LUMIERES. The eyes.

LUMPHAD. See Lymphad.

LUNA. The moon. In blazon is used to express argent.

LUNEL. Four crescents in cross, with their horns all turned in towards each other.

L'UN EN L'AUTRE. Same as counterchanged.

L'UN SUR L'AUTRE. Signifies in pale.

LUPAR. A wolf.

LURE, or Leure. The Lure was a figure stuffed like the bird which the hawk was designed to pursue. It's use was to tempt him back after he had flown. The Lure in armory is drawn as P. 43, f. 16.

LURE in. Wings conjoined, with their tips turned downwards as P. 33, f. 28, are said to be in Lure.

LUTE. A musical instrument. P. 43, f. 21, No. 2.

LUTRA. See Otter.

LYBBARD. See Leopard.

LYLYE. Same as Lily.

LYMPHAD. An old fashioned ship, with one mast, and rowed with oars. P. 38, f. 25. Other examples on the same plate.

LYMPHAD with oars. f. 29.

LYMPHAD with sails furled. f. 26.

LYNX. An animal of a tawny brown colour. P. 28, f. 15.

LYON, Lyoncel, or Lioncel. A lion.

LYON King of Arms. The chief of the Heralds Office for Scotland.

LYRE, Lyra, or Lire. A musical instrument. P. 43, f. 21, No. 3.

LYS, or Lis. A fleur-de-lis.

M

MACE. An ornamental staff. P. 35, f. 20, 21 and 22. Borne as an ensign of honour before magistrates, and is frequently given to such when they obtain a grant of arms.

MACE, spiked. P. 41, f. 48.

MACKEREL. A fish. P. 32, f. 17.

MACLES, or Mashes. See Mascles.

MACONNE. The same as Masoned.

MADDER Bag. P. 40, f. 21.

MAGNETIC-NEEDLE. P. 38, f. 34.

MAGPIE. A bird. P. 34, f. 40.

MAHOGANY-TREE. P. 45, f. 49.

MAIDEN'S-HEAD. Always depicted as the head and neck of a woman couped below the breast,. A Maiden's-Head wreathed about the temples with a garland of roses, and crowned with an antique crown, as borne in the arms of the Mercers' Company, London. P. 22, f. 24.

MAIL. Defensive-armour, represented like scales of fish, as the Habergeon. P. 38, f. 8 ; and Arm, P. 36, f. 21.

MAILED. Clothed with mail.

MAIN. A hand.

MAIN-MAST. P. 38, f. 39.

MAINTENANCE, Cap of; also termed a Chapeau. P. 40, f. 54.

MAJESTY, in his. Applied to the eagle when crowned and holding a sceptre.

MALE-GRIFFIN. Also termed an Alce. P. 27, f. 6.

MALE-TIGER. See Heraldic Tiger. P. 28, f 19.

MALLARD. A wild duck. P. 34, f. 22.

MALLET, Beetle, or Maul. P. 41, f. 33.

MALLOW. Plant of, and leaves. P. 44, f. 43.

MALTA, Cross of, or Maltese Cross. P. 11, f. 42.

MALTA, The Knight of. See Hospitallers.

MALTALE. A Maunch, as borne by Hastings, P. 40, f. 32, is called by Legh, a Maunch Maltale, i.e., illshaped, or cut.

MAN with one or more wives. P. 46, f. 1 to 8. See Marshalling.

MAN, and parts of his body in various attitudes, are common in Coat Armour. Each part will be found under its respective term. As Man's Head, Arm, Leg, Hand.

Observe that when the temples, or body of a man or woman are encircled with laurel, oak, etc., you are to say wreathed with laurel, oak, or whatever it may be; and in describing the upper parts of a man as cut, or torn off, you must say that he is couped, or erased at the neck, shoulders, or knees, as the case may be. When cut off about the middle he is called a Demi-man. For examples of blazon of Men. See P. 35; also terms Arm, Hand, Head, and Legs.

MAN's head. A Man's Head in Heraldry is always understood to be an old-man's head, with beard, etc., if not otherwise expressed. P. 36, f. 36.

MAN's head affrontée. f. 34.

MAN's head affrontée erased at the neck. f. 35.

MAN's head affrontée couped below the shoulders. f. 39.

Bust, and bust in profile. f. 36 and 37.

MAN's head conjoined. f. 40.

MAN's head couped below the shoulders. f. 37.

MAN's head couped at the neck in profile. f. 38 and 50.

MAN's head couped at the shoulders. f. 45.

MAN's head crowned. f. 39.

MAN's head distilling blood. f. 50.

MAN's head enwrapped. f. 49.

MAN's head in profile, f. 45, 37 and 38.

MAN's head, three conjoined. f. 41 and 44.

For other examples see P. 36.

MAN's head on a dish. Called the head of St. John the Baptist. P. 35, f. 33.

MAN-WOLF. Seé War-Wolf.

MANACLES, or Handcuffs. Single and double. P. 42, f. 39 and 40.

MANAGE-BIT. P. 37, f. 54.

MANCHE, or Maunch. An old fashioned sleeve. P. 40, f. 31.

A Manche as borne by Hastings f. 32; antique examples 33, 34, and 35.

MANCHE with a hand and arm in it, the hand clenched, borne by Glanville. P. 40, f. 36. One borne with the hand open by Mohun.

MANCHERON. A sleeve.

MANCHET, or Mancher. Cake of bread. See Wastel-cake.

MANDRAKE. A vegetable root. P. 44, f. 60.

MANED. Said of any beast having a mane of a different tincture to the body. Also termed Crined.

MANGONEL. See Swepe.

MANTEGRE, or Manticora. See Man-Tiger.

MANTELLE, or MANTELée. See Chappe and P. 21, f. 36.

MAN-TIGER, or Manticora. P. 27, f. 54.

MANTLE. A flowing robe worn over the armour. See Lambrequin and Robe.

MANTLE, or Cloak. Whereon the achievements are depicted in blazon must be said to be doubled. i.e. lined throughout with some one of the furs, etc. That of the Sovereign being gold doubled with ermine. Those of the Nobility gules, doubled ermine. Those of the Gentry gules doubled with white silk, or miniver. In blazoning this latter the doubling must be termed white not argent. See Robe.

MANTLE, or Royal Cloak. P. 40, f. 29.

MANTLET. A short wide cloak, with which Knights formerly covered their shields.

MANTICORA, or Man Tiger. P. 27, f. 54.

MANTLING. A term applied to the eagle when stretching out both legs and wings. P. 33, f. 11.

MANTLING, Cappeline, or Lambrequin. Which see.

MANTYLL. See Mantle.

MAP. A representation of any part of the surface of the earth drawn on paper or other material; also termed a Chart. P. 43, f. 33.

MAPLE-LEAF. P. 45, f. 24.

MARCASSIN. A young wild boar, distinguished from the old by his pendent tail. The tail of the old boar is always curled. P. 29, f. 31.

MARCHIONESS. The wife of a Marquis.

MARGARETTE Daisy. The Badge of Margaret of Anjou the consort of King Henry VI. P. 44, f. 26.

MARIGOLD. See Marygold.

MARINED. A term used for an animal with the lower parts of the body like a fish, as a Sea-lion. P. 26, f. 53. Most animals are found so joined to the tail of a fish, and are blazoned a Sea-horse. P. 29, f. 55. A Sea-Unicorn, a Sea-Wolf, Sea-Bear, etc.

MARINE-WOLF. A seal. P. 29, f. 51.

MARK, St. Lion of. P. 26, f. 51.

MARKS of Cadency   See Cadency and Distinction of Houses.

MARLET. See Martlet.

MARLIONS, or Merlions-wings. The wings of a Martlet. Two Marlions wings conjoined and expanded, as borne in the arms of Mills. P. 19, f. 21.

MARQUESS, or Marquis. Hereditary title, next in rank to a Duke. The eldest son of a Marquis, by courtesy, is called Earl, or Lord of a Place, and the younger sons Lords, with the addition of their christian name. All the daughters of a Marquis are Ladies. The armorial bearings of a Marquis are distinguished by his Coronet, P. 24, f. 43; and Mantle, P. 35, f. 16.

MARQUESS, Coronet of. P. 24, f. 43.

MARS. In blazon signifies red. P. 1.

MARS. The astronomical character of Mars is borne in the Arms of Stockenstrom, Bateman, Wimble, etc. P. 23, f. 45.

Mars signifies red, in blazoning arms by planets.

MARSHAL of England. The chief officer of arms, as the Earl Marshal, a great officer of the crown, who takes cognizance of all matters of the law of arms. The office belongs, by hereditary right, to the Duke of Norfolk. See Earl Marshal.

MARSHALLING. Is the right disposing of more than one Coat of Arms in one Escutcheon, either by impaling or quartering, and of distinguishing their parts, and contingent ornaments, in their proper places, thereby shewing alliances, descents, etc. See Pedigree. In Marshalling quarterings, the shield of the earliest *Heiress*.whom the bearers ancestor has married, is placed first after the paternal coat; then succeed any quarterings her descent may bring in; the same is to be observed in respect to the second *Heiress*, and so on in chronological order. When a daughter becomes *Heiress* to her mother, also an *Heiress*, and not to her Father, which happens when the Father has a Son by another Wife, she bears her Mother's Arms with the shield of her Father on a Canton, taking all the quarterings to which her Mother was by descent entitled. When married, she conveys the whole to be borne on an Escutcheon of Pretence by her Husband, and transmit them at her death to be borne as quarterings by her descendants. A GRAND QUARTERING is generally designed to denote the representation of a family different from that from which the possessor is descended in the linear male line; it usually accompanies the assumption of a second name, and unites the two associated coats so inseparably, that if they come to be Marshalled with other quarterings they are no longer (as in other cases) spread out among them, but they still remain together as a Grand Quartering. There is no general rule which coat shall take the first place. The paternal coat frequently retains it, but in many cases the assumed arms are borne as the first quarter.

No person can claim a Coat of Arms of inheritance who is not lineally descended from the person to whom the arms were first granted, and no one can claim any right by inheritance until the death of his ancestor, but with some modification derived from the usage of arms. e.g. The Heir apparent is entitled, according to the custom of arms, to use his ancestor's coat with a label of three points. P. 46.

It will be as well to observe that no Husband can impale his Wife's arms with his own, on a Surcoat, Ensign, or Banner; nor can a Knight of any Order, when surrounding the shield with the motto of his Knighthood, bear his Wife's coat therein. See P. 16, Husband and Wife called Baron and Femme. P. 10, f. 21.

Husband and Wife when she is an Heiress or Coheiress, the husband carries her arms in an escutcheon of pretence. P, 11, f. 21.

Husband with two or more Wives. P. 46, f. 2 to 8.

When a Widow marries a second Husband he impales her paternal arms.

See *Funeral Achievements*. P. 46.

MARSHAL'S Staff. See Baton.

MARTIN, or Marten. A kind of weasel sometimes called a Martin-cat. P. 30, f. 13.

MARTEL. A hammer.

MARTLET, Merlion, or Martinet. French Merlette, or Merlot. Latin Mercula. Is a bird shaped like a swallow with a forked tail, and two tufts instead of legs. These tufts are shaped like erasures. P. 2, f. 45; P. 34, f. 59; and P. 47. It is the distinctive mark of the fourth house. P. 46.

MARTLET volant. P. 34, f. 60.

MARYGOLD. A flower. P. 44, f. 22. A French Marygold. i.d. f. 28, as in the arms of Tyssen.

MASCLE. Is of a lozenge form, but always perforated. P. 40, f. 16.

MASCLE-HEAD, or top. A chev. with the top fretted over, in the form of a Mascle. P. 16, f. 28.

MASCLE-CROSS. P. 8, f. 7.

MASCLES conjoined. i.e., the points touching each other, as four mascles conjoined in cross. P. 8, f. 7.

MASCLES-FRETTED. P. 40, f. 18.

MASCLES, seven conjoined, three, three and one. P. 40, f. 17.

MASCULEE, or Mascally. See Masculy.

MASCULY, covered with Mascles. P. 2, f. 27; P. 3, f. 39; P. 18, f. 6.

MASCULY-BENDY. P. 18, f. 33.

MASCULY-CONJOINED. P. 2, f. 23.

MASCULY-NOWY. A cross so termed. P. 11, f. 23.

MASONED, Masonry, or Maconné. Represents the cement in stone buildings. P. 3, f. 11; P. 12, f. 13.

MASON'S square. P. 41, f. 23.

MAST with sail hoisted. P. 38, f. 38 and 39.

MASTIFF. A dog. P. 29, f. 25.

MATCH. Formerly used to fire cannons, depicted as P. 37, f. 60, and borne in the Arms of Leet.

MATCH-LOCK of a gun as borne by Leversage. P. 37, f. 34.

MATELEY-CROSS. A Cross Aiguise, or Urdée. P. 9, f. 45.

MAUL, or Beetle. A wooden hammer. P. 41, f. 33.

MAUNCHE, Maunchenale, Maunchmale, or Monchée. See Manche.

MAURICE, St. Cross of. P. 10, f. 20.

MAW, or Sea-Mew. The common gull. P. 34, f. 13.

MAWRITANIANS HEAD. A moor's head. P. 36, f. 42.

MAY-FLOWER, a sprig of. P. 2, f. 3.

MAYOR. Lord Mayor of London, collar of. See Collar of S.S., and P. 24, f. 29.

MAYOR, formerly Major. i.e. the first or senior alderman.
The Lord Mayor of London, as the chief magistrate is called ; is properly speaking, on'y Mayor of London and Lord of Finsbury. This latter title was conferred, on the gift of the manor of Finsbury, by Richard II., in consequence of Sir William Walworth (then Mayor of London) killing Wat Tyler in Smithfield.
State cap of the Lord Mayor of London. P. 40, f. 56.

MEAREMAID. See Mermaid.

MEASURING-YARD, or Yard-measure. P. 41, f. 41.

MEDAL. A badge of metal, struck in honour of some valiant achievement, or to commemorate some great event, or remarkable discovery.
It is borne suspended from the shield, and is frequently given as a charge in Coat Armour.
ALBERT MEDAL. This decoration was instituted 7th March, 1866, to be awarded, in cases where it shall be considered fit to such persons as shall endanger their own lives in saving, or endeavouring to save the lives of others from shipwreck or other perils of the sea.
There are two classes.
The Medal of the First Class is of gold, enamelled dark blue with Monogram V and A interlaced with an anchor erect in gold, surrounded with a Garter in bronze, inscribed in raised letters of gold " For Gallantry in Saving Life at Sea," and surmounted by a Crown representing that of Prince Albert. The Ribbon is dark-blue, 1¾ inch width, with four white longitudinal stripes. P. 25a, f. 3.
In the Second Class the medal is entirely of bronze, the Ribbon ½inch wide with two white stripes only.
In April 1877, by the especial desire of Her Majesty the Albert Medal was to be given for saving life on Land.
The First Class, the badge is gold, enamelled crimson, with Monogram V and A. The Second Class, the Medal is entirely of bronze.
The Ribbon for both is crimson. P. 25a, f. 4.
Naval and Military Medals.
P. 25, f. 10, 12, 18 and 20.
P. 25a, f. 16 and 17.

MEDIÆVAL. Relating to the middle ages.

MEDUSA Head on a shield. P. 43, f. 58.

MEIRE, or Meirre. The same as potent-counter potent. P. 3, f. 7.

MELTING Pot. See Furnace, and P. 39, f. 33.

MELUSINA. Said to be half a woman, and half a serpent, after the fashion of a mermaid.

MEMBERED. Explained under the term Bird.

MEMBRE, or Membrez. Same as membered.

MENIVER. See Miniver.

MENU of Vair, or Menuvair. When the vair consists of six or more rows, it is so termed.

MERCHANT-BRIG. See Ship.

MERCHANTS' Marks. Devices adopted by wealthy merchants of the middle ages.

MERCHANT Service, Ensign of. See Ensign.

MERCURY. In blazon, expresses the colour Purpure. P. 1.

MERCURYS-CAP, or Mercurial cap. The Petasus or winged cap. P. 38, f. 4.

MERIDIAN. See Globe, and P. 39, f. 2.

MERILLION. An instrument used by hat-band makers, and borne as part of their Arms. P. 41, f. 44.

MERLE. A blackbird. P. 34, f. 44.

MERLET, Merlette, or Merlion. A Martlet. P. 34, f. 59.

MERLETTE-DISPLAYED. The same as Allèrion. P. 33, f. 30.

MERLION. See Merlet.

MERLIN. A hawk. See Falcon.

MERLOTTE. A martlet.

MERMAID. Half a woman and half a fish, usually depicted with comb and mirror. P. 35, f. 12.

MERMAN. Represented as half a man and half a fish. Also termed a Neptune and Triton. P. 35, f. 11.

MERTLET. See Martlet.

MERTRIXES. Also termed a Martin, or Martin-Cat. P. 30, f. 13.

MESLE. A term used by Ferne, signifying *Mingled*, and applied by him in the same sense as *Triangled*.

MESLES. A term to describe the field when of metal and colour in equal proportions, as paly, bendy, etc.

METALS. Two only are used in heraldry, viz., gold and silver. See Tinctures, and P. 1.

METAMORPHOSED. When some portion of an animal has assumed a form different from the proper one.

MEW. A kind of Sea-Gull. P. 34, f. 13. Sea-Mew.

MEW. A Mew was a place of confinement for hawks.

MEWED-HAWK. i.e. a hawk with hood on.

MICHAEL S., and S. George, Order of Knighthood. See Knighthood.

MI-COUPPÉ. Signifies the escutcheon parted per-fesse half way across, some other partition line meeting it.

MIDAS-HEAD. A man's head with ass's ears. P. 36, f. 47.

MIDDLE base point, Middle chief point, etc. See Points of the Escutcheon.

MILL-BILL. See Mill Pick.

MILL-CLACK. P. 38, f. 50.

MILL-INKE. See Fer-de-Moline.

MILL-PICK. A tool used in dressing mill-stones. P. 38, f. 52.

MILL-RIND, Mill-rine, or Mill-ink. Is the iron affixed to the centre of the mill-stone, by which it is turned by the wheel; also termed Fer-de-Moline. P. 38, f. 53 and 54.
The first shewn in the engraving is that usually met with, the other examples are antique ones sometimes met with. See Mill-rind on the Mill-stone. f. 51.

MILL-STONE, charged with a Fer-de-Moline. P. 38, f. 51.

MILL-WHEEL. P. 38, f. 51.

MILLER-CROSS. P. 10, f. 24.

MINERVAS Head. P. 36, f. 33. Minerva the goddess of wisdom and the fine arts, commonly represented with helmet, spear, and shield.

MINIVER. A plain white fur.

MINNOW. A small fresh-water fish. P. 32, f. 39.

MINSTER, or Cathedral. See Church.

MIPARTEE, or Mi-party, the division of the escutcheon half way down the pale, and then crossed by some other partition. See Mi-taille.

MIRROR. A looking glass. P. 43, f. 34.

MI-TAILLE. A term to express that the escutcheon is cut only half way across, in bend sinister. If divided dexterways it is termed *Mi-tranché*.

These divisional lines, together with those called *Mi-party*, and *Mi-couppe*, form three gyrons. P. 19, f. 43.

MITRE. The cap of dignity borne over the arms of the Archbishops and Bishops of the Established Church of England. P. 24, f. 15.
The Mitre is sometimes borne as a charge and also as a crest.

Mitre of the Bishop of Durham issues from a ducal coronet. P. 24, f. 10.

MITRY. A bordure so termed when charged with Mitres.

MITUS. A bird of the pheasant kind.

MODILION, Catoose, or Scroll. The foliage ornament of a pillar.

MOILE. An ox without horns.

MOLE. Usually borne as in the arms of Mitford. P. 22, f. 43.

MOLE-HILLS. See Hills, and P. 42, f. 60.

MOLE-SPADE. P. 39, f. 13, No. 1.

MOLET, or Mollet. See Mullet.

MOLINE Cross. P. 10, f. 1. Also termed Molyne-cross.

MONASTERY, or Abbey in ruins. P. 23, f. 27. Borne by the name of Maitland; a monastery with two wings borne by Monkhouse.

MONCHEE. See Manche.

MONK. See Hermit.

MONKEY. See Ape, and P. 29, f. 58.

MONKEY-WINGED. i.d. f. 60.

MONOGRAM. A cypher composed for the most part of the initials of the bearers name intertwined. P. 39, f. 15.

MONTANT. The same as erect in pale.

MONTEGRE. See Man-tiger.

MONTESE, or Mountain-cross. Is a plain cross humettée. P. 8, f. 28.

MONUMENTS and Tombs. All nations have in some way or another honoured valiant men and noble races by distinguished places of sepulture.
But we now only treat of the time when it became customary to bury in churches, and when certain distinctive marks were devised to denote the estate and condition of those who lay in the several places of repose.
Kings and Princes were represented lying on their tombs (which were made in the shape of altars), in their armour, with their escutcheons, crowns, and all other marks of royalty about them.
Knights and Gentlemen could not be so represented unless they died on the field or within their own lordships.
Those who died victorious in battle were depicted with sword naked, point upwards, on the dexter side; their shield on the sinister; their helmets on their heads.
Those of the vanquished side who were slain,

were represented without their surcoat, their sword in its scabbard; vizor raised, hands joined, as in prayer. on their breast; their feet on a dead lion. N.B. Those who died on their lordships were represented in a similar way, only that they had on their surcoat of arms.

The son of a General, or Governor of a fortress, dying, while the place was besieged, was depicted in armour, with his head resting on a helmet instead of a pillow.

If a Knight or Gentleman entered any religious order when old, he was represented armed, but with the habit of his order instead of a surcoat.

A Knight, or Gentleman, slain in single combat, was represented in armour, his axe out of his hand, his left arm crossed over his right. The Victor was similarly represented, but with his axe in his hand, and his right arm over his left. Those who had gone to the Holy Land were depicted with the right leg crossed over the left, and their sword drawn by their side; those who had vowed to go, but who died without accomplishing their vow, were depicted with their left leg over the right, and with their sword in its scabbard.

Those who died prisoners are said to have been represented without spurs, helmet, or sword, though there is little warrant for this.

By degrees these rules fell into disuse, and persons placed figures in any position they pleased upon monuments to suit their own fancy. See Crest.

MOON. See P. 23, f. 36 and 37, and the term Crescent.

MOOR-COCK. P. 34, f. 41.

MOOR-HEN, or Moor-fowl. P. 34, f. 42.

MOOR'S head, Black's head, African, or Negro's head, are all drawn alike in Heraldry. P. 36, f. 42.

MOOTED, or Moulted. The same as Eradicated. P. 45, f. 31.

MORFEX. A bird. P. 34, f. 36.

MORION, a steel cap. P. 38, f. 1, 2 and 3.

MORISCOE's head, a Negresses-head. P. 36, f. 43.

MORNE, or Mortne. Applied to a lion ramp. having neither tongue, teeth, nor claws. P. 26, t. 5.

MORSE. The sea-lion. P. 26, f. 53.

MORSE. A clasp usually ornamented.

MORTAR. A thick short cannon mounted on a low carriage. P. 37, f. 12.

MORTAR and Pestle. P. 41, f. 50.

MORTCOURS, Morteres, Morterres, or Morteries-Royalls. P. 39, f. 28, No. 2.
A candlestick used at funerals and borne as part of the arms of the Wax Chandlers' Company.

MORTHEAD. See Mort's-head.

MORTIER. A cap of estate.

MORTNE. See Morne.

MORTISED. See Enclave.

MORT'S-HEAD. A death's head. P. 35; f. 34, and P. 36, f. 32.

MOSES'-Burning-bush. P, 45, f. 59.

MOSES-HEAD. A man's head with two rays of light, issuant from the temples like horns.

MOSSU, or Moussue. Rounded at the ends, as a cross mowrned, or blunted. P. 8, f. 41.

MOTTO, or mot. A word or saying added to the Arms. placed in a scroll, either under the shield, or above the crest, and sometimes in both places. P. 11, f. 21, and P. 47.
The motto is of universal use among all nobility and gentry. It does not exclusively belong to Heraldry, and is not hereditary, but may be taken, varied, or relinquished at pleasure. Still there is a pride in using a time honoured sentiment, particularly when it is commemorative of some deed of chivalry. —Mottoes are for the most part either in Latin or French; but they are met with in Hebrew, Greek, Italian, Spanish, German, Welsh, Irish, Scotch, etc. See Elvin's Handbook of Mottoes.

MOULIN, Fer-de. See Fer-de-Moline. P. 38, f. 53.

MOULINE-Cross, See Cross-Moline P. 10, f. 1.

MOULTED. See Eradicated.

MOUND, from Mundus the world. It is also called the Golden Orb, and is the emblem of Sovereignty, Authority, and Majesty. It forms part of the regalia of an Emperor or King.
It is represented as a ball encircled with a horizontal band, from the upper edge of which springs a semicircular band, both are enriched with diamonds and precious stones, and placed on the top of the ball is a cross-pattée. P. 42, f. 37.

MOUNT. The bottom of the shield represented green and curved, as P. 22, f. 7, 10, 11, and 12. P. 2, f. 51.
Animals and heraldic figures are very frequently placed on a mount and borne as Crest.

MOUNT-GRIECED, or in degrees. i.e. cut in the form of steps.

MOUNTAIN-CAT. See Cat-a-Mountain.

MOUNTAIN, or Hill. P. 42, f. 56.

MOUNTAIN-INFLAMED. It is also termed a burning hill or mount. P. 42, f. 57.

MOUNTAIN, or Montese Cross. A plain cross humettee. P. 8, f. 28.

MOUNTED. A term applied to a cross placed on grieces, or steps. P. 8, f. 23. Also to the horse bearing a rider.

MOUNTING, applied to beasts of chase when in the position of rampant.

MOURN, or mourned. Blunted applied to the spikes in the top of the Cronel.

MOUSE-RERE. See Reremouse.

MOUSUE, or Mossu. Rounded at the extremities as a Cross Blunted. P. 8, f. 41.

MOWRNED. See Mousue.

MULBERRY, the fruit of. P. 44, f. 58. The leaf. P. 45, f. 22.

MULE, or Moyle. An animal. P. 27, f. 43.

MULLET. Supposed to be the rowel of a spur, should consist of five points. P. 37, f. 47. When of more than five points should be blazoned a Star of six, eight, or more points, the number being named. P. 23, f. 43, and 44.

MULLET, the fish so called. P. 32, f. 38.

MURAILLE, or Murallée. When an ordinary is represented walled, embattled and masoned. P. 3, f. 11.

MURAL Crown. See Crown.

MUREX-FERREUS. See Galtrap.

MURR. See Auk.

MURREY-COLOUR, dark brown, the same as sanguine. P. 1. The Lion in the arms of Thos. de Berton, of Shropham in Nor., is of this colour.

MUSCHETORS, black spots similar to ermine, the three dots being omitted. P. 12, f. 26.

MUSCOVY-DUCK. P. 34, f. 21.

MUSIC LINES, or BARS, as borne in the arms of Tetlow. P. 5, f. 12.

MUSIMON. An animal with a goat's body and feet, ram's head and four horns. P. 27, f. 57.

MUSION. Ancient name for cat. See Cat-a-mountain.

MUSKET. A fire-arm. P. 37, f. 5.

MUSK-ROSE, branch of. P. 44, f. 3.

MUZZLED. Said of any animal whose mouth is banded to prevent its biting. Bears are always borne muzzled, if not expressed to the contrary. P. 29, f. 40.

MYRTLE branch, with flower and buds. P. 45, f. 10.

MYRTLE, or Oval Garland. Given to those who were victorious at the Julian Games.

N

NAG'S-HEAD. See Horse's Head.

NAIANT, Natant, or Nageant. Swimming; applied to fish in that position. P. 32, f. 15.

NAIANT counter naiant. Swimming in a contrary direction. i.d. f. 16.

NAIL. A closing, and passion nail. P. 37, f. 45, and P. 41, f. 31.

NAILED. See Lattice.

NAISANT, or Naissant. Coming out, as a lion naisant of a fesse. P. 26, f. 26.

NAPOLEON, Badge of. P. 25, f. 8.

NARCISSUS. A flower consisting of six petals, each resembling the leaf of a cinquefoil. P. 44, f. 17, No. 1.

NASCENT. See Naisant.

NATAND, or Natant. The same as Naiant.

NATIONAL Banner, or Ensign. See Union Flag.

NAUNCE. The same as Nebule.

NAVAL-CROWN. See Crown, and P. 24, f. 16.

NAVAL-MEDALS. See Medal, and P. 25, f. 10; P. 25a, f. 16.

NAVAL, Royal Ensign of, and Naval Reserve. P. 25a, f. 5 and 6.

NAVAL-POINT. See Points of Escutcheon. P. 1.

NAVETTY, or Navette. Semée of Shuttles.

NEBULE, Nebula, Nebuly, or Nebulée. Also termed Nebular and Nebulose. A crooked line to which all the ordinaries and partition lines are subject; it is intended to represent clouds, and is drawn as P. 3, f. 4; P. 12, f. 11; P. 19, f. 7.

NEEDLE. See Magnetic-needle, and P. 38, f. 34.

NEGRO. See Moor, and P. 35, f. 28.

NEGRO's head. P. 36, f. 42.

NEGRESS. A Negress's head is borne by several families. P. 36, f. 43.

NEPTUNE, or Triton. Half a man, and half a fish, generally drawn with a Trident. P. 35, f. 11.

NEPTUNE's-MACE, or Trident. A fork of three prongs barbed. P. 38, f. 45.

NERVED. When the fibres of leaves are of a different tincture from the leaf, they are said to be nerved.

NEST of Birds. P. 31, f. 18, borne by Drummond, Knevet, etc.

NETTLE-LEAF. P. 45, f. 28.

NEVE, or Newe. Fretted, or Nowed.

NEWFOUNDLAND Dog. P. 29, f. 29.

NEWT. Also termed Eft, or Effet. An animal of the lizard kind. P. 36, f. 12.

NIGHTINGALE. A bird that sings at night. P. 34, f. 52.

NIMBED. Having the head encircled with a Nimbus, as the child's head. P. 35, f. 1.

NIMBUS, Aureole, or Glory. A circle of rays, P. 35, f. 1, sometimes represented by a plain circle. See P. 26, f. 47; see also P. 28, f. 31, and term Glory.

NIPPERS. See Glazier's-nippers.

NISLEE, or Nyllée, narrow, slender, La croix nylée is by some considered to be the cross-cercellée. P. 11, f. 32; by others a cross-moline depicted very slender.

NOAH'S ARK. P. 38, f. 42. See Ark.

NOBILITY. Those who hold a rank above the degree of a Knight, and are distinguished by titles and privileges.

NOMBRIL, or Navel-point. See Points of Escutcheon. P. 1.

NORMAN-SHIELD, also termed the Heater-shield. See Escutcheon.

NORRY. The title of one of the King's of Arms, whose jurisdiction extends over England, North of the river Trent.

NOTCHED. See Cross-pattée notched. P. 9, f. 8.

NOVA SCOTIA, Baronets of. Instituted by James the First of England and Sixth of Scotland, for the planting of that country by Scottish colonies; as he created Baronets of England for the conquest and planting of the province of Ulster in Ireland. The Nova Scotia Baronets are distinguished by the Badge, P. 31, f. 13, viz., ar. a Saltire az., thereon an escutcheon of the arms of Scotland, with an imperial crown above the escutcheon; all encircled with the motto, on a blue ribbon, edged with gold. The motto is "Fax mentis honestæ gloria," in gold letters, suspended from the shield by an orange coloured ribbon. These Baronets are all allowed to wear Supporters. Arms of a Nova Scotia Baronet. P. 15, f. 21.

NOUED. See Nowed.

NOURRI. Applied to flowers when a part is cut off, and signifies couped.

NOWED. Tied in a knot, as a serpent nowed. P. 30, f. 25. A lion with tail-nowed. P. 26, f. 4.

NOWY. See Partition lines. P. 1. Three bars Nowy. P. 2, f. 14.

NOWYD. When the projection is not in the centre, but in each of the limbs as a Cross nowyd grady fixed. P. 7, f. 43.

NUAGE. See Nuée.

NUANCE. The same as Nebulée.

NUCE. A cloud.

NUEE, or Nuage. See Bend Nuée. P. 17, f. 24.

NUEE-GOARED. See Fesse Arondy, Nuée-goared. P. 4, f. 6.

NUNS-HEAD. P. 36, f. 30, borne by Daveney.

NUT, Nut-tree, and Nut-branch, are all found in Heraldry. P. 44, f. 55.

NUTE. See Newt.

NUTHATCH. A bird. P. 34, f. 38. Crest of Feilden.

NYLLE. See Nislée.

NYMPH. A female figure is sometimes blazoned a Mymph.

O

O. This letter stands for Or, in sketches.

OAK. A Tree, the Oak and parts of it are variously borne, and of very frequent use in Coat Armour. An Oak Tree eradicated and fructed ppr.; i.e., torn up by the roots, and having acorns upon it. P. 45, f. 31. An Oak Leaf. i.b. f. 19. An Oak Branch fructed should consist of four leaves; if unfructed, of nine; a sprig should have five leaves, and a slip only three. P. 44, f. 53, and f. 52. The Oak Tree is the emblem of virtue and strength.

OAR. A long pole with a flat thin end, by which vessels are driven along in the water. P. 32, f. 27.

OATS. A grain. A Sheaf of, borne by the name of Ottley. P. 45, f. 15.

OBSIDIONAL Crown, or Garland. See Crown Obsidional. P. 43, f. 2. This Crown was made of grass and twigs of trees interwoven.

OCTOFOIL. A double quaterfoil, as P. 46, No. 9, in distinction of houses.

OCULARIUM. The narrow opening for sight in the helmet.

ODIMOLIONT Fish. See Remora.

OFFICERS of Arms. See Heralds' College.

OFFICIAL Arms. See Arms of Office.

OGE, or Bouse. A Water-bouget. P. 42, f. 20 to 24.

OGRESS. The same as Pellet, P. 1, representing a ball or flint-stone for cannon.

OLIVE-CROWN. See Crown-Olive. P. 43, f. 5.

OLIVE-GUTTÉE de. See Gutté.

OLIVE-TREE, and Olive-Branches, are of very common occurrence as

Heraldic bearings. See Dove with Olive-branch. P. 31, f. 25; P. 33, f. 42.

OMBRE. Shadowed. See Adumbrated.

ONDE, or Undé. Same as Wavy, or Undy.

ONGLE. A term for the claws of birds or beasts; the same as armed.

ON, placed upon as "On a Fesse three lozenges." P. 4, f. 30. "On a Cross five fleur-de-lis." P. 7, f. 3. "On a Chief two mullets." P. 12, f. 2. "On a Chevron three escallops." P. 16, f. 24. "On a Bend three bezants." P. 47.

ON-SETT, or DOUBLE ON-SETT. It is also termed Downsett, Rampée, Coppée, Ramped, Copped, and Rompu, as a Fesse Rompu. P. 4, f. 25. A Chevron Downset, or Rompu. P. 16, f. 1.

OPEN-CROWNS. The Ducal-coronet when borne as a charge in the arms is sometimes blazoned " Open Crown."

OPEN in the head, Disjoint, or Brisse. See a Chevron disjointed. P. 16, f. 4.

OPIATE-ROD. See Caduceus.

OPINICUS. A beast with the body and fore legs of a lion, the head, neck and wings of an eagle, with the tail of a camel. It is sometimes borne " sans wings." P. 27, f. 8.

OPPRESSED, or Oppressing. The same as Debruised, or Surmounted. See Debruised.

OR, gold, or yellow. See Tinctures. The term Gold may be used in blazoning a coat. In engraving, " Or" is expressed by dots. See P. 1.

ORANGE. A roundle tenné. P. 1. See also Tenné.

ORANGE-TREE. P. 22, f. 12.

ORARIUM, a Banderole. P. 42, f. 46.

ORB-GOLDEN. See Mound.

ORB. The Globe, as P. 39, f. 5.

ORBICULAR. i.e. Circular; as seven stars placed orbicular, are found in the arms of D'Urban. P. 5, f. 39.

ORBIT. Round or Circle.

ORDERS. See *Distinguished Service Order*. There are two Orders confined to Ladies; *The Order of Victoria and Albert*, and *The Imperial Order of the Crown of India.* Members are entitled to no special precedence. Badges. P. 24, f. 25 and 30. Order of the Indian Empire. i.b. f. 24.

ORDER of the Dooranée Empire, Badge of. P. 25, f. 19.

ORDER of St. John of Jerusalem. See Hospitallers.

ORDERS of Knighthood. See Knighthood.

ORDINARIES. So called because they are the most ancient and common amongst the various cognizances used in Heraldry, are divided (although on this point the opinions of Heralds are greatly at variance) into the honourable and subordinaries, which are all subject to the accidental forms of the lines composing them, as engrailed, invecked, etc., etc. The honourable ordinaries according to the present practice should always occupy one third of the field, and are the Bend, Bend Sinister, Chevron, Chief, Cross, Fesse, Pale, Quarter, and Saltier, which, with their diminutives, will be found under their proper heads.

All ordinaries may be charged; i.e., have figures upon them, their diminutives should not, but in many shields they are charged with figures. See Subordinaries.

ORDINARY of Arms. Heraldic Bearings, classified and arranged in accordance with the charges, and having the name of the bearer attached.

OREILLE. Eared.

OREILLER. A cushion, or pillow. P. 40, f. 24.

ORGAN-PIPE. P. 43, f. 20.

ORGAN Rest. See Rest.

ORARIUM, or Vexillum. See Banderoll.

ORIENTAL-CROWN. See Eastern-Crown.

ORIFLAM, Oriflamme, or Oriflambe. A square banner, made of flame coloured silk, and always appeared at the head of the French armies, from the 12th to the 15th century. See Auriflamme.

ORLE. One of the subordinaries is composed of lines passing round the shield, forming an inner border, and derive its name from Ourler to hem. P. 5, f. 31.

The Orle is subject to all the accidental forms of Lines as Engrailed, Invecked, etc. f. 32.

Orle of clouds. P. 22, f. 24.

Orle of three pieces. P. 22, f. 25.

Orle fretted with a pallet. P. 5, f. 34.

In Orle. i.b. f. 36.

Within an Orle. i.b. f. 38.

An Orle of Estoiles. P. 5, f. 36.

Double Orle. f. 33.

ORMOND-KNOT. P. 43, f. 10, No. 2.

OSTRICH, and parts of it, are common bearings in Coat Armour. The Ostrich is usually represented in Heraldry with horse-shoe or key in its mouth. P. 33, f. 40.

OSTRICH, head couped between two ostrich wings. P. 33, f. 41.

OSTRICH Feathers are borne single, and in plumes. See *Plume*, and P. 6, f. 21 ; P. 25, f. 22 and 23 ; also P. 43, f. 37 to 40.

OTTER. An amphibious animal. P. 29, f. 54.

OTTER's Head. P. 29, f. 53.

OUNCE. A fierce animal. P. 28, f. 18.

OUNDY. Same as Wavy.

OUTSTICKER, as borne in the arms of the Basket Makers' Company, London. P. 22, f. 28.

OVER. The word over in Heraldry must never be taken to mean *above*, but *upon*.

OVER-ALL. Surmounted. P. 7, f. 4.

OVERLAID. A Pale fracted and overlaid. P. 14, f. 15.

OVERT, or Overture. Terms applicable to the wings of birds, etc., when spread open on either side of the head as if taking flight. P. 33, f. 3. It is also applied to inanimate things, as a purse overt; i.e., an open purse. P. 40, f. 41.

OVERTURE-ELEVATED. Differs from the last by having the points of the wings elevated. P. 33, f. 2.

OWL. The owl is always depicted full faced, P. 34, f. 55, and is the emblem of prudence and wisdom.

OWL-HORNED. i.b. f. 56.

OWNDY. The same as Wavy, or Undée.

OX. As borne in the arms of the city of Oxford. P. 22, f. 15. Ar. a chev. gu. betw. three oxen pass. sa. armed or. The Arms of Oxenden.

OX-YOKE. P. 37, f. 57.

Ox's foot couped. P. 31, f. 23.

OYSTER Catcher, or Sea-Pie. P. 34, f. 17.

OYSTER-DREDGE. P. 38, f. 59.

P

P. Sometimes used for the word Purpure.

PACK. See Wool-pack.

PACK-SADDLE. P. 37, f. 51.

PACO. See Alpaca.

PADLOCK. P. 42, f. 13.

PAIL. See Bucket.

PAILLE. Diapered, and variegated.

PAIRLE. The same as a Cross Pall.

PAIRLE-IN, as gu. three swords in Pairle hilts inwards ar. P. 31, f. 31.

PAISSANT. See Browsing.

PALATA. In pale.

PALE. One of the honourable ordinaries, formed by two perpendicular lines drawn from top to bottom of the shield as Ar. a Pale sa. P. 14, f. 1. Arms of Erskine.

PALE-ANGLED. f. 27.

PALE Angled-quartered. f. 35.

— ARCHED-DOUBLE. f. 19.

— ARONDIE. f. 19.

— BETWEEN two eagles. f. 6.

— BETWEEN two indorses. f. 4.

— BEVILED, or Beveled. f. 23.

— BRETESSED. f. 17.

— CHAMPAINE. f. 22,

— COUNTERCHANGED. f. 5. and 29.

— DANCETTE. f. 16.

— ENDORSED. f. 4.

— ENGRAILED. f. 10.

— FIMBRIATED. f. 9,

— FITCHEE. f. 20.

— FLORY. f. 12.

— FRACTED. f. 25.

— FRACTED-REMOVED. f. 26.

— IN-BASE. f. 37.

— INDENTED. f. 15.

— INDORSED. f. 4.

— INVECKED. f. 11.

— LOZENGY. f. 41.

— NUEE, or Nuage. f. 19.

— NOWY Quadrate, or square. f. 35.

— OVERLAID and removed. f. 25.

— RADIANT. f, 18.

— RAGULY. f. 13.

— REMOVED, etc. f. 25.

— RETRACTED. f. 24.

— SURMOUNTED. f. 7.

THREE Pales. f. 32.

Two Pales. f. 31.

Two Pales couped in Fesse, etc. f. 34.

PALE voided. f. 8.

PALE wavy. f. 14.

PALE, in pale. P. 14, f. 36, 41 and 43.

PALE, on a pale. P. 14, f. 18.

PALE, per or Per-pale. When the field or charge is divided by a centre line drawn perpendicularly from top to bottom. P. 2, f. 1 ; P. 14, f. 40 and f. 45.

PALED. The same as Impaled.

PALET, or Pallet. A diminutive of the Pale being one half of it. P. 14, f. 2. Three Pales or Pallets. i.b. f. 42, and 45 ; P. 2, f. 18,

PALEWISE, or Paleways. When figures are placed in Pale, as P. 14, f. 43 ; P. 31, f. 35.

PALES. See Park-pales. P. 43, f. 36.

PALISADES. See Park-pales.

PALISADO-CORONET. Composed of upright pieces, like pales, pointed and fixed upon a rim. P. 24, f. 37.

PALISSE, or Palissy. Represents a stockade, or row of stakes with intervals between them, placed before a fortification. P. 22, f. 36.

PALL. An archiepiscopal vestment, P. 22, f. 2, and 3, is borne as a charge in the arms of the Sees of Canterbury, Armagh and Dublin.

PALL-CROSS. P. 8, f. 14. This is the arms of Pauling, viz.: or a Pall gu.

PALL, per. A division of the field by a single line in the form of a pall.

PALLAS' HEAD. A woman's head in armour. P. 36, f. 33.

PALLAS. The Shield of. See Ægis and P. 43, f. 58.

PALLET or palet. A dimunitive of the Pale. P. 14, f. 2.

PALLICUM. See Pall.

PALM-BRANCH. P. 45, f. 55; P. 31, f. 42.

PALM-TREE. P. 45, f. 52.

PALMER or Pilgrims were soldiers that had served in the Crusades or holywar. They were so called because they generally brought home a branch of palm of the growth of Palestine, and wore it as a sacred badge and token that they had performed their vows, either by fighting against the infidels, or visiting the Holy Sepulchre.

PALMER'S SCRIP or Wallet. P. 40, f. 39.

PALMER'S-STAFF. P. 42, f. 44.

PALMER'S-STAFF and Scrip. P. 40, f. 40. Pilgrims to the Holy City carried each a staff and leather scrip.

PALMER WORM. P. 30, f. 24.

PALY. A term to express the field or any bearing when divided into any number of equal pieces by perpendicular lines, as paly of six. P. 2, f. 16. Paly of eight, f. 17.

PALY-BENDY. P. 22, f. 21; P. 2, f. 32.

PALY-BENDY sinister. P. 2, f. 33.

PALY-BARRY. P. 2, f. 42.

PALY-COUNTERPALY. Same as paly per-fesse counterchanged. P. 14, f. 33.

PALY and Fesse of nine, is the shield divided into nine equal squares. P. 2, f. 19.

PALY Lozengy. P. 2, f. 32.

PALY of three parted per-fesse. P. 14, f. 30.

PALY of six, ar. and gu., a bend sa. P. 14, f. 44.

PALY of six, per fesse. ib. f. 33.

PALY of six, per fesse counterchanged. P. 22, f. 42.

PALY of six Saltrery, or Paly Saltiery. P. 14, f. 38.

PALY-PER-FESSE. ib. f. 33.

PALY-PILY. P. 6, f. 39.

PAME. Langued.

PAMPILLETTEE. See Papelonné.

PANACHE. An upright plume of more than three rows of feathers, generally of a Cock or Swan, was not unfrequent, particularly at the period shortly before the assumption of more distinctive crests. P. 43, f. 41. Crest of Mortimer. The Panache of Peacocks' feathers is the Crest of Sir Edmund de Thorpe, 1418. P. 43, f. 42. A Panache of Turkeys feathers the Crest of Harsicke, of Southacre, co. Norfolk.

PANDALL, or Pendall. Also termed a Spindle Cross. P. 11, f. 43.

PANES. Pieces. The same as chequy of nine panes, or paly and fesse of nine. i.e., the shield divided into nine equal squares. P. 2, f. 19.

PANNES. Same as Pean.

PAPINGOE, Papegay. See Parrot.

PANOPLY. Complete armour.

PANSEY, Pansy, or Hearts' Ease. P. 44, f. 23.

PANTHER. In Heraldry, always drawn guardant, and incensed; i.e., with fire issuing from its mouth and ears. P. 28, f. 7.

PAPAL-CROWN, Tiara, or Triple-Crown. A long red cap, surmounted by a mound and cross pattée; round this cap are three Marquesses coronets of gold, placed one above the other; from the inside issue two ribbons fringed. P. 40, f. 59.

PAPAL-STAFF, or Pope's Cross-staff. P. 42, f. 48.

PAPEGAY. See Parrot.

PAPELONNE, or Pampillettée. A term to denote the field or charge, covered with a figure like the scales of a fish. P. 18, f. 7; P. 2, f. 22.

PAPILLONE. See Papelonne.

PARADISE, bird of. P. 34, f. 6.

PARADISE, tree of. P. 22, f. 7.

PARCHMENT, roll of. P. 36, f. 10.

PARER. Same as Butteris.

PARING Knife. A currier's shave. P. 41, f. 2.

PARK-PALES. P. 43, f. 36.

PARK-PALES in a circular form. P. 28, f. 55.

PARK with stag lodged. P. 28, f. 55.

PARLANTES, Arms of. See Allusive Arms.

PARLIAMENT Robe. P. 40, f. 30.

PARAQUET. A small sort of parrot. See next term.

PARRAKEET. One of the prettiest and most interesting birds of the parrot tribe. P. 34, f. 58.

PARROT, Popinjay, or Papegay. A gregarious bird. P. 34, f. 57. The parrot, when blazoned proper, is green, beaked and membered gules.

PARTED. Divided.

PARTED, double or biparted, triple or triparted, quarter or caterparted, and cinqueparted. Terms used for the field, or charge divided into two, three, four, or five parts.

PARTI. Same as Parted per pale.

PARTIE, or Party. Signifies divided, applied to all divisions of the field, or any figure when divided by those particular lines, as Party per pale, Party per fesse, etc. P. 2, f. 1 to 10; P. 4, f. 32 to 39; P. 16, f. 30 to 32; and P. 19, f. 1 to 25.

PARTISAN, or Partizan. See Halbert.

PARTITION Lines. See Divisions of the shield. P. 2, f. 1 to 10.

PARTITIONS. Are the several divisions made in a coat when the arms of several families are borne in one shield. See Quarterings.

PARTIZAN. See Halbert.

PARTRIDGE. A bird of game. P. 33, f. 47.

PARTY. Signifies divided, as Party per pale, etc. P. 2, f. 1 to 10.

PASCHAL Lamb, or Holy Lamb. Is depicted, pass. carrying a flag charged with the cross of St. George, and circle of glory over its head. P. 29, f. 4.

PASCUANT, or Pasquant. A term used for stags, sheep, etc., when feeding. See Browsing. P. 28, f. 48.

PASSANS. See Passant.

PASSANT. A term used for lions or other beasts in a walking position. P. 26, f. 23; P. 27, f. 1; P. 28, f. 19. Passant does not apply to the deer kind. See Trippant.

PASSANT, Counter-passant Two beasts walking in opposite directions. P. 26, f. 36.

PASSANT Guardant. Walking with head affrontée. i.d. f. 35.

PASSANT Reguardant. Walking and looking back. i.d. f. 24.

PASSANT Repassant. The same as Counter passant; that is one animal

walking to the sinister, and the other to the dexter. P. 26, f. 36.

PASSAUNZ. Passant.

PASSE EN SAUTOIR. A term to express any thing borne in saltier.

PASSION Cross. A long cross. P. 9, f. 38.

PASSION-NAIL, always drawn as P. 41, f. 31; and P. 10, f. 15.

PASSION, SHIELD of the. See Instruments of the Passion.

PASTORAL-STAFF. P. 42, f. 46. This is often, but erroneously, called a crozier.

PATEE. See Pattée-cross. P. 9, f. 1.

PATERNAL Arms. The original arms of a family.

PATER-NOSTER, or Nostrée. A cross of beads. P. 42, f. 41.

PATONCE Cross. P. 10, f. 13.

PATRIARCHAL Cross. P. 22, f. 23.

PATRICK, St. Cross of, is a saltire gu. P. 7, f. 21.

PATRICK, St. Order of Knighthood. See Knighthood.

PATRONAGE, Arms of. See Arms of Patronage.

PATTEE. See Cross Pattée. P. 9, f. 1 to 27.

PATTEE fitchée, etc. ib. f. 14.

PATTEN. A clog, as borne in the arms of the Patten-Makers' Company. P. 41, f. 15.

PATTES. The paws of any beast.

PAUL, St., Sword of. The dagger in the arms of the City of London is sometimes so called, St. Paul being the patron saint of the city. P. 27, f. 27.

PAULDRON. Armour for the shoulder.

PAUMY. See Apaume.

PAVACHE, or Targate. Was a large buckler, forming an angle in front like the ridge of a house, and large enough to cover the tallest man from head to foot. Sometimes they were emblazoned and borne in state, and were usually introduced into funeral trophies.

PAVAS, or Pavise. A large shield which almost covered the person.

PAVEMENT. Depicted as paly barry in perspective. P. 22, f. 39.

PAVER, Pavier, or Paviour's Pick. P. 41, f. 29.

PAVILION, or Tabernacle. An oblong tent, with projecting entrance. P. 40, f. 28.

PAVON. A long flag tapering from about half a yard to a point.

Paw. The foot of a lion, bear, seal, etc., cut off at the first joint. See Seal's paw erased. P. 29, f. 52.

Peacock, and parts of this bird are frequently borne in Heraldry. P. 34, f. 5.

Peacock in his pride. P. 34, f. 4 ; and Peacock close, f. 5.

The Peacock is used in ecclesiastical decoration, and symbolises power and omniscience. A Plume, or Panache of Peacock's feathers. P. 43, f. 42.

Pea-Rise. A pea stalked with leaves and flowers.

Pea-cod, or Pea-pod pendant. P. 44, f. 59.

Peal, or Peel. A tool used by bakers for drawing bread out of the oven. P. 41, f. 12.

A peal in pale, thereon three cakes, borne by the name of Pister. An oval-peel is borne by the name of Kill.

Pean. One of the furs, the ground of which is black, powdered with ermine spots of gold. P. 1.

Pear. Always borne as P. 44, f. 56, unless blazoned reversed, or other position, a Pear slipped. i.d.

Pear Tree fructed. P. 45, f. 39.

Pearched, or Pearching. See Perched.

Pearl. In Heraldry is used to express white.

Pecys. An old term meaning quarters.

Peded. A term to express the feet of aquatic birds when of a different tincture to the body.

Pedistal. The compartment, or carved ornament, upon which supporters stand. P. 19, f. 21 ; P. 31, f. 11.

Pedigree. A register of a line of ancestors. e.g. See below.

For abbreviations used in Pedigrees vid term Genealogy.

Pedigree of Athow, of Brisley, Co. Norfolk.

Arms. Sable a chevron between three carpenters' squares argent.

Thomas Athow, of Brisley, co. Norfolk = Audrey, da. & cohr. of Robert Curson, of Letherensett co. Norfolk.
Arms. Erm. a bend compony ar. & sa.

Thomas Athow, of Brisley, ob. 6. Edw. IV. =

John Athow, of Brisley. = Anna, da. of ... Gogney, of Brisley, ob. wid. 1536.
Arms Quarterly, 1 & 4. | Arms Per Chev. invecked or. & gu. three lions heads erased,
Athow, 2 & 3. Curson. | counterchanged.

Christopher Athow, of Brisley = Joan, da. and hr. of   John, a Priest.   Thomas, a Priest.
... Goldwell, of the
Isle of Ely.
Arms, Gu. a chief az.
over all a lion ramp. erm.

Christopher Athow, of Brisley. = Dorothy, da. of Thomas Jennyson.
| Arms, Az. a bend wavy, or betw. two swans ppr.

(A)

(A)

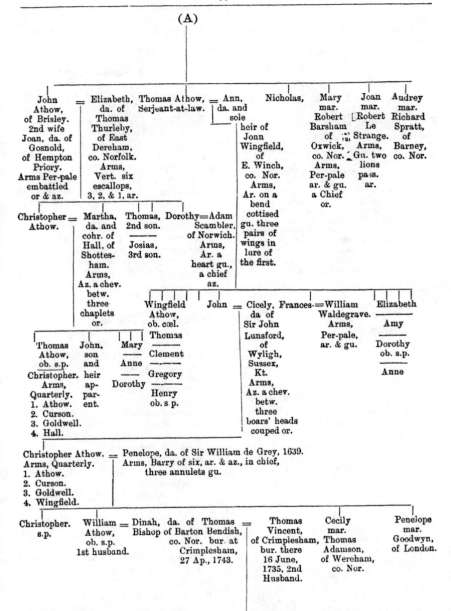

| John Athow, of Brisley. 2nd wife Joan, da. of Gosnold, of Hempton Priory. Arms Per-pale embattled or & az. | = | Elizabeth, da. of Thomas Thurleby, of East Dereham, co. Norfolk. Arms, Vert. six escallops, 3, 2, & 1, ar. | Thomas Athow, Serjeant-at-law. | = | Ann, da. and sole heir of Joan Wingfield, of E. Winch, co. Nor. Arms, Ar. on a bend cottised gu. three pairs of wings in lure of the first. | Nicholas, | Mary mar. Robert Barsham of Oxwick, co. Nor. Arms, Per-pale ar. & gu. a Chief or. | Joan mar. Robert Le Strange. Arms, Gu. two lions pass. ar. | Audrey mar. Richard Spratt, of Barney, co. Nor. |

Christopher Athow. = Martha, da. and cohr. of Hall, of Shottesham. Arms, Az. a chev. betw. three chaplets or.

Thomas, 2nd son. — Josias, 3rd son.

Dorothy = Adam Scambler, of Norwich. Arms, Ar. a heart gu., a chief az.

| Thomas Athow, ob. s.p. Christopher. Arms, Quarterly. 1. Athow. 2. Curson. 3. Goldwell. 4. Hall. | John, son and heir apparent. | Mary — Anne — Dorothy | Wingfield Athow, ob. cœl. Thomas — Clement —·— Gregory — Henry ob. s p. | John | = | Cicely, da of Sir John Lunsford, of Wyligh, Sussex, Kt. Arms, Az. a chev. betw. three boars' heads couped or. | Frances = William Waldegrave. Arms, Per-pale, ar. & gu. | Elizabeth — Amy — Dorothy ob. s.p. — Anne |

Christopher Athow. = Penelope, da. of Sir William de Grey, 1639.
Arms, Quarterly.   Arms, Barry of six, ar. & az., in chief,
1. Athow.   three annulets gu.
2. Curson.
3. Goldwell.
4. Wingfield.

| Christopher. s.p. | William Athow, ob. s.p. 1st husband. | = | Dinah, da. of Thomas Bishop of Barton Bendish, co. Nor. bur. at Crimplesham, 27 Ap., 1743. | = | Thomas Vincent, of Crimplesham, bur. there 16 June, 1735, 2nd Husband. | Cecily mar. Thomas Adamson, of Wereham, co. Nor. | Penelope mar. Goodwyn, of London. |

V

PEER. A Nobleman who has a seat and vote in the House of Lords; and, although the Peers differ in order of precedence, yet as Peers of the Realm they are equal in all political privileges.

PEER'S Robe. See Robe.

PEG, or Wedge. As borne by the name of Peg. P. 41, f. 42.

PEG. As borne in the badge of Lawrence. P. 43, f. 15.

PEG-TOP. P. 42, f. 29.

PEGASUS. A winged-horse. P. 27, f. 41. The Emblem of Fame.

PELICAN. P. 33, f. 37.
The Heraldic Pelican is represented with her wings endorsed, if not mentioned to the contrary, her neck embowed, pecking her breast, from whence issue drops of blood; and in blazon is termed vulned, or vulning. When depicted in her nest is termed in her piety. f. 38. The Emblem of Charity.

PELLET, or Ogresse. Roundle-sable. P. 1. Also termed Gunstones.

PELLETTEE, Pelletty, or Pelletye. Strewed with Pellets, also termed Semée of Pellets.

PEN. A quill pen, borne by Aldridge. P. 36, f. 29.

PENCEL, Pencell, or Pensell. A small streamer or pennon.

Pendal, Pandall, or Spindle Cross. P. 11, f. 43.

PENDANT. A term applied to anything hanging down, as the badge of any order pendent to the collar or ribbon. P. 24, f. 7, 18, 28, etc.

PENDANT. A small Standard.

PENGUIN. A web-footed marine bird. P. 34, f. 35.

PENNANT. A long narrow banner with the Cross of St. George in the head. P. 46, f. 17.
The Broad Pennant is a swallow-tailed flag.

PENNED. See Quilled.

PENNER and Ink-Horn. A case for holding pens and ink. P. 41, f. 17 and 18.

PENON, or Pennon. A Lance Flag, ending in one or more sharp points. P. 46, f. 12, 14, 17, and 22.

PENNONCLES, Pennoncelle, or Pencils. Small streamers or flags. P. 46, f. 15.

PENNY-YARD-PENCE. A small coin, stamped with a cross moline betw. twelve balls. P. 42, f. 29.

PENS. Such as are used to write with. P. 36, f. 29.

PENSILE. See Pennoncles.

PENTAGON, also termed the Mystic Pentagon. A star of five points composed of five A's interlaced with the word SALUS inscribed at its angles. P. 42, f. 30.
The Pentagon the symbol of health.

PEPINGOE. See Popingay.

PER CLOSE. A Demi Garter. P. 42, f. 18.

PER. Denotes a partition of the field or charge, as Per-Bend, Per-Chevron, Per-Fesse, Per-Pale, etc. P. 2, f. 1 to 10 and 49 and 50.

PERCEE. Same as Cleeché.

PERCH, or rest for Falcon. P. 43, f. 18.

PERCH. A fish. P. 32, f. 31.

PERCHED, or Perching, said of a bird when in a sitting position upon a branch, or other thing. P. 33, f. 19.

PERCLOSE, or Per-Close. A Demi Garter. P. 42, f. 18.

PERCULACED. The same as latticed.

PERCUSSANT, or Percussed. A term applied to the tail of an animal when lying on the back or side. P. 28, f. 32.

PERFLEWED, Purfled, or Purflewed. See Purfled.

PERFORATED. The same as pierced. P. 16, f. 16.

PERI, or Pery. Perished. Term used to denote that the thing to which it is applied is deficient in some of its parts.

PERIWINKLES, or Welks (shells). P. 32, f. 54.

PERPENDICULUM. An angle and plumbline. P. 41, f. 40.

PERSPECTIVE. Used to express division lines as barry-paly in prospect or perspective. P. 22. f. 39.

PERSIA. Badges of the Lion and Sun. P. 25a, f. 7.

PERTRANSIENT. Passing through.

PERUKE. P. 40, f. 47.

PESTLE and Mortar. P. 41, f. 50.

PETASUS, or Mercurys cap. P. 38, f. 4.

PETRONEL. An ancient name for a pistol. P. 37, f. 9.

PEWIT. A bird. P. 33, f. 55.

PHEON. The barbed head of a dart, or an arrow, frequently borne in Coats of Arms, depicted in various ways, but if not differently described is always represented as P. 37, f. 15.
A Pheon engrailed on outer edges. f. 16.
A Pheon mounted on a staff, and feathered a's), blazoned an arrow Pheoned. f. 14.
A Pheon per pale. P. 14, f. 4).

PHŒNIX. An imaginary bird, always represented issuing from flames.

P. 33, f. 25.
Emblematic of the resurrection.

PHEASANT. A bird of game. P. 33, f. 46.

PHYAL, Phial, or Vial. A small glass bottle. P. 41, f. 59.

PHYSICIANS Cap. See Cap.

PIC. See Pick-axe.

PICK-AXE. P. 41, f. 30.

PICOTE. Speckled.

PIE. See Sea-Pic.

PIDDLE, or Dunpiddle. A Kite, borne by the name of Piddle. See Kite. P. 33, f. 60.

PIEDMONT Silk, a Bale of. P. 40, f. 21.

PIED. Spotted. A bull pied, borne by Braybrooke.

PIERCED. When any ordinary or charge is perforated, the piercing is always understood to be circular, unless otherwise described. P. 8, f. 31. Quarter pierced. P. 7, f. 16. Square pierced. P. 8, f. 44. Lozenge pierced. P. 10, f. 2. The term Pierced is also applied to animals when wounded with an arrow, spear, etc. Examples of a chevron pierced. See P. 16, f. 15, 16 and 17.

PIERCER. See Wine Piercer.

PIETY. A Pelican in her piety. P. 33, f. 38.

PIGEON. A bird. P. 34, f. 39.

PIGNON. The same as per-chev., embattled.

PIGNONNE. Turreted.

PIKE, or Luce. A fish. P. 32, f. 6.

PIKE-DEMI. f. 7.

PIKE-STAFF, or Staves, P. 42, f. 43.

PILCHARD. A fish. P. 32, f. 37.

PILE. See Roman-pilum.

PILE, or PYLE. One of the ordinaries. P. 6, f. 1.

— BETWEEN. f. 17, 18 and 35.

— CHARGED with another. f. 12.

— COTISED. f. 13.

— COUNTERCHANGED. f. 32 and 36.

— CROSS pattée at point. f. 24.

— EMBATTLED. f. 6.

— EMBOWED. f. 15.

— ENGRAILED. f. 35.

— FITCHED. f. 7.

— FLANCHED. f. 9.

— FLORIED. f. 26.

— FLEUR-DE-LIS at point. f. 25.

— GOAREE. f. 8.

— INDENTED. f. 4.

— IN Point Bendwise. f. 11.

— ISSUING. f. 3, 13, 19 and 27.

— ON a. f. 34 and 35.

— PIERCED. f. 11.

PILE REVERSED. f. 2 and 28.

PILE REVERSED Indented. f. 5.

— SURMOUNTED. f. 22 and 33.

— AND Saltire counterchanged. f. 36.

— SQUARE. f. 40.

— TETRAGONELL. f. 40.

— TRANSPOSED. f. 2.

— TRANSPOSED between two reversed. f. 18.

— TRAVERSE. f. 38.

— TRIANGULAR. f. 41.

— TRIPLE-POINTED. f. 10.

— TRIPLE. f. 26.

— WAVY. f. 20 and 23.

— WAVY Fitched. f. 42.

— WITHIN a bordure. f. 37.

PILES, Two. f. 14, 15 and 28.

PILES, THREE. f. 16, 17, 18 and 27.

PILES, Five. f. 29.

PILES traversed barwise. f. 30.

PILE-PER and Chevron. f. 43.

PILE-PER and Fesse, or Per-Bar and Pile. P. 2, f. 10.

PILE-PER reversed. P. 6, f. 44.

PILE-PER transposed. P. 6, f. 45.

PILY-BARRY, or Pily Traverse. P. 6, f. 31.

PILY counter pily of seven traits. P. 6, f. 24.

PILY of eight. i.d. f. 31.

PILY-PALY. i.d. f. 39. A division of the field in the form of piles, reaching from the top to the bottom.

PILGRIMS' staff. See Palmer's staff.

PILLAR. The same as Column. P. 43, f. 50.

PILLOW, Cushion, or Oreilliers. P. 40, f. 24. Is a cushion with tassels. The Norman Cushions were called Carreaux, from their square or diamond shape, as you see them placed under the heads of the recumbent effigies of the twelfth and thirteenth centuries.

PINCERS. A tool. P. 41, f. 1.

PINE-APPLE, or Ananas. P. 44, f. 56.

PINE-BRANCH. P. 44, f. 47.

PINE-CONE. P. 44, f. 54.

PINE Tree. P. 22, f. 10.

P.NIONED. Refers to the quill of a wing when of a different tincture from the feathers. P. 25, f. 23.

PINK, slipped and leaved. P. 44, f. 20.

PINNACE. In Heraldry, an open boat with oars.

PINZON. A finch, or chaffinch. P. 34, f. 54.

PIPE. A musical instrument. P. 43, f. 21. No. 2.

PISMIRE. See Ant.

PISTOL. P. 37, f. 9.

PITCHER. Same as Ewer. P. 42, f. 27.

PITCHFORK. P. 39, f. 14. No. 3.

PITCH-POT. See Beacon.

PITHON. A winged serpent.

PLACCATE. A piece of armour worn over the breast-plate to strengthen it.

PLACQUE. An Herald's Tabard.

PLAICE. A fish. P. 32, f. 20.

PLAIN. An ordinary is sometimes (although not necessarily) blazoned plain, when charged with another) engrailed.

PLAIN Point. P. 21, f. 5.

PLAISSE, or Plaissa. See Palisse.

PLAITED. Fretted or interlaced.

PLANE. A Joiner's tool. P. 41, f. 36.

PLANET. The Astronomical symbol of Mars, Uranus and Venus, are borne by the families of Wimble, Herschel and Thoyts. P. 23, f. 45.

PLANETS. Used by some heralds to blazon the arms of Kings. See P. 1.

PLANTS. In great variety are found in coat armour. e.g. Cyanus, Fern, Tobacco, etc. P. 44.

PLANTA-GENISTA, or broom, sprig, and flower. P. 25, f. 6 and 9.

PLASTERERS' hammer. P. 41, f. 26.

PLATE. A round, flat piece of silver. P. 1.

PLATTEE. Strewed with Plates. Same as semée of plates.

PLATTED, or Plaited. Interlaced, or tied.

PLAYING TABLES. P. 42, f. 32. Also termed Back-gammon tables.

PLAYING TOP. P. 42, f. 29.

PLENITUDE. This term is applied to the moon when in her complement. P. 23, f. 37.

PLIE. The same as close applied to birds with the wings close to the body.

PLOUGH. P. 39, f. 7.

PLOUGH-PADDLE. P. 39, f. 8.

PLOUGH-SHARE, or Coulter. P. 39, f. 10.

PLOYE. Bowed or bent, sometimes applied to a serpent when nowed.

PLOVER. P. 34, f. 49.

PLUMB-RULE, and Plumb-Rule reversed. See Plummet. P. 41, f. 38.

PLUMBERS' cutting knife. P. 41, f. 19.

PLUMBERS' Triangular soldering iron. i.d

PLUMBY. Same as purple.

PLUME of Ostrich Feathers. P. 43, f. 38.
A Plume of Feathers consists of three. If more, it must be expressed as a plume of such a number. The plume of five feathers is also termed a bush of feathers. Sometimes one plume is placed above another, it is then termed either a double plume, or a plume of two heights. If composed of three rows, one above the other, it is termed a triple plume, or a plume of three heights, and should be composed of twelve feathers, of which five are placed in the bottom row, four in the next, and three in the top row. If the quills are of a different tincture from the feathers the tincture must be named, and the feather is termed either quilled, penned, or shafted. P. 25, f: 22 and 23. See also P. 43, f. 38, 39 and 40. The Badge of the Prince of Wales consists of a plume of ostrich feathers ar. qnilled or., enfiled with a prince's coronet of the last, with an escroll az, thereon the words " Ich Dien " in gold. P. 6, f. 21. See Panache.

PLUMED. Feathered.

PLUMETTY. When the field is divided into fusils, filled with the ends of feathers, and depicted in metal and colour, alternately. The proper blazon of which, says Edmondson, is fusily or. and gu., diapered with feathers counterchanged.

PLUMING, or Pruning. Applied to birds when dressing their feathers. An eagle pluming, borne by the name of Rous.

PLUMMET. An instrument used by masons, etc. P. 41, f. 38.

POD, or Cod. The case of seeds. P. 44, f. 59.

POESY. A motto.

POIGNARD. A short sword.

POINT, Base, Baste, or Base-Bar. Is the base of the shield cut off by a horizontal line, and blazoned a Plain Point. P. 21, f. 5.
The Point may be of any of the accidental forms of lines, as a Point wavy, borne by the name of Hawkins. f. 43.
When borne Pointed it should be so expressed, as a Point Pointed. f. 2. It may be on either side of the escutcheon, and is then termed a Point dexter, or sinister.

POINT Based. f. 24.

POINT Champaine, Champion, or a Base-chausse. f. 6.

POINT Convexed. f. 19.

POINT Dexter, or a Point Dexter-parted. f. 1.

POINT Escartelled. f: 17.
A plain Point with a square piece cut out, or notched in the centre of the upper line. A Point with one embattlement differs from the last in having a projection of a square form instead of an indenture. f. 18.

POINT in Point. Also termed a Graft and Gusset. f. 4.

POINT pointed fleury. f. 16.

POINT pointed Invecked. f. 9.

POINT pointed on the top a pommel. f. 14.

POINT pointed Removed. f. 8.

POINT pointed Reversed. f. 3.

POINT pointed reversed bottony at end. f. 15.

POINT shapourne. Same as Point Champaine.

POINT sinister and dexter base indented. P. 21, f. 20.

POINTS four, or Lozengy in Point. f. 23.

POINTS four, Pointed and Nowy on the top in pale. f. 22.

For other examples see P. 21.

POINTS, three, four, or five. The Ancient blazon of the field, divided into as many parts, but each part must be of a distinct colour.

POINT in point. A term applied to indentings, when extending from one side of the ordinary to the other, as a Fesse per fesse indented point in point. P. 3, f. 26.

POINT. A tool used by wire- drawers. P. 41, f. 4, and P. 42, f. 33.

POINTE. A term for leaved.

POINTED. Same as fitched. P. 9, f. 42, to 44.

POINTER. See Dog.

POINTS. The rays or points of a star, or mullet, etc.

POINTS of the Escutcheon. The different parts of the shield denoting the position of the charges. Explained on P. 1.

POINTZ DE SIX. As ung escu de six pointz, the same as paly of three parted per fesse. P, 14, f. 30.

POISSON. See Marined.

POIX, guttée de. Black drops. P. 1.

POLE-AXE. P. 37, f. 27.

POLECAT. P. 30, f. 17.

POLE-STAR. The same as Estoile. P. 23, f. 42.

POLEYNS, or Genouillières. Steel Knee-pieces. P. 39, f. 20, No. 6.

POMEE, Pommettée, Pommellée. or Pommy. When the extremities terminate in knobs. See Cross Pomettée. P. 10, f. 28.

POMEIS. Green roundles. P. 1.

POMEGRANATE. Always represented as P. 44, f. 57.

POMEL, or Pommel. The round knob at the extremity of the handle of a sword. See Sword.

POMELT and Hyltte anowyd. An old term for pommel and hilt gold.

POMELLED Cross. P. 10, f. 28.

POMETTE, or Nowed. Having circular projections in the middle of each arm on a cross. P. 7, f. 43.

POMEY, or Pome. A roundle vert. P. 1.

POPE's Crown, Papal Crown, Tiara, or Triple Crown. P. 40, f. 59.

POPINJAY. A small green parrot, with red beak and legs. See Parrot, and P. 34, f. 57.

POPLAR Tree. P. 45, f. 47.

POPPY-BOLE. P. 45, f. 12.

PORCUPINE. A rodent quadruped, furnished with spines. P. 27, f. 55.

PORTANTE, or Portrate. See Portate.

PORTATE. A cross so called, from its position being saltierways. P. 8, f. 15.

PORT, or Portal. The door or gate of a castle. P. 23, f. 13.

PORTCULLIS, or Herse. A machine composed of cross bars. P. 37, f. 37. It was hung by chains before the gates of fortified places, and its perpendicular bars were spiked at the bottom, the chains by which it hung are usually attached.

PORTCULLIS. The title of one of the Pursuivants of Arms.

PORTCULLISED. P. 22, f. 38.

PORTHOLE. Same as Loop-hole.

PORTUGAL-LAUREL. P 45, f. 20.

PORTUGUESE Badge of the Tower and Sword. P. 25a, f. 8.

POSE, or Posed. Same as Statant.

POSED. As three fish interchangeably posed. P. 32, f. 25.

POSSENET. See Water-bouget.

POT-INFLAMED. Same as Fire-chest. P. 37, f. 3.

POT. Also termed Porridge Pot. A vessel with three feet. P. 41, f. 16.

POT. A term sometimes applied to a steel-cap.

POTENCE. Same as Potent.

POTENCY counter-potency, or Potency in point. The same as potent counter potent. P. 3, f. 7.

POTENT counter-potent. P. 1, and P. 5, f. 16.

POTENT. Resembles the head of a crutch. P. 1.

POTENT-CROSS, or Cross Potent. P. 11, f. 7.

POTENT. Repotent in four points. P. 11, f. 14.

POTENTED or Potentée. Applied to ordinaries when the outer edges are formed into potents. P. 5, f. 15; P. 17, f. 35, and 36.

POUCH. A Purse. As P. 40, f. 38.

POULDRON. The name of that part of a suit of armour which covers the shoulders.

POUNCE. A perforated sketch used by Herald Painters by means of which the drawing is transferred unto a panel, silk, or other material.

POUNCE. The talon of a bird of prey.

POUNCING. See Preying.

POUNDERS. The tufts of Erminites so termed.

POUR enquirir. See Armes pour enquirir.

POWDERED. Same as Semée.

POWDER-HORN, or Powder-Flask. P. 40, f. 42.

POWDYRDYE. Same as powdered, or Semée.

POWTS, or Tadpoles. Young frogs.

POYNT. An old term for per-cheveron.

PPR., or ppr. A contraction of proper.

PRANCING. Same as rearing, applied to the horse. P. 27, f. 26.

PRASIN. A term used by some heralds for vert, or green.

PRAWN. See Shrimp. P. 32, f. 40a.

PRAYING. An angel in the act of praying. P. 36, f. 55.

PRECEDENCE. The taking place according to the degree, rank, or station in life.

THE ORDER OF PRECEDENCY.

The Sovereign.
The Prince of Wales,
The Queen's younger Sons.
Grandsons of the Sovereign.
The Archbishop of Canterbury.
The Lord High Chancellor.
The Archbishop of York.
The Lord President of the Council.
The Lord Privy Seal.
The Lord Great Chamberlain.
The Earl Marshal.
The Lord Steward of Her Majesty's Household.
The Lord Chamberlain.
The last four rank above all Peers of their own degree.
Dukes, according to their Patents of Creation.
1. Of England. 2. Of Scotland. 3. Of Great Britain. 4. Of Ireland.
5. Those created since the Union.
Marquises according to their Patents, in the same order as Dukes.
Dukes' eldest Sons.
Earls, according to their Patents, in the same order as Dukes.
Marquises' eldest Sons.
Dukes' younger Sons.
Viscounts, according to their Patents, in the same order as Dukes.
Earls' eldest Sons.
Marquises' younger Sons.
Bishops of London, Durham, and Winchester.
All other English Bishops, according to their seniority of Consecration.
Bishops of the Irish Church, created before 1869, according to seniority.
Secretaries of State, if of the degree of a Baron.
Barons, according to their Patents, in the same order as Dukes.
Speaker of the House of Commons.
Treasurer of H.M.'s Household.
Comptroller of H.M.'s Household.
Master of the Horse.
Vice-Chamberlain of Household.

Secretaries of State under the degree of Barons.
Viscounts' eldest Sons.
Earls' younger Sons.
Barons' eldest Sons.
Knights of the Garter.
Privy Councillors.
Chancellor of the Exchequer.
Chancellor of the Duchy of Lancaster.
Lord Chief Justice Queen's Bench.
Master of the Rolls.
The Lords Justices of Appeal.
Lords of Appeal.
Judges according to seniority.
Viscounts' younger Sons.
Barons' younger Sons.
Baronets of England, Scotland, Ireland, and United Kingdom, according to date of Patents.
Knights of the Thistle.
Knights of St. Patrick.
Knights Grand Cross of the Bath.
Knights Grand Commanders of the Star of India.
Knights Grand Cross of St. Michael and St. George.
Knights Grand Commanders of the Indian Empire.
Knights Commanders of the Bath.
Knights Commanders of the Star of India.
Knights Commanders of St. Michael and St. George.
Knights Commanders of the Indian Empire.
Knights Bachelors.
Judges of County Courts.
Companions of the Bath.
Companions of the Star of India.
Companions of St. Michael and St. George.
Companions of the Indian Empire.
Companions of the Distinguished Service Order
Eldest Sons of the younger Sons of Peers.
Baronets' eldest Sons.
Eldest Sons of Knights:—1. Garter.
2. Thistle. 3. St. Patrick. 4. The Bath.
5. Star of India. 6. St. Michael & St. George.
7. Indian Empire. 8. Knights Bachelors.
Younger Sons of the younger Sons of Peers.
Baronets' younger Sons.
Younger Sons of Knights in the same order as eldest Sons.
Esquires.
Persons holding the Queen's commission in Civil, Naval, or Military capacity.
Members of the Royal Academy of Arts.
Barristers.
Masters of Arts and Bachelors of Law.
Clergymen.
Gentlemen entitled to bear arms.

Women take the same rank as their husbands, or as their brothers; but the daughter of a peer marrying a Commoner retains her Title as Lady or Honourable. Daughters of Peers rank next immediately after the wives of their elder brothers, and before their younger brothers' wives. Daughters of Peers marrying Peers of lower degree take the same order of precedency as that of their husbands; thus the daughter of a Duke marrying a Baron degrades to the rank of Baroness only, while her sisters married to commoners retain their rank and take precedence of the Baroness. Merely official rank on the husband's part does not give any similar precedence to the wife.

LOCAL PRECEDENCY. No written code of county or city order of precedence has been promulgated, but naturally in the county the Lord-Lieutenant stands first, and secondly the High Sheriff. In London and other Corporations the Mayor stands first, after him the Sheriffs, Aldermen. Chief Officers, and Livery. At Oxford and Cambridge the High Sheriff takes precedence of the Vice-Chancellor.

PRECIOUS Stones. It was formerly the practice of some heralds to blazon the arms of the Nobility by gems, instead of metals and colours, and arms thus blazoned are to be met with in old records. See Explanation at Plate 1.

PREENE. An instrument used by clothiers. P. 40, f. 9.

PREMIER. Fr. for first. Used by English Heralds to denote the holder of the most ancient hereditary title in each degree of Nobility.

PRESTER JOHN, or Presbyter John, depicted as P. 35, f. 4.

PRETENCE. See Escutcheon of Pretence.

PREYANT. See Preying.

PREYING. When any beast or bird is standing on its prey in the act of tearing or devouring it. It is sometimes blazoned "Seizing," and when applied to birds "Trussing." P. 33, f. 12.

PRICK, or Pryck-spur. A spur with a single point. P. 37, f. 47; and P. 39, f. 20, No. 7.

PRICKETT. A buck in his second year, the points of whose horns are just appearing, borne by the name of Prickett.

PRIDE, In his. Said of the Peacock with his tail extended. P. 34, f. 4. Also of the Turkey-Cock. P. 34, f. 3.

PRIME. An instrument used by Basket Makers, and borne in their armorial ensigns. P. 22, f. 28.

PRIMROSE. An ancient term for the quaterfoil. P. 41, f. 16.

PRIMROSE-NATURAL, stalked and leaved. P. 45, f. 9.

PRINCE. A title of honour, properly belonging to sovereigns or their sons, and anciently given even to Dukes.

PRINCE's Coronets. P. 24, f. 2 and 3.

PRINCESS. A title of honour belonging to a lady next in rank to a queen. The Daughter of a Sovereign, and Sovereigns son's wives are Princesses.

PRINCESS' Coronet. P. 24, f. 4.

PRIOR'S-STAFF. P. 42, f. 45.

PRISONER'S BOLT. See Manacles and P. 42, f. 39.

PROBOSCIS. The trunk of an elephant. P. 29, f. 50.

PROMENING. Same as pluming.

PROPER. A term applied to everything when borne of its natural form and colour.

PROSPECT. See Barry paly in Prospect. P. 22, f. 39.

PROYNING and Pruming. The same as Pluming.

PRUNING-HOOK or Pruning-knife. P. 41, f. 22.

PRUSSIAN CROWN. P. 25a, f. 13.

PUFFED. See Slashed.

PUNJA. P. 39, f. 42. No. 3.

PUNNING ARMS. See Aarm Parlantes.

PURFLE, or Purflew. Is the embroidery of a bordure of fur, shaped exactly like vair. When of one row, it is termed Purflewed. When of two counter-purflewed, and when of three, vair. P. 1.

PURFLED, trimmed, or garnished. A term for the studs and rims of armour being gold.

PURPURE. Purple, expressed in engraving by diagonal lines, from left to right. P. 1.

PURSE. P. 36, f. 7.

PURSE OF STATE. P. 40, f. 37.

PURSE, stringed and tasselled. i.d. f. 38.

PURSUIVANT OF ARMS. An officer lowest in degree in the College of Arms.

PYCCHE. An old term for fitched.

PYE. See Sea-Pie.

PYLE. See Pile.

PYNANT AND SAYLAND. The old term for pommel and cross of a sword.

PYOT. A magpie. P. 34, f. 40.

PYRAMID. An edifice in shape as. P. 43, f. 60.

PYRAMIDWAYS. Of a pyramid form, or rising like a pyramid.

PYTHON. A winged serpent, or dragon

Q

QUADRANGULAR. Four cornered, or square. A Quadrangular, or square castle. P. 23, f. 6.

QUADRANS. A quarter. P. 19, f. 34.

QUADRANT. An instrument for taking the altitudes of the sun and stars. P. 38, f. 47.

QUADRANT fer-de-moline. A mill-rind with a square centre.

QUADRATE. Square. As a Cross Quadrat in the centre. P. 11, f. 13.

QUADRATURE In. When four charges are placed at the angles of an imaginary square, generally blazoned, two and two.

QUARTER. An ordinary, containing one fourth of the shield. P. 19, f. 34.

QUARTER FRANC. A Plain Quarter.

QUARTER Sinister. P. 19, f. 35.

QUARTER-ANGLED. Same as quadrat. See Cross. P. 11, f. 13.

QUARTER PIERCED. See Quarterly Pierced.

QUARTER-POINTED, or Quarter Per saltier. Also termed a squire, or point removed. P. 21, f. 25.

QUARTER-STAFF. A long straight pole.

QUARTERED. When the shield is divided into four equal parts. P. 1. Sometimes applied to the cross when voided in the centre. P. 7, f. 16.

QUARTERING. The regular arrangement of various coats in one shield.

QUARTERINGS. The arms of different families arranged in one shield to shew the connection of one family with another; and the representation of several families by combining their respective bearings according to priority of accession.

QUARTERINGS Grand. See Marshalling.

QUARTERLY. The field or charge divided into four equal parts. P. 2, f. 9, and P. 29, f. 7.

QUARTERLY-QUARTERED. A cross quarterly quartered. P. 22, f. 22.

QUARTERLY quartered, or grand-quarters. See Marshalling.

QUARTERLY, Quarter-pierced, or quarter voided. Perforated in a square form. A cross quarter-pierced. P. 7, f. 16. A cross moline quarter-pierced. P. 10, f. 3.

QUARTERLY in Saltire. The same as per-saltier. P. 2, f. 5.

QUARTIER-FRANC. A plain quarter.

QUATERFOIL, or Quatrefoil. Four-leaved grass. P. 44, f. 16; P. 11, f. 17.

The Quaterfoil was an imitation of the primrose, which being one of the first flowers of the spring, was considered as the harbinger of revivified nature, and was adopted by the church architects to signify, emblematically, that the gospel, the harbinger of peace and immortality, was there preached. The Trefoil was the emblem of the Trinity.

QUATERFOIL slipped. P. 44, f. 16. No. 2, and 3.

QUATERFOIL double. The same as Caterfoil. P. 44. f. 13, and 18.

QUARTYLLE. Same as quarterly.

QUATREFEUILLE. A Quaterfoil.

QUATREFOIL, or Quaterfoil. P. 11, f. 17.

QUATUFORFOLIA. Same as Quaterfoil.

QUEEN. A Queen regnant is the only female who is entitled to bear her arms in a shield with helmet, crest, lambrequin, motto, and the order of knighthood.

QUEUE ERMINE. An ermine spot.

QUEUE, Queve, or Quevye. See Queued.

QUEUE-FORCHEE, or fourche. Same as tail forked. P. 26, f. 3.

QUEUED. A term for the tail of an animal.

QUEUED Inflected. When the tail comes between the legs. P. 26, f. 45.

QUEVE, or Queued Renowned. Having the tail elevated over the head. P. 31, f. 26.

QUILL, or Wheel-Quill of Yarn. P. 40, f. 4.

QUILL empty. P. 40, f. 9.

QUILL of Yarn. P. 40, f. 4.

QUILL of Gold. or Silver thread. See Trundle. P. 40, f. 4,

QUILL PEN. P. 36, f. 29.

QUILLED Penned, or Shafted. Applied to the quill of a feather when borne of a different tincture from the feather itself. P. 25, f. 23.

QUINCE. A sort of apple. P. 44, f. 57.

QUINTAIN. A plank about six feet high, fixed firmly in the earth. At this, men on horseback tilt with poles. P. 37, f. 58.

QUINTAL. See Quintin.

QUINTERFOIL. The same as Cinquefoil.

QUINTEFUEIL, or Quintefeuille. The same as Cinquefoil.

QUINTIN, or Quintal. An upright pole with a cross beam on the top, which works on a pivot. At one end of the cross beam is a shield painted with rings, and at the other end is a log of wood, suspended by a stout chain. Men on horseback tilted at the shield, and unless they passed very quickly were struck by the log as the beam revolved. P. 37, f. 59.

QUINTISE. A covering for the helmet, supposed to be the origin of the mantling. P. 25a, f. 9.

QUINYSANS. See Cognisance.

QUISE, A LA. See A-la-quise.

QUIVER of Arrows. A case filled with arrows. P. 37, f. 13.

R

R. A text **r** is borne in several coats. See Letters.

RABBIT, or Coney. P. 29, f. 19.

RACCOURCY, or Recourcie. The same as Coupée, or Couped.

RACK-POLE-BEACON. P. 37, f. 2.

RADIANT, or Rayonne. Any ordinary edged with beams like those of the sun. See Fesse-radiant. P. 3, f. 25. A Pale-radiant. P. 14, f. 18.

RADIATED, Rayonated, or Rayonée. The same as Rayonce, Radiant, Rayonnant, and Rayoonne. Terms all used to express the same thing, viz., Rays, or shining beams issuing from an ordinary or charge. P. 7, f. 17; P. 12, f. 12.

RADIATED Crown. The Eastern Crown. P. 24, f. 32.

RAGGED. Same as Raguly.

RAGGED-STAFF. P. 41, f. 57.
The bear and ragged staff Badge of the Earls of Warwick. P. 29, f. 42.

RAGULEE. Same as Raguly.

RAGULY, or Raguled. P. 1. P. 3. f. 18. Is when the bearing is uneven or ragged, like the trunk or limb of a tree lopt of its branches. P. 17, f. 27. A Cross Raguly. P. 7, f. 6.

RAGULY-STAFF, or Staff Raguly. P. 29, f. 42; P. 41, f. 57.

RAINBOW. A semicircle of various colours, arising from clouds. P. 16, f. 21; P. 39, f. 6.

RAIONEE. Same as Radiant.

RAKE, or Tillage-rake. Depicted as P. 39, f. 11.

RAKE-HEAD, and Thatch-rake. i.d. f. 12.

RAM. A male sheep. P. 28, f. 56.

RAM's head erased. i.d. f. 57.

RAM's head affrontée, or Cabossed. i.d. f. 58.

RAME. A term for branched, or attired.

RAMPANDE. Same as Rampant.

RAMPANT. A term to express the Lion, Tiger, etc., when in an upright position standing on the near hind leg. P. 26, f. 1, etc.

RAMPANT, guardant, and regardant, etc. P. 26.

RAMPEE, Ramped, or Rompu. Broken. P. 16, f. 1.

RAMPING. The same as Rampant.

RANGANT. An old term for the bull etc., enraged, or furiosant.

RANGE. A term signifying many. Mullets, or other charges, placed in bend fesse, cross, etc.

RAPIER. A narrow sword.

RAPIN, or Raping. Applied to ravenous animals when feeding, or devouring their prey.

RASED, or Razed. The same as erased.

RASEE. Erased.

RASIE. Having rays, or being rayed.

RASYD. Same as erased.

RAT. A fierce and voracious animal, borne by several families. P. 30, f. 12.

RATCH-HOUND, or Beagle. A small species of hound. P. 29, f. 26.

RAVEN. Also termed a Corbet, and Corbie. A bird. P. 33, f. 52.
The emblem of Divine Providence.

RAVISSANT. A term to express the posture of a wolf, etc., half raised, and just springing forward upon his prey. It is also applied to all ravenous animals when devouring their prey.

RAYONNANT. Sending forth rays. See Radiant and Radiated. P. 14, f. 18. Also termed Rayed and Rasie.

RAYON. A ray. See Rayonne.

RAYONNE, or Rayonée. Same as Radiant.

RAYS. Beams of light. Rays issuing from a cloud. P. 23, f. 28.

RAYS issuing from dexter chief point. i.d. f. 30.

RAYS Illuminated, or Inflamed. i.d. f. 34.

RAZED. Same as erased.

RAZOR-BILL, or Eligugs. A web-footed bird. P. 33, f. 59.

REAPING-HOOK, or Sickle. P. 39, f. 13, No. 2.

REAR-MOUSE. See Rere-mouse.

REARING. Applied to a horse when standing upon the hind legs. P. 27, f. 26.

REBATED. When a part is cut off, as a cross rebated. P. 9, f. 32.

REBATEMENT. The same as Abatement.

REBENDING. The same as Bowed-embowed.

REBENT. Bowed-embowed, or reflexed.

REBOUNDANT, or Rebounding. Applied to the tail of a lion when turned up, with the end inwards. P. 26, f. 37.

REBUS. In Heraldry, "Non verbis rebus loquimur," a device alluding to the name of the bearer, as the device of Arblaster. Erm. a cross bow (arblast) in pale gu.
Fletcher. az. a chev. betw. three arrows or.
Martell. gu. three (martels) hammers or.
Sykes. ar. a chev. betw. three sykes ppr.
Yate. ar. three yates sa.

RECERCELLEE, Recercelled, and Recersile. A cross Cercelée. P. 11, f. 32.

RECLINANT. The tail of a serpent when upright, without any waving, is said to be reclinant.

RECOPYD, or Recouped. Same as Couped.

RECOUPEE. Reparted per-fesse.

RECOURCIE, Clechée, or Percée. Same as a chev. recoursie. P. 15, f. 7. A Cross-recourcie. P. 7, f. 19.

RECOURSE. Same as Clechée.

RECROISE. Crossed, as a crosslet crossed; i.e. a cross-crosslet. P. 8, f. 18.

RECROSSED. See Cross double crossed. P. 8, f. 22.

RECROSSETTEE, or Recrossie. A cross-crosslet. P. 8, f. 18.

RECT, or Right-Angle. Is the angle which one straight line makes with another straight line, upon which it falls perpendicularly. P. 12, f. 20.

RECUMBENT. Same as lodged.

RECURSANT. Applied to the eagle, shewing the back part. P. 33, f. 16 and 17.

RECURSANT Overture, or Inverted displayed. As an eagle displayed, with the back turned towards the beholder. P. 33, f. 18.

RECURSANT Volant, in pale. As an eagle flying upwards, showing the back the reverse of f. 17. P. 33.

RECURSANT Volant, in fesse, wings overture. i.e. flying across the field fesseways, showing its back.

RECURSANT Volant, in bend, wings overture. i.d. f. 16.

RECURSANT displayed, wings crossed. i.d. f. 18.

RECURVANT. Bowed embowed, or curved and recurved. P. 30, f. 34.

RED CROSS. See Royal Red Cross.

RED, gules.

REDOUT. The cross potent rebated. P. 11, f. 39.

REED, Slay, or Slea. An instrument used by weavers. P. 42, f. 32.

REEDS. Long hollow knotted grass. P. 44, f. 48.

REEL. See Spindle. P. 40, f. 2.

REFLECTED, or Reflexed. Curved, or turned round, as the chain or line from the collar of a beast, thrown over the back. P. 29, f. 15; P. 18, f. 21.

REGALIA. Ensigns of Royal dignity, as Crowns, Sceptres, Mounds, etc.

REGARDANDE. Same as reguardant.

REGARDANT. Looking back. See Reguardant.

REGUARDANT. Looking behind. A Lion reguardant. P. 26, f. 10 and 4. An Eagle reguardant. P. 33, f. 4. A Dove reguardant. P. 31, f. 25.

REGUARDANT REVERSED. Applied to serpents when nowed in the form of a figure of 8 laid fesseways, the head turned under from the sinister, and the tail bending upwards. P. 30, f. 25.

REGULE. See Raguly.

REIN-DEER. A stag with double attires. P. 28, f. 37.

REIN-DEER's head cabossed. i.d. f. 38.

REIN-GUARD. That part of armour which guards the lower part of the back.

RELIEF. See Adumbrated.

REMORA, or Fish Odimoliont. The Sucker-Fish.

In Fo. 103 Bossewell gives the Coat of Roscarroche. Vert three scythes argent. For Crest, " the fishe odimoliont haryant (haurient) sable." The dexter supporter to the arms of Baron Soarsdale is a female figure, holding in the sinister hand a javelin, entwined with a Remora, which Burke and Foster in their Peerage's describe as a serpent.

REMOVED. Shifted from its place as a chief removed, or lowered. P. 12, f. 31. A chev. removed. P. 15, f. 37. If a Fesse, Chevron, Bend, etc., is placed higher in the shield than its proper place it is termed Enhanced. P. 3, f. 6.

REMPLI. When a chief is filled with any other tincture, leaving only a border round it. P. 12, f. 24.

RENCONTRE, or Au-Rencontre. The same as Cabossed. See P. 28, f. 52 and 58.

RENDING. As two hands rending a horse shoe. P. 19, f. 29.

RENVERSE, Reversed, or Reverse. Turned contrary to its natural position. P. 15, f. 43.

REPASSANT. The same as Counterpassant. P. 26, f. 36.

REPLENISHED. Stocked with. As a quiver filled, or replenished with arrows. P. 37, f. 13. This term is also used for Semee, or Powdered. P. 2, f. 38.

REPOSING. See Resting.

REPTILES. The most common in Coat Armour is the snake. The following are also found: The Asp, Lizard, Adder, Viper, Crocodile, etc. P. 30.

RERE-MOUSE. A bat. P. 30, f. 4.

RESARCELEE. A cross is so termed when voided and open at each end. P. 10, f. 10; P. 11, f. 40.

RESIGNANT. Applied to the tail of a lion when it is hid.

RESPECTANT, or Respecting. Applied to tame animals, birds, or fish, when placed face to face. P. 32, f. 28; P. 31, f. 27.

RESPLENDENT. Applied to the sun when surrounded with rays of glory. P. 23, f. 32.

REST, Clarion, or Claricord. P. 43, f. 27 and 28.

A difference of opinion exists as to what this charge represents. Some blazon it a horseman's rest, and assert that it was the rest in which the tilting-spear was fixed. Others contend that it was a wind instrument, and blazon it Clarion, or Claricorde. Some consider them to be Sufflues, instruments which transmit the wind from the billows to the organ, while others term them brackets or organ rests. See Clarion.

REST. See Perch, or Rest for a Falcon. P. 43, f. 18.

RESTING, or Reposing. Said of a hind or other animal resting a foot upon any object, as a lion resting his dexter foot upon a book. P. 26, f. 51.

RESTRIALL. An ancient term for barry-paly, and pily.

RETAILLE. Cutaway, and an Escutcheon is termed Retaillé when cut into three traits by two lines in bend-sinister.

RETIERCE. The field divided into three parts fesseways, each of which is again divided into three parts paleways, making nine equal squares, and properly expressed as paly and fesse nine. P. 2, f. 19.

RETORTED. Applied to serpents when fretted, in the form of a knot. P. 30, f. 25.

RETRACTED. Cut off. A pale retracted. P. 14, f. 24.

RETRANCHE. A term, signifying that the escutcheon is twice cut athwart bendways, or doubly cut in bend dexter, when it is said to be tranché and retranche.

REVERBERANT. Same as Reboundant.

REVERSED, or Inverted. Contrary to each other, or contrary to the usual position, as a Leopard's face jessant-de-lis reversed. P. 28, f. 6.

REVERSED-ENDORSED. Turned back to back. P. 39, f. 13.

REVERSIE. Reversed or transposed. P. 15, f. 43.

REVERTANT, or Reverted, flexed and reflexed, or bending in the form of an

S. Reverted also used to express anything turned upside down, as an arrow, etc., with point upwards.

REVESTU. The same as Vestu.

REVEYNS. An old term for Ravens.

REYNARD. A fox.

RHINOCEROS. A large animal having a horn in his front, and a skin full of wrinkles, which is so hard that it can scarcely be pierced by a sword. P. 27, f. 51.

RIBAND, or Ribbon. A subordinary containing the eighth part of the bend. The Ribbon applied as a difference of the younger sons is of very high antiquity. P. 17, f. 4.

RIBBON. Part of the insignia of an order of Knighthood. P. 24, f. 19; f. 20, 23, and 28; P. 25, and 25a.

RING. Called a Gem-Ring. P. 37, f. 42.

Iron-Ring. P. 42, f. 29. See Iron Ring.

RINGANT, or Rangant. An old term for the Bull, etc.—Enraged.

RINGDOVE. A species of pigeon. P. 34, f. 37.

RINGS-INTERLACED. See Annulets.

RISING. A term applied to birds when preparing to fly. P. 33, f. 3.

RIZOM. The corn or fruit of the Oat is not generally termed the ear, but the rizom.

ROACH. A fish. P. 32, f. 30.

ROBE. Sometimes called the Mantle, distinguishes the rank of the bearer by the number of guards or rows of Fur on the dexter side. That of a Duke should have four guards of ermine, that of a Marquis three and half. P. 35, f. 16. An Earl three, a Viscount two and half, a Baron two. The two last should be plain Fur.

The arms within this mantle are those of the Marquess of Queensbury, quarterly 1st and 4th, ar. a human heart gu. imperially crowned ppr. for Douglas; 2nd and 3rd, az. a bend betw. six cross crosslets fitchee or. for Marr, all within a border of the last, charged with the double tressure of Scotland.

ROBE of Estate. P. 40, f. 29.

ROBE of Parliament. P. 40, f. 30.

ROBIN, or Robin Redbreast. A pretty little bird with a red breast. P. 33, f. 44.

ROCK. A stony mass. P. 42, f. 56. Emblem of Security.

ROD OF ESCULAPIUS. P. 30, f. 57.

ROE, or Roebuck. A species of deer. P. 15, f. 21.

ROELE. See Rowel.

ROELSE. See Gurges.

ROLL of Parchment. P. 36, f. 10.

ROLL, or Row. A wreath.

ROLL OF ARMS. Heraldic records of armorial insignia.

ROMAN &. Borne by the name of *And*.

ROMAN FASCES. P. 43, f. 6.

ROMAN LAMP. P. 39, f. 26. No. 2.

ROMAN PILUM, or pile. A javelin. P. 37, f. 22.

ROMAN SOLDIER. P. 35, f. 27.

ROMPE, or Rompu. Broken. See chev. rompu. P. 16, f. 1.

RONDEUS. See Roundles.

ROOFED. When a building has a roof of a different tincture to the other part.

ROOK, or Crow. P. 33, f. 53.

ROOKS, pieces used in the game of Chess. P. 43, f. 49.

ROOT. A golden-root. P. 25, f. 24. The badge of John Duke of Bedford, brother to Hen. V.

ROOT of a Tree couped and erased. The same as a stump or stock couped and eradicated. P. 45, f. 57.

ROPE, a coil of. P. 43, f. 13. A Rope. f. 15.

ROPE-HOOK. P. 40, f. 12.

ROPE TASSEL and ring. A *Lure* is sometimes thus blazoned.

ROSE. Is borne depicted naturally, and heraldicly. P. 44, f. 1 and 3.
The Heraldic Rose is always shewn full blown, with the petala, or flower-leaves expanded, seeded in the middle, and backed by five green barbs, or involucra; this Rose, when gules, is never to be called proper, whereas the rose borne naturally, is always when gules termed proper, and is always stalked and leaved, and termed a Rose slipped. The Heraldic Rose may be of any tincture, and is said to be barbed and seeded of such a colour, which must be expressed, unless the seeds are yellow and the barbs vert, when it is blazoned a Rose of such a colour, seeded and barbed proper. The Rose is used as a distinction for the seventh son. See Distinction of Houses. P. 46.

ROSE HERALDIC. P. 44, f. 1.
The White Rose the badge of the House of York, and the Red Rose the badge of the House of Lancaster. P. 25, f. 2 and 4, The White and Red-Rose united and imperially crowned is the Badge of England. P. 3, f. 21. Also termed a Double-Rose,

ROSE-LEAF. P. 45, f. 29.

ROSE, stalked and leaved. P. 44, f. 3. Also termed a Damask-rose, stalked and leaved. A Damask rose, with leaves and thorns. P. 25, f. 27.

ROSE, wild, or Bramble. P. 44, f. 27.

ROSE AND THISTLE conjoined and imperially crowned the Badge of James I. P. 25, f. 3.

ROSE AND THISTLE conjoined. P. 44, f. 4

ROSE-EN-SOLEIL. A white rose, surrounded by rays.

ROSELETTES. Single roses, having five leaves each, as the Rose, P. 44, f. 27.

ROSEMARY. A plant. P. 45, f. 2.

ROSARY. A chaplet of beads, with cross attached. P. 42, f. 41.

ROSTRAL CROWN. Lipsicus, in his treatise on the Roman milita, fancies the *Corona Navalis* and the *Rostrata* to have been two distinct crowns, though generally believed to be one, and the same crown. See Crown Naval.

ROUGE-CROIX, or Rouge Cross. The title of one of the Pursuivants of Arms.

ROUGE-DRAGON. The title of one of the Pursuivants of Arms.

ROUND TOPS OF MASTS. Represented so as to show the particular part of the mast to which it belongs, and are sometimes blazoned pieces of masts, with their round tops. P. 38, f. 35.

ROUNDELLY. Strewed with roundles.

ROUNDLES. Round figures which may be charged with any figure, (e.x., P. 2, f. 45). In blazon change their names according to the different tinctures of which they are composed, except when they are counter-changed as e.x. P. 2, f. 39, when or, they are called Bezants. P. 1.

argent	„	Plates.
gules	„	Torteaux.
azure	„	Hurts.
vert	„	Pomeis.
sable	„	Pellets, or Ogresses.
purpure	„	Golpes.
tenné	„	Oranges.
sanguine	„	Guzes.

Barry wavy, ar. and az. Fountains.
These figures are all globular, except the bezant, plate, and fountain.

ROUNDLES counterchanged. P. 2, f. 39.

ROUND-PIERCED. See Cross. P. 8, f. 31.

ROUSANT, or Rowsand. Rising. When applied to the Swan the wings are to be endorsed. P. 34, f. 25.

ROWEL, or Roele. The point of a spur turning on an axis. P. 37, f. 47.

ROW-GALLY. A Lymphad. P. 38, f. 25.

ROWAN-TREE. A mountain ash.

ROWSAND. Rising.

ROWSING. Putting up, and driving a hart from its resting place.

ROWT. A term to express a number of wolves together.

ROYAL ANTLER. The third branch of the attire of a buck, that shoots out from the rear, or main horn above the bezantlier.

ROYAL-ARMS. P. 31, f. 1 to 11. From William I. to Victoria.

ROYAL CADENCY. P. 16, f. 40 to 45, and P. 25a, f. 1 and 2. See Label.

ROYAL CROWN. The Imperial Crown. P. 24, f. 1; P. 26, f. 27.

ROYAL EAGLE. Same as Imperial Eagle. P. 33, f. 6.

ROYAL NAVY, ensign of. P. 25a, f. 5.

ROYAL RED CROSS. A decoration instituted 23rd April, 1883, for rewarding services rendered by certain persons in nursing the Sick and Wounded of the Army and Navy.

The Decoration may be conferred upon any Ladies, whether subjects or foreign persons, who may be recommended to Her Majesty's notice by the Secretary of State for War for special exertions in providing for the nursing, or for attending to, sick and wounded soldiers and sailors.

This Decoration may be conferred upon any Nursing Sister, whether subjects or foreign persons, who may be recommended to Her Majesty's notice by the Secretary of State for War, or, as the case may be, by the First Lord of the Admiralty through the Secretary of State, for special devotion and competency which they may have displayed in the nursing duties with the Army in the Field, or in the Naval and Military Hospitals.

Badge of the Decoration, a Cross enamelled crimson, edged with gold, having on the Arms thereof the words, Faith, Hope, Charity, with the date of the institution of the Decoration; the centre having thereon the Queen's Effigy.—On the reverse side Her Majesty's Royal and Imperial Cypher and Crown shown in relief on the centre. The Riband is dark blue edged red, one inch in width, tied in a bow, and worn on the left shoulder. P. 31, f. 43.

ROYAL ROBE, or Mantle. P. 40, f. 29.

ROYAL STANDARD of Great Britain and Ireland is a Banner containing the arms of England, Scotland, and Ireland, quartered. P. 7, f. 21.

ROYAL TENT, as borne in the arms of the Merchant Tailors' Company. P. 40, f. 25.

ROYALTY, Ensigns of. As the Crown, sceptre, swords, mound, or orb, etc.

ROYS. Old English for rows or lines.

ROYNE. See Grose.

RUBY. A precious stone, used to express gules. P. 1.

RUE. A small shrubby plant. P. 44, f. 45.

The collar of the most ancient Order of the Thistle is composed of thistles and sprigs of rue. P. 24, f. 18.

RUE CROWN. P. 16, f. 40.

The Arms of Saxony on an inescutcheon Barry of ten or. and sa., a Rue Crown in bend vert.; also termed a bend trefle.

RUFFLES. Frills worn over the wrists. P. 36, f. 10.

RUDDER of a Ship. Should be represented hooked. P. 38, f. 40.

It is sometimes borne with a handle. i.d.

RUDDOCK. A robin, or redbreast.

RULE, or Yard-measure. P. 41, f. 41.

RULES OF BLAZON. See Blazon.

RUNDLES. See Roundles.

RUSHES. Plants with long slender stems, which grow in watery lands. P. 44, f. 48. A Bull-rush.

RUSSET. A grey colour.

RUSTRE, or Ruster. A lozenge pierced round in the centre. P. 40, f. 16.

They are called by some incorrectly Mascles pierced round.

RUTHER. See Helm.

RYE, Ear of. Generally called rye-stalk, or stalk of rye, with the ear bent downwards. P. 45, f. 16.

S

S. and Sa. Are both used to denote sable.

S. A Text S is borne by the name of Kekitmore. See Letters.

SABLE. Black; in engraving is represented by perpendicular and horizontal lines crossing each other. P. 1.

SABRE. See Scymetar.

SACRE, or Saker. A kind of falcon with grey head, the legs and feet bluish, and the back a dark brown.

SADDLE. A seat for a horseman fitted to a horse's back. A saddle, as borne in the arms of the Saddlers' Company, Newcastle. P. 37, f. 49.

SADDLE, with stirrups and leathers. P. 37, f. 50. Saddlers' Company, London.

SADDLE-PACK. i.d. f. 51.

SAGITTARIUS, or Sagittary. An Archer. See Centaur, and P. 27, f. 40.

SAIL OF A SHIP. P. 38, f. 35. f. 38, as borne in the arms of Enderby. f. 39. As borne by Tennant.

ST. ANDREW'S CROSS is a white saltire. P 7, f. 21.

ST. ANTHONY'S CROSS. The Cross Tau. P. 9, f. 30.

ST. COLUMBIA. As in the arms of the See of the Isles. P. 38, f. 37.

ST. CUTHBERT'S CROSS. P. 11, f. 1.

ST. GEORGE'S CROSS is a red cross. P. 7; f. 21.

ST. GEORGE'S ENSIGN. See Ensign.

ST. JAMES'S CROSS. P. 11, f. 2.

ST. JOHN'S HEAD in a charger. P. 35, f. 33.

ST. JOHN OF JERUSALEM, the Order of. The Arms, distinguished by a red chief charged with a white cross. P. 23, f. 21. See Hospitallers.

ST. PATRICK'S CROSS is a red saltire P. 7, f. 21.

ST. PAULINUS, Cross of. See Saxon Wheel-Cross.

ST. STEPHEN'S CROSS. P. 10, f. 1.

ST. THOMAS'S CROSS, P. 8, f. 28, with the addition of an escallop shell on the centre.

SAKER. A hawk. See Sacre.

SALAMANDER. An imaginary animal, represented as P. 27, f. 52.

SALIENT, or SAILLANT. The position of all beasts of prey, when leaping or springing. P. 26, f. 20.

SALIENT, counter-salient. P. 29, f. 10.

SALIY. A willow tree. P. 45, f. 35.

SALLED HEADPIECE, or Salade. An ancient name for the helmet.

SALMON. A fish. P. 32, f. 18.
Three Salmons fretted. f. 26.

SALMON-SPEAR. A name sometimes given to the harpoon. P. 38, f. 45.

SALT, Salt-cellar, Salts-covered, or Sprinkling-salt, P. 39, f. 39, as in the arms of the Salters' Company.

SALTANT. A term applied to the Ape, Cat, Greyhound, Monkey, Rat, Squirrel, Weasel, and all Vermin; when in a position of springing forward.

SALTERYE. See Saltire.

SALTIRE, Saltier, or Saltes. One of the honourable ordinaries. P. 20.
The Saltire is subject to all the accidental forms of lines, as Embattled, Nebule, Wavy, etc.
When figures are borne on the saltire, it is said to be charged, or the charges are said to be, on a saltire. When the saltire is between four figures it is said to be cantoned

SALTIRE ARCHED NOWY. P. 20, f. 25.

— BETWEEN. f. 37.

— BOTTONEE. f. 31.

— BRETTESSED. f. 23.

— CANTONED. f. 38.

— OF CHAINS. f. 44.

— CHECKY. f. 7.

— COMPONY. f. 9.

— COMPONY, counter-compony. f. 8.

— CONJOINED. f. 43.

— COUNTERCHANGED. f. 6 and 40.

— COTTISED. f. 34.

— COUPED. f. 22 and 28.

— EDGED. f. 4.

SALTIRE ENGRAILED. f. 36.

— FIMBRIATED. f. 4.

— FLANKS OF. f. 38.

— FRETTED IN SALTIRE. f. 16.

— OF FUSILS. f. 14.

— FUSILY. f. 11.

— INDENTED. f. 17.

— INVECKED. f. 34.

— IN SALTIRE. f. 29, 39, and 16.

— INTERLACED. f. 43.

— LOZENGY. f. 10.

— OF LOZENGES. f. 13.

— OF MASCLES. f. 15.

— MASCULY. f. 12.

— NOWY. f. 24.

— NOWY ARCHED. f. 25.

— NOWY LOZENGY. f. 27.

— NOWY QUADRAT. f. 26.

— ON A SALTIRE. f. 36 and 42.

— PER PALE. f. 40.

— PER QUARTERLY COUNTERCHANGED. f. 5.

— PIERCED. f. 35.

— PIERCED LOZENGY. f. 26 and 28.

— POTENTEE. f. 20.

— QUARTERED QUARTERLY. f. 5.

— RAGULY. f. 19.

— SALTERED AND FLORY. f. 33.

— SALTERED PATTEE. f. 30.

— SURMOUNTED. f. 3.

— TOULOUSE AND POMETTEE. f. 32.

— TRIPARTED AND FRETTED. f. 18.

— VOIDED. f. 2.

— WITHIN A BORDURE. f. 42.

SALTIRE-PER. Applied to the field of a coat of arms, or any charge when divided by two diagonal lines crossing each other. P. 2, f. 5; P. 20, f. 21.

SALTIREWISE, Salterwise, or In Saltier. Any figures placed in the form and position of a Saltire. P. 20, f. 39.

SALTIERY. Parted per saltier. P. 14, f. 38.

SALTORELS. Saltires.

SALTS. Also termed Salt-cellars and Sprinkling salts. P. 39, f. 39.

SANDAL. A kind of shoe, sometimes called brogue. P. 19, f. 38.

SANDGLASS, or Hourglass. A glass for measuring the hours, by the running of sand from one part of the vessel into another. P. 39, f. 44, No. 2.

SANDGLASS or Hourglass winged i.d. f. 45.

SANG, Gutte de, drops of blood. P. 1.

SANGLANT. Bloody.

SANGLIER. A wild boar. P. 29, f. 31.

SANGUINE. A term to denote murrey colour; and is expressed, in engraving, by diagonal lines crossing each other. P. 1.

SANGUINATED. Bloody. The same as embrued. P. 37, f. 11.

SANS. Without. Applied to animals, or birds, deprived of some member; e.g. a wyvern sans wings. P. 27. f. 13. A Wyvern, sans legs. f. 14. A Dragon sans wings and legs. f. 23. An Eagle displayed sans legs. P. 33, f. 9.

SANS-NOMBRE. The same as semée, only that no part of the figures are cut off. See semée. P. 2, f. 38 and 40.

SAPPHIRE. Used to express blue in blazon. P. 1.

SARACEN. See Savage.

SARCELLED. Cut through. See a Cross Sarcelled. P. 7, f. 20.

SARCELLED DEMI. Same as a Cross Escartelle pattée. P. 9, f. 8.

SARCELLY, or Cercelée. See cross Circelée. P. 7, f. 20.

SARDINE. A fish. P. 32, f. 42.

SARDONYX. In blazon represents murrey colour. P. 1.

SASH. A band or belt. P. 36, f. 19.

SATAN'S HEAD. P. 36, f. 48.

SATURN. In blazon implies sable. P. 1.

SATYR, or Satyral. A beast having the body of a Lion, the face of an old man, with the horns of an an antelope. P. 26, f. 57.

SATYR. See Man-tiger.

SATYR'S-HEAD couped at the neck in profile. P. 36, f. 47.
This is also termed the head of Midas.

SAUTOIRS. Are supposed to be cords formed of silk which hang from the saddle to be grasped by the hand of the rider when mounting.

SAUTOIR. A Saltire.

SAVAGE. Wild-man, Green-man, Woodman, and Saracen, are all depicted the same, and generally with a wreath of leaves round the temples and waist. See Term Man and the following examples at P. 35.
A savage ppr. wreathed about the loins and temples vert. holding in his dexter hand a spiked club. f. 24. A Demi savage wreathed round the temples and waist, holding in his dexter hand a club all ppr. f. 25. A savage ambulant ppr. in the dexter hand a club resting on the shoulder, and in the sinister hand a shield ar. charged with a cross gu, f. 26.

SAVIN TREE. P. 45, f. 59. From Burke's Heraldic Illustrations.

SAW, or Frame-Saw. P. 41, f. 35.

SAW, or Hand-Saw. P. 41, f. 34.

SAWLTEREY, or Sawtry. An old term for per-saltier.

SAXON'S HEAD. See Head.

SAXON SWORD. See Seax.

SAXON-WHEEL-CROSS. A Plain Cross within a circle the outer edge of which is indented.

SCALE-ARMOUR, or Mail Armour. P. 36, f. 21.

SCALES. See Balance.

SCALED, or Escalloped. Covered over, as if with the scales of a fish; it is also termed Papellonné, as a bend so termed. P. 18, f. 7.

SCALES-SCALED, or Escallops-escalloped, differs from the last, each scale being as it were jagged or fringed after the manner of diapering, with a deeper colour than that of the field.

SCALING-LADDER. P. 37, f. 7.

SCALLOP-SHELL. The same as Escallopshell. P. 42, f. 42.

SCALLOPED, or Escalloped, the same as Escallopée. See Papelonne. P. 18, f. 7

SCALP. Skin of a man's head with the hair. P. 36, f. 18.
Also the skin of the forehead of an animal. If the animal have horns they are attached to the scalp, as at P. 15, f. 21. A Stag's scalp. A Bull's scalp. P. 31, f. 17. Hare's scalp. P. 31, f. 15.

SCALPEL. See Lancet.

SCALY-LIZARDS. P. 39, f. 24.

SCARABEE. A Beetle, borne by the name of Thorndike. P. 25, f. 27.

SCARCELLY, Sarcelly, Sarcelled, or Recarcelle. P. 7, f. 20 and 22.

SCARF. A small ecclesiastical banner hanging down from the top of a Pastoral Staff. P. 42, f. 46.

SCARPE, or Escarpe. A diminutive of the bend sinister being one half its breath. P. 17, f. 6.

SCATEBRA, or Water-pot. The Urn or Vase on which Water Gods are depicted leaning.

SCEPTRE. A royal-staff. The golden sceptre. P. 35, f. 13.
The Sceptre and Dove. f. 14. The Sceptre of Queen Mary. f. 18. Sceptre called St. Edward's Staff. f. 17. Sceptre. f. 19. The Sceptre is of greater antiquity than the Crown.

SCEPTRES. P. 42, f. 47.

SCEPTRE or Mace of the Lord Mayor of London. P. 35, f. 21.

SCHALLOP. Same as Escallop.

SCIMITAR. A sword with a convex edge. P. 38, f. 22; and P. 36, f. 31.

SCINTILLANT. Sparkling, applied to anything having sparks of fire about t.

SCOOP. A kind of ladle. P. 39, f. 21.
A Scoop with water therein wavy. Borne by the name of Scopham, In the blazon of the arms Scopholme it is termed a *Scolpe*.

SCOPPERELLE. See Escallop.

SCORPION. P. 32, f. 53.
The largest and most malignant of all the insect tribes. It somewhat resembles the lobster; is generally borne erect. When borne with the head downwards is described as reversed.

SCOTCH SPUR. P. 37, f. 47.

SCOTCHEON. See Escutcheon

SCOTLAND. The Badge of. P. 3, f. 21.
Crest of P. 26, f. 28.
Crown of. P. 25, f. 29.
Bordure of. P. 35, f. 16.

SCOURGE. A whip, in blazon the number of lashes must be named. A scourge with three lashes. P. 42, f. 41.

SCRIP, Wallet, or Pilgrim's pouch. A bag formerly carried by pilgrims. P. 40, f. 39 ann 40.
Scrip, or Wallet open. f. 41.

SCROG. A term used by Scotch Heralds for a small branch of a tree.

SCROLL. That part of the achievement on which the motto is placed. P. 18, f. 21. See Escroll.

SCRUTTLE. A winnowing basket. P. 39, f. 16.

SCULL-HUMAN. P. 36, f. 32.

SCULL in a cup. P. 35, f. 34.

SCUTCHEON. The same as Escutcheon.

SCYMETAR. See Scimitar.

SCYTHE. An instrument of husbandry. P. 39, f. 10.
The handle of the scythe is still called, in some counties, a *Sned*, and is so blazoned in the arms of Sneyd as allusive to their name.

SCYTHE-BLADE. i.d. f. 10, No. 3.

SEA-APE. P. 29, f. 59.

SEA-AYLET. See Aylet.

SEA-BREAM. Same as Hake-fish. P. 32, f. 36.

SEA-DOG. P. 29, f. 56.

SEA-BULL, Sea-Bear, Sea-Cat, Sea-Dragon, Sea-Horse, Sea-Lion, etc.
The anterior portions of the bodies of these are all depicted in the forms which the several names denote; but like the Sea Horse. P. 29, f. 55, and the Sea-lion. P. 26. f. 53, they have fishes tails and webbed paws.

SEA-DOG. P. 29, f. 56.

SEA-GULL. P. 34, f. 13.

SEA, or Marine Wool, is depicted as P. 29, f. 51.

SEA-MEW. See Sea Gull.

SEA-MONKEY. P. 29, f. 59.

SEA-PIE. P. 34, f. 17.

SEA-URCHIN. P. 32, f. 49.

SEAL. A carnivorous and amphibious animal. P. 29, f. 51.

SEAL. A device, or an engraved inscription; also an impression made on wax.
Personal Seals may be regarded among the most trustworthy evidences of armorial bearings. Indeed, when a seal attached to a charter bears the same name as that of the person granting the charter, its authority for a shield of arms is almost indisputable.

SEALS attached to a book. P. 43, f. 32.

SEAL'S PAW erased. P. 29, f. 52.

SEAX. A scimitar with a semicircular notch, hollowed out of the back of the blade. P. 38, f. 20 and 22.

SECOND TITLE. See Courtesy Title.

SEDANT. The same as Sejant.

SEEDED. Applied to the seeds of roses, lilies, etc., when borne of a different tincture to the flower.

SEGMENT. A portion cut off by a line from a circle.

SEGRANT. See Segreant.

SEGREANT. A term applied to the Griffin when standing erect upon its near hind leg, with the wings elevated and endorsed. It is the position of a lion rampant. A Griffin Segreant. P. 27, f. 2.

SEIZING. Applied to birds of prey when feeding on their prey. P. 33, f. 12.

SEJANT. Sitting. P. 26, f. 41 ; P. 27, f. 3 ; P. 29, f. 15.

SEJANT ADDORSED. Setting back to back. P. 29, f. 44.

SEJANT CONTOURNE. P. 26, f. 18.

SEJANT RAMPANT. i.d. f. 19.

SEJANT GUARDANT in aspect. i.d. f. 43.

SEJANT EXTENDED in full aspect. i.d. f. 44.

SEJANT IN HIS MAJESTY, as the crest of Scotland. f. 28.

SEJANT DEXTER paw raised. f. 42.

SEJANT REGUARDANT. P. 28, f. 10.

SELCH, or Sealch. Seal, an amphibious animal. P. 29, f. 51.

SEMEE, Semme, or Seme. Aspersed, or Powdered. P. 2, f. 38.
The terms Averlye, Gerattie, and Strewed, are also used for the same thing, which implies that the Field, Charge, Crest, or Supporter, is strewed over with figures, such as roses, stars, etc. When strewed with fleur-de-lis it is then termed Semee-de-lis.

SEMY. Same as Semée.

SENESTROCHERE. The sinister arm.

SENGREEN, or House-Leek, as borne in the arms of Caius College, Cambridge. P. 22, f. 17.

SENTRIE. An old term for Piles.

SEPT-FOIL. A figure of seven foils. See Foils.

SEPT-INSULAR LION. A winged lion passant guardant, holding seven arrows in his paw, and over his head a nimbus. P. 26, f. 47.

SEPULCHRAL MONUMENTS. See Monuments, and Brasses Sepulchral.

SEPURTURE. The same as Endorsed, as Wings Endorsed, or Sepurture. P. 27, f. 17; P. 33, f. 26, No. 2.

SERAPH'S HEAD. Depicted as the head of a child with three pairs of wings. P. 36, f. 57.

SERAPHIM. The same as Seraph's Head.

SERGENT, or Sergreant. The same as Segreant.

SERPENT. A snake. P. 30.
In Blazon, the position of the Serpent must be particularly expressed. As a Serpent Nowed. f. 25. Nowed in Pale. f. 60. Targent. f. 28.
A full description of other positions will be found at Plate 30, f. 25 to 60, and Plate 22, f. 7 and 17.

SERRATED. Indented. P. 39, f. 14, No. 2.

SERUSE. A torteau.

SESANT. See Issuant.

SEVERED. Disjointed. See Chevron Disjointed. P. 16, f. 4.

SEX-FOIL, or Sise-foil. A plant with six leaves. See Narcissus. P. 44, f. 17.

SEXTANT. P. 38, f. 47. See Quadrant.

SHACK-BOLT. Borne both single and double. P. 42, f. 40.

SHACKLE, or Oval link of a fetter. P. 37, f. 42.

SHAFFERON. See Chaperon.

SHAFTED. Arrows, Spears, etc., are said to be shafted when the shaft is of a different tincture from the head. See Pheon Shafted. P. 37, f. 14.

SHAG. A cormorant. P. 34, f. 34.

SHAKE-FORK. Is in form like the cross pall, but does not touch the edges of the shield, and is depicted as P. 39, f. 19.

SHAMBROGUS. A shoe. P. 19, f. 38.

SHAMBROUGH. A kind of ship. P. 38, f. 26.

SHAMROCK. The same as Trefoil, three leaved grass. P. 44, f. 14.
The Badge of Ireland. P. 3, f. 21.

SHANKBONE, or Shinbone. P. 42, f. 52.

SHAPEAU. See Chapeau.

SHAPERNES, or Shapourns. The same as Shapournet.

SHAPOURNATED. P. 12, f. 40.

SHAPOURNE. A curved line. P. 21, f. 6.

SHAPOURNET. See Chapournet. P. 12, f. 39.

SHARK. A voracious fish. P. 32, f. 51.

SHAVE. See Curriers' Shave. P. 41, f. 2.

SHAVE-HOOK. P. 41, f. 19.

SHAVING-IRON, as in the arms of the Fanmakers' Company. P. 41, f. 36.

SHEAF. See Garb.

SHEAF OF ARROWS. P. 37, f. 19.

SHEAVES. A term applied to a bundle of arrows. See Arrow.

SHEARS. A tool used by clothiers. P. 41, f. 43.

SHEEP. A quadruped always depicted as the lamb, P. 29, f. 4, without the banner and nimbus.

SHELDRAKE. A kind of duck. P. 34, f. 15.

SHELLS. See Escallop Shell and Welkshell.

SHEPHERD'S CROOK. P. 39, f. 11, No. 3.

SHERIFF. This title is a corruption from Shire Reeve, from the Saxon, meaning the Reeve or Governor of the Shire, he is the chief civil officer in each county, and has the title of Esquire for life.

SHETYLL. See Shuttle.

SHIELD, Buckler, Target, or Escutcheon. A weapon of defence, borne on the arm to turn off the blows of an enemy's weapon. P. 1; P. 36, f. 27.
As to the form or shape of shields there can be no rule; any form may be taken. See Escutcheon.

SHIN-BONES. Two in saltire, borne by the name of Newton, Baynes, Gale, Gatty, etc. P. 42, f. 52.

SHIPS of various kinds are met with in Heraldry, and also the different parts of ships, as the rudder. P. 38, f. 40. The mast. f. 35. A sail. f. 39. Helm. f. 40. The stern of a line of battle ship. f. 31.
An Heraldic ship is always drawn with three masts, and is termed a Lymphad; also blazoned a vessel, and a galley with oars, and sometimes a row-galley. P. 38, f. 25 to 30. Modern ships are of common occurrence, and, in blazoning, should be mentioned whether they have two or three masts, and whether under all sail, or full sail, and whether the sails are reefed or furled. P. 38, f. 32 and 33. In both the former and latter cases it must be mentioned whether pennons, streamers, or colours, are flying.

SHIP GUN CARRIAGE, on it a piece of Ordnance mounted. P. 37, f. 6.

SHIP-LANTERN. P. 39, f. 27. No. 2.

SHIVERED. Broken or splintered.

SHODS. Iron arrow heads.

SHOT. See Spar and Chain Shot. P. 37, f. 8, and 9.

SHOVEL. A kind of spade with broad blade slightly hollowed.

SHOVELLER. A species of water-fowl. P. 34, f. 23.

SHREDDING KNIFE. P. 41, f. 20.

SHRIMP, or Prawn. Depicted as P. 32, f. 40, a.

SHRUTTLE, Fan, or Winnowing Basket, used for winnowing corn. P. 39, f. 16.

SHUTTLE. An instrument used by weavers, and borne in the arms of their Company. P. 40, f. 2.
It is blazoned a shuttle tipped and quilled, and is very generally given as a bearing to those who have risen to affluence by it. As the family of Peel.

SICKLE. An instrument of husbandry used for reaping corn. Two inter-laced. P. 39, f. 13. No. 2.

SICKLE with teeth. i.d. f. 14. No. 2.

SIDE. A dexter-side. P. 22, f. 10. It may be dexter or sinister and not more than one sixth of the shield, cut off by a perpendicular line.

SIDE-FACE, or Side long face. A face in profile. P. 36, f. 38.

SIDETH. Same as Impaled. When a coat has two impalements as P. 46, f. 4; the second is frequently termed a *Siding*.

SIGNET ROYAL. A swan so called when gorged with a Coronet and chain.

SILK-HANKS. As borne in the arms of the Silk Throwers' Company. P. 40, f. 5.

SILK-THROWERS' MILL. P. 40, f. 6.

SILVER. Argent. In painting repre-sented by white. P. 1.

SINCKFOIL. See Cinquefoil.

SINISTER. The left. i.e. the right to the spectator. See Shield Impaled. Dex-ter and Sinister. P. 1.

SINISTER BEND. See Bend Sinister. P. 17, f. 5.

SINISTER BASE POINT, See Points of Escutcheon. P. 1.

SINISTER QUARTER. P. 19, f. 35.

SINISTERWAYS. Turned to the sinister.

SINOPLE. Green or vert.

SIR. The title of a Baronet and Knight.
This title in former times, was given to all who had taken a degree, or had entered into orders. Aubrey's Letters, 1, 117.

SIREN. A Mermaid. P. 35, f. 12.

SISTRUM. A musical instrument used in the rites of Isis. P. 38, f. 48.

SITFOILE. See Sixfoil.

SITHE. See Sythe.

SIXFOIL. A Narcissus. P. 44, f. 17.

SKEIN, Skean, or Skeen. A short sword, or dagger.

SKELETON, or Deadman's head. P. 36, f. 32.

SKELETON, Human holding an arrow. P. 35, f. 35.
The emblem of mortality. A crowned skeleton, is the emblem of christian death.

SKIFF. A Galley. See Lymphad.

SKIPPING. Erected, mounting, or leap-ing.

SKULL HUMAN. P. 35, f. 34, and P. 36, f. 32.

SKY-LARK. P. 33, f. 57.

SLASHED. Sleeves of garments were formerly cut open lengthways, and these openings were filled with a puffing of another colour. See arm so vested, viz., a cubit arm vested or., cuffed and slashed ar., hand ppr. holding a scymitar imbrued, gu., hilt and pommel gold. P. 36, f. 13.

SLAUGHTER-AXE. P. 22, f. 32, and P. 41, f. 19.

SLAY, Slea, or Reed. An instrument used by weavers, and borne as part of the arms of the Weavers' Company of the City of Exeter. P. 42, f. 32.

SLEDGE. A vehicle moved on runners used in husbandry. P. 42, f. 28.

SLEDGE-HAMMER. A large heavy ham-mer. P. 41, f. 25.

SLEEVE. See Maunche.

SLING with a stone in it. P. 41, f. 55.

SLING. As borne in the arms of Cawarden. i.d. f. 56.

SLIP. A twig should be depicted with only three leaves; as a pear slip. P. 44, f. 56.

SLIPPED or Slipt, applied to flowers, fruit, etc., when depicted with a stalk. P. 44, f. 52.

SLOE-BUSH. See Crequer-plant.

SLOGAN, or Slughorn. The Scottish Cri-de-guerre.

SMALLAGE-GARLAND. Given to victors at the Nemean Games.

SMELT. A small fish. P. 32, f. 34.

SMEW, or White-Nun. P. 34, f. 33.

SNAFFLE. See Barnacle.

SNAFFLE-BIT. P. 37, f. 53.

SNAGGED. Couped so, the edge is seen in perspective, as P. 45, f. 56.

SNAIL, or House-snail, also termed a Snail in his Shell. P. 30, f. 6.

SNAKE. See Serpent.

SNAKEY-STAFF. See Caduceus.

SNED. The handle of a Scythe to which refer.

SNIPE. A bird. P. 34, f. 50.

SNIPPERS. See Glaziers'-nippers.

SOARANT, or Soaring. Flying aloft.

SOCIETIES, ARMS OF. See Arms of Community.

SOCK, or Ploughshare. See Coulter.

SOL. The sun, by which or, or gold is expressed in blazoning arms by the Planets. P. 1.

SOLDERING-IRON. A tool used by plumbers, and borne in the arms of their company. P. 41, f. 1.

SOLDERING-IRON TRIANGULAR. See Plumbers' Knife.

SOLE. A flat fish. P. 32, f. 10a.

SOLEIL. A Rose en Soleil is a rose surrounded with rays.

SOLON GOOSE, or Gannet. P. 34, f. 20.

SOMERSET HERALD. See Heralds College.

SOMME. Horned, applied to the stag when the branches are not less than thirteen, but if more it is blazoned Sommé Sans Nombre. The term Sommé, is also used by some in the sense of surmounted.

SONG THRUSH. See Thrush. P. 34, f. 45.

SORE. A term for the young of the buck in its fourth year.

SOREL. A young buck in its third year.

SOUSTENU, Soutennée, or Soutenu. When a chief is represented supported by a small part of the escutcheon beneath it, of a different colour, or metal from the chief, and reaching as the chief doth, from side to side, being as it were a fillet on the bottom part of the chief, of another colour. P. 12, f. 33.

SOUTHERNWOOD, Branch of, borne by the name of Sotheron. P. 45, f. 55.

SOVEREIGN'S HELMET. P. 24, f. 8.

SPADE. P. 39, f. 18. A Half-spade. i.d. No. 4.

SPADE IRON, or the Shoeing of a Spade. i.d. f. 18, No. 2 and 3.

SPANCELLED. See Horse Spancelled. P. 27, f. 31.

SPANIEL. A dog with long shaggy coat. P. 29, f. 27.

SPARLING, or Smelt. A small fish. P. 32, f. 34.

SPARROW. A bird. P. 33, f. 51.

SPARROW-HAWK. See Hawk.

SPAR-SHOT. P. 37, f. 9.

SPATULA, as borne in the arms of the Barbers' Company. P. 22, f. 19; and P. 42, f. 50.

SPAYADE. A young stag, in his third year.

SPEAR. An instrument used in warfare. P. 37, f. 22. Broken Spear. f. 11.

SPEAR-EEL. See Eel Spear.

SPEAR-HEAD imbrued. P. 37, f. 11.

SPEAR-REST. See Rest.

SPEAR. See Tilting-spear.

SPEAR-SALMON. See Harpoon.

SPECKLED. Spotted with another tincture.

SPECTANT. At gaze, or looking forward, sometimes termed in full aspect. P. 28, f. 44, and P. 26, f. 44.

SPELLERS. The small branches shooting out from the flat part of the buck's horn, at the top.

SPERVER, or Spurver. A kind of tent, as borne in the arms of the Upholders' Company. P. 40, f. 28.
It is also termed a Pavilion, or Tabernacle.

SPHERE. Armillary, Celestial, and Terrestrial Sphere. P. 39, f. 4, and f. 5.

SPINK. A small bird. P. 34, f. 54.

SPHINX. A fabulous monster, with the head and breasts of a woman, body of a lion, and the wings of an eagle. P. 30, f. 2.

SPHINX couchant, sans wings. i.d. f. 3.

SPILTED. Covered with. Same as Powdered.

SPIDER and WEB. Borne by the name of Chettle. P. 22, f. 5.

SPIKED. Studded with points, as a club spiked. P. 41, f. 48.

SPINDLE. As borne by Miller. P. 40, f. 2. See also Wharrow-spindle. i.d. f. 3. Borne by Badland, etc.

SPIRE, or Steeple of a Church. P. 23, f. 23.

SPIRES. Blades of grass

SPIRED, having raised points.

SPLAYED. The same as displayed.

SPLENDOUR, a term for the Sun, when represented with a human face, environed with rays. P. 23, f. 33.

SPLINTERED. Broken.

SPOKESHAVE. Also termed Grazier. See Grater.

SPOOL. See Spindle.

SPOTTED. The same as speckled.

SPRAT. A small fish. P. 32, f. 40.

SPREAD EAGLE. Same as an Eagle with two heads displayed. P. 33, f. 6.

SPRIG. A twig, as P. 44, f. 40.

SPRING-BOK. P. 29, f. 23.

SPRINGING. Applicable to beasts of chase, in the position in which wild beasts are called salient. It is also applied to fish when placed in bend. See Stag Springing. P. 28, f. 45.

SPRINKLING-SALT. See Salt.

SPROUTING. Shooting forth leaves. P. 45, f. 56, and 57.

SPUR. An ancient or Scotch spur. Also called a prick-spur. P. 37, f. 47.

SPUR. Generally borne with the straps. Termed a spur leathered.
A Spur and Spur-leather, depicted as P. 37, f. 48.

SPUR-ROWEL, or Spur-reule. i.d. f. 47.

SPUR-ROWEL BLEMISHED. i.e. having the points cut off. f. 47.

SPURRED. Equipped with spurs, as a boot spurred. P. 38, f. 15.

SPURVER. See Sperver.

SQUARE. As borne in the arms of Attow, Bevill, Edmonds, etc. P. 41, f. 23.

SQUARE-PIERCED, or Quarterpierced. P. 7, f. 16; P. 8, f. 44.

SQUAT. A term used for a rabbit sejant.

SQUIRE BASE. P. 21, f. 24. See also Equire.

SQUIRREL. An animal always borne sejant, and often cracking a nut. P. 29, f. 43.

SQUIRRELS sejant endorsed. i.d. f. 44.

SRUTTLE. See Winnowing-fan. P. 39, f. 16.

S.S., COLLAR OF. See Collar of S.S. and P. 24, f. 29.

STAFF. A Bishop's Staff, or Pastoral-staff. P. 42, f. 46.
The Staff of a Patriarch is a double cross, P. 22, f. 23; and that of the Pope a triple one. P. 42, f. 48.

STAFF-CROSS, or Fore Staff. P. 38, f. 43.

STAFF, Episcopal, or Bishop's staff. P. 42, f. 46.

STAFF Palmers. i.d. f. 44.

STAFF-PIKE. See Pike-staff.

STAFF RAGGED, or Raguly. P. 41, f. 57

STAFF-TREE leaf. P. 22, f. 33.

STAFFORD-KNOT. The Badge of Stafford. P. 43, f. 9.

STAG and Stag's head are common bearings in coat armour.
The Stag is blazoned at Gaze, Tripping, Springing, Courant, (or in full course) Browsing and Lodged. See P. 28, f. 43 to 48. And when the head is cut off, showing no part of the neck, and placed full faced, it is termed Cabossed. f. 52. But when the neck is shown with the head, and full faced, it is termed a stag's head and neck Affrontee, couped or erased at the neck. If shown in profile, it is blazoned a stag's head couped, or erased, the profile being understood. f. 49 and 50. When the horns (antlers) and hoofs are of a different tincture, it is said to be Attired

and Unjuled. If the antlers have more than five projections on each, it is blazoned attired with so many (mentioning the number) tynes.

STAG or Hart, cumbent, or Lodged in a Park-paled. P. 28, f. 55.

STAGGARD. A Stag in the fourth year.

STAINED, or Stamand. According to Guillim such colours as having no body do only stain, as Murrey and Tawny.

STALKING. Walking applied to long-legged birds.

STALL-PLATES. A square or oblong plate of gilt copper, upon which the Arms of Knights of the Garter and the Bath are emblazoned, and fixed in their stalls in the Chapels of St. George at Windsor, and of Henry VII, at Westminster. The arms of the Esquires of the Knights are similarly displayed and recorded in the lower range of Stalls.

STALL, or Canopy. P. 43, f. 53.

STANDARD. An ancient military ensign, long and tapering towards the end, which is split and rounded; on the upper part appears the Cross of St. George, the remainder being charged with Motto, Crest, or Badge, but never with arms. P. 46, f. 20. The term Standard is now applied to the ensign carried by the Cavalry, those of the Infantry being called Colours.

STANDARD ROYAL. See Royal Standard.

STANDARD CUP. See Cup-covered.

STANDING-DISH. See Dish.

STAPLE. An iron fastening. P. 42, f. 14.

STAR. An Ensign of Knightly Rank, common to the Heraldry of all nations. See Knighthood.

STAR. See Estoile.

STAR-BLAZING. See Comet.

STAR-CROSS. P. 8, f. 45.

STAR OF SIX, AND EIGHT POINTS. P. 23, f. 43 and 44.

STAR OF INDIA. See Knighthood Orders of.

STAR-FISH, as borne in the arms of La-Yard. P. 32, f. 55.

STAR-PAGODAS, as borne in the arms of Blades. P. 42, f. 29.
The Star-Pagoda is an Indian coin.

STARLING. A bird; sometimes termed a Sterne, or Stare. P. 33, f. 50.

STARS AND STRIPES of the United States of America with the Eagle. P. 25a, f. 15.

STARVED, or Blighted. A tree, or branch, without leaves, as a Blighted Tree and Starved Branch. P. 45, f. 58.

STATANT. A term applied to animals standing with all their feet on the ground, except to those of the Deer kind. See P. 26, f. 39 and 40; P. 27, f. 8 and 19.

STATE, CAP OF, as borne by the Lord Mayor of London, termed the Civic Cap. P. 40, f. 56.

STATERA ROMANA. A steelyard. P. 39, f. 22.

STATES GENERAL, Hat worn over the Arms of the. P. 40, f. 52.

STAVE OF ESCULAPIUS. P. 30, f. 57.

STAVES, used by Palmers or Pilgrims. P. 42, f. 43.

STAVES OF AN ESCARBUNCLE. Are the eight rays which issue from the centre. See Escarbuncle.

STAVES OF A WHEEL. The spokes, which unite the nave to the felloes. P. 41, f. 53.

STEEL FOR STRIKING FIRE. Also termed a Furison. P. 22, f. 45.

STEEL-CAP. See Morion.

STEEL-GAD. See Gad. P. 42, f. 35.

STEELYARD. A kind of balance. P. 39, f. 22.

STEEPLE OF A CHURCH. When borne in arms, is drawn with a part of the tower or belfry. P. 23, f. 23. Blazoned a "Church Spire," name of Bakeham, Backcombe, etc.

STELLION-SERPENT. A Serpent with the head of a weasel, borne by the name of Bume.

STEM, or Trunk of a Tree. P. 45, f. 56 and 57.

STEPHEN, St. Cross of. P. 10, f. 1.

STERN. The hinder part of a ship is frequently met with in Coat Armour. It is borne by Nelson, P. 38, f. 31, Carneige, Campbell, etc.

STERNE, or Stare. A Starling. P. 33, f. 50.

STILL. A utensil of the distillery as borne in the arms of Wennington. P. 39, f. 30, No. 1.

STILT. An instrument made to walk with. P. 41, f. 59.

STIRRUP AND LEATHER. P. 37, f. 52. When borne without the leather it should be blazoned stirrup iron.

STOCK, or Stump of a Tree. P. 45, f. 56.

STOCK-CARD. An instrument for carding wool. P. 40, f. 7.

STOCKFISH. P. 32, f. 47.

STOCKE. A Falcon's-rest. P. 43, f. 18.

STOLE. Part of the vestment of a priest. P. 40, f. 45.

STONE. See Flag-stone. P. 42, f. 34. A Tombstone. f. 53.

STONE-BILL, or Wedge. Used to split timber. P. 41, f. 42.

STONE-BOWS. A cross bow for shooting stones. P. 37, f. 23.

STONE-MASON'S MALLET. P. 41, f. 33.

STORK. A large bird allied to the Heron. P. 34, f. 9.

STREAMER. A flag; the length may be from 20 to 40 yards, on which may be put a man's conceit, or device.

STREAMING. A term used to express the stream of light darting from a comet, or blazing star. P. 23, f. 45.

STREWED. Scattered. The same as Semée. P. 2, f. 38.

STRING-BOW. P. 37, f. 18.

STRINGED, or Strung. Terms used to express the strings of harps, bows, and bugle-horns, and when these are depicted without strings they must be blazoned "Sans strings."

STUDDED. Adorned with studs.

STUMP, or Stock of a Tree. P. 45, f. 56.

STURGEON. A large kind of fish. P. 32, f. 32.

SUB. Applied to an ordinary when the bottom edge is different from the top, as a Fesse Nebuly, Sub Invecked. P. 4, f. 26. A Fesse Sub-Crenellée is a Fesse with plain line at top, and the bottom embattled.

SUB-ORDINARIES. The following are commonly so called, viz.: The Bordure, Canton, Flanch, Fret, Gyron, Inescutcheon, Orle, Pile, Tressure, and Voider.

SUBVERTANT, or Subverted. Reversed turned upside down. P. 15, f. 43.

SUCCEEDANT. Following one another.

SUCCESSION, ARMS OF. See Arms of Succession.

SUFFLUE. A rest, or clarion. See Clarion.

SUGAR-CANE. The plant from which sugar is obtained. P. 44, f. 33.

SUGAR-LOAF. A conical mass of sugar, borne by the name of Sugar.

SUN. Usually borne with a human face and rays. P. 23, f. 32.

SUN IN SPLENDOUR, or in Glory. P. 23, f. 33.

SUN IN SPLENDOUR, each ray illuminated, or inflamed. f. 34.

SUN ENCIRCLED with clouds distilling drops of rain. f. 29. Borne in the arms of the Distillers' Company.

SUN RESPLENDENT, rays issuing from clouds in chief. P. 23, f. 28.

SUN RESPLENDENT, rays issuing from dexter chief point. f. 30.

SUN RISING IN SPLENDOUR, or issuing from clouds. f. 31.

SUN IN SPLENDOUR, charged with an eye. f. 35.

SUN AND LION OF PERSIA, BADGE OF. P. 25a, f. 7.

SUNDIAL on a Pedestal. P. 39, f. 44, No. 1.

SUPER-CHARGE. A term used to express one figure borne upon another; more properly blazoned *Surmounted*. P. 20, f. 3.

SUPER. The top. e.g. A fesse super nebuly, i.e. nebuly only on the top, as in the arms of Blancharden, which is also Sub invecked, i.e. the bottom only is invecked. P. 4, f. 26.

SUPPLANTING. Treading under-foot.

SUPPORTED. Said of an Ordinary that has another under it, by way of support. P. 3, f. 33.

SUPPORTERS. Are figures represented on each side of the shield, and appear to support or hold it up. P. 18, 19 and 20, f. 21; P. 31, f. 11.

Supporters are used by the Sovereign, Princes, Peers, and Peeresses, Knights of the several Orders, and Nova Scotia Baronets. The English Baronets are not allowed this privelege, except a very few, who for distinguished services have received a licence to use them.

The Sons of Peers, although using supporters, have no legal right to them, and I would remark that a somewhat foolish custom has lately sprung up. If a Peer intermarries with a lady belonging to a family whose arms have supporters, he places one of the supporters of his own coat on the dexter, and one of the supporters of the coat belonging to her family on the sinister side of his shield; yet it is certain by all the rules of Heraldry that a woman can in no case convey supporters to her husband, and that even to convey them to her children she must at least be a Peeress in her own right.

SUPPORTING. Sustaining, or holding up. P. 8, f. 21, P. 31, f. 21.

SUPPRESSED. The same as Debruised.

SUR. On, upon, or over.

SUR-ANCREE, or Sur-Anchored. P. 10, f. 34.

SURCOAT. A loose frock without sleeves, worn by Military men over their Armour, on it, their Arms were sometimes painted or embroided. P. 39, f. 20. No. 5.

"The Surcoat, originated with the crusaders for the purpose of distinguishing the many different nations serving under the banner of the cross, and to throw a veil over the iron armour, so apt to heat excessively when exposed to the direct rays of the Sun." Meyrick.

SURCHARGED. Charged or Surmounted.

SURGIANT, or Surgeant. Rising. P. 33, f. 3.

SURGIANT, or Surgeant-tergiant. The wings expanded on each side of the head, the points not elevated, and the dexter wing showing behind, and the sinister before the bird. P. 33, f. 10.

SUR-LE-TOUT. En-Surtout, Surmounted, or over-all. See Surtout.

SURMOUNTED, Surmonté. Terms to express any charge having another placed over it. It is also expressed by the term Debruised. P. 7, f. 4.

A Lion surmounted or debruised of a fesse. P. 26, f. 21.

SURPOSE. Same as, in pale.

SURROY, or Southroy. The ancient title of the King of Arms for the south parts of England, now called Clarenceux.

SURROYAL TOP. The broad top of a stag's horn, with the branches or small shoots from it.

SURSUANT. The same as erected and elevated, but without being waved or turned. See Reclinant.

SURTOUT, or Sur-le-tout. A term for Over-all. Generally applied to a small escutcheon, containing a Coat of Augmentation. P. 16, f. 40; P. 31, f. 42.

SUSPECTANT, or Spectant. Looking upwards. P. 33, f. 14.

SUSTAINED. See Soustenu.

SUSTAINING. Supporting, or holding. P. 31, f. 21.

SWALLOW, Hirondelle, or Hirundo. When represented flying, is termed volant. P. 34, f. 60.

SWAN. Always borne with the wings endorsed, unless it is expressed otherwise.

A Swan close. P. 34, f. 27.

A Demi Swan, wings expanded. f. 28.

A Swan Rousant; i.e., standing with wings endorsed. f. 25.

A Swan in Pride, is a Swan represented swimming. f. 26.

A Swan's Head erased. f. 29.

SWEEP, Swepe, or Balista, also termed Mangonel; an engine used by the ancients for throwing stones. P. 37, f. 38.

SWIVEL. Two iron links which turn on a bolt. P. 42, f. 39.

SWORD. P. 38, f. 19.

In blazoning a sword in coat armour, its position must always be mentioned; whether the point is upwards or downwards, towards the dexter or sinister, etc. See examples. P. 31, f. 30, to 35, and P. 9, f. 21. When the handle and pommel (i.e. the knob affixed to the handle) are of a different tincture, it it is termed hilted and pommelled. The hilt includes the entire handle and guard, but if the hand part is of a different tincture it is blazoned as the grip. e.g. a sword erect ar. grip vert. hilt and pommel or. the crest of Pollard. The Crest of Roundell is a sword in pale ar. hilt and pommel or, grip gu.

If the blade is wavy it is termed a sword wavy P. 38, f. 19. If with fire round the blade, it is said to be inflamed, or flammant, sometimes it is called a flaming sword. f. 21. If blood is depicted upon the blade, it is said to be imbrued. P. 36, f, 13.

See Terms. Broadsword, Curtana-sword, Cutlass, Rapier, Scimitar, Seax, Tuck, etc, The sword is frequently used as the Emblem of Power. See Curtana. Two Swords in Saltire, the Emblem of St. Paul.

SYKES. Fountains. See Heraldic Fountain.

SYMBOL. An emblem, type, or figure, the sign or representation of any moral thing by the images or properties of natural things as " the lion is the *symbol* of courage "; " a trident is the *symbol* of Neptune."

SYNAMUR. See Sanguine.

SYNETTYS. An old term for Swans.

SYNOBOLT. Sinople, or vert.

SYRCOTT. See Surcoat.

SYREN. Or Siren, a Mermaid. P. 35, f. 12.

T

T. A Roman T is borne by Gryme, an old English 𝕿 by the family of Toft. See Letters.

TABARD, or Tabert. A coat without sleeves, whereon the armorial ensigns were anciently depicted, from whence the term Coat of Arms. P. 38, f. 16.

The Tabard with wide sleeves reaching to the elbow is now used as a habit of ceremony, being embroidered with the Royal Arms, worn by Heralds and Pursuivants upon great festivals and other public ceremonies. See Tunic.

TABERNACLE. Same as Pavilion. P. 40, f. 28.

TADPOLES, or Powts. Young frogs.

TAIL. The tail of the lion, and the tail of a Beaver, are sometimes borne in Coat Armour. P. 29, f. 50.

The following are the different names for the Tails of several animals, viz.: That of the Deer is called single; of the Boar, the wreath; of the Fox, the brush; of the Wolf, the stern; and of the Hare and Coney, the scut.

TAIL FORKED, or Queue Fourché. P. 26, f. 3.

TAILLE. The same as party per bend sinister.

TAILOR'S-BODKIN. P. 42, f. 28.

TALBOT. A hound with long ears, and of very common use in Coat Armour.

A Talbot Statant. P. 29, f. 13.
A Talbot Sejant. i.d. f. 15.
A Demi Talbot Ramp. i.d. f. 14.
A Talbot's Head erased. i.d. f. 16.
A She-Talbot, borne by the name of Gottington.

TALENT. A bezant. P. 1.

TALON, or Claw. An Eagle's Talon reversed in pale ppr., as in the Crest of Marchmount. P. 33, f. 21.

TANKE. A kind of deep round cap, called a cap tanke; it is sometimes represented with strings, to tie under the chin.

TAPER-CANDLESTICK, with candle inflamed. P. 39, f. 27.

TAPER-CANDLESTICK, as borne in the arms of the Founders' Company. P. 39, f. 28, No. 1.

TARE, or Tarre. Affrontée, or fullfaced.

TARGANT. See Torqued.

TARGET, or Targe. A circular shield.

TASCES, Tasses, or Tassetts. That part of the armour which covers the thigh.

TASSEL. An ornament of silk or gold fringe, used as an addition to the strings of mantles, etc. The arms of Barnes are ar. a Tassel az. P. 40, f. 23. The Arms of Wooler are gu. three tassels or.

Roman Catholic ecclesiastics of high rank are distinguished by tassels pendant from a cord of silk issuing from either side of a hat which is placed over their shield. These tassels are arranged in rows, and the number of tassels in each row exceeds by one the number in that above it, so that the whole form an equilateral triangle. A Cardinal has five rows of scarlet tassels pendant from a scarlet hat. P. 40, f 60. Archbishops have a green hat, and four rows of green tassels. Bishops and Prothonotaries of the Pontifical Court, three and two rows respectively of green tassels.

TASSELLED. Adorned with tassels.

TASS-VAIRY. The same as Potent counter potent. P. 1.

TAU, a Cross Tau, or Taucross. P. 9, f. 30.

TAVALURES. Ermine spots.

TAWNY, or Tawney. See Tenne.

TEAL. A water fowl. P. 34, f. 18.

TEA-LEAVES. P. 44, f. 34.

TEA-PLANT. P. 44, f. 34.

TEAZEL. The head or seed-vessel of a species of Thistle. P. 45, f. 6.

TEMPLE. Borne by the name of Temple. P. 23, f. 26.

TEMPLARS. See Knights Templars.

TENAS, or more properly Tenans. A term applied to inanimate objects on the side of the shield, but not touching it.

TENANT, holding. A term to express that the shield is held by one man or beast. Supporters, when there are two.

TENANTEE, or Tenanted. See Cross Tenantée. P. 10, f. 36.

TENCH. A fish. P. 32, f. 14.

TENNE. The same as Tawny. It is by some heralds called Brusk; and in engraving, it is expressed by diagonal lines drawn from sinister chief points, and traversed by horizontal ones. P. 1.

TENT. P. 40, f. 25.
Figure 26 is a Tent as borne by Lindsey, viz., A Tent az. fringed and semée of stars or, ensigned with a pennon gu. See also Pavilion and Sperver.

TENT-ROYAL, or Royal Tent. P. 40, f. 27.

TENTER-HOOKS, two different shapes. P. 41, f. 24.

TERGANT, or Tergiant. The same as Recursant.

TERRAS, or Terrasse. The representation of a piece of ground at the base of the shield, and generally vert.

TERRESTRIAL GLOBE. See Globe, and P. 39, f. 2 and 5.

TERWHITT. A Lapwing. P. 33, f. 55.

TESTE A LA QUEVE, Quise, or Queue. Three fishes, etc., lying one upon the other, so that the head of each is between the other two, may be blazoned two fishes, in saltire, debruised by another in pale, the tail erect.
It is also called a *Trien* of fishes, lying cross, the heads and tails interchangeably posed; it is also termed *Testes aux queues*, i.e. heads to tails. P. 32, f. 25.

TETE. The head.

TETRAGONAL PYRAMIDS. Piles are generally considered to represent wedges; but they are sometimes borne triangular, and also square, in which latter case they may be termed square piles, or tetragonell pyramids reversed. P. 6, f. 40.

TEXT-LETTERS are borne in several Coats of Arms. See Letters.

THATCH-RAKE. An instrument used in thatching, P. 39, f. 12, borne by the name of Zakesley.

THATCHER'S HOOK. Same as Thatch-Rake.

THEMIS. The Goddess of Justice. P. 35, f. 7.

THEUTONS, Teutonic, German, Tholose, or Thoulouse Cross. P. 8, f. 39.

THIGH-BONE. See Shin-bone.

THISTLE. The Badge of Scotland. P. 3, f. 21.

THISTLE, slipped and leaved. P. 44, f. 5.

THISTLE, ORDER OF. See Knighthood.

THOISON, or Toison d'or. The golden fleece. P. 22, f. 29

THOMAS, ST. CROSS OF. P. 8, f. 28, with an escallop in centre.

THONG. A strap of leather for fastening anything; also the lash of a scourge. P. 42, f. 41.

THORN TREE. P. 45, f. 42.

THORN, CROWN OF. P. 43, f. 3.

THORR'S HAMMER, Fylfot, or Gammadion. q.v.

THOULOUSE-CROSS. The Crosses at P. 8, f. 36 and 39 are both so termed by Randle Holme.

THREE, Two, and One. Terms to denote the position of six charges, viz.: Three in chief, two in fesse, and one in base. P. 2, f. 39.

THREE. Three charges of any kind on a field are always placed two and one, P. 22, f. 45, unless otherwise described as three stirrups in pale. P. 14, f. 43.

THREE-QUARTERED, or In train aspect. Shewing three fourths of an animal.

THRESTLE, or Trestle. A hawk's perch. P. 43, f. 18.

THROUGHOUT. Extending to the sides of the escutcheon as a Cross Pattée throughout. P. 9, f. 7.

THRUSH. A song bird. P. 34, f. 45.

THUNDER, CROSS OF. P. 37, f. 43.

THUNDERBOLT. The emblem of Jupiter. P. 37, f. 44.
It is sometimes blazoned Jupiters Thunderbolt.

THYRSUS. A rod surmounted with a fir-cone, or a bunch of vine leaves or ivy, with grapes or berries, carried by Bacchus, and the Satyrs, Mænads, and others, during the celebration of religious rites. Beneath the garland or fir-cone the Thyrsus ends in the sharp point of a spear, a puncture from which induces madness. Two Thursi in Saltire, borne by the family of Fructuozo.

TIARA, or Triple Crown. The Papal Crown. P. 40, f. 59.

TIARA, or Triple Crown, with clouds in base, issuing rays as borne in the Arms of the Drapers' Company. i.d. f. 55.

TIERCE, Tiercée, or Tierced. Divided into three equal parts.

TIERCE IN BEND. P. 21, f. 39.

TIERCE IN FESSE. f. 37.

TIERCE IN GIRONS, or Gyrons. f. 40.

TIERCE IN GYRONS ARONDIA. P. 19, f. 45.

TIERCE IN MANTLE. P. 21, f. 36.

TIERCE IN PAIRLE. f. 35.

TIERCE IN PALE, or en Pal. f. 38.

TIERCE IN PILE. f. 41.

TIERCE'S THREE. Sa Three Tierces or; the Arms of Bourbourg. P. 22, f. 34.

TIGER AND MIRROR, borne by Sibel. P. 28, f. 14.

TIGER NATURAL. i.d. f. 13.

TIGER HERALDIC. Is depicted with a hooked talon at the nose, and with tufts as P. 28, f. 19.

TIGER HERALDIC, head of erased. f. 20.

TIGES AND FEUILLES. Terms applied to fruits when represented with stalks and leaves.

TILLAGE RAKE-HEAD. P. 39, f. 12.

TILT. See Tournament.

TILTING SPEAR. Always depicted, if not named to the contrary, with bur and vamplate. P. 35, f. 15.

The Bur is a broad ring of iron behind the place made for the hand on the tilting spear ; which bur is brought to the rest, when the tilter charges his spear; serving there to secure and make it easy to direct. The Vamplate is the broad piece of steel that is placed at the lower part of the staff of the spear for covering the hand, and may be taken off at pleasure. It sometimes resembles a funnel in shape. f. 23.

TILTING SPEAR, broken, or broken tilting spear ; in blazon, implies the bottom part only. P. 37, f. 11.

TIMBERED. See Anchor.

TIMBRE, or Tymbre. According to J. G. Nichols in the Herald, and Genealogist is a "Crest," but C. Boutell, in his Heraldry, Historical and Popular, gives Timbre as the Helm when placed above the shield in an achievement of arms.

Heaume and Timbre are also used to express

those things that are without the Escoucheu to distinguish the Degree of Honour and Dignity, such as Crowns, Coronets, etc. It is taken in particular for the Helmet.

TIME, The Emblem of. P. 35, f. 29.

TINCTURES. Under this term are included the colours used in Coat Armour, which are divided into three classes.

1st. *Metals*; i.e. *Or*, the metal gold; and *Argent, Silver*, the former is represented in engraving by dots, the later is left quite plain.

2nd. *Colours*; *Gules*, expressed in engraving by perpendicular lines. *Azure*, by horizontal lines from side to side. *Sable*, by horizontal and perpendicular lines crossing each other. *Vert*, by diagonal lines from dexter to the sinister. *Purpure*, by diagonal lines from sinister to dexter. *Tenne*, by diagonal lines from sinister to dexter, crossed by horizontal lines. *Sanguine*, by diagonal lines from dexter to sinister, and from sinister to dexter, crossing each other.

3rd. *Furs*: Which are generally reckoned to be six in number, but some writers have made them amount to eleven.

Ermine: A white field, with black tufts.

Ermines: Black field, with white tufts.

Erminois: A gold field, with black tufts.

Pean: Black field, with gold tufts.

Vair: White and Blue, represented by figures of small escutcheons, ranged in lines, so that the base argent is opposite to the top azure.

Counter-Vair: The same as the above, only the figures of escutcheons are placed base against base, and point against point.

Vaire en point: Figures standing exactly one upon another point upon flat.

Vaire or Warrie: When the escutcheons forming the Vair are of more than two tinctures.

Vaire ancient: Represented by lines nebuly separated by straight lines.

Potent: Resembles the head of crutches.

Potent, Counter-potent: Also termed *Cuppa*, or *Varry Cuppa*. (P. 22, f. 40.)

All these examples are on Plate 1. You must observe that it is not usual to place metal on metal, nor colour on colour. There are some exceptions to this rule, but it is considered bad heraldry.

Some Authors blazon the Arms of Sovereigns by Planets, of Peers by Precious stones, etc. See Paradigm at Plate 1. When any beast, bird, or charge is represented in its natural colour, it is blazoned proper, abbreviated ppr.

TINES, or Tynes. Antlers upon the horns of a stag. In blazoning, their number, and tincture must be named.

TIPPED. When the ends of a truncheon, etc., are of a different tincture from the other part. P. 36, f. 16.

TIRA. See Tiara.

TIRRET. A manacle, or handcuff. P. 42, f. 39.

TIRWHIT. See Lapwing.

TITYRUS. See Musimon.

TOAD. A small batrachian reptile. P. 30, f. 10.

TOBACCO PLANT. P. 44, f. 31.

TOBACCO LEAF, borne by Hutton. i.d.

TOD. A Fox, borne by the name of Todhunter.

TOISON D'OR. The golden fleece. P. 22, f. 29.

TOMAHAWK. An Indian war-axe, depicted as a Pole-axe. P. 37, f. 27.

TOMBS. See Monuments.

TOMB-STONE. P. 42, f. 53.

TONGS. See Closing Tongs. P. 41, f. 23.

TONGYS. Langued, or tongued.

TON. See Tun.

TOOTH. A fanged tooth. P. 42, f. 52.

TOPAZ. A precious stone, used to express gold in blazoning by precious stones.

TOP-BOOTS. P. 38, f. 15.

TOPS. Also termed playing tops. P. 42, f. 29.

TOR, or Conical-hill.

TORCE, or Torse. See Wreath.

TORCH. A flambeau, or firebrand. P. 41, f. 47.

TORGANT. See Torqued.

TORN. An ancient name for spinning wheel.

TORQUED. Wreathed, bowed-embowed. P. 30, f. 28, No. 2, and f. 55.

TORQUED. A dolphin haurient is sometimes said to be a Dolphin Torqued. P. 32, f. 2.

TORQUENED. The same as torqued.

TORTEAU, (plural Torteaux) a red roundle, termed in French cerises, cherries. P. 1. By some termed Wastell-cake.

TORTEYS. An old term for Torteux.

TORTILLE. Nowed, twisted, or wreathed. P. 30, f. 25.

TORTOISE. Always depicted as. P. 30, f. 5, if not expressed to the contrary.

TOUCHSTONE. See Flintstone.

TOURNAMENTS, Tilts, and Justs. These exercises were always performed on horseback, (although the riders when both were dismounted, might continue the combat on foot,) and were called Justs, because they partook of the nature of regular battle, or because the knights directed their horses straight at each other—and Tournaments—from the French "Tourner," because great skill was required in wheeling and handling the charger.

Single Knights tilted with each other, but when two parties engaged in a sort of general action it was termed a tournament. The weapons used were lances, swords, maces, and axes. The lances were sometimes sharp, but more usually had a blunted head, called from its peculiar shape a Cronel. Combats fought entirely on foot are by some writers termed tournaments but improperly. They were always judicial combats, fought "en champ clos" with axes and daggers.

When any knights wished to distinguish themselves by holding a Tournament they caused notice to be given that they would be ready at such a place to meet all comers in the lists, sometimes even naming how many courses they would run with the lance, and how many strokes exchange with sword or axe.

Both those who gave and those who accepted these challenges, appeared armed cap-a-pie, with their Surcoats, Wreaths, Crests, Mantles, Shields, and with their horses Barbed and Caprisoned; their Esquires carrying their pennons of arms before them.

A Knight on coming near the barriers, blew a horn in token of defiance, when the attendant Heralds received his name, bearings, and proof of his gentle blood; though these points were not always insisted on. This being settled, the champions charged each other from opposite ends of the lists after having saluted the President of the Tourney and the Ladies, and if either of them was unhorsed, lost his lance, stirrup, helmet, or wounded his opponents horse, he was vanquished; if both parties broke fairly their lances on each other, in the courses which they had agreed to run, they parted on equal terms.

TOURNE. Turned towards the sinister.

TOWER AND SWORD. Badge of. P. 25, a. f. 8.

TOWER. Always depicted as P. 23, f. 8, unless differently blazoned.

A Tower is said to be *Masoned* when the cement is of a different tincture from the stones.

Az. a fess or. betw. three Towers ar. are borne by Dasent of Ascott. Berks.

TOWER AVANT MUR. P. 23, f. 1.

TOWER BREACHED. i.d. f. 8.

TOWER DOMED. i.d. f. 12.

TOWER INFLAMED. i.d. f. 12.

TOWER with Scaling ladder. i.d. f. 9.

TOWER-TRIPPLE towered chain transverse. i.d. f. 11.

TOWER-TRIPPLE towered. i.d. f. 10, and P. 4, f. 21. See other examples at plate 23.

TOWERED or Turretted. Having towers or turrets.

TOWRE, Pynakelyd and Imbatayled. Old English for Tower, roof and embattlements.

TRACE, Tract, or Traile. The Tressure is so termed by Upton.

TRAFALGAR-MEDAL. P. 25, f. 10.

TRAMELS. A kind of shoe. See Brogue.

TRAMMELS. Same as the above.

TRAILING-PIKE, or leading staff, tasselled as in the armorial bearings of the Artillery Company, London. P. 41, f. 59.

TRAITS. Pieces. See P. 6, f. 24.

TRANCHE. The same as Per Bend.

TRANGLE. A diminutive of the fesse; by some it is called a *bar*, by others a *closet*.

TRANSFIXED. Pierced through. P. 16, f. 17; P. 42, f. 3.

TRANSFLUENT. Applied to water as if running through a bridge. P. 23, f. 19 and 20.

TRANSMUTED. Counterchanged.

TRANSPARENCY, or Transparent. Painted in shadow. See Adumbrated.

TRANSPIERCED. The same as Transfixed.

TRANSPOSED. Reversed, or turned contraryways.

TRANSVERSE, Traverse, or Doublet. According to Guillim is a bearing resembling a cheveron, which issues from two angles of one side of the shield, and meets in a point about the middle of the other side. P. 21, f. 41. It may issue from either side, dexter or sinister, the point should be mentioned in the blazon.

TRAVERSE, or Transverse. Across the escutcheon horizontally.

TRAVERSE IN POINT. P. 6, f. 31.

TRAVERSED. Facing the sinister.

TRAVERSED. Lying across, as two sceptres in saltire, traversed by a sword in pale. P. 42, f. 47.

TREBLE-CROSS STAFF, or Papal-staff. P. 42, f. 48.

TREBLE-FLAT-BRUSH. P. 41, f. 42.

TRECHEUR. See Tressure.

TREE. Trees in great variety are met with in Coat Armour, e.g. The *Alder, Almond, Apple, Aspen, Ash, Banyan, Beech, Birch, Box, Cedar, Cherry, Cocoa, Cotton, Cypress, Date, Elm, Fir, Hawthorn, Linden* or *Lime, Mahogany, Oak, Olive, Orange, Palm, Pear, Pine, Pollard-Willow, Paradise (Tree of), Poplar, Salix, Savin, Thorn, Walnut, Willow, Yew,* etc. See P. 45, f. 31 to 60, and P. 22, f. 7.

In blazoning a Tree you must observe in what condition it appears, whether spread, or blasted; and what kind of Tree it is, whether bearing fruit; if so, it is termed *Fructed*. If a part only is borne, that part must be named as *Stem, Stock,* or *Stump, Branches, Fruit, Leaves,* The Stem, Stock,

or Stump, must be described, if standing, as "*erect*"; if fallen, as "*jacent*"; if torn up by the roots, as "*eradicated*"; if shooting forth leaves, as "*sprouting*," etc. P. 45, f. 56 and 57. A branch with fruit is said to be fructed; if with leaves only, it is termed a branch; when without leaves, it is said to be withered, f. 58; if torn off, it is called slipped. P. 44, f. 56. A branch, if fructed, is always supposed to consist of four leaves. P. 44, f. 53. If unfructed of nine leaves, i.e. three slips set together on one stem. A sprig should have five leaves, and a slip only three. P. 44, f. 52.

TREE, Stem of, erased and sprouting. P. 45, f. 56.

TREE, Stock or Stump of, snagged and erased. i.d.

TREE, Stock of, jacent eradicated. i.d. f. 57.

TREE, Stem of, couped, eradicated, and sprouting. i.d.

TREE, Starved or Blighted. i.d. f. 58.

TREFLEE. A bend treflée, as in the arms of the Prince of Wales. P. 16, f. 40. See Rue Crown.

TREFLEE OF TREFOILS. Semée of Trefoils

TREFOIL. Three leaved grass. P. 44, f. 14, No. 1. Trefoil fitched. No. 2. Slipped and Raguled. No. 3. Treble slipped. No. 4. Double slipped. No. 5.

TREFOIL, double slipped raguled couped. P. 44, f. 15, No. 1. Trefoil stalked, fixed to a twig fesseways. No. 2.

TREILLE, or Trillise. A Lattice, or Trellis, a pattern resembling fretty, but always nailed at each intersection; also termed Trellised cloué. P. 22, f. 37.

TRENCHANT. Cutting, or brandishing.

TRENCHING KNIFE, as borne by Trenchard. P. 41, f. 22. Same as Pruning Knife.

TREPAN. A surgical instrument. P. 42, f. 50.

TRESSURE, or Treschur. The tressure passes round the field in the same shape as the field. When impaled, it is always to be omitted on the side next the line of impalement. P. 31, f. 9. It is always borne double and flory counterflory as in the royal Arms of Scotland. This is sometimes blazoned the Royal Tressure, or the Tressure of Scotland. P. 2, f. 43; P. 31, f. 11; P. 35, f. 16.

TRESSURE FLEURE. Same as Tressure.

TRESSURE FLORY COUNTERFLORY, on a bordure. P. 35, f. 16.

TRESSURE COUNTER FLOWERED. Same as Tressure-counter-flory.

TRESTLE, Tressel, or Trussel. A three legged stool. P. 41, f. 15.

TREVET, or Trivet. A circular, or triangular frame of iron with three feet. P. 41, f. 13 and 14.

TREWYT. See Trevet.

TRI-ARCHEE. Triple, or Treble-Arched, having three arches. P. 23, f. 19 and 20.

TRIAN ASPECT, IN. Three quartered. See Aspect Trian.

TRIANGLE-IRON. P. 41, f. 10.

TRIANGLE. Cross of Triangles. P. 8, f. 13.

TRIANGLE, IN. Disposed in the form of a triangle.

TRIANGLE, Counter-Triangle, Triangled, or Trianglée. The same as Barry Indented one into the other, or Barry Bendy Lozengy counterchanged. P. 2, f. 36.

TRIANGULAR CASTLE. A castle with three towers. P. 23, f. 4.

TRIANGULAR. Emblem of the Trinity, with the legend. P. 22, f. 1.

TRIANGULAR FRET. P. 42, f. 38. The badge of Tyrell.

TRIANGULAR HARROW. P. 39, f. 9.

TRIANGULAR SOLDERING IRON. Depicted as Plumbers Knife. P. 41, f. 19.

TRIANGLES-INTERLACED. P. 43, f. 56.

TRANSMUTED. Same as Counterchanged.

TRANSPOSED. Reversed.

TRICKING OF ARMS, Arms in Trick, or Tricked. Terms to denote a concise and easy method used by Herald Painters and Engravers in taking down Arms by Abbreviations. P. 2, f. 46.

TRICOLORE, or Tricolour. The emblem of France, of three colours, Blue, White, and Red, and has been successively those of the French Standard for many centuries.

TRICORPORATE. Three bodies conjoined to one head, as three lions Incorporate, or Tricorporated. P. 26, f. 17.

TRIDENT. A three-pronged barbed fork. P. 38, f. 45.

TRIEN. Three. A Trien of fish-fretted. P. 32, f. 26.

TRIMELLS. Az. three Trimels, or Tierces or. the Arms of Warner. P. 22, f. 34.

TRINACRED. See Triquetra.

TRINITY. This Heraldic device which represents the Holy Trinity in an azure field was the heraldic ensign of the monastery of Grey Friars, called Christ church, in the city of London. It is also blazoned " The Triangular Emblem of the Trinity with the legend." The field is generally gu. P. 22, f. 1.

TRIPARTED. Parted into three pieces, applicable to the field as well as ordinaries and charges. A Cross Triparted. P. 7, f. 30.

TRIPARTED BARWISE. P. 21, f. 37.

TRIPARTED IN BEND. i.d. f. 39.

TRIPARTED FLORY. P. 10, f. 26.

TRIPLE, thrice repeated. As triple towered. P. 23, f. 10.

TRIPLE CROWN. See Tiara.

TRIPLE PLUME OF FEATHERS. Is composed of three rows, one above the other. P. 43, f. 40.

TRIPLE TOWERED GATE, double leaved. P. 23, f. 16.

TRIPPANT, or Tripping. A term applied to beasts of chase, as passant to those of prey. A Stag Tripping. P. 28, f. 43.

TRIPPANT COUNTER, or Counter Trippant. When two animals are walking past each other in opposite directions. P. 28, f. 53.

TRIQUETRA, or Trinacria, of Sicily. The ancient symbol of Sicily, as represented on the gold medal for the Victory of Maida. Three naked legs, in the same form as those at P. 36, f. 26.

TRISTRAM, or Truelove Knots. See Knots.

TRITON. A Sea God. P. 35, f. 11. Neptune with trident.

Triton sometimes, but improperly blazoned Neptune, should be represented blowing a Murex (a shell), the Crest of Sykes.

TRIUMPHAL CROWN, or Garland. See Crown Triumphal.

TRIVET. A frame of iron with three supports. P. 41, f. 13 and 14.

TROGODICE'S HEAD ERASED. P. 29, f. 3.

TROIS. Three.

TROMPYTS, or Trompyls. Old English for trumpets.

TRONCONNE. Shivered.

TRONONNE. See Tron-onné.

TRON-ONNE ET DEMEMBREE. Cut in pieces, or dismembered, yet the pieces are so placed as to preserve the outline. e.g. A Cross Trononné. P. 8, f. 16.

TROUT. A fish. P. 32, f. 19.

TROWEL. A tool used by bricklayers. P. 41, f. 30.

TRUE-LOVE KNOT. See Knot. P. 43, f. 14.

TRUMPET. A wind instrument. P. 43, f. 22 and 23, No. 4.

TRUNCATED. See Trunked.

TRUNCHEON. A short staff. See Baton.

TRUNDLE. A quill of gold thread, used by Embroiderers, and borne in the arms of their Company. P. 40, No. 1, at f. 4. Trundle, or Quill. No. 2. The centre figure at f. 3 is also termed a Trundle.

TRUNK OF A TREE. See Stock.

TRUNKED. When the main stock of a tree is borne of a different tincture from the branches.
It is also used in the same sense as *Cabossed.*

TRUSSED. A term to express that the wings of birds are closed. It is an unnecessary term, as all birds are always understood to have the wings close to the body, if not otherwise expressed. P. 33, f. 1, 31, etc.

TRUSSEL. See Trestle.

TRUSSING. See Preying.

TUB. See Tun.

TUBB-FISH, or Tubbe. P. 32, f. 39a.

TUBERATED, Gibbuns, Knotted, or Swelled out, as the middle part of the serpent. P. 30, f. 41.

TUCHE-STONE. See Touchstone.

TUCK. A long narrow sword.

TUDOR-ROSE. Is the red rose of Lancaster, and the white rose of York, sometimes quarterly of the two tinctures, or the red rose charged with a white one. See the rose under shield in title page, and P. 3, f. 21.

TULIP. A flower. P. 44, f. 21.

TUFT. A bunch of grass, etc.

TUFTED. A term applied to the small bunches of hair on the Heraldic Tiger, Antelope, etc. P. 28, f. 19.

TUN. A barrel; if not named to the contrary is depicted in a lying position. P. 39, f. 37, No. 1.

TUN AND BOLT, or Bolt in Tun. i.d. f. 37, No. 2.

TUN ERECT, inflamed at the top. i.d. f. 38, No. 1.

TUN, Issuing from the Bung hole of a, five roses, stalked and leaved. P. 31, f. 28.

TUNIC, Tunique, or Tabard. The surcoat worn by heralds and other officers of Arms distinguished by the general name of Tabard; but the tabard of a King of Arms is properly called a Tunique; that of a Herald, a Placque; and that worn by a Pur-

suivant, a Coat-of-Arms. All were alike, emblazoned with the Arms of the Sovereign or Noble whom the wearer served, and for this reason a surcoat was also termed 'Houce des Armes.'

TURBOT. A sort of flat fish. A Turbot Naiant. P. 32, f. 8. A Demi Turbot, tail erect, crest of Lawrence. i.d. f. 9.

TURKEY-COCK. A large domestic bird. P. 34, f. 3.

TURKEY-FEATHERS, a Panache of, borne by the family of Harsicke, of South-acre, co. Norfolk. P. 43, f. 41.

TURKS HEAD. See Savage.

TURNED UP. When a cap or cuff is supposed to be folded back so as to show its lining it is said to be turned up. e.g. A Chapeau gu., turned up Ermine. P. 40, f. 54.

TURNIP. A plant. P. 44, f. 59.
The Arms of Damnant are sa. a turnip ppr. a chief or., gutte-de-larmes.

TURNPIKE, or Turnstile, borne by Skipwith. P. 39, f. 40, No. 2 ; by Woolston. f. 41.

TURQUINE. Azure.

TURRET, as borne in the Arms of Johnson. P. 41, f. 43.

TURRET. A small tower on the top of another. P. 23, f. 10.

TURRETTED, Donjonnée. Applied to a tower or wall having small towers upon it. See Castle and Tower, towered or turretted. P. 23, f. 2 and 14.

TURTLE-DOVE. See Dove.

TUSHED. See Tusked.

TUSKED, denté. A term used in blazonry, when the tusks of an animal are of a different tincture from its body.

TWISTED. Wreathed in various ways, as a serpent targent tail wreathed, or a serpent torqued. P. 30, f. 28 and 34.

TWISTING. The same as Twisted, or Torqued. See a Serpent Twined, Twisted, or Twisting; i.e. entwined, or turned round any thing. P. 30, f. 58.

TWO AND ONE. When three charges are borne on a field, two in chief, and one in base, they are sometimes blazoned two and one.
This disposition of three charges is always so understood, if not ordered otherwise, and therefore it is unnecessary to use the term two and one ; but if more than three charges of the same description are borne in a field their position must be named. e.g P. 40, f. 17. Seven mascles conjoined, or conjunct

three, three and one. P. 20, f. 39. Five roses in saltier. P. 12, f. 3. For examples of three charges in a field, see P. 31, f. 3, and f. 30 to 35.

TWO HEADED EAGLE. See Eagle, displayed with two heads. P. 33, f. 6.

TWYFOIL, or Dufoil. Two leaved foil, shaped like those of the Trefoil.

TYGER. See Tiger.

TYGER AND MIRROR. See Tiger and Mirror.

TYMBRE. See Timbre.

TYNES. A name given to the branches of the horns of stags. In blazoning their number and tincture must be named; a stag's head attired with ten tynes is borne by the family of Gordon.

TRYING. Same as Preying. P. 33, f. 12.

TYRWHITT. A lapwing. P. 33, f. 55.

U

ULLUM, as in the Arms of Lake. P. 39, f. 42, No. 2. See also P. 32, f. 48.

ULSTER BADGE. A shield ar., thereon a sinister hand apaumée, couped at the wrist, and erect gu. P. 31, f. 12. This is the Badge of a Baronet of Great Britain. See Baronet.

ULSTER KING OF ARMS. See Heralds College.

UMBRACED. The same as Vambraced.

UMBRATED. Shadowed. See Adumbrated.

UN CRI DE GUERRE. The War Cry, or Motto.

UNDATED. Same as Waved.

UNDATYD. Used by Upton for undée.

UNDE, Undée, or Undy. The same as Wavy. P. 17, f. 12.

UNDULATED. Wavy.

UNE DEVISE. The motto.

UNFRUCTED. Slips of laurel, bay, etc., consist of three leaves; the sprig, of five leaves; and the branch, of nine leaves; if fructed, four leaves are sufficient to term it a branch. P. 44, f. 53.

UNGLET. See Unguled.

UNGULED. A term applied to the hoofs of the horse, stag, bull, goat, etc., to express that they are of a different tincture from that of the body of the animal.

UNICORN. An imaginary animal, represented as having the head, neck and body of a horse, the legs of a buck, the tail of a lion, and a long straight horn growing out of the middle of the forehead. It is well known as the sinister supporter of the present Royal Arms. P. 31, f. 11.

UNICORN PASSANT. P. 27, f. 36. Demi Unicorn. i.d. f. 37. Head couped. f. 39. Head erased. f. 38.

UNIFOIL. A plant with a single leaf, like a leaf of the trefoil.

UNION FLAG. The National Ensign of Great Britain, commonly called the Jack, or Union Jack. In this Union-Flag we have three crosses, viz., that of St. George for England, of St. Andrew for Scotland, and St. Patrick for Ireland; properly combined according to the rules of heraldry, as follows :—On a field az., the cross saltier of St. Andrew ar., surmounted by that of St. Patrick, gu., over all the red cross of St. George, fimbriated of the second. P. 7, f. 21. See Elvin's Anecdotes of Heraldry.

UNION, Cross of the. This form was settled as the badge of the Union between England and Scotland, and is blazoned az., a saltire ar. surmounted of a cross gu. edged of the second.

UNITED STATES OF AMERICA, Ensign of. P. 25a, f. 15.

UNIVERSITIES, Arms of. See Arms of Community.

UPON, or Above Another. Lying upon it. Also the placing of Arms in pale

UPRIGHT. Erect. Applied to all shellfish instead of haurient, and to reptiles instead of rampant.

UPSILON. The Greek Y, borne by the name of Clark. Westenius, de linguâ Græcâ, tells us that Pythagoras invented the Y of the original alphabet, as a representation of the path of life. The foot is said to represent infancy, the two forks, two paths, the one leading to good, the other to evil.

URANUS, or Georgium Sidus. An astronomical sign. P. 23, f. 45.

URCHIN, or Hedgehog. P. 30, f. 11.

URCHIN SEA, or Sea-Urchin. P. 32, f. 49.

URDE. According to Randle Holme, is the singular of Urdée, and implies one projection, as per bend urde. P. 19, f. 8. A Bend Urdée. P. 17, f. 19.

URDEE-CHAMPAINED. P. 15, f. 20.

URDEE. A Cross Urdée is a cross pointed, Champaine, or Aiguisée. P. 9, f. 45.

URDEE, in point paleways. P. 21, f. 29.

URDEE IN POINT, or Contrary Urdée. P. 21, f. 28.

URINANT. Diving. Applied to fish with the head downwards. P. 32, f. 12.

URLE. See Orle.

URN. A vessel, usually largest in the middle. P. 39, f. 39, No. 1.

URUS'S HEAD. A bull's head.

URVANT, or Urved. Turned, or bowed upwards.

V

V. This letter is used to express vert.

VAIR. One of the furs being party-coloured ar. and az., and always so understood, if not named to the contrary. P. 1.

VAIR ANCIENT. Represented by lines nebulée, separated by straight lines in fesse. P. 1.

VAIR COUNTER, or Counter-Vair, or Vairy. Resembles Vair, but the escutcheons are of like tincture immediately under each other. P. 1.

VAIR CUPPA, or Vair Tassy. Is the same as Potent Counter Potent. P. 1.

VAIR IN POINT, formed like vair, but with the bottom points of the shield, falling on the centre of the flat tops of those beneath. P. 1.

VAIR TAFFE. Same as Cuppa.

VAIR EN PAL. The same as Vair.

VAIREE. The same as Vair, with this difference that it may consist of any number of colours, which must be expressed in the blazon as *Vaire* erm., gn. and az. the Arms of Broase. P. 1.

VAIRY, or Vaire. Same as Vair.

VAIRY-CUPY. Same as Potent Counter Potent. P. 1.

VALLARY CROWN, or Garland. See Crown Vallary. P. 24, f. 17.

VALORY CROWN. Same as Preceding.

VAMBRACED, Vambrace, or Avant bras. Vambrace is armour for the arm, entirely covering it, but *Avant bras*, covering for the fore part only. *Vambraced* implies that the whole limb is covered with armour. P. 36, f. 16, 17 and 19.

VAMPLATE. A gauntlet, or iron glove. P. 38, f. 17.

VAMPLATE, or Vamplet, of a Tilting Spear. The broad piece of steel that is placed at the lower part of the staff of the spear for covering the hand.

VAMPS, or Vampays. An odd kind of short hose, which came down no lower than the ancles.

VANDYKED. A term applied to the cuff or collar of a dress when indented. P. 36, f. 12.

VANE, or Van. A winnowing basket. P. 39, f. 16.

VANE. A small flag, as P. 23, f. 19 and 20. See Weather-cock.

VANNET. Escallop, so termed when depicted without ears. P. 42, f. 42.

VARIEGATED. Diversified with a variety of colours.

VARRIATED, Warriated, or Variated. It is also termed Champagne, cut in the form of Vair. P. 17, f. 19.

VARRY CUPPE. See Cuppa.

VARRY, VARREY. Same as Vair.

VARREY IN POINT. The same as perfesse Urdée in point palewise. P. 21, f. 29.

VARVELLS, Vervels, or Wervels. The rings attached to the ends of the jesses of a hawk. P. 33, f. 34. See Jesses.

VARVELLED, or Vervelled. Having rings at the ends of the jesses of a hawk. P. 33, f. 34.

VASE. See Chalice.

VEIL. A cover. P. 22, f. 15; P. 36, f. 30.

VELLOPED. See Jelloped.

VENUS. In blazoning by planets, implies vert.

VENUS. The astronomical symbol of Venus is borne by Thoyts. P. 23, f. 45.

VERBLEE. A hunting horn, edged round with metal of different tinctures from the other part.

VERDEE. See Cross Verdée. P. 8, f. 34.

VERDON-KNOT. The same as Harrington Knot. P. 43, f. 9.

VERDOY. An unnecessary term used to denote a bordure charged with eight flowers, leaves, fruit, or vegetables of any kind. P. 13, f. 39.

VERGETTE, or Verget. The same as an Endorse.

VERGETTE. French term for Paly.

VERMEIL. Gules.

VERREY, or Verry. The same as Vair.

VERSANT, Reclivant, or Sursuant. Erected, or Elevated.

VERSE, or Reverse. Reversed.

VERT. Green; expressed in engraving by diagonal lines, drawn from the dexter chief to the sinister base. See terms, Emerald, Sinople, and Venus. P. 1.

VERTANT AND REVERTANT, or Verted and Reverted. The same as Flexed and Reflexed; i.e. formed like the letter S.

VERULES, Vires, Ferruls, or Ferrils. Rings of metal.

VERULED, or Ferruled. Terms used to express the ornamental rings round hunting horns, etc. P. 43, f. 24.

VERVELLED. Hawks when the leather thongs which tie on the bells to their legs are borne flotant, with rings at the ends, are said to be jessed, belled, and vervelled. P. 33, f. 34.

VERVELS, or Wervels. Small rings used by Falconers, and to which the jesses of the hawk are fastened.

VESTED. Habited, or clothed. See an Arm Vested. P. 36, f. 9 to 13.

VESTU. When an ordinary has some division on it only by lines, and signifies clothed, as if some garment were laid upon it. P. 12, f. 34 and 35.

VEXILLUM. See Banderoll. P. 42, f. 46.

VICTORIA AND ALBERT, The Royal Order of. Badge. P. 24, f. 25.
This Order was Instituted 10th February, 1862. Enlarged 10th October, 1864; 15th November, 1865; and 15th March, 1880.

THE IMPERIAL ORDER OF THE CROWN OF INDIA.
Instituted 1st January, 1878, to commemorate the assumption of Her Majesty's Imperial title of Empress of India.
Badge. P. 24, f. 30.
These two Orders are confined to Ladies, the Members are entitled to no special precedence.

VICTORIA CROSS. V.C. A Military and Naval Badge is a bronze cross, with the Royal Crest in the centre, and underneath which an escroll with the motto "*For Valour*," Instituted by Queen Victoria, 8th Feb., 1856. It is the decoration of *Eminent personal valour*, in actual conflict with the enemy.
The Cross P. 25, f. 11, is suspended by a Blue ribbon, if worn by a Sailor and a Red ribbon if by a Soldier. The date of the act of bravery is inscribed on the centre of the reverse with the name and date of the Action or Campaign in which the honour was won. On the reverse side of the Bar to which the ribbon is attached the Rank and Name of the Recipient is engraved. For every fresh act of bravery equal to the first an additional Bar is granted. A Pension of £10 per annum is bestowed upon non-commissioned officers, and men who receive the Cross; and a further pension of £5 a year is given with each Bar.
By Warrant, bearing date Dec. 13th, 1858 it was declared that Non-Military persons, who, as Volunteers, had borne arms against the Mutineers in India should be considered eligible to receive the decoration of the Victoria Cross.

VIGILANT. Applicable to the cat when borne in a position as if upon the watch for prey.

VILAINIE. A lion sans vilainie is the upper half of a lion rampant, by which the hinder part is to be understood by the word vilainie, as being in the base point.

VINE-BRANCH FRUCTED. P. 45, f. 8; P. 47

VINE-SLIP FRUCTED. P. 20, f. 21.

VINE.HOOK. See Pruning hook.

VINE LEAVES. P. 45, f. 8.

VIOLA. The tenor violin and violoncello. P. 43, f. 25.

VIOLET. Stalked and leaved. P. 44, f. 24.

VIOLIN, as borne in the Arms of Sweeting. P. 43, f. 25.

VIPER, or Vipera. See Snake.

VIRES. See Verules.

VIRGIN AND CHILD, depicted as P. 35, f. 1.

VIROLE. The ring or mouth-piece of the bugle-horn.

VIROLLED. See Veruled.

VIROLS. The rings which commonly encircle bugle-horns.

VISARD, or VIZARD. A mask, borne by the name of Vizard.

VISCOUNT. Hereditary title next to an Earl. A Viscount is Right Honourable, and is styled "My Lord." His sons and daughters are "Honourable."

VISCOUNT'S CORONET. P. 24, f. 45.

VISITATIONS. The Clarenceux and Norroy Kings of Arms were empowered by their commission to hold Visitations in their respective provinces, either personally or by deputy.
Accordingly they were accustomed to issue notices to the bailiffs of the different hundreds in each county, warning them to summon the Knights, Esquires, and Gentlemen resident therein to appear before the King of Arms or his Deputy at the time and place by him appointed. They were to bring with them such Arms and Crests as they used and wore, with their descents, pedigrees, and patent of Arms, and the necessary evidence to justify them; in order that the King of Arms might duly record them if found correct; or on the other hand, to reject, and degrade all such persons as falsely, and without good reason had taken the title of Esquire and Gentleman upon them, and cause their names to be proclaimed as infamous at the Assize of Arms, or General Session, held by him at some central place in his province. Those who failed

to answer to this summons were warned to appear personally, on a day specified, before the Earl Marshal, under a penalty of ten pounds.

In case of a petition to the Earl Marshal for a grant of Arms, an order was directed by him to the King of Arms of the province in which the petitioner resided, who accordingly formed a fitting coat, which, with the sanction of the Earl Marshal, was duly blazoned and registered at the Visitation. The King of Arms also, during his progress, might visit all Churches, Castles and Houses in his province, and there pull down or deface any bearings contrary to the laws of Arms which he might find. The records of these Visitations are perhaps the most comprehensive of all our repositories of genealogical information; inasmuch as they contain an authoritative list of pedigrees, and the exact blazon of each coat as it was issued or confirmed by the Heralds. The original of these records are for the most part in the College of Arms; but some few of the originals, and copies of most of the others, are to be found in the Library of the British Museum, which is very rich in Heraldic M.S.S.

The first Visitation on record took place A.D. 1528, in Staffordshire, but in the majority of the other counties they are not mentioned till 1530. The last Visitation was held in Middlesex, 1687.

VISOR. See Vizor.

VIUDE. Voided.

VIURE, Wiure, or Wyer. See Wiure.

VIVRE. A narrow fillet dancette, and may be placed in fesse or otherwise. P. 12, f. 28.

VIZARD. See Visard.

VIZOR, Garde-Visure, Beaver, or Beauvoir. That part of the helmet which defends the face, and which can be lifted up or put down at pleasure. A Helmet, with vizor raised. P. 38, f. 10. An Esquire's Helmet, with vizor down. P. 24, f. 12.

VOIDED. A term applicable to any ordinary when the middle is removed so that the field is seen through it, as a Cross Voided. P. 7, f. 20; P. 10, f. 29, and f. 10. P. 14, f. 8, a Pale Voided. P. 15, f. 11, a Chevron Voided.

VOIDER, or Voyder. An ordinary resembling a flanch, but is not so circular. P. 5, f. 41.

VOL. In blazon, implies two wings conjoined as P. 33, f. 26, No. 2. A Demi Vol is a single wing. f. 26, No. 1.

VOLANT, or Volans. Flying. P. 34, f. 60.

VOLANT DIVERSELY. Flying about indiscriminately as P. 30, f. 20.

VOLANT EN ARRIERE, and Volant tergiant, when flying, shewing the back. P. 33, f. 18.

VOLENTES VOLARE, or Assorant. Is said of buzzards, or such like birds, with long legs, that are depicted as if rising.

VOLUTED. Spirally curled. A Serpent Voluted. P. 30, f. 49.

VOMITING. Sending forth. P. 28, f. 12; P. 27, f. 24.

VORANT, Swallowing, Devouring, or Gorging. Terms applied to animals, fish, etc., in the act of swallowing anything. P. 30, f. 55, and P. 32, f. 5.

VOYDED. See Voided.

VOYDES DU CHAMPS. Mascles.

VULNERATING. The same as Vulning.

VULNED. Wounded, and bleeding. P. 42, f. 1.

When an animal is wounded with an arrow, the arrow should not pierce through the animal; the proper term in that case is transfixed.

VULNING. A term applied to the pelican, which is always depicted wounding her breast. P. 33, f. 37.

VULTURE. A rapacious bird. P. 33, f. 36.

W

WAGON. A four-wheeled carriage. P. 41, f. 52.

WAKE'S KNOT. P. 43, f. 10. No. 2.

WALES, Arms of. Quarterly or. and gu. four Lions passant guardant counter changed. See Title Page.

WALES, Badge of. A Dragon passant wings elevated and endorsed gu., upon a mount vert. P. 5, f. 21.

WALES, Prince of. Badge of the. P. 6, f. 21.

WALL embattled in bend sinister. P. 18, f. 43.

WALLED, or Murallée. Covered with a representation of Masonry. P. 3, f. 11.

WALLET. See Scrip. P. 40, f. 39.

WALLET OPEN. P. 40, f. 41.

WALLET and Staff. i.d. f. 40.

WALNUT-LEAF. P. 45, f. 28.

WALNUT TREE. P. 45, f. 38.

WAR-BILL. The centre figure at P. 41, f. 22.

WAR-CRIE, Cri-de-guerre. See Motto and Cri-de-guerre.

WAR MEDALS. See Medals.

WAR-WOLF. Also termed a Were-Wolf, Wher-Wolf, or Wolf-Man, P. 30, f. 18. As borne by the name of Dickeson, or Dickison.
Supposed to be a man living a wolf's nature—a genus I imagine far from being extinct.

WARDEN. A pear; sometimes so called in armory, borne by the name of Warden, in allusion to the name.

WARRIATED, Champagne, Urdée, etc. A Cross so termed. P. 9, f. 45. A Bend Warriated. P. 17, f. 19.

WASSAIL-BOWL. Same as Bowl.

WASTEL-CAKES. Round cakes of bread. P. 39, f. 17. According to Guillim, the same as Torteaux. See Manchet.

WATER. There are two ways of representing this in Heraldry; anciently, it was symbolized by the field, or a portion of it being barry wavy, argent, and azure. P. 22, f. 15 and 16.
It is now however frequently borne proper as at f. 13, and 14.

WATER-BUBBLES. See Bubble.

WATER-BOUGET, or Water-budget. A vessel anciently used by soldiers for the conveyance of water to the camp. The Water-budget is depicted in different ways, as P. 42, f. 20 to 24. The last is the most common. See Water bags

WATER-BAGS, or pair of Dossers. Also termed Water-bags, hooped together, and borne by the name of Banister. P. 42, f. 21.

WATER-CRESS AND LEAVES. P. 44, f. 41.

WATER-LIZARD. See Asker.

WATER-POT. A fontal, called a Scatebra, out of which naiads and river-gods are represented as pouring the waters of rivers, over which they are fabled to preside.

WATER-SPANIEL. See Spaniel. P. 29, f. 27.

WATER-WHEEL. P. 38, f. 51.

WATERLOO MEDAL. P. 25, f. 12.

WATERY. The same as Wavy, or Undée. P. 7, f. 9.

WATTLED. When the gills of a Cock, or Cockatrice, are of a different tincture from the head it is said to be Wattled.

WAVED. Same as Wavy.

WAVED-SWORD. P. 38, f. 19.

WAVES OF THE SEA. P. 22, f. 13.

WAVY, or Wavée, Undée, or Undy. P. 1.

WEAR, Weare, or Weir. A dam or fence against water, made with stakes and twigs of osier, wattled, or inter-woven. By some Heralds, termed a Haie. P. 2, f. 47. A Weir in fesse, borne by the name of Williams.

WEASEL. A small carnivorous quadruped. P. 30, f. 14.

WEATHER-COCK, or Vane, as borne in the arms of Fitz-Alwyn, the first Mayor of London. P. 43, f. 55.

WEAVERS-SHUTTLE. P. 40, f. 2.

WEDDING-FAVOURS, as borne in the Arms of Latter. P. 43, f. 14.

WEDGE, or Stone-bill. A tool used to split timber. P. 41, f. 42.

WEEL, or Fish-Weel, for catching fish. P. 38, f. 55.
Fish-Weel, with handle. f. 56 and 58. The Weel as f. 57 is borne by the family of Wylley.

WEIR. See Wear.

WELK, Welke, Whelk, or Wilke. A shellfish, borne by the name of Shelley. P. 32, f. 54.

WELL. As borne by the name of Caldwell, P. 31, f. 19, without the Vine and Columbine.

WELL, with frame and handle, borne by Coucher. P. 39, f. 34.

WELL, with Vine and Columbine branches as borne by Goldwell. P. 31, f. 19. Termed a Golden-well.

WELL-BUCKET, as borne by the name of Pemberton. P. 39, f. 35, No. 1.

WELT, or Edge. A narrow bordure.

WELTED, or Edged. Having a narrow bordure. P. 4, f. 3. Observe the difference between Edged and Fimbriated. f. 5.

WERE. An old term for Vair, or Varry.

WERVELS, or Varvells. See Vervels.

WHALE. A Whale haurient. P. 32, f. 3.

WHALE's head erased. i.d. f. 4.

WHARROW - SPINDLE. An instrument formerly used by women to spin with, whilst walking, by sticking the distaff in their girdles, and whirling round the spindle pendent to the thread. Borne by the name of Clinton. P. 40, f. 3.

WHEAT. Of frequent use in Armory. A wheat ear, a wheat stalk bladed and eared. When in a sheaf is termed a Garb. P. 45, f. 13 and 14.

WHEAT Big. An old provincial term for Barley borne by the name of Bigland. P. 45, f. 16.

WHEAT Guinea, An Ear of. A kind of bearded wheat similar to the last, borne by the name of Graindorge. f. 16.

WHEAT-SHEAF. A Garbe, or Garb. See Garb.

WHEEL, or Cart Wheel. P. 41, f. 53. Demi, or half wheels, are wheels divided pale-ways; three such are borne by the name of Wheeler.

WHEEL-CATHERINE, or Katherine-wheel. See Catherine-Wheel and P. 41, f. 54.

WHEEL, or Fish-Wheel. See Fish-Weel.

WHEEL of a Mill. See Mill-Wheel.

WHEEL SHUTTLE. See Shuttle.

WHET-HERYS. An old term for Wheat ears.

WHINTAIN. See Quintain.

WHIPS stringed and knotted. As in the Arms of Crowland Abbey. Also termed a Scourge. P. 42, f. 41.

WHIRLPOOL, or Gurges. Represents water, argent and azure, and invariably covers the whole field as P. 22, f. 6, borne by the name of Gorges. The family of Chellery bear ar, a whirlpool gu.
The Whirlpool is sometimes represented by a number of rings one within another.

WHISTLE. See Boatswain's-Whistle. P. 38, f. 43.

WHITE. A word used instead of Argent, for the lining of Mantles, which is of a pure white fur, which some call the livits skin. White is used in painting for argent, or silver.

WHITE ENSIGN, or St. George's Ensign. See Ensign.

WHITING. A fish. P. 32, f. 23.

WHITTAL'S, or Wittal's head. A man's head with short horns. P. 36, f. 46.

WILD-BOAR. See Boar.

WILD-CAT. See Cat a Mountain.

WILD-MAN. See Savage.

WILLOW, or Salix. P. 45, f. 35. A Pollard Willow. f. 36.

WIMBLE, or Wine-piercer. P. 41, f. 32.

WINDMILL. P. 38, f. 49, and f. 50.

WINDMILL Sails. i.d. f. 50.

WINDOW GRATING. P. 40, f. 22.

WINDSOR HERALD. See Heralds College

WINE-PIERCER, or Wine-broach. An instrument to tap wine casks. P. 41, f. 32.

WING. A single wing is termed in Armory a Demi vol; and two wings when endorsed are termed a Vol. P. 33, f. 26.
Wings are always undertood to be those of the eagle unless named otherwise.

WING-SINISTER. The same as demi vol. P. 33, f. 26.

WINGS conjoined in base, or Wings erect conjoined. P. 33, f. 27.

WINGS conjoined in lure, or Wings inverted. P. 33, f. 28.

WINGS endorsed. The Dragons wings. P. 5, f. 21, are endorsed.

WINGED. Having wings, or adorned with wings as a winged heart. P. 42, f. 5.

WINGED COLUMN. P. 43, f. 51.

WINNOWING BASKET, or Shruttle. P. 39, f. 16.

WISALLS, or Wisomes. The leaves or tops of carrots, parsnips, or other edible roots; are so blazoned by Randle Holme

WITHERED BRANCH. Also termed a Starved branch. P. 45, f. 58.

WITHERED TREE. Blighted or starved. i.d. f. 58.

WITHIN. When an ordinary, or charge is entirely surrounded by anything, it is said to be within. e.g. A Saltire within a bordure. P. 20, f. 42. A Manche within an orle of fleur-de-lis. P. 5, f. 37.

WITTAL'S HEAD. A man's head with short horns, couped below the shoulders. P. 36, f. 46.

WIURE, Wyer, Viure, and Viurie. A narrow fillet, generally nebuly, it may be placed in bend, in fesse, or otherwise. P. 4, f. 17. P. 22, f. 35.

WIVRE, or Vivre. A Diminutive of the dancette. See Vivre.

WIVERN, Wiveron, or Wyvern. An imaginary animal, the upper part resembling what is called a Dragon; with two legs; and the lower, a serpent. P. 27, f. 11.

WIVERN, tail nowed. i.d. f. 12.

WIVERN, sans wings. i.d. f. 13.

WIVERN, sans legs. i.d. f. 14.

WIVERN'S HEAD COUPED. P. 27, f. 25.

WOLF-HERALDIC. P. 28, f. 8.

WOLF. i.d. f. 9.

WOLF-SEJANT. i.d. f. 10.

WOLF'S HEAD ERASED. i.d. f. 11.

WOLF, Marine. The seal. P. 29, f. 51.

WOLF-TRAP. P. 41, f. 4.

WOLF-WERE, or Wolf-man. See Warwolf.

WOMAN. Woman's head, and demi-woman; also blazoned by the term Lady.
A woman's head and neck when couped below the breast, the head wreathed with a garland of roses, and crowned with an antique crown is always blazoned a maiden's head. P. 22, f. 24. When the hair is depicted as loosely flowing, it is termed dis-

hevelled; as the Crest of Ellis, viz,, a woman naked, her hair dishevelled ppr. P. 35. f. 6. See a'so term Lady.

WOMAN'S BREAST, distilling drops of milk. P. 43, f. 34.
Borne by the name of Dodge and Piddock.

WOOD, or Hurst. A small group of trees. P. 45, f. 60.

WOOD-BILL, Wood-hook, or Forest-bill. P. 41, f. 22.

WOODBINE. The same as Honeysuckle. P. 45, f. 1.

WOODBINE LEAF. P. 45, f. 27.

WOODCOCK. A bird of passage. P. 34, f. 48.

WOOD-LOUSE. P. 30, f. 7.

WOODMAN. The same as Wild-man, or Savage. P. 35, f. 24.

WOODMARTIN. See Martin.

WOODPECKER. A bird. P. 33, f. 45.

WOOD-PIGEON. P. 34, f. 39.

WOODWIFT. A wild man, or savage. P. 35, f. 24.

WOOL-CARD. An instrument for carding wool. P. 40, f. 10.

WOOL-COMB, or Jersey Comb. P. 40, f. 12.

WOOL-PACK, or Wool-sack. P. 40, f. 19.

WOOL-PACK, corded. i.d. f. 20.

WORDS. Are used as charges in many Coats of Arms. e.g. Netherlands in the Arms of Jones, Bart. Trafalgar in the Arms of Collingwood. Orthes, in those of Harvey, etc.

WOUND. A term used by Bossewell, to express the roundle when tinctured purpure.

WOUNDED. See Vulned.

WOYDYD. Same as voided.

WOYDYRS. Old term for four quarters.

WRAPPED, Wrapt, Enwrapped, or Enveloped. The same as Entwined.

WREATH, Torse, or Torce. Is a garland, chaplet, or attire for the head.
The wreath, upon which the Crest is placed, is of silk, composed of two different tinctures twisted together, and showing six folds., three of each tincture, and the tinctures of the wreath are with few exceptions, those first mentioned in blazoning the coat of arms. The Wreath is placed between the helmet and the crest which are fastened together by it. P. 47. In some instances crowns or coronets supply the place of the wreath, P. 21, f. 21, but Crests are always understood to be placed upon a wreath, when not ordered to be borne upon a Crown, Coronet, Cap, or Chapeau. When a wreath composed of silk, is placed round the temples of a man, it should have two bows with strings at the sinister end. P. 36, f. 37.

WREATH CIRCULAR. As borne in the Arms of Jocelyn. P. 43, f. 45.

WREATHED. Encircled with a wreath; as a head wreathed. P. 36, f. 37.
Savages are frequently wreathed about the temples and loins with oak leaves, ivy, etc., but laurel leaves are always understood if not mentioned to the contrary. A Demi Savage wreathed about the loins. P. 35, f. 25. Ordinaries are sometimes wreathed, as a Fesse wreathed or tortile gules and azure. P. 3, f. 28.

WREN. A small insessorial bird. P. 34, f. 51.

WRESTLING-COLLAR, as borne by the family of Gurney, co. Norfolk. P. 43, f. 43.

WRINCLE-SHELL. See Welk.

WYN. A vane, or little flag. P. 23, f. 19 and 20.

WYVERN. See Wivern.

WYVRE. A viper.

Y

Y. See Upsilon.

YARD, or Yard-measure. Depicted as a round rod, with divisions of measurement marked thereon. P. 41, f. 41.

YARE. See Weir, and P. 2, f. 47.

YARN, Quill of. See Quill.

YATES. An old term for Gates.

YELLOW. Used in painting, instead of gold.

YEOMAN. The degree below that of Gentleman, and above that of Artificer, or labourer.

YEW-TREE. P. 45, f. 47.

YNDE, or Inde. Azure.

YOKE, or Ox-Yoke. P. 37, f. 57; also termed a Double Ox-Yoke.

YORK-HERALD. See Herald's College.

YORK, Rose of. A white rose. P. 25, f. 2.

YORKIST Badge and Collar, formed of Suns and Roses, linked together with chains. The *White Lion Badge* is generally attached to the Collar, and forms a pendant to it.

YSSUINGE. Issuing.

Z

ZODIAC. The Zone of the celestial sphere. A bend sinister, with the three signs of Libra, Leo and Scorpio upon it. P. 18, f. 26. A Fesse Zodiac, or Hemisphere. P. 3, f. 29.

ZULE, or Zulis. A chess-rook. P, 43, f. 49.

Errata to Plates.

P. vi. q.v. *for* quad *read* quod

Pl. 1. Line 33, *for* Sardonix *read* Sardonyx

„ 3. No. 23, *for* Fruille *read* Feuille

„ 4. No. 2, *for* Recouise *read* Recoursie

No. 9, *for* Grice *read* Griece

„ 6. No. 13, *for* Fimberiated *read* Fimbriated

No. 20, *after* Piles *add* Wavy

„ 13. No. 21, *line* 5 *after* ar. *add* Crest

„ 18. No. 15, *for* Grice *read* Griece

„ 19. No. 8, *after* Point *add* Urdé

Pl. 22. No. 15, *for* arranyed *read* arrayed

„ 24. No. 22, *for* Knight's *read* Knight

„ 26. No. 8, *for* Cone *read* Coue

No. 34, *for* guard. *read* reguard

„ 29. No. 25, *for* Mastaff *read* Mastiff

„ 33. No. 46, *for* Phesant *read* Pheasant

„ 35. No. 23, *for* Joustiug *read* Jousting

„ 36. No. 22, *for* Spear *read* Spur

„ 38. No. 8, *for* Habergon *read* Habergeon

„ 40. No. 59, *for* Tara *read* Tiara

Addenda and Corrigenda to the Dictionary.

P. 6 2nd col., line 47, *for* shot *read* short

„ 10 Line 31, *for* Combant *read* Combatant

„ 13 2nd col., line 8, *for* insigna *read* insignia

„ 19 Line 49, *after* with *add* in

2nd col., line 52, *after* BLANCH-LYON *add* anciently

„ 22 2nd col., line 49, *for* Gardbras *read* Garde-de-Bras

„ 23 Line 35, *for* Habergon, *read* Habergeon

2nd col., *for* Gaminiverous *read* Graminivorous

„ 26 Line 53, *for* fn *read* in

„ 30 Lines 24 and line 30, *for* LABLE *read* LABEL

„ 31 2nd col., line 31, *for* CLONE *read* CLOUE

„ 33 Line 20, *for* Tan *read* Tau

„ 37 2nd col., line 3 *from the bottom, for* as *read* at

„ 38 2nd col., line 24, *for* Tan *read* Tau

„ 39 2nd col., line 22, *for* Cooped *read* Couped

„ 42 2nd col., line 1, *for* quadrant *read* quadrat

„ 64 2nd col., 6 lines *from bottom, for* gronnd *read* ground

„ 66 Line 25, *for* and *read* as

„ 73 2nd col., line 35, *for* HOSPITALLARS *read* HOSPITALLERS, *and add at the end of the Article the following, viz.:* On the 11th March, 1889, Her Majesty the Queen was graciously pleased to allow the Members and Honorary Associates of this Order in England to wear generally the Insignia of their respective grades in the said Order, as provided for in the Royal Charter of Incorporation of the 14th May, 1888

P. 75 2nd col., line 30, *for* INSIGNA *read* INSIGNIA

„ 80 2nd col., line 24, *for* huadred *read* Hundred

„ 84 Line 11, *for* Dovetaiied *read* Dovetailed

2nd col., line 47, *for* SEJANT DEXTER. Paw raised, *read* SEJANT. Dexter paw raised

„ 85 Line 53, *for* Quadranglar *read* Quadrangular

„ 88 2nd col., line 6, *for* derivcd *read* derived

2nd col., line 21, *for* pretencc *read* pretence

2nd col., line 26, *for* Fnneral *read* Funeral

„ 93 Line 21, *for* NORRY *read* NORROY

„ 94 2nd col., line 24, *for* Subordinaries *read* DIMINUTIVES

„ 105 2nd col., line 16, *for* Aarm *read* Arms

„ 112 2nd col., 10 lines *from bottom, for* runnnig *read* running

„ 117 Line 18, *for* SOLON *read* SOLAN

„ 120 Line 34, *for* privelege *read* privilege

„ 129 Line 36, *for* gn. *read* gu.